The Illustrated Directory of

DINOSAURS

AND OTHER PREHISTORIC CREATURES

The Illustrated Directory of

DINOSAURS

AND OTHER PREHISTORIC CREATURES

Edited by
Ingrid Cranfield

PUBLISHED BY
SALAMANDER BOOKS LIMITED
LONDON

A Salamander Book

Published by Salamander Books Ltd.,
8 Blenheim Court,
Brewery Road,
London N7 9NT,
United Kingdom

A member of the Chrysalis Group plc

ISBN 1 84065 241 1

Credits

Project Manager: Ray Bonds
Designed by: Interprep Ltd
Color reproduction by: Studio Technology
Printed in Slovenia

The Editor

Ingrid Cranfield is author of *Animal World, 100 Greatest Natural Wonders, The Archaeology Kit* and several other books. She was editor and project manager of a major recent series, *The Age of the Dinosaurs.*

Contents

Introduction

Dinosaurs lived during the so-called Mesozoic Era of earth history. The Mesozoic (literally 'middle life') comprises the Triassic, Jurassic and Cretaceous Periods, which lasted from about 225 until 64 million years ago. Animals that lived before the Mesozoic, such as the large sail-backed reptiles of the Permian Period, for example *Dimetrodon*, or after the Mesozoic, such as the woolly mammoths, were *not* dinosaurs.

Dinosaurs were also *reptiles* - not fish, amphibians, birds or mammals. They were all land-living creatures. Thus the gigantic sea monsters of the Mesozoic - the plesiosaurs, ichthyosaurs and mosasaurs - were not dinosaurs. Similarly, no dinosaurs were airborne fliers. Therefore the flying reptiles of the Mesozoic, the pterosaurs, were not dinosaurs either.

Dinosaurs are in fact members of a group of reptiles known as archosaurs ('ruling reptiles'), which include well-known creatures such as crocodiles, pterosaurs, birds and thecodontians.

As Richard Owen, who coined the term 'dinosaur', rightly pointed out in 1841, the dinosaurs are distinct from other archosaurs for one main reason: they are able to walk and run extremely efficiently, their legs being tucked in beneath the body rather than held out from the sides. This difference has left tell-tale marks in their fossils in the form of changes in the structure of the hip, knee and ankle joints, which distinguish dinosaurs from other archosaurs.

Since the last half of the 19th century the dinosaurs have been split into two groups, the *saurischian* ('reptile-' or 'lizard-hipped') and the

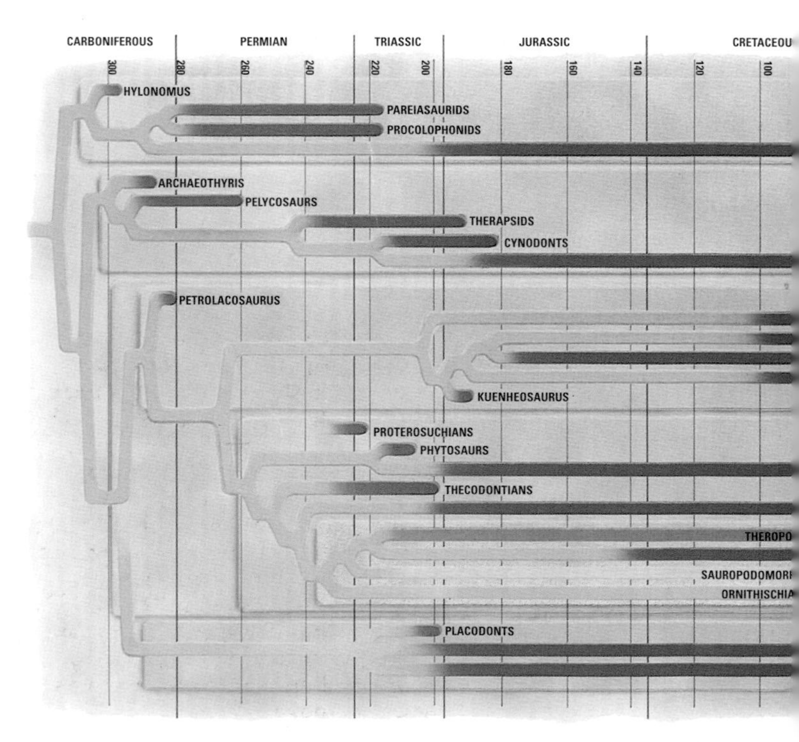

ornithischian ('bird-hipped'). In saurischian dinosaurs the three bones on each side of the hip radiate outward from the hip socket. The upper bone (ilium) contacts the backbone, forming a very firm attachment, while the two lower bones (pubis and ischium) point forward and backward respectively and provide areas for the attachments of large, leg-moving muscles. Examples of saurischian dinosaurs are the large plant-eating sauropods *Diplodocus* and *Brachiosaurus* and the meat-eating theropods *Allosaurus* and *Tyrannosaurus*.

In early ornithischian dinosaurs the pubis lies back against the ischium. In later ornithischians the pubis points forward. Ornithischians were all herbivores so far as we can tell and tended to have a distinctive turtle-like beak at the tips of the jaws. Examples include ornithopods such as *Hypsilophodon*, ceratopians (*Triceratops*) and stegosaurs (*Stegosaurus*).

It has been estimated that the earth is about 4,600 million years old. The oldest rocks so far discovered are about 3,600 million years old. Precise dating of rocks is important to palaeontologists because it tells them the age of fossilised organisms contained within them. There are two ways of dating rocks, *comparative* dating and *absolute* dating. Comparative dating involves such means as comparing the characteristic fossils of one rock sample with those of another: if they are similar, it is a fair supposition that they are of similar age. Time sequences can be constructed in this way but they give no idea of the actual age of the fossils. Absolute dating can be done by analysing radioactive isotopes, which are known to decay at an established rate. ▶

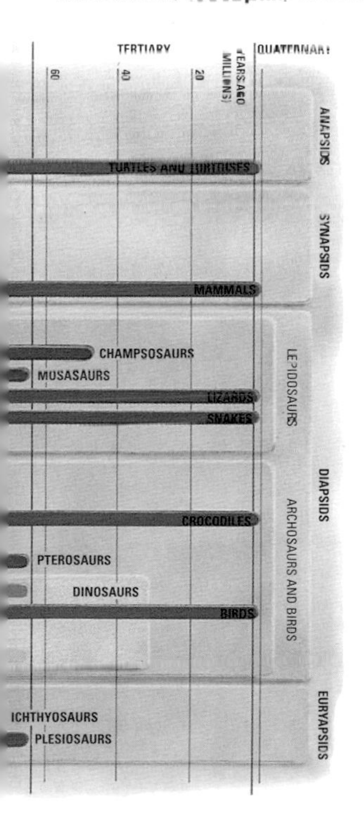

Left: Reptiles can be divided into four major groups on the basis of the pattern of openings in the back of the skull. Anapsids have no skull openings. Synapsids have one low opening and euryapsids one high opening. Diapsids, with two skull openings, can be further divided into two groups: lepidosaurs (lizards and snakes) and archosaurs (crocodiles, dinosaurs and their kin). The Triassic was the time of origin of all major archosaur groups from the thecodontians to the aerial pterosaurs and the dinosaurs.

The proportions remaining in the rocks allow the age of the rocks to be calculated.

Dinosaurs are not the oldest known fossils. The oldest forms of life so far discovered are tiny, bacteria-like creatures whose remains have been preserved in rocks 3,000 million years old. More complicated life forms appear about 2,500 million years later. The vast expanse of time before the first complex organisms start to appear is known as the Precambrian ('before the Cambrian'). Beyond the Precambrian, the last 600 million years of life on earth is termed the Phanerozoic ('visible life'), which is in turn divided into three eras - the Palaeozoic ('ancient life'), Mesozoic ('middle life') and Cenozoic, or Kainozoic ('recent life').

The **Palaeozoic Era** (600-225 million years ago) marks the appearance of most of the major groups of animals and plants that we recognise today, such as shellfish, insects, spiders, fish, amphibians, reptiles and most plant types except for the flowering plants.

The **Mesozoic Era** (225-64 million years ago) marks the arrival of several modern groups, notably the mammals and birds as well as flowering plants and many modern groups of insect. More importantly from our point of view, the Mesozoic marks the arrival of dinosaurs and their rise to dominance throughout this era.

The Mesozoic is divided into three periods: the Triassic Period (225-200 million years ago), the Jurassic Period (200-135 million years ago) and the Cretaceous Period (135-64 million years ago). At the start of the Triassic there were no dinosaurs. Mammal-like reptiles were particularly abundant; these, however, died out towards the end of the Triassic to be replaced by the dinosaurs. Many kinds of dinosaur appeared throughout the remaining 140 million years of the Jurassic and Cretaceous Periods but they all mysteriously became extinct at the

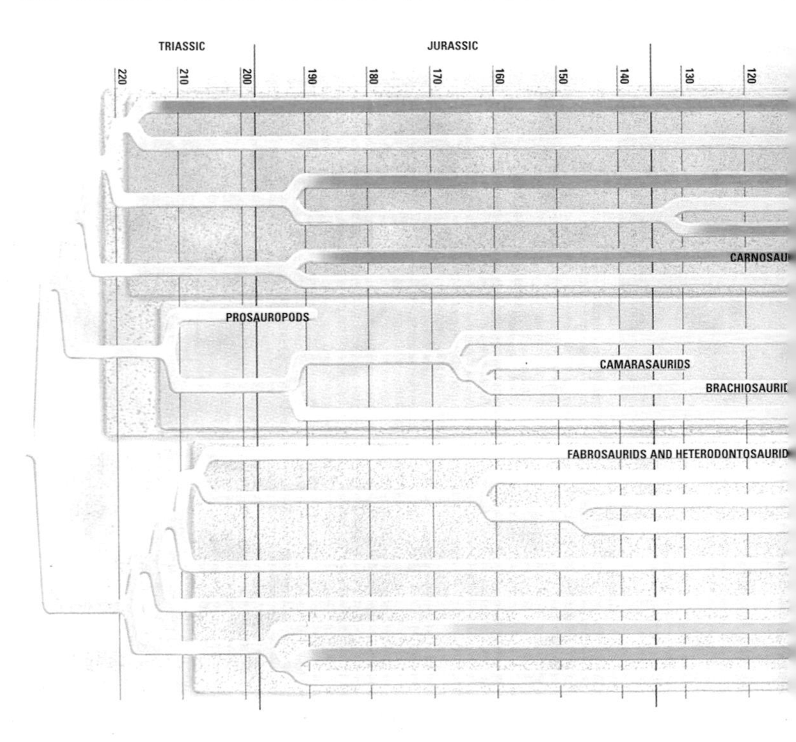

end of the Cretaceous.

The **Cenozoic (Kainozoic) Era** (64 million years ago to the present day) saw the change to animals and plants more typical of today. Mammals, birds, insects and flowering plants spread everywhere and the first humans appeared. Early Man, however, did not appear on earth until a mere two to three million years ago - long after the dinosaurs went extinct!

The notion of continental drift is relevant to the study of dinosaurs. The great sheets of the earth's crust, known as tectonic plates, are slowly moving, carrying the continents about on them. The continents have moved around quite considerably in geological time. In the Triassic Period all the continents were joined together to form the supercontinent of Pangaea. This began to split in the Jurassic Period. A narrow Atlantic Ocean formed and sea separated Europe and Asia. By the early Cretaceous, the continents were further removed and shallow seas started to divide the southern continents. By the late Cretaceous, South America and Africa had begun to separate, India was rafting away across the Indian Ocean and Europe and North America were moving apart. Seaways also divided Europe and Asia *and* western from eastern North America. This resulted in some curiously isolated fauna. The positions of the continents and the connections or barriers between them are major factors that have affected the evolutionary history and geographical distribution of particular groups of dinosaurs.

As noted above, the major division of the dinosaurs is into the Saurischia and Ornithischia, based primarily on differences in hip structure. The Saurischia are further subdivided into Theropoda and Sauropodomorpha. The theropods included a wide variety of carnivorous ▶

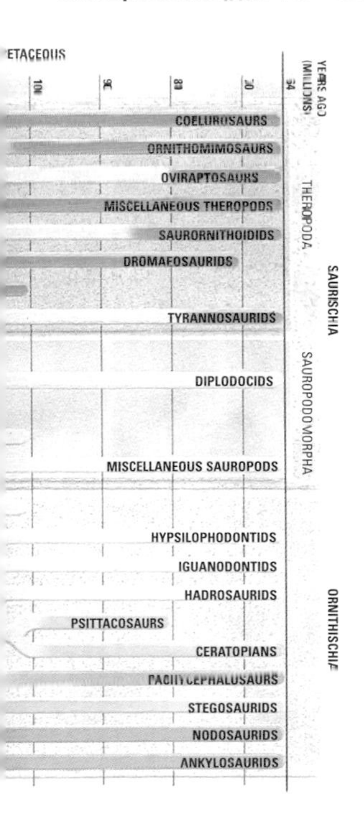

Left: The major division of the dinosaurs is into the Saurischia and Ornithischia. The Saurischia are further subdivided into Theropoda and Sauropodomorpha. The theropods were bipedal carnivores. The sauropodomorphs were herbivores, as were all the Ornithischia.
If we can have one of these family trees and not both, I think this one - dinos. - is the one to prefer.

dinosaurs all of which were bipedal. They range from small fast runners such as coelurosaurs to the larger carnosaurs and tyrannosaurids of the late Cretaceous. The sauropodomorphs were the large, plant-eating dinosaurs of the Mesozoic. They include the partially bipedal prosauropods of the late Triassic and early Jurassic and the massive quadrupedal sauropods of the later Jurassic and Cretaceous.

The Ornithischia were all herbivores. They can be further divided into a series of distinctive types: Ornithopoda, Ceratopia, Pachycephalosaurs, Stegosauria and Ankylosauria. Ornithopods first appeared in the early Jurassic with small, lightly built creatures such as the fabrosaurids. They culminate in the late Cretaceous hadrosaurids. Ceratopians were a late Cretaceous group characterised by peculiar parrot-like beaks, horns and frills. Pachycephalosaurs were a strange group with oddly thickened skulls, while the stegosaurs and ankylosaurs were distinctively armoured types.

Fossilised dinosaur remains have been found all over the world. The first descriptions were made by the Reverend William Buckland and Dr Gideon Mantell in England in the 1820s, although neither realised the significance of their discoveries. It was Richard Owen, a comparative anatomist, whose review of British fossil reptiles in 1841 revealed that *Iguanodon, Megalosaurus* and *Hylaeosaurus* were so unlike living lizards that they deserved to be recognised as a separate group which he called Dinosauria ('terrible reptiles').

Top right: The first stage in a restoration of Iguanodon is the reconstruction of the skeleton. It is possible to position the muscles and ligaments correctly thanks to 'scars' left on the bones where they were attached. Once the skeleton has been clothed in muscles, it can be wrapped in skin to provide a restoration of the animal as a living creature.

Below right: In these diagrams the pubis is shown in blue, the muscles in red. In *Ticinosuchus*, a thecodontian included for comparison, the normal hip muscles operate effectively because the femur is angled inwards. In the quadrupedal sauropod *Diplodocus* muscle 1 still operates because the femur does not swing far forward. Muscle 1 works more effectively for a bipedal theropod like *Ceratosaurus* because the pubis is tilted up and away from the femur. In *Scelidosaurus*, an early quadrupedal ornithischian, the pubis has moved backwards and muscle 1 is attached to the ilium. In the bipedal *Hypsilophodon* the new pubic bone has grown for the attachment of muscle 1.

Below: This sequence shows the sprawling posture of most living reptiles (left). In the centre is the semi-erect posture adopted by thecodontians and living crocodiles. On the right is the fully erect posture typical of dinosaurs, birds and mammals.

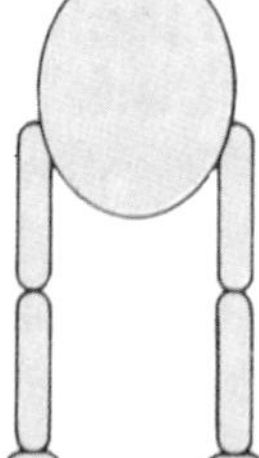

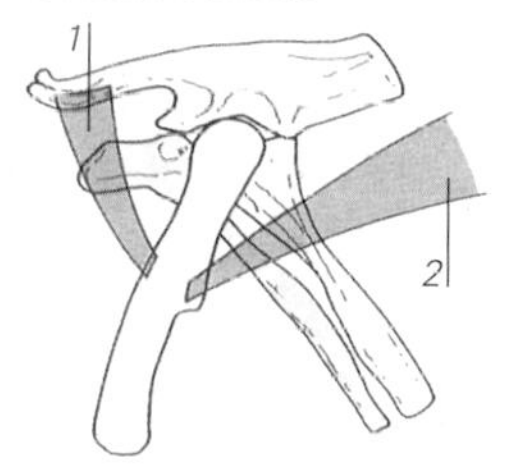
Scelidosaurus
1
2

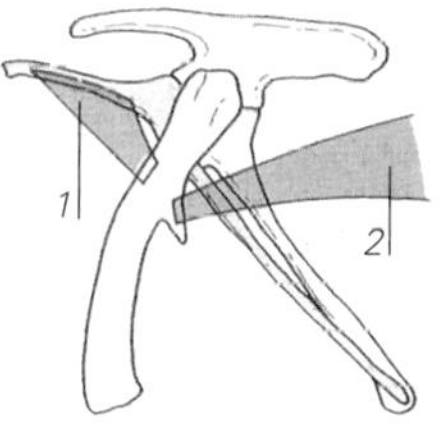
Hypsilophodon
1
2

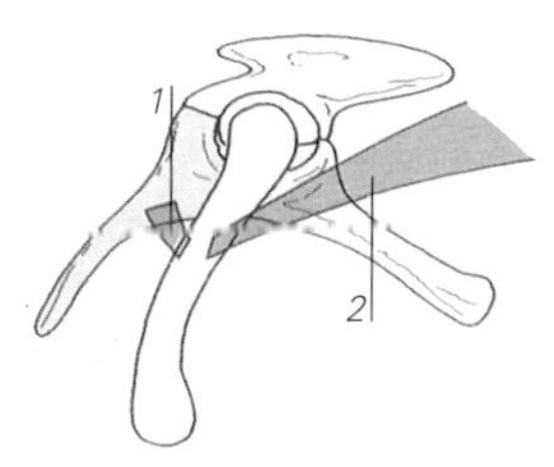
Ticinosuchus
1
2

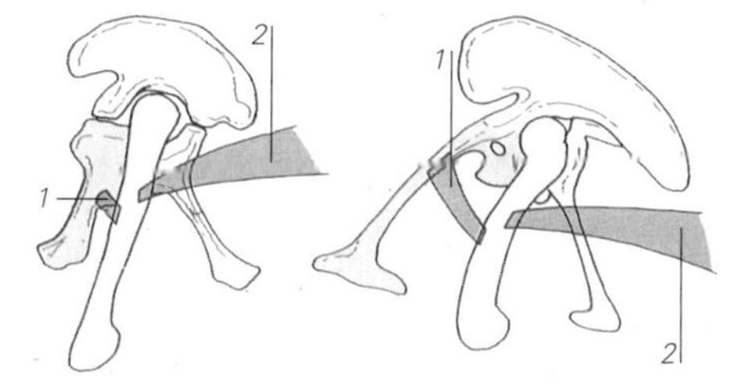
Diplodocus
2
1
Ceratosaurus
1
2

Coelurosaurs

The saurischian ('lizard-hipped') dinosaurs were a fairly mixed group of animals, which all shared the organisation of the hindlimb and pelvis for a fully erect position. The saurischians fall into at least two distinct groups: the Theropoda (or theropods; 'beast feet') and Sauropodomorpha (sauropodomorphs; 'reptile-type feet'). The theropods tended to be bipedal carnivores, while the sauropodomorphs tended to be either omnivores (i.e. eating a mixed diet) or herbivores.

The theropods were an enormously varied group of carnivorous dinosaurs, having in common some predatory habits and associated skeletal form. Unfortunately their relationships are not at all clear because good theropod fossils are relatively rare. There are many isolated theropod fossil bones and teeth, which tend only to add to the confusion.

All theropods were carnivores (although there are one or two examples such as the ornithomimosaurs which lacked teeth and may have had a rather specialised diet); they also all tended to be two-legged (bipedal) runners. It is difficult to find obvious counterparts for this kind

of body plan among living animals. The most familiar living carnivores are the quadrupedal (four-footed) mammals such as dogs, bears and cats. The only two-legged carnivores are found among the birds (kestrels, kites, eagles, etc), but these winged and feathered animals can hardly be compared to the ground-dwelling theropods of the dinosaur era. This poses the question why there were so many obviously successful ground-dwelling bipedal predators among dinosaurs whereas today the ground-dwelling predators are all quadrupeds.

The coelurosaurs ('hollow-tailed reptiles') were a rather odd mixture of generally small, lightly built theropods. Though not all close relatives, they are described together here simply as a matter of convenience. All of these theropods were slender, fast-running predators with small heads (the jaws of which were lined with small, sharp teeth), long flexible necks and long arms with sharply taloned grasping hands. Unfortunately, few of their fossils have been preserved. Small animal carcasses tend to rot very quickly and their skeletal remains are liable to be scavenged and scattered or destroyed.

Left: **An intriguing suggestion has been advanced that one species of the coelurosaur *Compsognathus* (C. corallestris) may have been equipped with flipper-like forelimbs, which would have allowed it to adopt an amphibious way of life, venturing into lagoons to find food or avoid its natural enemies. Recent study of the skeleton, however, casts doubt on the evidence of flippers.**

Compsognathus

Period: Late Jurassic. **Family:** Coelurosaurs.
Where found: Southern Europe.
Estimated length: 28in-4ft 7in (70cm-1.4m)

Compsognathus ('pretty jaw') remains have been discovered in rocks of late Jurassic age from southern Germany and France. It was a small creature, probably between 28in and 4ft 7in (70cm-1.4m) in length.

The first remains of *Compsognathus* to be discovered were a beautifully preserved, virtually complete skeleton from lithographic limestone in Bavaria, southern Germany, found by a Dr Oberndorfer in the late 1850s. Since then only two other specimens of *Compsognathus* have been reported. One consists of a few toe bones from the same area. The other is an almost complete skeleton discovered in 1972 in rocks of a similar age near Nice in southern France.

The first *Compsognathus* skeleton is by far the best-known specimen. It represents an animal about 28in (70cm) long, preserved lying on its right-hand side. The skeleton is virtually undisturbed. The animal died with its head and neck strongly arched over the back, a position often found in skeletons. The likely cause of this contorted posture is the contraction in rigor mortis of the neck muscles and ligaments, which would have been very powerful in these long-necked animals.

Above: **One of the smallest dinosaurs of all, some *Compsognathus* reached a total length of only 28in (70cm) or so. Most of this length was made up by the long, slender tail. An adult was no heavier than a present-day hen. The tail was used as a balancing rod during fast running. The neck was quite long and the hand had only two clawed fingers, an unusual feature.**

The proportions of *Compsognathus* are very similar to those of *Coelophysis.* A long tail counterbalances its front and the hindlimbs are strong and slender, indicating that it was a fleet-footed biped. The forelimbs deserve particular mention, first because they are unusually short for an animal that presumably used them to grasp prey and second because they exhibit only two clawed fingers on each hand, whereas *Coelophysis* had three and a remnant of a fourth.

It is reasonably self-evident that *Compsognathus* was a fleet-footed, bipedal predator of small animals: presumably insects and small vertebrates of various types. We can, luckily, be fairly certain of the probable feeding habits and abilities of *Compsognathus* because the remains of its last meal are preserved within its ribcage. The stomach contents showed that it consisted of the skeleton of a small lizard named Bavarisaurus. Judging by the proportions of its limbs and its long tail, Bavarisaurus must have been an extremely fast running, agile, ground-dwelling lizard. Since *Compsognathus* undoubtedly caught creatures like *Bavarisaurus* it must have had keen sight, rapid acceleration, high speed, manoeuvrability and quick reactions.

In 1972 a new species of *Compsognathus (C. corallestris)* was described, based on a fairly complete skeleton of a larger animal in almost the same preserved position, found on a slab of rock. The new ▶

specimen was given the new specific name because it was larger than the German skeleton and also because it seemed to have flipper-like front legs. At first it was envisaged that this species of *Compsognathus* lived in and around coral lagoons and that the 'flippers' on its forelimbs enabled it to swim more efficiently, either in pursuit of prey or to avoid predators. However, the forelimbs of this skeleton are quite poorly preserved, and the area of rock that is supposed to show the flipper impression does not look very different from other areas of the rock. It has now been proved fairly conclusively that the French specimen was simply a larger version of the same species of *Compsognathus* from Germany and that there was no good evidence for a flipper on the forelimb.

Top right: **This lightly built skull is typical of a predator that caught small, active animals such as insects or small vertebrates. The teeth are sharply pointed but not particularly strong and the jaw-closing muscles are fairly generalised.**

Right: **The hand of *Compsognathus* is peculiarly short for an animal that presumably grasped its prey. Also, only two of the fingers are clawed and the third is very small indeed. The foot, however, is quite typical of most coelurosaurs, with three long, slender, forward-pointing toes and a fourth pointing backwards.**

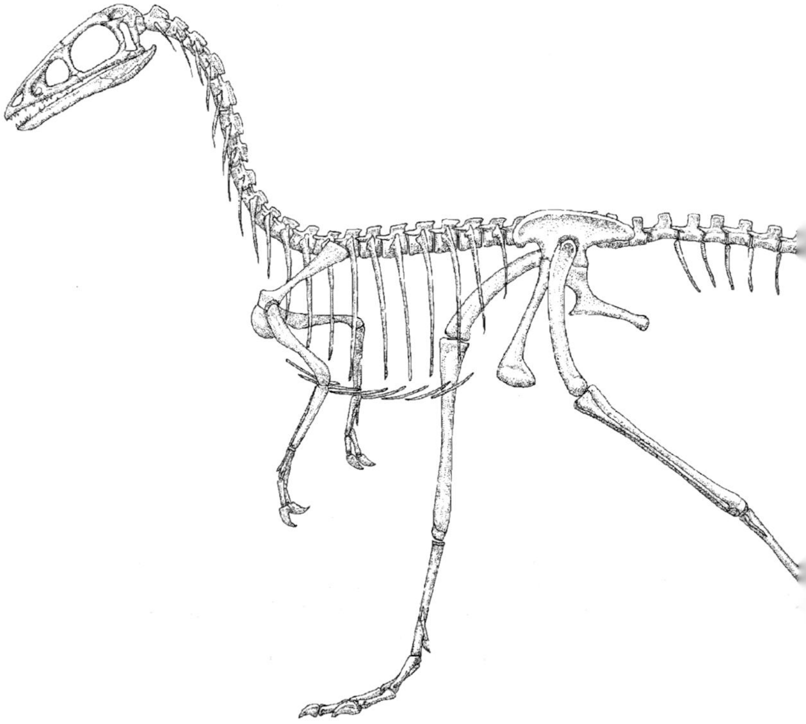

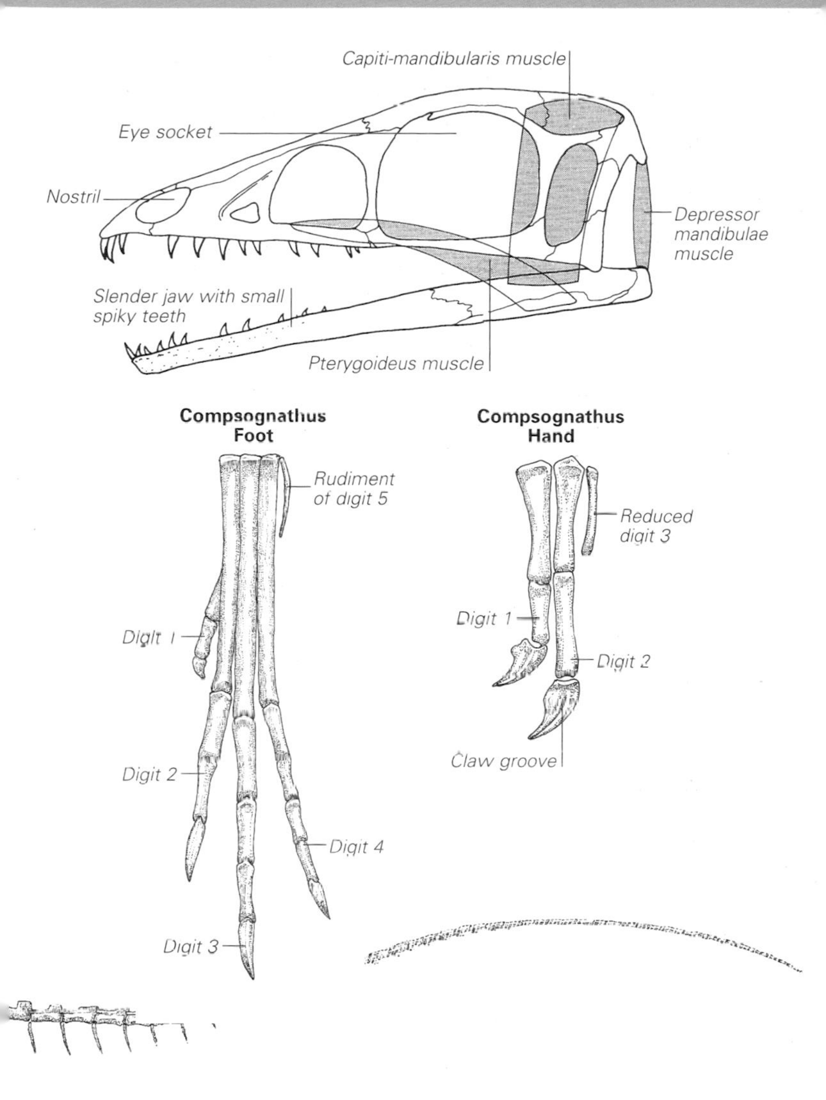

Left: Compsognathus **displayed typical coelurosaur features. These animals were comparatively small for dinosaurs. The neck was long and flexible and joined on to a rather compact body. The animal was bipedal with strong, slender back legs and reduced, but still useful front legs. The fingers were armed with strong claws for grasping prey. The long tail acted as a counterbalance for the front of the body.**

Coelophysis

Period: Late Triassic. **Family:** Coelurosaurs.
Where found: North America.
Estimated length: 10ft (3m).

The incomplete remains of *Coelophysis* ('hollow form') were first discovered in 1881 by an amateur fossil collector named David Baldwin in New Mexico, where there are good exposures of Permian and Triassic rocks. Experts recognised them as the bones of a small, very lightly built, carnivorous dinosaur. The bones – various vertebrae, leg bones and pieces of pelvis and rib – remained all that was known of one of the earliest discovered dinosaurs for the next sixty years.

An expedition organised by the American Museum of Natural History revisited the area in 1947 and, using Baldwin's field notes, discovered the original *Coelophysis* locality, now on a property known as Ghost Ranch. The team found large numbers of bone fragments but no good skeletons and eventually decided to excavate a large section of the hillside, down to the layer where the bones seemed to be weathering out. As this layer was exposed, it revealed one of the most amazing dinosaur graveyards. Literally dozens of skeletons were discovered, all lying across one another. It seems as though some local catastrophe had struck a herd of these animals; perhaps they were caught in a flash flood and their carcasses were swept downriver on to a sand bar. Whatever the reason, the phenomenon has left some of the best evidence of any Triassic dinosaur. In this remarkable accumulation of skeletons can be seen animals of all ages from very young to fully grown.

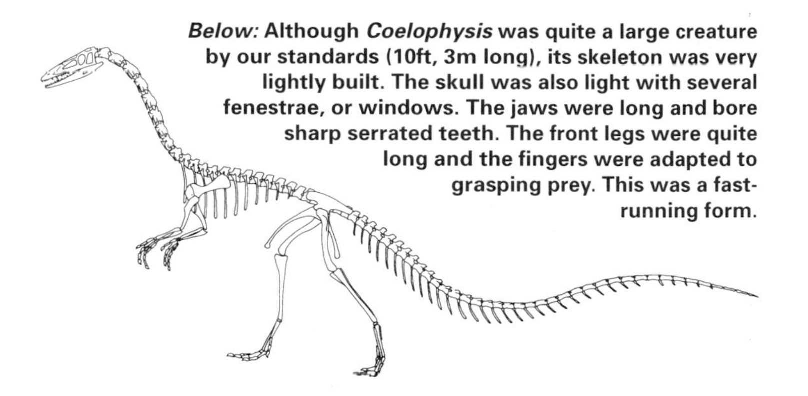

Below: **Although *Coelophysis* was quite a large creature by our standards (10ft, 3m long), its skeleton was very lightly built. The skull was also light with several fenestrae, or windows. The jaws were long and bore sharp serrated teeth. The front legs were quite long and the fingers were adapted to grasping prey. This was a fast-running form.**

Coelophysis was a slender creature; its skeleton was very lightly built, with a long tail counterbalancing the front part of its body. The head was long and pointed, the eyes were large and the long jaws were armed with sharp, serrated teeth. As with all coelurosaurs, the neck was very slender and flexible. The arms were moderately long and had sharp, clawed hands for grasping prey. The back legs were quite long and slender, clearly designed for running fast in pursuit of prey.

The general lifestyle of *Coelophysis* is fairly obvious. With its light build, grasping hands and mouth lined with sharp teeth, it was undoubtedly a nimble predator of the late Triassic. Growing to a maximum length of 10ft (3m), *Coelophysis* may well have preyed upon the small, fleet-footed ornithopods of the time: *Lesothosaurus*, *Heterodontosaurus* and *Scutellosaurus*, all of which were no more than 3-5ft (1-1.5m) long. In fact, they probably had a fairly varied diet, as many carnivores do today, taking large and small insects, amphibians and lizards. The Ghost Ranch discoveries also give a rather gruesome insight into the feeding habits of *Coelophysis*. Some of the skeletons reveal the presence of small *Coelophysis* skeletons inside the ribcage of adult animals. At first it was supposed that the young skeletons were those of unborn infants. But all dinosaurs seem to have laid eggs, rather than bearing live young. The skeletons are too large and well-formed to have been embryos inside eggs; they must therefore represent the last meal of the adult *Coelophysis*! So it seems likely that *Coelophysis* adults were cannibals, eating any small creatures that they could catch – even their own kind!

Left: **This is one of the earliest and most primitive dinosaurs. *Coelophysis* was very slim and it could have run on its hind legs or walked on all fours. The hands were equipped with three strong fingers that were probably used for attacking smaller prey such as the small lizard-like reptiles that lived at the same time. Some of the skeletons of *Coelophysis* that were found in a mass burial at Ghost Ranch, New Mexico, in 1947 contained the bones of juveniles of the same species. It was thought that these were babies ready to be born, but they are rather too big for that, so *Coelophysis* may have been a cannibal.**

Ornitholestes

Period: Late Jurassic. **Family:** Coelurosaurs.
Where found: North America.
Estimated length: 6ft 6in (2m).

Ornitholestes ('bird robber') was discovered in late Jurassic rocks at Bone Cabin Quarry near Como in Wyoming, USA, in 1900. This specimen, which consists of a partial skeleton including the skull, jaws and many other parts, was first described by Henry Fairfield Osborn in 1903 and in more detail in 1916. To this day it is still only known from this specimen and an incomplete hand from another individual.

A quick glance at *Ornitholestes, Coelophysis* and *Compsognathus* reveals the very strong similarity between them. The body is balanced at the hips and the neck is slender and flexible. In *Ornitholestes,* however, the skull and forelimbs are sufficiently different to merit some brief comments. The skull is rather more robustly constructed than in the other two examples, being both deeper and shorter-snouted. The teeth are also numerous and quite large. This arrangement of skull and teeth suggests *Ornitholestes* had greater mechanical strength and thus a rather more powerful bite than the other two. If so, *Ornitholestes* was probably capable of tackling larger and more active prey than either *Compsognathus* or *Coelophysis*. ▶

Below: Ornitholestes **was an active predator and may have fed on small animals such as lizards, frogs and early mammals. It had strong jaws and grasping hands.**

The hand, which was represented by several finger bones in the original skeleton and two other complete fingers from another individual, is rather unusually proportioned. The second and third fingers are long, slender and almost equal in length, while the first finger is very short. The arm is also relatively long compared with that of *Coelophysis* and *Compsognathus*. Both of these features suggest an enhanced prehensile ability of the forelimb for reaching and grasping prey more powerfully and effectively The difference in length between the first and the second and third fingers is linked to the ability to turn the first finger inwards against the other two like a thumb. The hand could therefore grip its prey very powerfully indeed. The structure of the hand is rather similar to that of dromaeosaurids.

***Below: Ornitholestes* was another small, lightly built theropod, with a long, slender neck, large back legs and small front legs and the long, counterbalancing tail.**

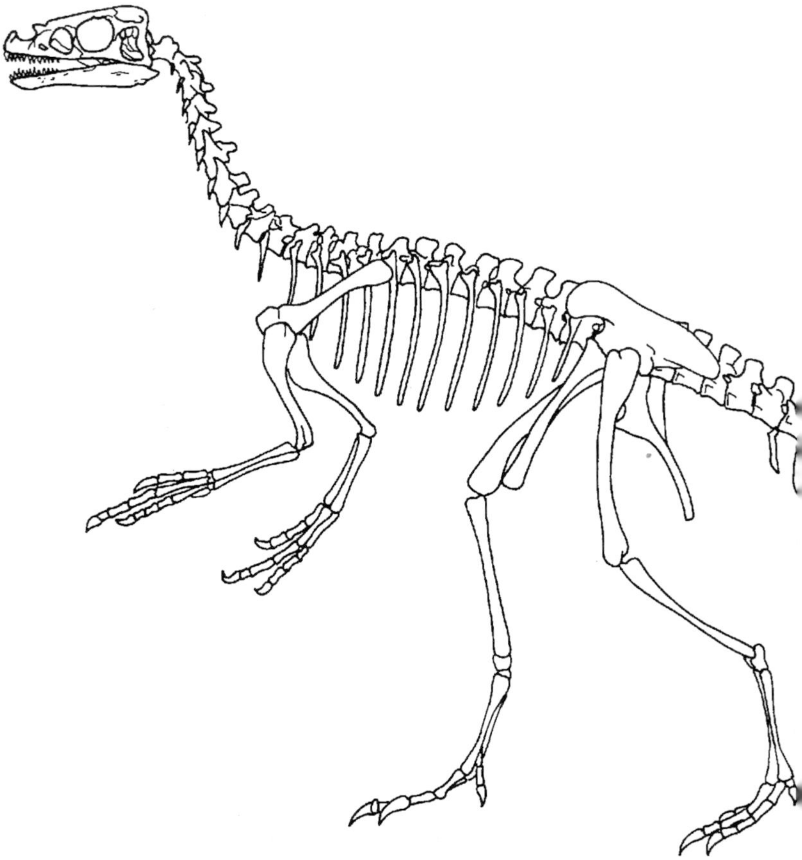

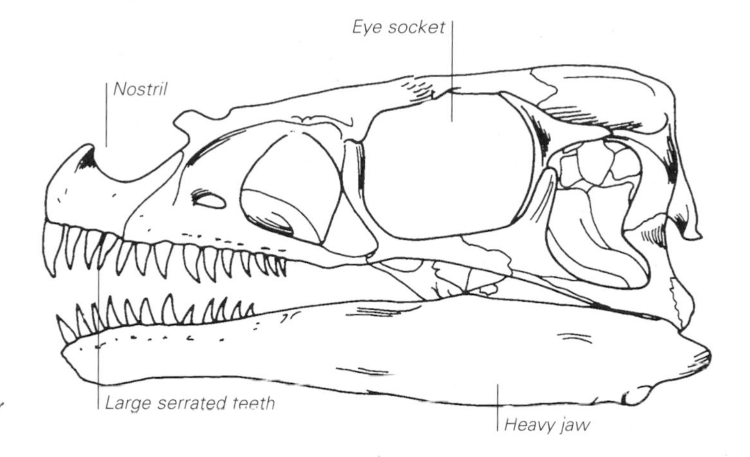

Above: This predator had a comparatively heavy skull, with shortish jaws and robust teeth, which clearly equipped the animal with quite a powerful bite.

Right: The hand of _Ornitholestes_ is unusual for coelurosaurs in having two especially long fingers and a short first finger. It is possible that this short finger could be turned in towards the others, as we do with our thumb, providing a very effective mechanism for gripping prey.

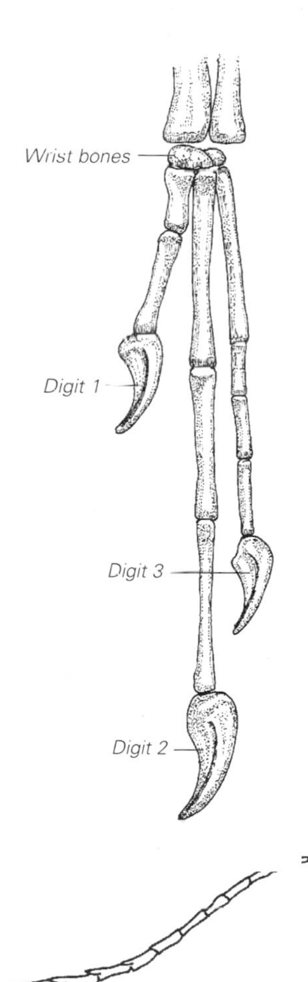

Ornithomimosaurs & Oviraptorosaurs

The remains of ornithomimosaurs ('ostrich dinosaurs') are reasonably abundant in late Cretaceous rocks of western North America and eastern Asia (Mongolia). Ornithomimosaurs seem to have been very similar in size and appearance, reaching body lengths of about 10-13ft (3-4m) and strongly resembling modem ground-dwelling birds such as the ostrich, although the latter obviously lack a long, bony tail and clawed arms. The first ornithomimosaur remains (later named *Ornithomimus*, 'speedy bird mimic') consisted of the imperfect foot of a dinosaur, discovered in 1889 near Denver, Colorado. It was O. C. Marsh who realised that these animals were not ornithopods as originally suspected, but theropods of a hitherto unknown sort. Their precise relationship to other theropods was very uncertain; they represented relatively large animals and were therefore thought to belong to the carnosaurs rather than the smaller coelurosaurs.

The first reasonably complete skeleton of an ornithomimosaur was described in 1917 by Henry Fairfield Osborn. This skeleton consisted of a more or less completely preserved animal, lacking only parts of the head, some of the vertebrae and a few limb bones. Osborn suggested that a new generic name, *Struthiomimus* ('ostrich mimic') *altus* be used. Osborn recognised that *Struthiomimus* was from a geologically earlier period than

Ornithomimus and also differed in having a small, splint-like remnant of a fourth toe on its hindfoot, which *Ornithomimus* lacked.

The really unexpected characteristic of *Struthiomimus* was the absence of teeth in its jaws, which were probably sheathed in a homy beak. The thin and light structure of ornithomimosaurs' skull bones makes it highly likely that the skulls of these creatures were flexible and that the beaks could move separately from the jaws, as is the case in some living birds such as parrots.

The neck was long and slender and the bones were very flexibly jointed to permit great mobility, whereas the back and the end of the tail seem to have been held rather stiffly. Ornithomimosaurs were thus probably ground-dwelling, omnivorous dinosaurs, capable of running very fast – perhaps as fast as living ostriches (31 mph, 50 kph). This permitted them not only to escape larger predators, but also to catch fast-moving prey, such as lizards, small mammals or flying insects.

The oviraptorosaurs – 'egg-stealing reptiles' – were equally extraordinary creatures. They were toothless, theropod dinosaurs, whose remains have been found in Mongolia. Whereas the earliest ornithomimosaurs seem to have appeared in the late Cretaceous, the oviraptorosaurs were exclusively late Cretaceous in age.

Left: **The basic body shape of ornithomimosaurs would seem to be well adapted to a plant-eating lifestyle. The long arms and hands might be used to grasp branches while the beak could nip off buds and leaves. Of course these attributes would also suit a speedy omnivore with a wider and more catholic diet.**

Oviraptor

Period: Late Cretaceous. **Family:** Oviraptorosaurs.
Where found: Mongolia.
Estimated length: 5ft-6ft 6in (1.5-2m).

The first remains of oviraptosaur fossils were those named *Oviraptor* ('egg thief'). The remains consisted of one partial skull and skeleton discovered in 1923 at Shabarakh Usu, southern Mongolia. The skull, although rather badly fractured, was preserved in a nodule of sandstone, enabling a clear idea of its shape and the arrangement of its bones to be obtained. It is notable for the large number of openings in its sides and the curious horn-like prong on the tip of its snout. As in the ornithomimosaurs, this skull possesses no teeth and presumably compensated for this by having horn-covered jaws. However, unlike in ornithomimosaurs, the skull is rather short-snouted, with a very deep and strong lower jaw.

Other remains included fragmentary neck vertebrae, various ribs, the shoulder bones and parts of the hands. One hand exhibited three elongate fingers ending in large, sharp claws. Preserved in the shoulder was a modified collar-bone, or clavicle – an unexpected find because it had hitherto been believed that the bony collar-bone had been lost before dinosaurs evolved.

Five better-preserved skulls and skeletons of *Oviraptor* were discovered in 1972, confirming the presence of the unusual collar-bone. The curious feature is that, instead of comprising a pair of bones, one on each side of the shoulder girdle, the two bones are welded together to form a single curved bone. This arrangement is strikingly like that seen in living birds whose collar-bones are fused together to form the 'wish-bone' (furcula). This discovery has added much fuel to the debate over the origin and relationships of birds and dinosaurs.

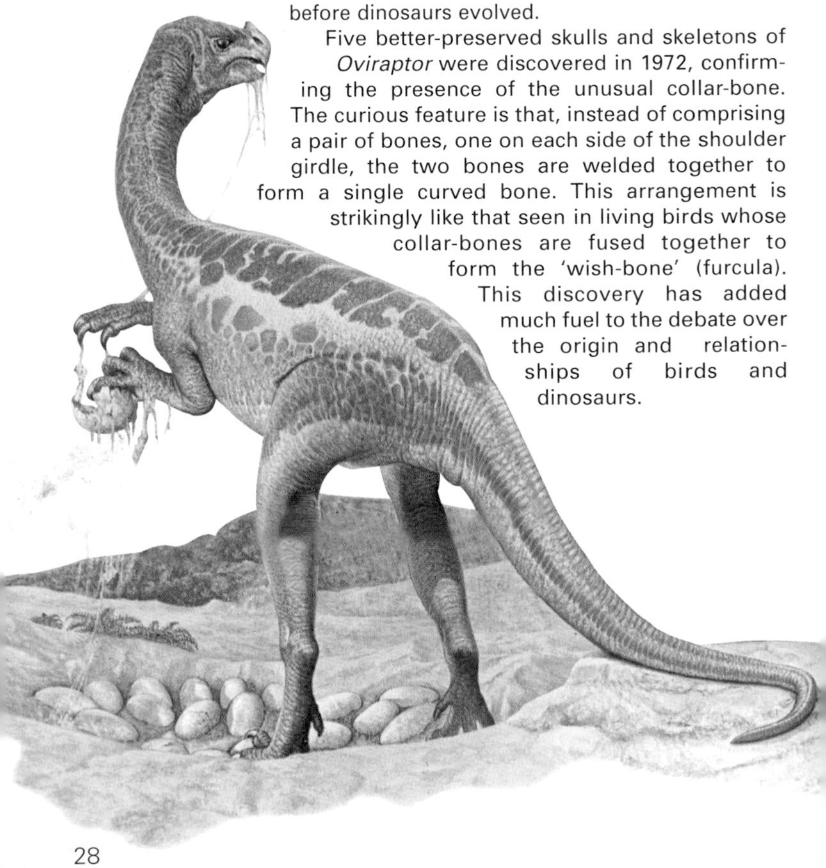

***Right:* Oviraptor skulls exhibit quite a lot of variety. The top two skulls have been assigned to the species *philoceratops,* yet one has a small bump in the nasal region, while the other has a large crest. The third and fourth drawings show another species from Mongolia. Its large eye sockets and smooth bone contours suggest that it is a juvenile animal.**

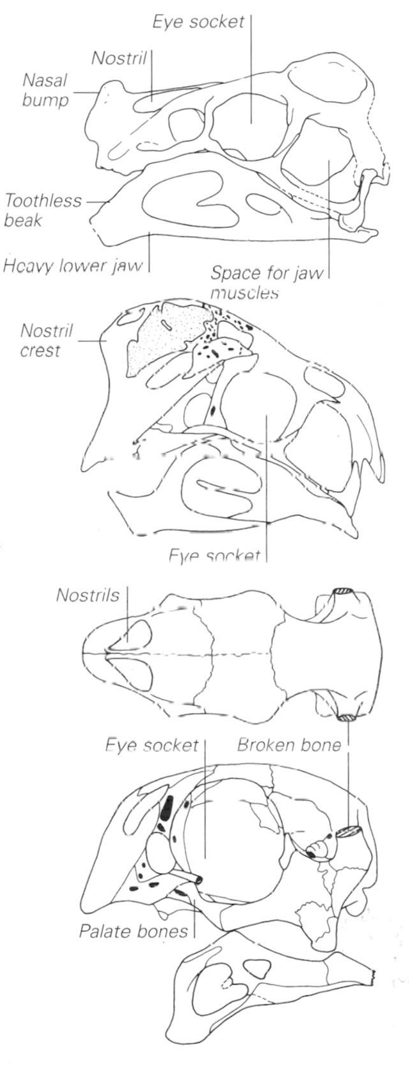

The remainder of the skeleton of *Oviraptor* appears to be very similar to that of most theropods. Differences in skull shape and degree of horn development in *Oviraptor* remains may be due to the degree of maturity of the specimen.

An unusual bird-like jaw from the late Cretaceous of Alberta, Canada, very probably represents a North American species of the oviraptorosaurs.

The circumstances of preservation of the original specimen of *Oviraptor* provided the reason for its name: *Oviraptor philoceratops* ('egg thief, fond of ceratopian eggs'). Its skull and skeleton were found lying on top of a clutch of *Protoceratops* eggs! Perhaps the unfortunate creature had died at the very moment of robbing a nest, or its skull was crushed after being caught by an enraged parent. We shall never know. It is certainly possible that *Oviraptor* preyed upon ceratopian eggs, which it cracked open with its horny beak. Perhaps, like the ornithomimosaurs, they were general predators or scavengers of anything dead or alive.

***Left:* Oviraptor may have fed on the eggs of other dinosaurs, which it crushed by biting. The jaws were relatively more massive than those of the ornithomimosaurs. The jaw bones were completely toothless, but may have been covered with a horny sheath.**

Struthiomimus

Period: Late Cretaceous. **Family:** Ornithomimosaurs.
Where found: Western North America.
Estimated length: 10-13ft (3-4m).

Struthiomimus resembled ostrich-like running birds in the structure of its head, neck and legs. Its forelimbs, however, were most similar to those of sloths, which hang from branches. That *Struthiomimus* was a running creature seems incontrovertible. Its tail counterbalanced the front part of its body and its end was very stiff since the prongs of bone that joined the vertebrae together were very long and so restricted movement. The stiffened back end was probably used as a dynamic stabiliser for rapid changes of direction, as well as straight running. This particular adaptation seems to be quite widespread among fleet-footed dinosaurs.

Right: **This was a medium-sized ostrich dinosaur, being 10-13ft (3-4m) long. The proportions of the body of *Struthiomimus* and many of the more detailed features of its anatomy are remarkably convergent with present-day ostriches. The most obvious differences are that *Struthiomimus* had no feathers (as far as we know) and that it used its long tail for balancing while running. Ostriches use their reduced wings for this purpose.**

As far as their diet is concerned, William Beebe proposed that ornithomimosaurs were insectivores, perhaps the equivalent of the anteaters of today. Henry Osborn, discoverer of the first partial skeleton of an ornithomimosaur, rejected this theory because the forelimbs of *Struthiomimus* were clearly not powerful enough to undertake the sort of digging activities needed to grub up anthills. Certainly there is no evidence of the powerful shoulder muscles characteristic of modem anteaters, nor was there any evidence of a long, sticky tongue. Furthermore, the hindlimbs were adapted for fast running rather than digging.

Another theory arose from the fact that the remains of ornithomimosaurs are usually found in coastal shore deposits. It was proposed that these creatures may have waded along shores feeding on small crabs and shrimps, which they caught by using their forelimbs for scraping sand, moving rocks and probing crevices. Osborn rejected this theory also, on several grounds. First, he suggested that the beak and hands were not adapted for catching shrimps and the like. Second, he stated that the forelimbs were not adapted either for digging or holding struggling prey. These two arguments were matters of opinion, rather than logical conclusions from the facts, and did not provide a conclusive rebuttal of the shore-bird proposal. Third, neither the structure of the beak nor that of the feet resembles that of living wading birds. Here at least Osborn was making a statement of comparison – although whether the structure and habits of small wading birds can be realistically compared with those of a shore-dwelling dinosaur 10-13ft (3-4m) long must be open to doubt.

Having reviewed and rejected previous theories, Osborn proposed his own - the ostrich theory - which was that *Struthiomimus* was a browsing herbivore. He suggested that the forelimbs were used as grapples for bending down branches, so that young shoots and buds could be bitten off. This type of lifestyle seems to explain the combination of long, grasping hands and arms and the long, flexible neck, which would have allowed the head to be moved with accuracy between branches and twigs, there to peck at food. The shape of the beak seems well suited to this type of feeding. And finally the feet are similar to those of the big ostrich-like birds.

A fourth interpretation of the habits of *Struthiomimus* was proposed by Dr William King Gregory. Gregory concurs with Osborn in envisaging these animals as very fast-running ground-dwellers, which used their arms and hands as grapples to obtain food. However, Gregory suggested that *Struthiomimus* was an omnivore, taking fruits and seeds as well as smal vertebrates (mammals, reptiles, amphibians) and larger invertebrates (millipedes, flying insects, etc). He also came up with the novel suggestion that they may have had skin flaps (patagia) between the arms and body, serving to prevent the animal from toppling forward when running fast with arms outstretched. This last suggestion has never really been taken seriously and could be proved only if a ▶

well-preserved skin impression were to be found.

Although the sea-shore theory has not been disproved, the general consensus today supports the opinions of Osborn and Gregory. Ornithomimosaurs were probably ground-dwelling, omnivorous dinosaurs, capable of fast running – perhaps as fast as living ostriches (31 mph, 50 kph). Their fleetness of foot and probable great manoeuvrability permitted them not only to escape larger predators but also to catch fast-moving prey, such as lizards, small mammals or flying insects.

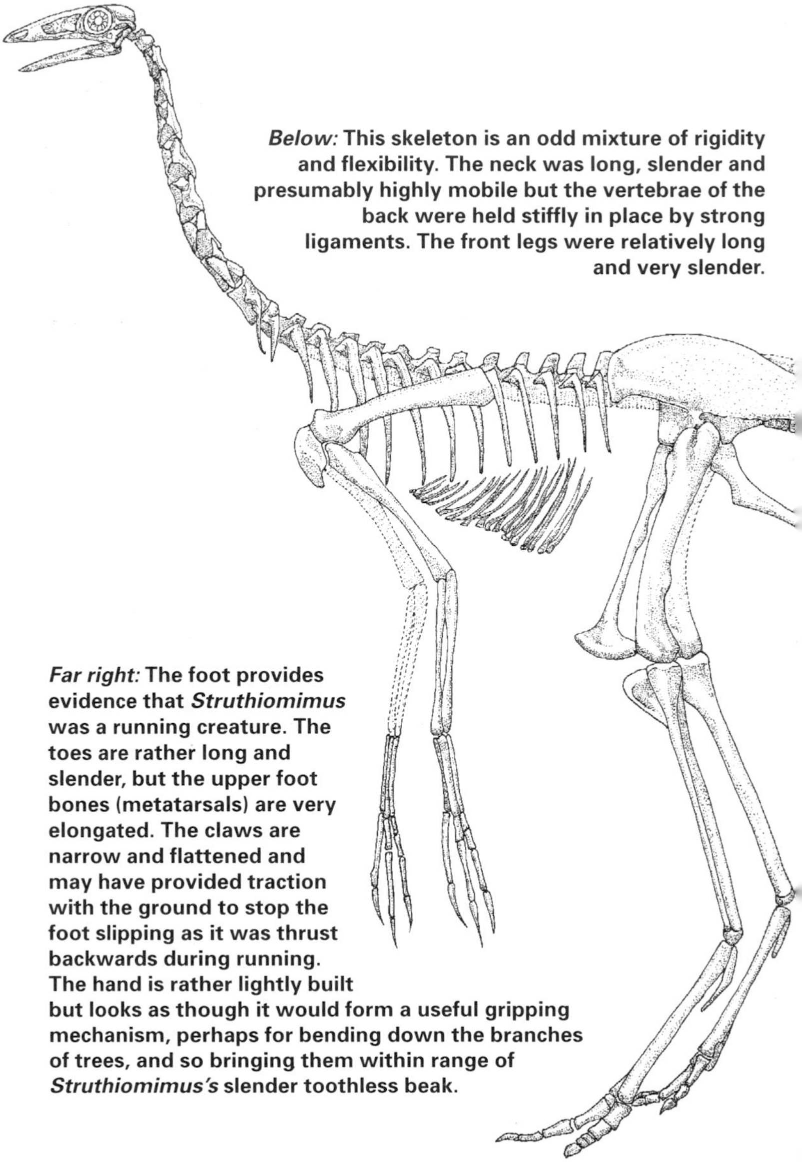

Below: **This skeleton is an odd mixture of rigidity and flexibility. The neck was long, slender and presumably highly mobile but the vertebrae of the back were held stiffly in place by strong ligaments. The front legs were relatively long and very slender.**

Far right: **The foot provides evidence that *Struthiomimus* was a running creature. The toes are rather long and slender, but the upper foot bones (metatarsals) are very elongated. The claws are narrow and flattened and may have provided traction with the ground to stop the foot slipping as it was thrust backwards during running. The hand is rather lightly built but looks as though it would form a useful gripping mechanism, perhaps for bending down the branches of trees, and so bringing them within range of *Struthiomimus's* slender toothless beak.**

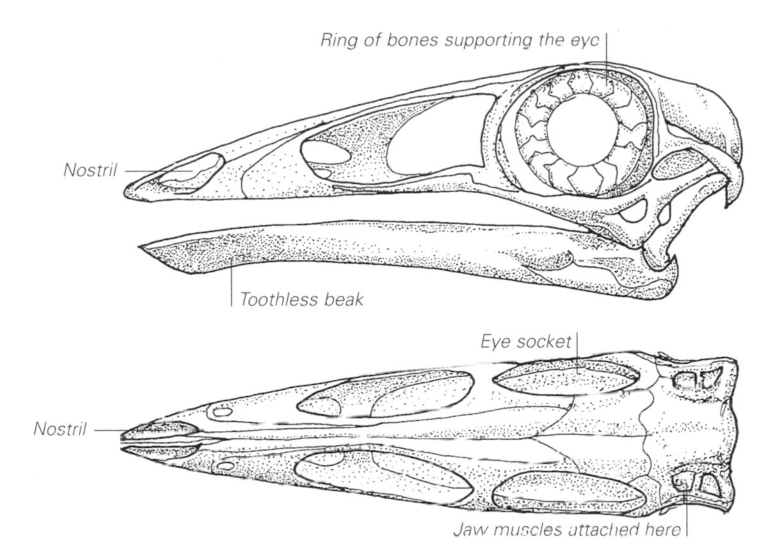

Above: **The long, slender, toothless jaw and large eyes give this skull a very bird-like appearance. It is also probable that the jaws were covered with horn. The lightness and thinness of the skull bones suggest that they may have been flexible, allowing movement in the skull, as in modern birds.**

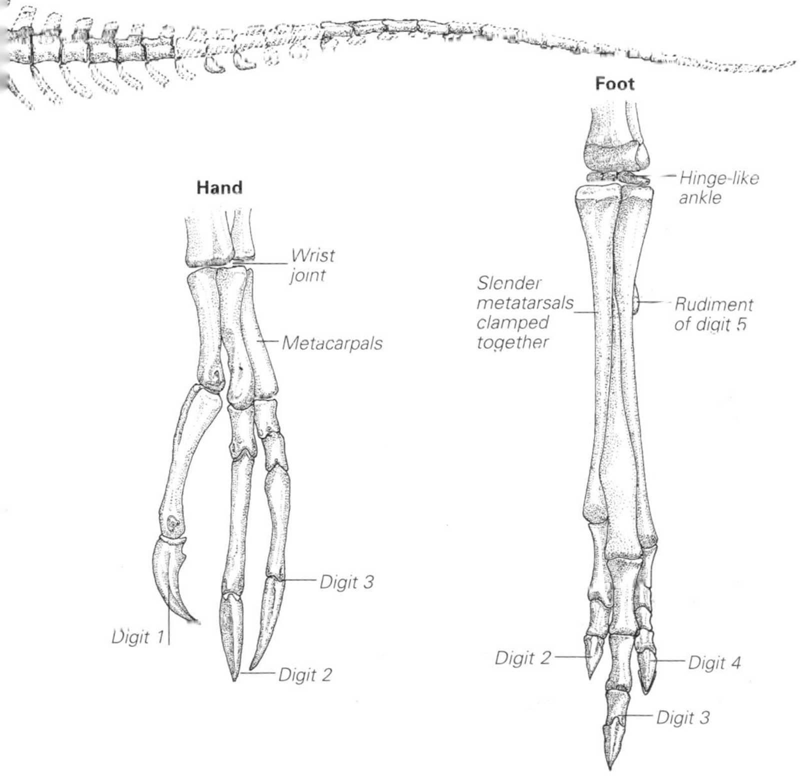

Dromiceiomimus

Period: Late Cretaceous. **Family:** Ornithomimosaurs.
Where found: North America.
Estimated length: 10-13ft (3-4m).

Since the early years of the twentieth century, several significant discoveries of ornithomimosaurs have been made both in North America and Asia. In the early 1920s a fragmentary skeleton, *Struthiomimus brevitertius*, came to light. Then in 1926 a new specimen was discovered near Steveville on the Red Deer River, Alberta, Canada. This new find consisted of the front part of the skeleton (including a fine head) of an ornithomimosaur, which was described and named *Struthiomimus samueli* in 1928. It was the first ornithomimosaur with a well-preserved skull. In the early 1970s a completely new ornithomimosaur – *Gallimimus* ('chicken mimic') from Mongolia – was described.

In 1972 Dale Russell of Ottawa provided a much-needed review of the North American ornithomimosaurs and reassessed the various species that had been proposed since the 1890s. His research revealed that there were three genera of ornithomimosaurs in the late Cretaceous of North America: *Ornithomimus, Struthiomimus* and *Dromiceiomimus* ('emu mimic'). *Dromiceiomimus* was based on material from Alberta originally described as *Struthiomimus* brevitertius and *Struthiomimus samueli. Dromiceiomimus* had a relatively short back, a comparatively slender and long forearm and hand and somewhat differently arranged pelvic bones.

Russell also reviewed the possible habits of ornithomimosaurs and proposed that they may well have been solely carnivorous, perhaps feeding on eggs and other small animal material obtained by scooping from the ground or digging. Being defenceless, they would have relied upon their sprinting abilities (and possibly camouflage) to avoid predators, which may well have been the more heavily built but less agile tyrannosaurids.

In *Dromiceiomimus* the huge size of the eye socket may imply that these creatures possessed a particularly acute sense of vision. As to the likely feeding habits of ornithomimosaurs such as *Dromiceiomimus*, their basic body shape would seem to be well adapted to a plant-eating lifestyle. The long arms and hands might be used to grasp branches, while the beak could nip off buds and leaves.

Ornithomimosaurs may well have originated from the coelurosaurs such as *Elaphrosaurus*, a relatively large, lightly built theropod from the later Jurassic of Tanzania. Unfortunately the head of *Elaphrosaurus* is not known, so it is uncertain whether it possessed teeth in its jaws or had the horny bill typical of ornithomimosaurs. However, numerous small theropod teeth are known from the same locality.

Right: **This is a close relative of *Struthiomimus* and appears to have been very similar in size and general shape. *Dromiceiomimus* had quite a small head with enormous eye sockets and a relatively large brain.**

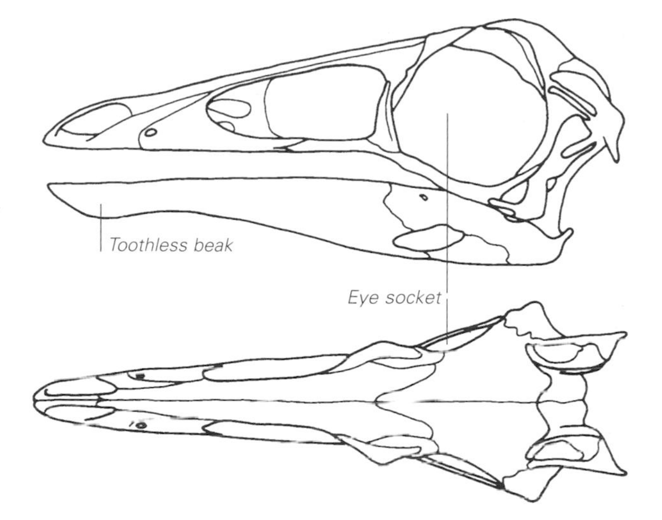

Above: **The skull of *Dromiceiomimus* was lightly built and very similar to that of *Struthiomimus*. In fact, it is the body skeleton of *Dromiceiomimus* that really distinguishes it from other ornithomimosaurs: the short back, slender front legs and slightly differently arranged pelvic bones.**

Theropods

Over the last decades a large variety of enigmatic theropods have been discovered and described. For the most part these have been rather poor or incomplete specimens of dinosaurs that do not seem to fit readily into any of the groups currently recognised. With further discoveries and study, many will fall into some of the better established groups; others may prove to be totally new dinosaur types. Some of these animals are described below, others on the following pages.

Chirostenotes

Chirostenotes ('slender hand') consists of two imperfectly preserved, sharply clawed hands discovered in late Cretaceous rocks of the Red Deer River, Alberta. The fingers are of unequal length and quite closely resemble those of the late Jurassic coelurosaur *Ornitholestes* and the dromaeosaurids. Indeed, *Dromaeosaurus* is known from the same area, so the material may well belong to this genus. Several teeth and a lower jaw found a few kilometres away have been cautiously referred to *Chirostenotes*.

Macrophalangia

Macrophalangia ('large toes') is another theropod from the Red Deer River. First described by Charles Sternberg in 1932, *Macrophalangia* is known from a partial foot, which looks very much like that of an ornithomimosaur. It has long, slender toes ending in flattened but quite pointed claws. However, unlike the three-toed ornithomimosaur foot, the foot of *Macrophalangia* has four toes: three long, slender ones and a smaller first toe typical of the great majority of theropods. Does *Macrophalangia* represent a primitive type of ornithomimosaur? If so, then its appearance in late Cretaceous rocks is unexpected. Alternatively, these remains may indicate a completely new group of slender-toed theropods in the late Cretaceous.

Elmisaurus

Elmisaurus ('foot reptile'), another poorly preserved theropod, this time from the late Cretaceous of the Gobi Desert, was described in 1981. Known from portions of hands, feet and odd leg bones, this new dinosaur may provide vital clues to the relations of both Chirostenotes and *Macrophalangia*. The hand of *Elmisaurus* seems, from its proportions, to resemble closely that of *Chirostenotes* (as well as that of *Ornitholestes* and dromaeosaurids). The foot, however, is most similar to that described as *Macrophalangia*; the toes are quite long and slender and are arranged very similarly to those of ornithomimosaurs, except that, as in *Macrophalangia*, there appear to be four toes.

It is possible that *Chirostenotes, Macrophalangia* and *Elmisaurus* may represent a new family of theropods in the late Cretaceous, which could be called elmisaurids. These dinosaurs seem to combine the grasping hands of the rapacious dromaeosaurids with the fleetness of foot of ornithomimosaurs. Very little is known about the skeletons or the skulls of these creatures, so accurate, lifelike restorations are impossible.

Below: **The hand of *Elmisaurus* resembles in its proportions that of dromaeosaurids such as *Deinonychus*. The foot by contrast is more similar to that of the ornithomimosaurs, having long, slender toes and no slashing claw.**

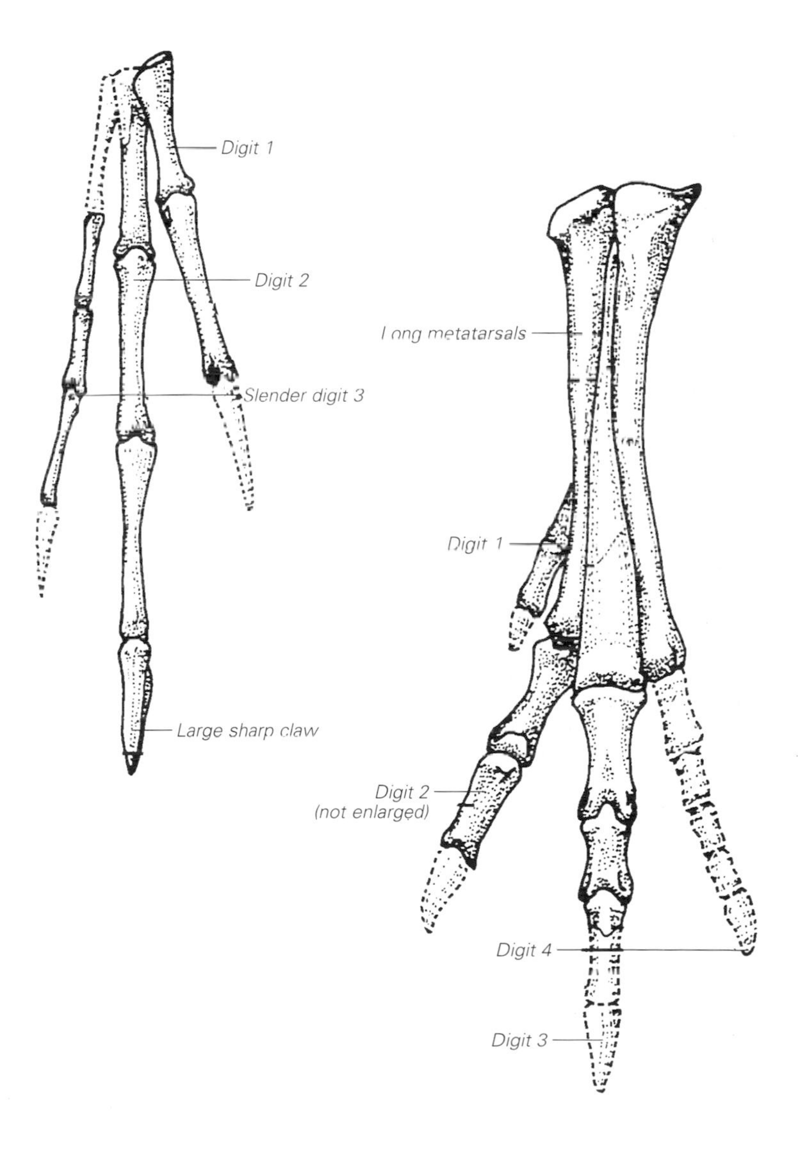

Segnosaurus

Period: Late Cretaceous. **Family:** Theropods.
Where found: Mongolia.
Estimated length: 20-23ft (6-7m).

The first segnosaurid remains were described in 1979 from material discovered during Soviet Mongolian expeditions. The fossil remains are incomplete and merely provide an interesting glimpse of other dinosaur types. So far three Mongolian segnosaurids have been identified: *Segnosaurus* ('slow reptile'), *Erlikosaurus* ('King of the Dead [Erlik] reptile') and an unnamed form.

Segnosaurus was described on the basis of a partial skeleton including a lower jaw, parts of the legs and backbone and a complete pelvis. Other fragments including a forelimb have also been discovered in the same area, providing a little more evidence of the structure of this animal. Several features of *Segnosaurus* deserve mention. First and most obviously, the pelvis is very unusual for a theropod. The pubis lies parallel to the ischium below the hip socket; this arrangement is very similar to that seen in ornithischian dinosaurs and birds. Second, the jaws are unusual for theropods in that the front part of the jaw is toothless and the teeth at the back of the jaw are quite small and pointed, rather than being like large serrated daggers. The front end of the jaws was probably covered by a horny beak, again like that of ornithischians. Judging from the size of the jaw, the head was quite small relative to the size of the body. The forelimb is short and ends in three slender, clawed fingers. The hindlimb is quite sturdy and ends in a rather short and broad four-toed foot. Again the foot is most unusual for a theropod, the toes of which were usually slender and bunched together in a distinctly bird-like arrangement. The remains indicate a slow-moving animal of 20-23ft (6-7m) in length.

Clearly *Segnosaurus* was a most unusual theropod. It has been suggested that it was an aquatic fish-eater; this may explain the small pointed teeth and broad (perhaps webbed) feet of this animal, although why it should possess a horny beak is a complete mystery.

Erlikosaurus is known from a skull, some neck vertebrae, a humerus and both feet. Smaller than *Segnosaurus, Erlikosaurus* has a greater number of teeth, a larger beak and narrower claws on its feet. The shape of the pelvis in *Erlikosaurus* is assumed to have resembled that of *Segnosaurus*.

***Right: Segnosaurus* had an unusual and perplexing combination of a toothless beak, bird-like hips, theropod hands and rather broad feet. One suggestion is that these creatures were fish-eaters and had webbed hind feet.**

Segisaurus

Period: Early Jurassic. **Family:** Theropods.
Where found: North America.
Estimated length: 3ft 4in (1m).

Over the last few decades a large variety of enigmatic theropods have been discovered and described. For the most part these have been rather poor or incomplete specimens of dinosaurs that do not seem to fit readily into any of the groups currently recognised. *Segisaurus* is one such new and enigmatic animal.

Discovered in 1933 in early Jurassic rocks of Arizona, *Segisaurus* ('reptile from Segi Canyon') was described by Dr Charles Camp in 1936. The fossil remains of this animal consist of a fragmentary, headless skeleton, which includes a few back vertebrae, some ribs, the shoulder girdle and incomplete arms, legs and parts of the pelvis. Although the head was missing, the other remains were reasonably well preserved. The animal as reconstructed is small (about 3ft 4in, 1m, long) and ran on slender hind legs. The fore legs were apparently short, with sharp-clawed fingers. The feet and hands are reminiscent of those of coelurosaur-type theropods. However, *Segisaurus* does have a collar-bone (clavicle) preserved on one shoulder, which is quite rare in dinosaurs. Until better material of *Segisaurus* is recovered it is probably best to regard it as a rather curious small theropod.

Segisaurus was quite small and was lightly constructed as a presumably agile runner. Most probably *Segisaurus* fed on small vertebrates such as lizards and amphibians or larger insects. The teeth were not preserved, so we cannot be absolutely sure of its diet.

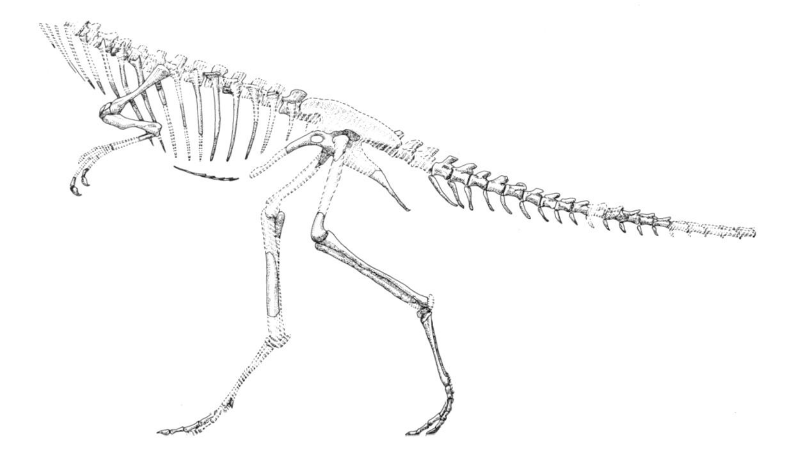

Above: Segisaurus has been restored by Dr Charles Camp. It was evidently a small, agile theropod with short arms and powerful grasping hands. The absence of the head is frustrating since it might have revealed its diet and its relationships to other theropods. It is assumed that *Segisaurus* fed on small vertebrates such as lizards and amphibians or on larger insects.

Below. Another unusual theropod is the early Jurassic *Segisaurus* from Arizona. It was small and ran on slender hind legs.

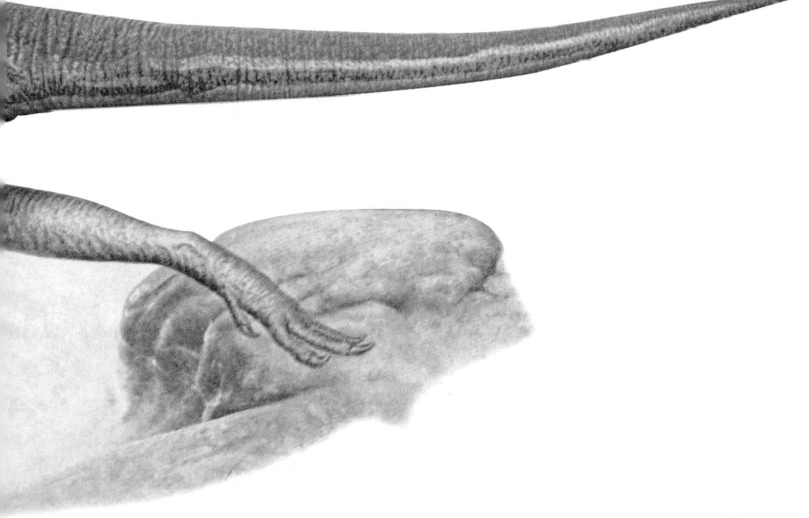

Avimimus

Period: Late Cretaceous. **Family:** Theropods.
Where found: Mongolia.
Estimated length: 5ft (1.5m).

In 1981 Dr Kurzanov of Moscow described the partial skeleton of a remarkably bird-like theropod dinosaur, *Avimimus* ('bird mimic'), discovered during the joint Soviet-Mongolian expedition. This dinosaur was of very slender build, with slim legs and long, bird-like feet, as well as a long, slender, bird-like neck. The tail was typically long and dinosaurian (unlike the short 'parson's nose' of a bird) so as to counterbalance the front part of the body. Dr Kurzanov noted that there were a considerable number of bird-like characteristics found in *Avimimus* and proposed that this was a small, feathered, bird-like dinosaur of the late Cretaceous.

Among the skeletal remains there is an incomplete forelimb, which is of particular interest. Kurzanov analysed the bones and demonstrated that the humerus (upper arm bone) was extremely bird-like with all the ridges and bumps for attachment of the main flight muscles and a wing-folding mechanism. In addition, Kurzanov demonstrated that one of the forearm bones (ulna) had a distinctive bony ridge running along its rear edge. No other theropod is known to possess such a bony ridge. Birds do, however, have a rather similar series of small bony 'pimples' running along this forearm bone. These 'pimples' are developed at the point of attachment of the flight feathers (secondaries). *Avimimus* does not have a series of pimple-like attachment points, but the bony ridge is nevertheless very suggestive of the presence of feathers on the forelimbs – although there is no direct evidence of feathers as there is in the case of the famous fossils of *Archaeopteryx*. Kurzanov proposes that *Avimimus* was a member of a very late group of bird-like theropod dinosaurs named avimimids; these were small, fleet-footed creatures living perhaps upon insects. The feather covering is supposed to be associated primarily with body insulation rather than flight.

Kurzanov believes that these were small, highly active creatures, which would have generated their own body heat internally, rather than relying upon the sun to keep them warm as reptiles usually do. They may have used feathers for insulation. As others have suggested in the past, a small, highly active, ground-running creature such as this may have been a first stage in the origin of powered flight. Kurzanov visualised *Avimimus* occasionally fluttering into the air when pursuing flying insects, or alternatively using short airborne jumps as a way of avoiding larger fleet-footed predators.

Left: This restoration of _Avimimus_ is inspired by Kurzanov's work of recent years. It is illustrated with a feather-like covering to its body, particularly along its 'arms'. Although many palaeontologists are sceptical about the 'evidence', Kurzanov believes that the bones of the arm in particular show traces equivalent to the feather attachment areas on the wing bones of birds, provoking the idea that maybe several theropods were feathered rather like birds.

Saurornithoidids

In 1923 Henry Fairfield Osborn described the incomplete remains of a bird-like theropod dinosaur from late Cretaceous rocks at Bayn Dzak (=Shabarakh Usu) in the Gobi Desert. This new dinosaur was named *Saurornithoides mongoliensis* ('bird-like reptile from Mongolia') and was at first supposed to be an early toothed bird, because its skull had a long, rather bird-like, narrow muzzle. The incomplete hind foot showed that the toes were arranged in typical theropod fashion with a small, spur-like first toe and three longer walking toes. The second toe of the foot had a somewhat enlarged claw, which could have been raised clear of the ground. Osborn concluded that *Saurornithoides* must have been a small, carnivorous theropod.

In 1932 some more bones were described by Charles Sternberg; these came from the late Cretaceous near Steveville on the Red Deer River, Alberta. The remains included a complete foot, several hand bones and a few vertebrae. The hand bones were rather similar to those of *Ornitholestes* and *Chirostenotes* with uneven finger lengths. The foot, however, was rather unusual because, although it showed the typical bird-like arrangement of toes, the second toe was somewhat shorter than the third and fourth toes and had an unexpectedly large, sharply curved claw. The third and fourth toes were both quite long and almost equal in length with smaller but still sharply curved claws. As in the case of *Saurornithoides*, the second toe was jointed in such a way that it could be held clear of the ground, instead of being used for walking upon. As before, however, the significance of the unusual second toe and its claw was missed. At the time Sternberg concluded that this foot belonged to a new type of theropod that may have evolved from animals like *Ornitholestes*; he named this material *Stenonychosaurus* ('slender-clawed reptile') *inequalis*.

It was not until the discovery of *Deinonychus* in the mid-1960s that the possibility of a relationship between *Saurornithoides* and *Stenonychosaurus* was appreciated. It was recognised that Deinonychus had a very large claw on the second toe of its foot, which could have been used as an offensive weapon. *Saurornithoides* and *Stenonychosaurus* were found to have similar, if smaller, offensive claws. At first, both of these dinosaurs were included with other dromaeosaurids. However, in 1974 more material of *Saurornithoides*, discovered at Bugeen Tsav in Mongolia, was described, prompting the proposal that *Saurornithoides* and *Stenonychosaurus* should not be included in the dromaeosaurid family but should be placed in a family of their own. They became known as saurornithoidids.

In 1978 *Saurornitholestes* ('reptile-like bird robber') was added to the saurornithoidid group, although this small, lightly built creature (found in Canada) may be a dromaeosaurid. Other supposed saurornithoidids include *Bradycneme* ('heavy shin') and *Heptasteornis* ('star bird'), both from Romania.

Right: **Dale Russell and R. Séguin of Ottawa published an article in 1982 postulating what *Stenonychosaurus* might have looked like if it had continued evolving to the present day – vertical posture, enlarged brain and no need for a tail.**

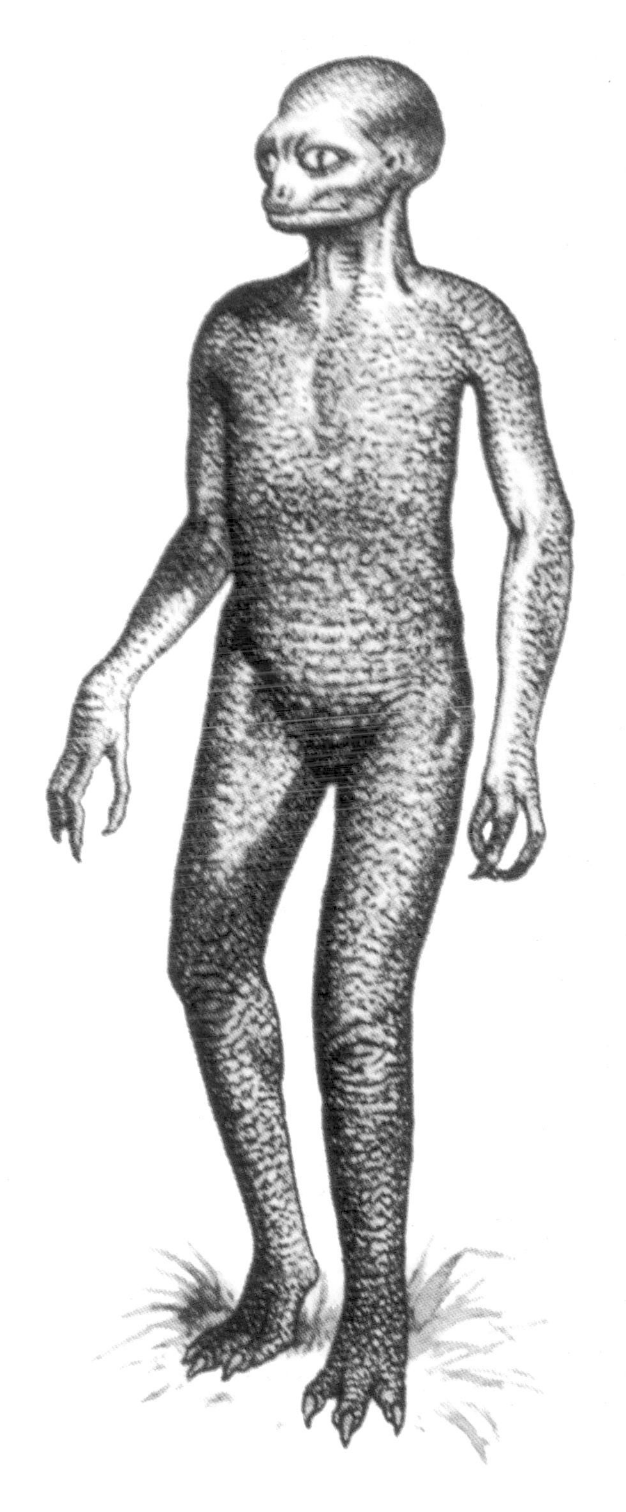

Stenonychosaurs

Period: Late Cretaceous. **Family:** Saurornithoidids.
Where found: Mongolia and Alberta, Canada.
Estimated length: 6ft 6in (2m).

In 1982 Dale Russell and R. Séguin (Ottawa) published an interesting article on *Stenonychosaurus* ('slender-clawed reptile'). A new partial skeleton of this dinosaur was discovered in Alberta in 1967, and this provided the basis for the first skeletal and flesh reconstruction of *Stenonychosaurus* and of a 'dinosauroid' – the animal that, they postulated, would have evolved from *Stenonychosaurus* if it had not become extinct at the end of the Cretaceous Period.

One interpretation of the probable habits of *Stenonychosaurus* (and saurornithoidids in general) is that they were lightly built, active hunters of small prey – perhaps small lizards and mammals. The long, grasping hands and the very large eyes, which pointed partly forwards and therefore gave reasonable stereoscopic vision, may indicate that these were nimble predators which were active at dusk or even at night, when many of the small nocturnal mammals of the time would have been active. The 'dinosauroid' was constructed by extrapolating from these attributes. It was visualised as a highly intelligent and 'manipulative' dinosaur. What it would have lacked in fleetness of foot (since it is more 'flat-footed' than *Stenonychosaurus*) it would have made up for through its greater intellect. This would have allowed it to avoid potential predators by 'outwitting' them rather than by showing them a 'clean pair of heels'. As a predator it may have been able to catch prey both by endurance running and perhaps by making simple weapons - much as primitive man must have done. Such an idea is an obviously fanciful, though provocative thought.

Stenonychosaurus had a relatively large brain and has been credited with being the most intelligent dinosaur, although most of its excess brain volume was probably not concerned with reasoning and other activities that we would call 'intelligence'. The brain was presumably concerned mainly with its highly developed senses, fine control of its limbs and fast reflexes, which were used in hunting small, elusive prey.

Right: **Some say this was the most intelligent dinosaur. It had a relatively large brain compared with other dinosaurs. The brain was probably concerned mainly with the animal's highly developed senses and motor activity.**

Saurornithoides

Period: Late Cretaceous. **Family:** Saurornithoidids.
Where found: Mongolia.
Estimated length: 6ft 6in (2m).

The first specimen of *Saurornithoides* ('bird-like reptile') was found in Mongolia in 1923. The remains included the major part of a skull found in one sandstone nodule and, a little way away, parts of the backbone, pelvis, legs and feet. In general shape and proportions its skull was rather similar to that of *Velociraptor*, which was incidentally described at the same time and came from the same area of Mongolia. However, the teeth, in particular, were rather different; those of *Saurornithoides* were smaller and more numerous. This creature had 38 teeth in the upper jaw, while *Velociraptor* had no more than 30 teeth. The teeth

***Right:* Like *Stenonychosaurus*, *Saurornithoides* had a large brain and a slender body. On its foot there was a slightly enlarged claw, which was normally folded back, but which could be used to slash at potential prey. In this it resembles *Deinonychus*.**

were also unusual in that only their back edges were serrated whereas both front and back edges of *Velociraptor's* were serrated.

However, in 1974 Rinchen Barsbold (Ulan Bator, Mongolia) described more material of *Saurornithoides*, which had been discovered at Bugeen Tsav in Mongolia. This material, ascribed the name *Saurornithoides junior* ('younger bird-like reptile), was found in slightly earlier rocks and was 30 per cent larger than the earlier species, while the number of teeth in the jaws was also greater. Apart from these differences, which may eventually prove to be simply due to growth, the two species seem remarkably similar.

The new *Saurornithoides* material included a well-preserved skull. The latter showed some rather curious swollen areas in the ear region and in the floor of the brain case. These features, plus the quite small size of the claw on the second toe of the foot, and the fact that their teeth were relatively smaller, more numerous and only serrated along their back edges, prompted Barsbold to propose that *Saurornithoides* and *Stenonychosaurus* should not be included in the dromaeosaurid family as proposed by Ostrom and belonged in a family of their own, the saurornithodids.

Saurornithoides had a large brain and a slender body. Its large, saucer-like eyes may have been used for hunting small mammals at dusk, when other predatory dinosaurs would have been unable to see properly.

Dromaeosaurids

The first dromaeosaurid remains to be described were those of *Dromaeosaurus* ('running reptile') *albertensis*, which were discovered near the Red Deer River in 1914. Unfortunately, the specimen was far from complete; it consisted of the partial head, lower jaws and an assortment of foot bones of a small carnivorous dinosaur. On that poor evidence alone, *Dromaeosaurus* was grouped by some people with the huge carnosaurs (the tyrannosaurids or megalosaurs), while others suggested that it was related to the small, slender coelurosaurs (e.g. *Compsognathus* or *Coelurus*). If anything, its small size tended to favour the latter interpretation.

This state of affairs was considerably improved by the discovery in 1964 of a new fossil locality in southern Montana. During the next two years excavations at the site unearthed several hundred bones of an entirely new carnivorous dinosaur: *Deinonychus* ('terrible claw) *antirrhopus*. The study of this dinosaur, which is now known from several almost complete (or complementary) skeletons, has revealed many new and exciting facts, not only about this extraordinary kind of dinosaur, but also about its kinship with *Dromaeosaurus*. Confusion had arisen because both *Dromaeosaurus* and *Deinonychus* share characteristics with both carnosaurs and coelurosaurs, as well as exhibiting features that are unique. One of their most characteristic features is the huge, sickle-like claw on the second toe of the foot. Once the unusual nature of the feet of these dinosaurs was appreciated, it became possible to draw comparisons with another dinosaur known since 1924, *Velociraptor* ('speedy predator') *mongoliensis*, which also had a sickle-like claw on its hind foot.

One of the most exciting discoveries was made in southern England. In 1982 a quarryman, Bill Walker, discovered a very large, sickle-shaped claw in a quarry in Surrey. The claw (12in, 31cm, around its outside edge and thus three times larger than that of *Deinonychus*!) engendered an excavation, which recovered the major part of a very large dromaeosaurid, now known as *Phaedrolosaurus*, or the Surrey dinosaur.

Above: To overcome large prey like *Tenontosaurus, Deinonychus* may have hunted in predatory packs. Some would slow the potential victim by grasping its tail and hind quarters while others would aim lethal kicks at its underside.

Below: This sequence shows how an individual *Deinonychus* may have hunted a similarly fleet-footed prey, such as the ornithopod *Hypsilophodon*, in a one-to-one chase. Both animals were capable of high speed running and jumping, but once *Deinonychus* had closed with its prey, it used its arms and teeth to subdue the struggling creature. The coup de grâce, however, was administered by the fearsome claws on *Deinonychus's* hind feet.

Velociraptor

Period: Late Cretaceous. **Family:** Dromaeosaurids.
Where found: Mongolia.
Estimated length: 6ft (1.8m).

Fossil remains of *Velociraptor* ('speedy predator') were first discovered in the Djadochta Formation of Shabarak Usa, in Mongolia, in 1924. Although found in similar regions to Dromaeosaurus and Deinonychus, remains of *Velociraptor* have not been found so far in geological deposits at the same sites as the other two, so in life they probably never met! *Velociraptor* can be distinguished from other dromaeosaurids by its very, low and narrow head. The difference in head shape and size may well reflect differences in the diets. Like Deinonychus, *Velociraptor* also had a sickle-like claw on its hind foot.

A remarkable find was uncovered by the 1971 Polish-Mongolian expedition at Toogreeg in the Gobi Desert. It revealed an almost complete skeleton of *Velociraptor* mongoliensis interlocked with that of Protoceratops andrewsi, its hands and feet apparently gripping the triangular-shaped skull of its victim. Did they die in combat, perhaps as *Velociraptor* was trying to plunder eggs from the ceratopian's nest? If so, this may be one of the few pieces of real evidence we have of the feeding habits of predatory dinosaurs.

Below: **The skull of *Velociraptor* differs in shape from that of *Deinonychus*; it has a long, low, depressed snout. The eye sockets are large, and the irregular array of teeth are sharply serrated as one might expect in a carnivorous predator.**

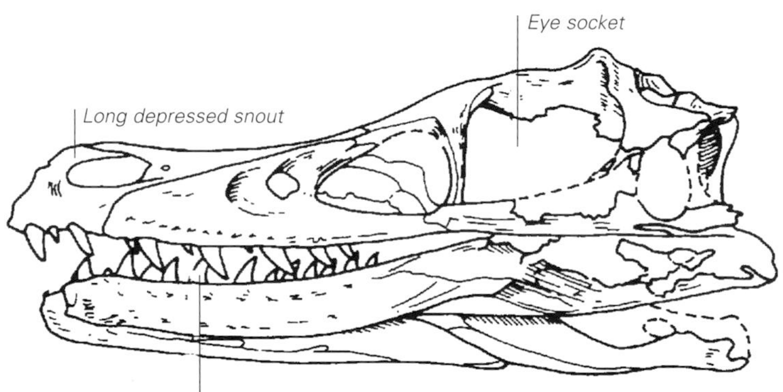

Below: **Fossil remains of this dinosaur have been discovered in the Djadochta Formation of Shabarak Usu, in Mongolia. Remains of *Velociraptor* have not been found so far in geological deposits at the same sites as *Dromaeosaurus* and *Deinonychus,* so it is not known whether these animals were actually co-inhabitants or contemporaries. *Velociraptor* can be distinguished from other dromaeosaurids by its very low and narrow head. The difference in head shape and size may well reflect differences in the diets.**

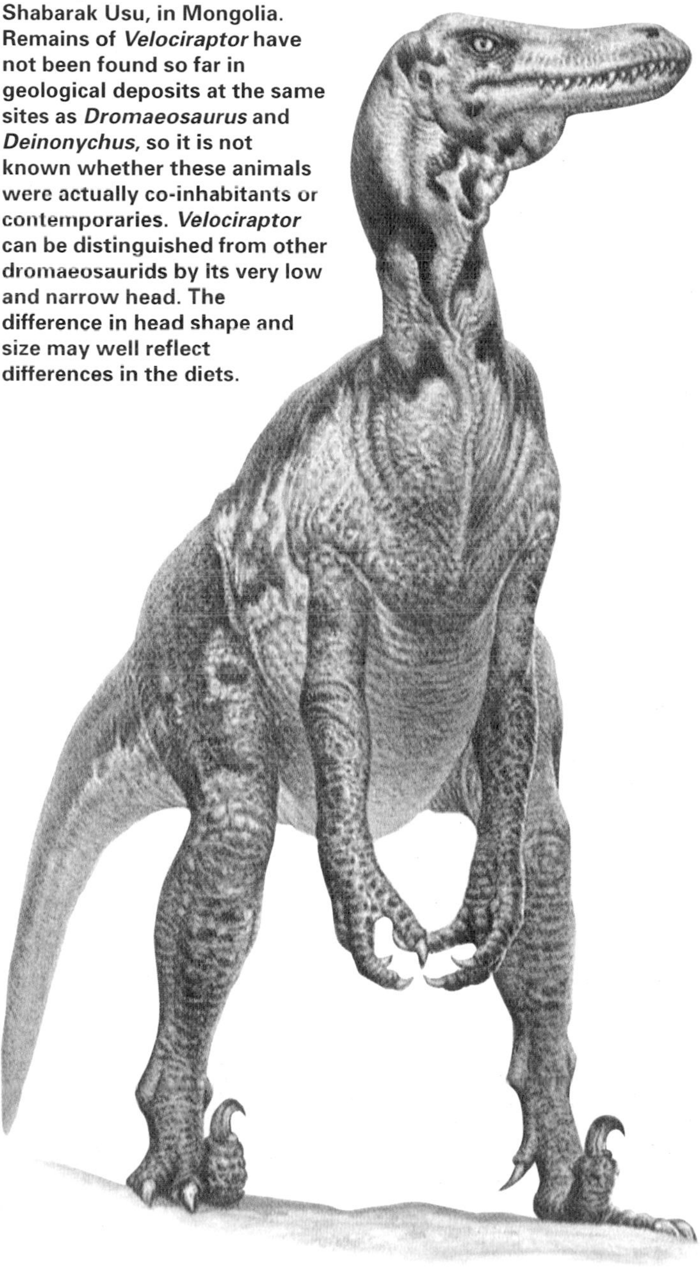

Deinonychus & Dromaeosaurus

Deinonychus:
Period: Mid-Cretaceous. **Family:** Dromaeosaurids.
Where found: North America.
Estimated length: 10-11ft (3-3.3m).

Deinonychus ('terrible claw'), the best-known dromaeosaurid, had a large head but it was quite lightly built with large openings in its sides for the eyes and muscles of the jaws. The jaw muscles were arranged so that one set was able to drive the jaws together powerfully when they were nearly closed, while another set (the pterygoideus) worked best when the jaws were wide open. The teeth were large, with serrated edges, and were curved backwards, suggesting that *Deinonychus* was able to tear large chunks of flesh from its prey by tugging backwards. The head on the slender, flexible neck had a wide range of

***Above: Deinonychus* is the best-known of all dromaeosaurids. The head is large with backwardly curved teeth; the arms are long and powerful and the feet have the extraordinary sickle-like second toe. The 'terrible claw' is shown raised off the ground.**

movement. The back, by contrast, was held quite stiffly by powerful ligaments. The arms were unusually long and the three-fingered hands were very large with powerful, sharply curved talons.

The hind leg of *Deinonychus* is clearly its most striking possession. The upper leg bone is shorter than the shank, which is a feature usually associated with animals that are capable of running very fast. The foot bones are, however, not as long as might be expected in a fast runner. Instead of having three forward-pointing toes of roughly equal length, the foot has two toes (the third and fourth), which it used for walking, while toe number two is modified into a large, sickle-shaped claw, and toe one is a small, backward-pointing spur. The large claw seems to have been used as a formidable weapon of attack.

Another unusual feature of *Deinonychus* was in the tail. Beneath and between the vertebrae were small, wedge-shaped bones called chevrons; these developed a pair of long, thin, forward-pointing rods of bone, which overlapped several vertebrae in front. Similarly, there were enormously elongated forward-pointing rods above the vertebrae. The effect of these rod like structures was to produce a sheath of bony rods almost completely surrounding the tail of the animal. The tail nevertheless remained flexible because the joints between the individual vertebrae were not welded together by bone.

Dromaeosaurus:
Period. Late Cretaceous. **Family:** Dromaeosaurids.
Where found: Canada.
Estimated length: 6ft (1.8m).

The first dromaeosaurid remains to be described were those of *Dromaeosaurus* ('running reptile') *albertensis*. The remains, discovered near the Red Deer River in Alberta, Canada, in 1914, consisted only of the partial head, lower jaws and an assortment of foot bones of a small carnivorous dinosaur. *Dromaeosaurus* remains surprisingly poorly known. The shape of the head, with its deep, rounded snout, is correct, as are part of the arms and legs, but, as far as the rest of the animal is concerned, any reconstruction has to be based on guesswork using *Deinonychus* and *Velociraptor* as models from which to work.

▶

***Left:* The first of the dromaeosaurids to be discovered, *Dromaeosaurus* ('running reptile') is really surprisingly poorly known. Apart from the head and fragments of the arms and legs, little else of the skeleton has been found. So the convincing-looking reconstruction here is largely conjecture.**

One part of the body that was present in the *Dromaeosaurus* find and not in that of *Deinonychus* was the top of the skull. In *Dromaeosaurus* a narrow hinge runs across the head just behind the eyes; this probably served as a shock-absorber, which may even have prevented it from jarring its brain when it snapped its jaws together to eat its prey.

Dromaeosaurus are at present known in the northern continents only – North America, Europe and Asia – and it is likely that they were restricted to these regions. The earliest record of dromaeosaurids is from about the middle of the Cretaceous, when Tethys, a large ocean, separated Europe and Asia from Africa, Australia and India. Seaways also separated North from South America and had probably done so for several million years. Their distribution may well be explicable in terms of their time of origin and the relative positions of continents then.

The relationship of dromaeosaurids to other carnivorous dinosaurs is still a vexed question. Their nearest relatives would seem to be the saurornithoidids, which also exhibit a smaller version of the peculiar sickle-shaped toe claw, although they do not possess the stiffened tail or the same hips as dromaeosaurids.

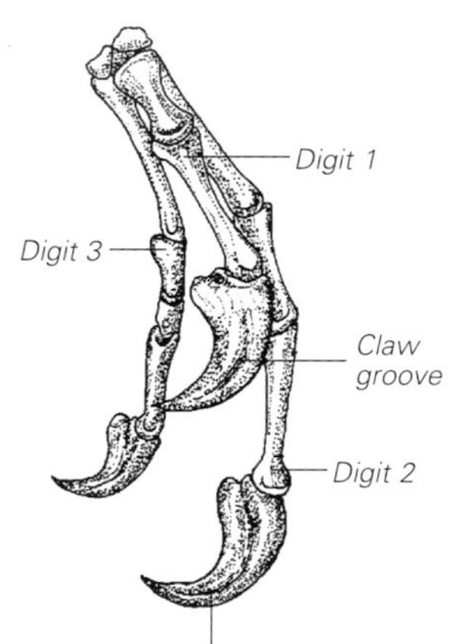

Top right: **The head of *Deinonychus* was composed of thin struts of bone. The jaw muscles (1, 2 and 3) were confined to the back of the head and stretched down to the lower jaw. Muscle 1 gave the jaw its powerful bite, while muscle 2 snapped the jaws shut quickly. Muscle 3 at the back of the head simply opened the jaws wide.**

Left: **The hand had only three fingers, which were very strong with exceptionally large, sharp claws. The small, pebble-like wrist bones allowed the hand to be strongly flexed.**

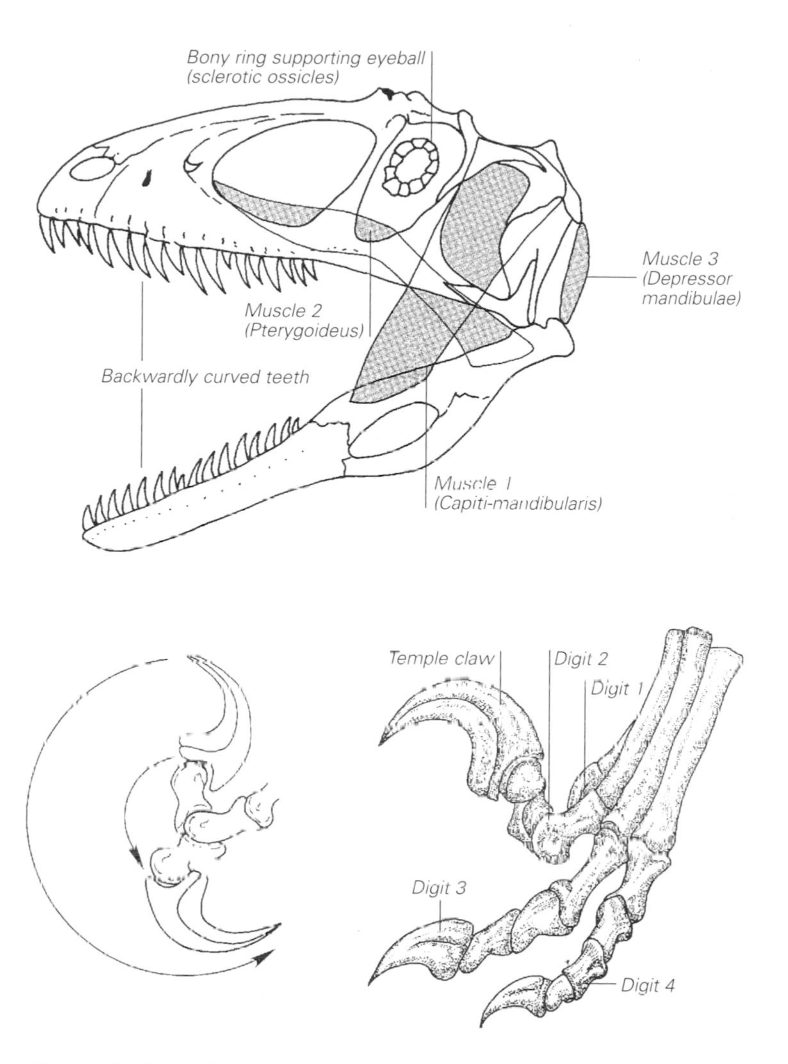

Above: **The foot of *Deinonychus* was one of the most extraordinary of any dinosaur. The first toe was a small, spur-like one; it was probably held clear of the ground and may have been used for gripping food or prey. The second toe was equipped with an enormous claw. The joints of this toe were specially enlarged so that the toe could be raised up and back to avoid damage while running. Toes 3 and 4 were of roughly equal length and were the only ones used for running upon.**

Left: **The large head of *Deinonychus* was balanced on a slender, almost bird-like neck. The chest was quite short and horizontal. The position of the pubis is not certain.**

Carnosaurs

The carnosaurs and the coelurosaurs are the two major groups of theropod dinosaurs described in most popular dinosaur books. They differ quite markedly in their bodily proportions from other types of theropod. Carnosaurs were typically large theropods, 20ft (6m) or more in length, and were heavily built, with stout, pillar-like hindlegs, rather feeble forelimbs and very large heads perched upon short, very powerful necks. Although most carnosaurs share these characteristics, there is very little agreement among palaeontologists about the degree to which they are all related to one another, partly because very few of these heavily built theropods are known from anything like a complete skeleton. It is also quite likely that smaller theropods tend to share common design features (i.e. slender legs, long arms, small heads, etc) while larger theropods all tend to have pillar-like legs, large heads and short arms. We may, therefore, simply be grouping together animals that share the same design constraints, rather than those that are closely related in a genealogical sense.

Allosaurus ('strange reptile') has rather confused origins, like many other dinosaurs. The remains of an *Allosaurus*-like theropod were first discovered in 1869 by Dr Ferdinand Hayden in Grand County, Colorado. This consisted of a single broken tail bone, which was described in some considerable detail by Joseph Leidy in 1870. Leidy was able to show that this single broken bone resembled those of other large carnivorous dinosaurs known from Europe, and at first he referred to it as *Poicilopleuron* ('varying cavity') after a European genus. A little later Leidy gave this bone the new name *Antrodemus*. In 1877 Benjamin Mudge, an assistant to Othniel Charles Marsh, discovered the partial remains of another large carnivorous dinosaur in Fremont County, Colorado. To these imperfect remains Marsh gave the name *Allosaurus*. Unfortunately Marsh then decided to abandon Mudge's quarry in Fremont County and return to Wyoming where better fossils were being found, with the result that little more of this animal was discovered. In 1883 another of Marsh's assistants (M. P. Felch) returned to the quarry and resumed where Mudge had left off – with spectacular results.

Between 1883 and 1884 Felch excavated an almost complete *Allosaurus* skeleton from this quarry as well as several partial skeletons and various isolated fragments. Since then more *Allosaurus* material has been recovered from late Jurassic rocks of North America. One of the most spectacular of these discoveries was made in Utah in 1927 at the so-called Cleveland-Lloyd Dinosaur Quarry.

Right: **Spinosaurids were an especially interesting group of carnosaurs, which developed long dorsal spines that seem to have acted as supports for a large sail of skin. In *Spinosaurus*, an *Allosaurus*-sized theropod from Niger, Africa, the spines grew to a length of 6ft (1.8m). It is possible that the spinal sail acted as a heat exchanger, allowing the dinosaur to warm its blood rapidly when standing in the sun or to dissipate heat when the sail was angled out of direct sunlight.**

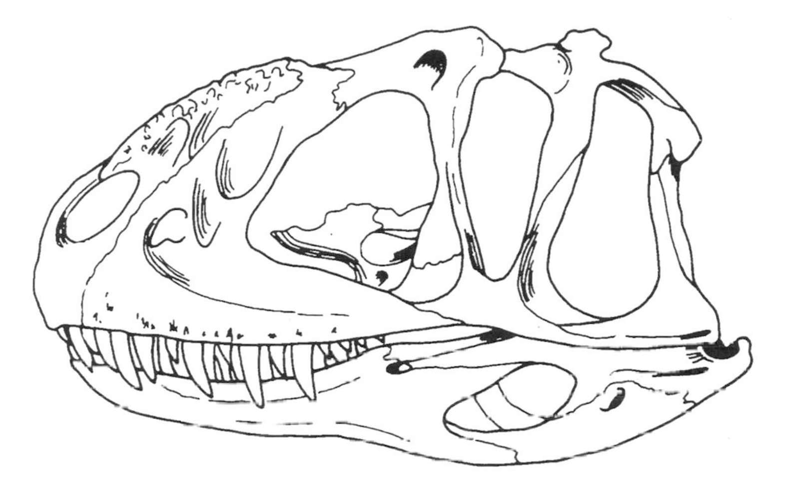

Above: This is the skull of a Chinese form from *Yangchuanosaurus,* the Jurassic deposits of Sichuan. It is very similar to that of *Allosaurus,* to which it may be related.

Allosaurus

Period: Late Jurassic. **Family:** Carnosaurs.
Where found: North America.
Estimated length: 39ft (12m).

The skull of *Allosaurus* was far longer than that of any of the other known theropods. Several skulls are known, which range in length from 24 to 36in (60-90cm). The jaws are very large and lined with many long, curved, serrated teeth. The skull, although large, is surprisingly lightly ▶

Left: Allosaurus lived in North America at the same time as the first bird, *Archaeopteryx,* lived in Germany. An adult *Allosaurus* was up to 39ft (12m) long, and the skull could be 3ft (90cm) long. The jaws were lined with recurved, dagger-like teeth, which had serrated edges back and front, just like the blade of a steak knife. *Allosaurus* had strong claws on its hands and feet with which to hold down and tear at its prey.

***Right:* The very large jaws bear many long curved, serrated teeth. However, the rest of the skull is lightly built with several fenestrae, or windows, to reduce its weight.**

constructed. There are several large lateral spaces in front and behind the eye. It seems most likely that they helped to lighten the skull so that it was easier for the animal to move its head around. There are really only two areas of skull that cannot be lightened much by removal of bone; they are the jaws, which have to anchor the teeth, and the area at the rear of the skull where the muscles that operate the jaws attach. Between these two areas of the skull there is a rather complicated series of bars or struts of bone, which presumably served to transmit the forces exerted on the bones of the skull during biting and tugging at prey.

It must seem a little curious that the very large skulls of predatory dinosaurs should have proportionately less bone in them than some of the smaller theropods. However, it does highlight the point that a skull of solid bone would have rendered the head incredibly heavy and unwieldy in life. Another curious feature of *Allosaurus's* skull is the large roughened ridge just above and in front of the eye. The centre of this bone is hollowed out, but no one is really sure why. It may have housed a salt gland or alternatively provided some sort of distinctive feature that allowed individual *Allosaurus* to recognise one another.

The body was typically carnosaur. The massive pillar-like legs supported the squat body, which was balanced over the hips by the massive tail. The neck, although short, was strongly curved so that the head was held almost above the shoulders rather than extended forward. The long ribs and blunt, roughened spines on the neck indicate that powerful muscles were attached here, which undoubtedly assisted with feeding. The back too was short and powerfully constructed, and the spines of each vertebra were broad and very roughened where powerful back muscles and ligaments were attached. The forelimbs were quite small compared with the hindlimbs but they were evidently very powerful, and ended in three viciously curved claws.

All in all, *Allosaurus* was an extremely well-equipped predatory dinosaur. The huge jaws were lined with large stabbing and cutting teeth, both for killing and dismembering their prey. The powerful neck and back would have aided the jaws in tearing off large chunks of flesh, and the large claws on the hands and feet undoubtedly helped to subdue victims. Precisely what their prey and predatory habits were is something of a mystery. Unlike the majority of coelurosaurs, these animals were not built for high-speed pursuit; they were much larger lumbering creatures. They probably fed on the larger ornithischians such as *Camptosaurus* and *Stegosaurus* as well as the larger sauropods such as *Diplodocus* and *Apatosaurus*. The large sauropods could well have been attacked by *Allosaurus* operating in hunting groups. It seems possible that several *Allosaurus* could bring down even the largest sauropods in a determined attack; although the main victims may well have been the less powerful juveniles. The evidence of strong herding tendencies among sauropods is probably a reflection of the threat posed by large predatory theropods such as *Allosaurus*.

Like the large predatory cats of today, *Allosaurus* were probably opportunistic scavengers of carrion – not only devouring long-abandoned carcasses, but also driving small theropods away from their own kills.

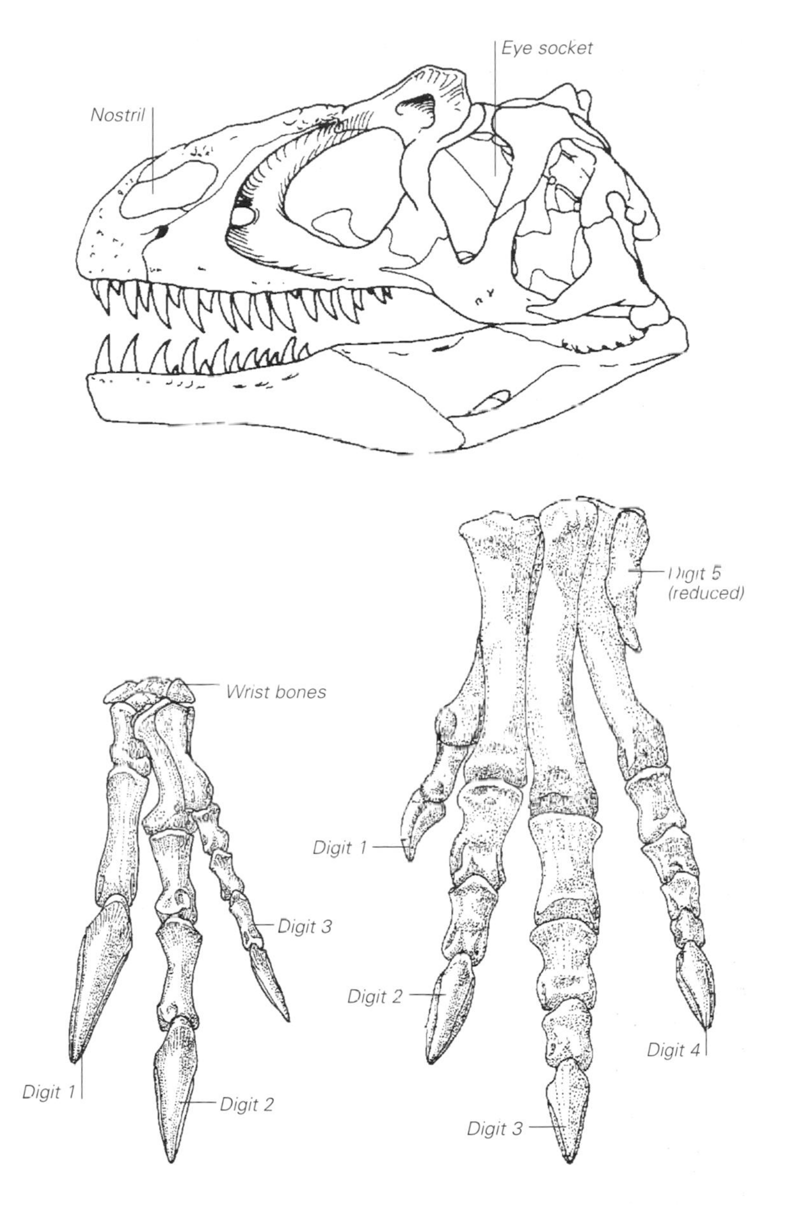

Above: **As in all carnosaurs, the front leg of *Allosaurus* is much weaker than the back one. The hand (left) has three fingers and bears three sharp, curved claws. It would have been very useful in helping to subdue prey and possibly also in tearing flesh off the bones of carrion. The feet (right) are much larger and have four toes each, of which three face forwards while the first toe points backwards. This configuration would have provided a large surface area for the foot – an adaptation for bearing the weight of this large, lumbering theropod.**

Ceratosaurus

Period: Late Jurassic. **Family:** Carnosaurs.
Where found: North America.
Estimated length: 20ft (6m).

Excavated in 1927, 1939 and then very extensively in 1960-65, the Cleveland-Lloyd Dinosaur Quarry has so far revealed a diverse fauna of dinosaurs: ornithopods, stegosaurs, ankylosaurs, sauropods and theropods of several types including *Allosaurus* and *Ceratosaurus*. *Allosaurus* is by far the most common dinosaur, being represented by at least 44 individuals. The one unfortunate feature of the Cleveland-Lloyd Dinosaur Quarry is that all the skeletal material is scattered. There is not one articulated skeleton.

The first skeleton of *Ceratosaurus* ('horned reptile') was discovered in 1883-84 by M. P. Felch at the same quarry in which the fine skeleton of *Allosaurus* had been excavated in Fremont County, Colorado, seven years earlier. A large part of the skeleton of this theropod was recovered. It provided O. C. Marsh with very good information with which to describe another new type of theropod, which was both smaller and clearly different from *Allosaurus*.

Ceratosaurus seems to have reached a maximum body length of 20ft (6m) and stood about 6ft 6in (2m) high. In its general proportions *Ceratosaurus* resembles *Allosaurus*. It has a large head, a short neck, relatively short arms and pillar-like legs. However, there are several notable differences. In the skull the jaws are massive and the teeth are sharp and curved. Again, the sides of the skull are cut away to produce large open spaces enclosed by a bony framework of struts. There is also a large, hollowed-out ridge just above the eye similar to that of *Allosaurus*. However, unlike *Allosaurus*, *Ceratosaurus* has a very prominent bony horn on the snout. This is indeed the most striking feature of *Ceratosaurus*. The bony bump on the snout is shaped rather like a rhinoceros horn. Its function is uncertain. It is unlikely to have served to protect the animal against other predators, but may have been used by males in fighting each other for mates. Another difference between ▶

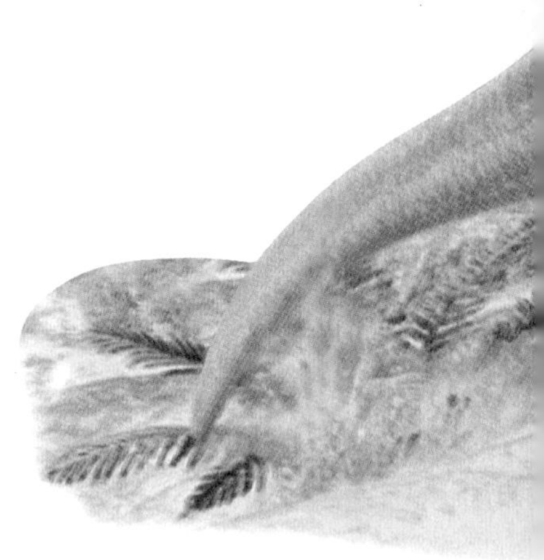

***Right:* Similar to *Allosaurus* in some respects, *Ceratosaurus* was smaller and had four-fingered hands. The most striking feature of *Ceratosaurus* is the sizeable bony bump on its snout, which was shaped rather like a rhinoceros horn. The function of the bony bump is uncertain. It probably was not for protection against other predators, but may have been used by males in fighting each other for mates. *Ceratosaurus* has fewer teeth than *Allosaurus*.**

Ceratosaurus and *Allosaurus* is that *Ceratosaurus* has fewer teeth in the jaws and the back of the skull is larger and deeper.

The remainder of the skeleton of *Ceratosaurus* also shows several subtle differences from that of *Allosaurus*. In particular, the hand has four well-developed fingers, unlike *Allosaurus*, which has only three. The hip of *Ceratosaurus* shows the arrangement typical of saurischian dinosaurs, with the front pelvic bone (pubis) pointing forwards. However, the hip is unusual in that the individual bones are firmly welded together, rather than being separate, as is more usual, and the sutures (areas of contact of the bones) are obliterated. Rather unexpectedly, the *Ceratosaurus* skeleton was also found to possess the remains of a narrow row of bony plates that seem to have run down the middle of the back. Typically for a carnosaur, *Ceratosaurus* has a long tail, which provides attachment for strong musculature and acts as a counterbalance.

Compared with *Allosaurus*, *Ceratosaurus* would seem to have been a smaller, more lightly built and more agile predator. Skeletal remains of *Ceratosaurus* are quite rare in late Jurassic rocks, and most probably this implies that it was a more versatile and perhaps solitary predator, unlike the gregarious *Allosaurus*.

***Below and right: Ceratosaurus* exhibits typical carnosaur features. The skull is rather large for the body and, although it has a very robust lower jaw, the rest of it is quite lightly built. The crest in the nasal region is a distinguishing feature of *Ceratosaurus*. The neck is rather short and, although the back leg is powerful and pillar-like, the front leg is feeble. The tail is long and provides attachment for strong musculature and acts as a counterbalance.**

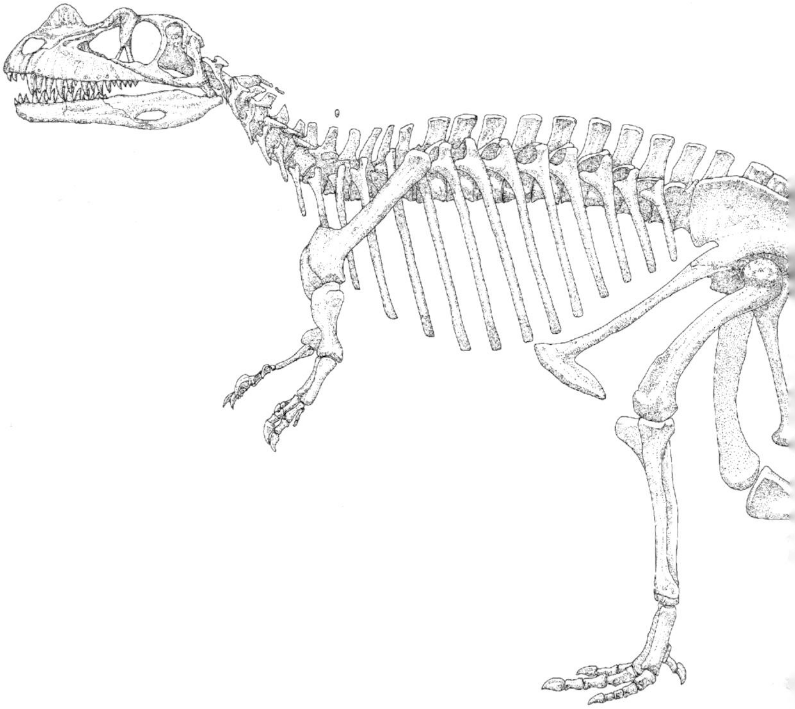

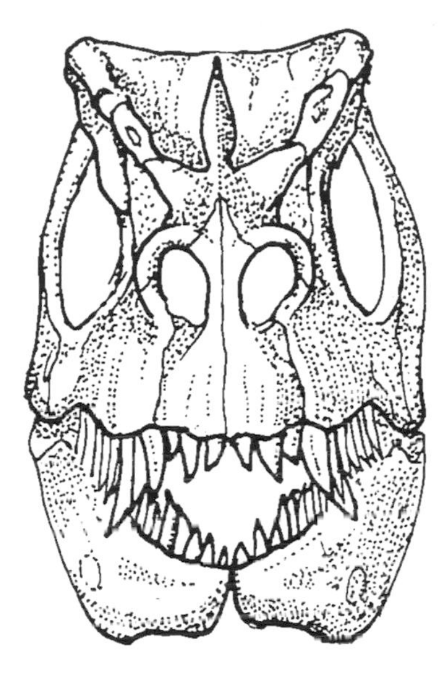

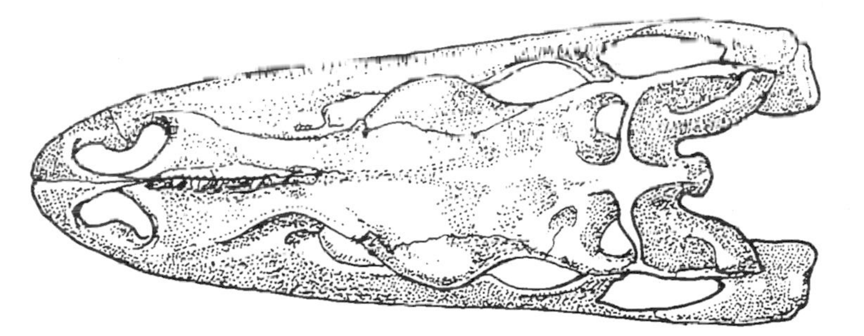

Dilophosaurus

Period: Early Jurassic. **Family:** Carnosaurs.
Where found: Western North America.
Estimated length: 20ft (6m).

Along with *Allosaurus* and *Ceratosaurus*, *Dilophosaurus* is one of the best-known examples of carnosaurs. *Allosaurus* and *Ceratosaurus* seem to have been contemporaries, their remains having been found in the same late Jurassic quarries of North America. *Dilophosaurus* ('two-ridged reptile') is one of the very few well-preserved early Jurassic dinosaurs. It also was found in North America.

Its remains were first discovered in 1942 during an expedition to northern Arizona organised by the University of California. The team were led to the site by a Navajo Indian, Jesse Williams, where they discovered the remains of three individuals: one was an almost complete skeleton 20ft (6m) long, the other two consisted of rather badly eroded fragments.

After careful preparation in the laboratory, this dinosaur was finally described by Dr Sam Welles in 1954 as a new species of *Megalosaurus*. *Megalosaurus* is a well-known but unfortunately very fragmentary large theropod dinosaur from the late Jurassic of England. First analysis of Welles's new dinosaur suggested strong similarities to the English theropod. In 1964 Welles returned to the area in which his *Megalosaurus* was found and was fortunate to discover another skeleton of a similar theropod. Unlike the previous examples, this skull was quite well preserved and revealed a pair of thin bony crests that ran along its top. Clearly this was no ordinary theropod, and in 1970 Welles gave it the new name of *Dilophosaurus* in recognition of the unusual crests on its head.

In 1984 Sam Welles published a very detailed description of *Dilophosaurus*. The skull is large in proportion to the body and is quite delicately constructed. Welles concluded that the long slender teeth at the front of the snout were probably used for plucking and tearing at the flesh of their victims rather than biting, while the more posterior teeth were used for cutting and slicing flesh. The function of the tall crests on the skull remains a mystery; most likely they were associated with some aspect of the behaviour of the animal – perhaps visual signalling for recognition purposes.

The neck, although long and flexible, was controlled by powerful muscles attached to the ribs and spines. The long tail counterbalanced the animal so that it could walk and run on its hind legs, which were long and powerful. The forelimbs were short but strong, and the hand had four fingers, the first three of which bore sharp claws. The first finger was shorter and more powerful than the other two.

Many other carnosaurs have come from the Jurassic and Cretaceous rocks of most countries. Unfortunately many of them are known from very scrappy material, such as odd serrated teeth or claws; ▶

Below: **This is the earliest large carnivorous dinosaur. *Dilophosaurus* had a crest on its head, which was made from two thin ridges of bone situated side by side and shaped rather like half dinner plates set up on end. *Dilophosaurus* was also different from *Allosaurus* and *Dilophosaurus* since its jaws were weak and slender. They probably could not have withstood the stresses of dealing with struggling prey, and it has been suggested that *Dilophosaurus* was a scavenger rather than an active predator.**

this has led to the naming of large numbers of species on very dubious evidence indeed. The renowned dinosaur *Megalosaurus* ('big reptile') is particularly famous because it was the first dinosaur to be named and scientifically described. The remains of *Megalosaurus* (*M. bucklandi* as it was later to be known) were discovered in a quarry at Stonesfield in Oxfordshire, England, in the early years of the 19th century; they represented parts of a large theropod dinosaur 23-26ft 2in (7-8m) long that lived in late Jurassic times. In the years following the original description, by William Buckland in 1824, any fragmentary remains of a carnivorous dinosaur found in Jurassic or Cretaceous rocks were referred to as *Megalosaurus*! Thus *Megalosaurus* remains were reported from Europe (France, Belgium, Germany, Portugal), Australia and North America (later to be renamed *Dilophosaurus*!). In fact much of this material is either obviously not referrable to *Megalosaurus* or too fragmentary to be diagnosed as anything more than 'the remains of a large theropod'. The widespread use of the name '*Megalosaurus*' as a 'dustbin' for any large theropod remains arose primarily because most theropod fossils are isolated fragments. Up to the present time at least 26 different names have been created for large, poorly preserved *Megalosaurus*-like theropods.

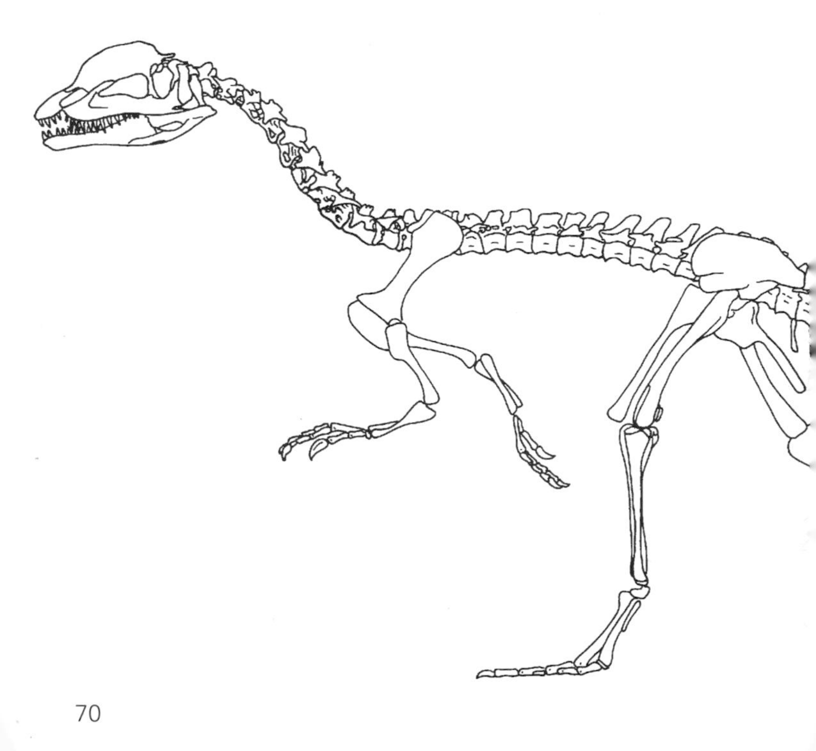

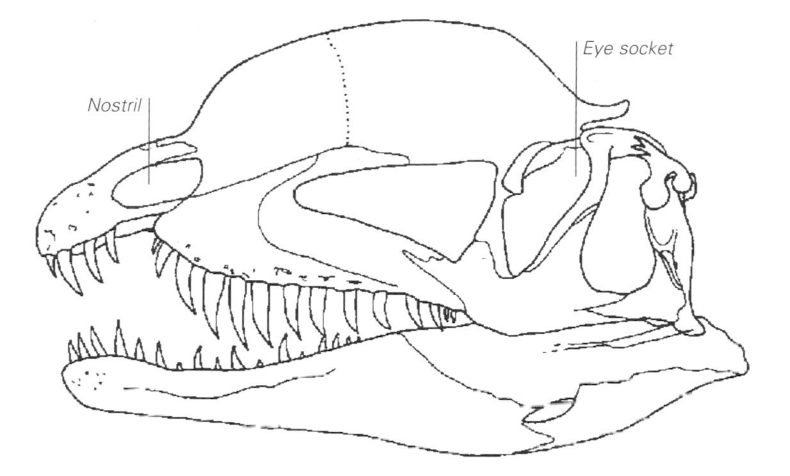

Above: This is a typical carnosaur skull, being large relative to the body and lightly built except for the strong lower jaw. The crests on the skull give this animal its name.

Below: Dilophosaurus was about 20ft (6m) long – about the same length as *Ceratosaurus*. Both were probably more agile than *Allosaurus*, which was very much larger. *Dilophosaurus* exhibited the typical carnosaur features of the large head, weak front leg, powerful back leg and long tail. In this form the neck was longer and more flexible than usual, but it was still controlled by powerful muscles attached to the neck and ribs. They were probably necessary to support the large head.

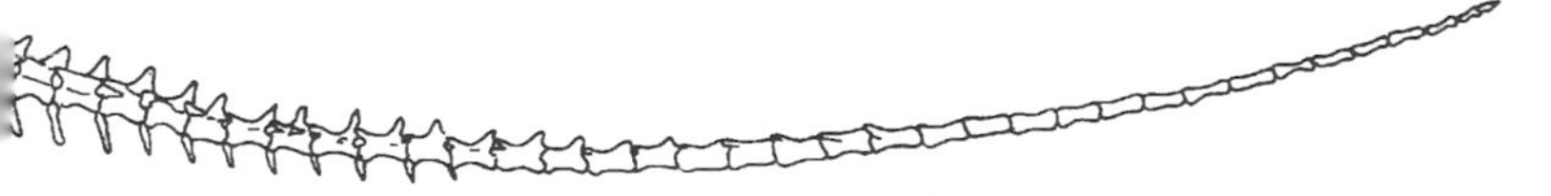

Tyrannosaurids

Tyrannosaurids, undoubtedly the best-known of all dinosaurs, are a family of large (20-46ft, 6-14m long) theropods whose remains have been found in late Cretaceous rocks in North America and Central Asia. There are four well-established species of tyrannosaurid: *Tyrannosaurus rex, Daspletosaurus torosus* and *Albertosaurus libratus*, from North America, and *Tarbosaurus bataar* from Mongolia.

The tyrannosaurids were not recognised as a distinct group of theropods until 1906, shortly after the first reasonably complete skeleton of *Tyrannosaurus* ('tyrant reptile') was discovered in Montana in 1902. *Tyrannosaurus* was first described in 1905 by Henry Fairfield Osborn, who also reconstructed its skeleton. Modern reconstructions do not differ very significantly from his attempt.

In 1908 another far more complete skeleton including a perfect skull was discovered in the same area of Montana. This made *Tyrannosaurus* one of the best-known of all theropod dinosaurs. The only remaining unknowns are the structure of the hand (the two-fingered hand is based on that of *Albertosaurus*) and the length of the tail.

Lawrence Lambe was one of the first palaeontologists to postulate the likely lifestyle of a tyrannosaurid (*Albertosaurus*). He proposed that *Albertosaurus* was a very slow-moving creature of sluggish habits. The well-developed belly ribs and the large 'foot' on the pubis could have been adaptations for lying prone on the ground. *Albertosaurus* was principally a scavenger.

Right: **Tyrannosaurids may have attacked their prey, such as this hadrosaurid, by running into it jaws agape, the shock of such a collision being absorbed by the heavily reinforced skull.**

However, the skeleton of *Tyrannosaurus* gives the impression of a fairly dynamic animal. The tail is massive and counterbalances the trunk and head effectively. The pillar-like legs do not necessarily mean that tyrannosaurids were slow, lumbering creatures. Speed in an animal depends not only on the proportions of its limbs, but also on their overall length. Longer-legged animals take long strides and can therefore cover the ground quickly. Thus tyrannosaurids may have been able to move quite fast, but only over short distances.

The heavily reinforced skull of tyrannosaurids also suggests that these animals were devastating predators. The head had to withstand the violent impact of the jaws against the body of the prey. Regions of flexibility at the back of the skull where the lower jaw is supported also indicate that the skull bones could move passively rather than break under great stress. For dismembering prey, the jaws, armed with large serrated teeth, would easily have sliced through skin and flesh.

One persistent puzzle of tyrannosaurid anatomy is the ridiculously small arms. The hands could not have been much use in dismembering prey, nor probably even reach the creature's mouth. Two suggestions only seem feasible. Osborn proposed that they may have been used as grapples during mating. Barney Newman has suggested that *Tyrannosaurus* used its arms when trying to rise from a prone resting position, anchoring the front part of the body against the ground so that it did not pitch forward on to its nose.

Albertosaurus

Period: Late Cretaceous. **Family:** Tyrannosaurids.
Where found: North America.
Estimated length: 29ft 6in (9m).

Like *Tyrannosaurus*, *Albertosaurus* ('reptile from Alberta') has had a rather chequered history. Two partial skulls of large theropods were discovered on the Red Deer River of Alberta in the early 1890s and twice mistakenly referred to other genera. In 1905 the remains of large theropods were reviewed by H. F. Osborn, who created the name *Albertosaurus sarcophagus*. Knowledge of this type of dinosaur was greatly improved by C. H. Sternberg's discovery in 1913, in the same area, of a very well-preserved skeleton of a large theropod dinosaur, consisting of a fine, if slightly squashed skull and much of the remainder of the skeleton including the forelimb. In 1914 this skeleton was given the name *Gorgosaurus* (*Albertosaurus*) *libratus* ('free dragon reptile').

The forelimb was sufficiently distinctive to merit some early comment. In most theropods the hand has three clawed fingers. In *Gorgosaurus* (*Albertosaurus*) only two clawed fingers (digits 1 and 2), both quite small, were noted and a remnant of the third finger. The very small forelimb and reduced hand are now distinguishing characteristics of tyrannosaurids as a whole.

In 1917 Lawrence Lambe provided a first skeletal reconstruction of *Gorgosaurus*. This revealed a theropod that was a little smaller than *Tyrannosaurus*, but its proportions were very similar. It was not directly related to *Tyrannosaurus* at the time because, on no evidence, Osborn had reconstructed the skeleton of *Tyrannosaurus* in 1916 with three clawed fingers on the hand. Like *Tyrannosaurus*, the skeleton of *Gorgosaurus* was that of a large and quite heavily built theropod with a massive skull, short forelimbs and heavy, pillar-like legs ending in bird-like feet. Similarly, the belly ribs were particularly well developed and the lower end of the pubis in the pelvis was distinctly enlarged ('footed').

In 1970 a review of the large theropods of western Canada concluded that *Gorgosaurus* material should be referred to *Albertosaurus libratus*. The differences were explicable in terms of juvenility of the *Gorgosaurus* specimens. The review also revealed the rather slender and delicate proportions of young tyrannosaurids.

Albertosaurus sarcophagus is now thought to represent a descendant species of *A. libratus*.

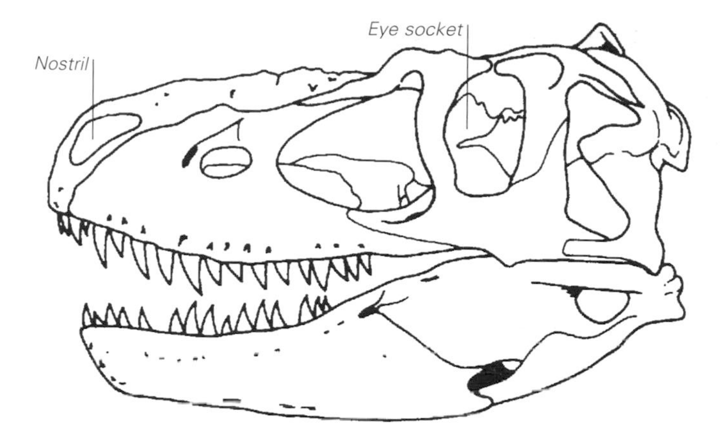

Above: The skull of *Albertosaurus* (top) is very similar to that of *Tyrannosaurus*. It is massively built with smaller skull windows surrounded by thicker struts of bone. The teeth are sharp and recurved (pointing backwards), typical of a carnivore.

Left: Albertosaurus may have been able to hunt the active hadrosaurids. *Albertosaurus* could have killed its unarmoured prey with a strong, bone-crushing bite on the back of the neck. In addition, it could probably have delivered a fierce and disabling kick with its sharply clawed hind foot when at close quarters.

Daspletosaurus

Period: Late Cretaceous. **Family:** Tyrannosaurids.
Where found: North America.
Estimated length: 29ft 6in (9m).

Daspletosaurus torosus ('frightful flesh-eating reptile') comes from the Red Deer River near Steveville, Alberta, Canada. Most of the skeleton was found by C. M. Sternberg in 1921. At first this was referred to as *Gorgosaurus*, being of about the same size as the *Albertosaurus* specimen described by Lawrence Lambe. However, the skeleton is that of a much more heavily built animal. The forelimb, although small as in all tyrannosaurids, is larger than that of all other known species.

Almost all *Daspletosaurus* remains are from large, presumably fully adult specimens, while the remains of more than half of the *Albertosaurus* skeletons found to date are of immature individuals. The coexistence of two species of large theropods may indicate that there were at least two discrete ecological niches for them. Dr Dale Russell proposed that *Daspletosaurus* preyed upon the larger and heavier ceratopids while the lighter and perhaps more fleet-footed *Albertosaurus* preyed upon the smaller, more agile hadrosaurids. It is certainly true that hadrosaurids and *Albertosaurus* were both very abundant at this particular time, while *Daspletosaurus* and the ceratopids were markedly less so, but whether these ratios are merely a matter of chance or indicate the biological interactions suggested is an open question.

Daspletosaurus was smaller than *Tyrannosaurus*, but it was still a fearsome carnivore. It had a massive head with strong jaws, which were lined with dagger-like teeth. It may have fed on the quadrupedal armoured ceratopids – difficult animals to overwhelm. *Daspletosaurus* would probably have tried to sink its teeth into the unprotected flanks of its prey: once it had locked its jaws shut, the ceratopid probably could not have shaken itself loose. The teeth of *Daspletosaurus* were fewer in number but larger than those of *Albertosaurus* or *Tyrannosaurus*. Like the other tyrannosaurids, it had a heavily reinforced skull.

Right: **This tyrannosaurid was smaller than *Tyrannosaurus*, but with a total body length of 29ft 6in (9m) it was still a fearsome carnivore. *Daspletosaurus* had a massive head with strong jaws, which were lined with dagger-like teeth. It has been suggested that it fed on the quadrupedal armoured ceratopids and these would have been difficult animals to overwhelm. *Daspletosaurus* would probably have tried to sink its teeth into the unprotected flanks of its prey: once it had locked its jaws shut, the ceratopid probably could not have shaken itself loose.**

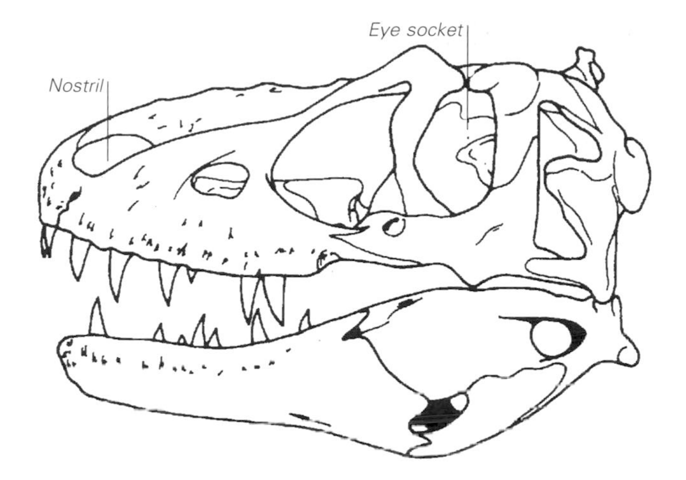

***Above:* Daspletosaurus has the typical tyrannosaurid build. It is distinguished by its teeth, which, although fewer in number than the skulls of *Albertosaurus* and *Tyrannosaurus*, are particularly large. All tyrannosaurid skulls show marked similarities.**

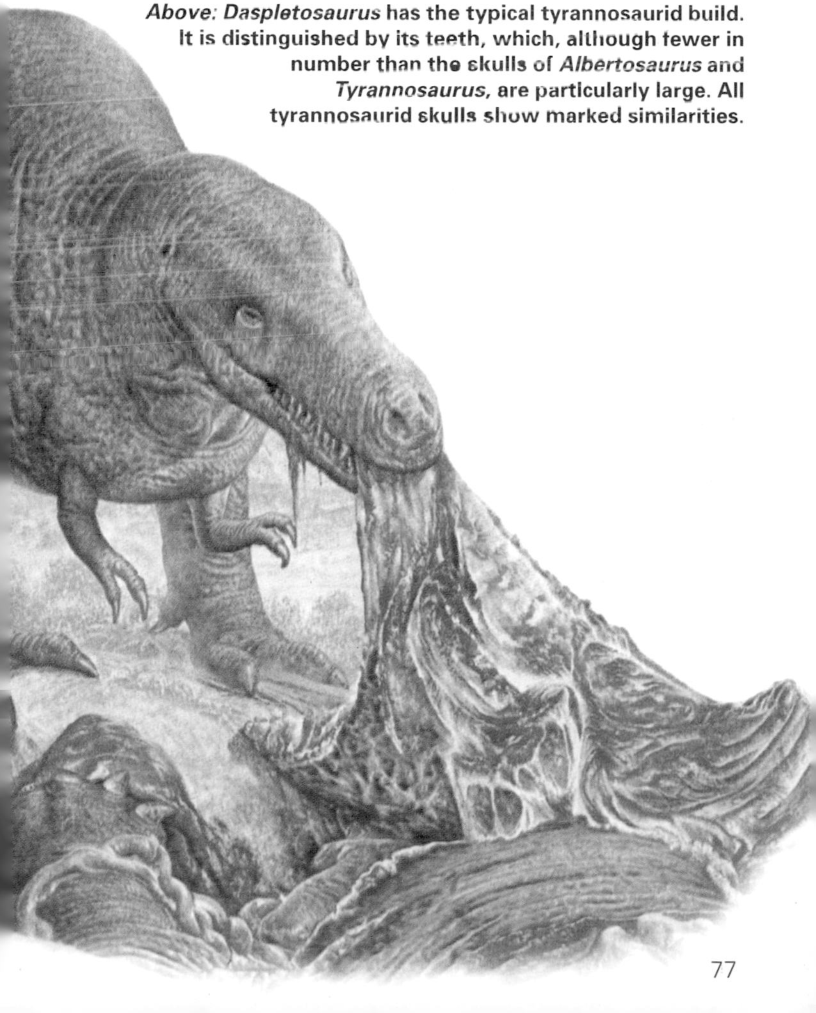

Tyrannosaurus

Period: Late Cretaceous. **Family:** Tyrannosaurids.
Where found: North America.
Estimated length (l), height (h) and weight (w): l: 46ft (14m); h: 18ft 6in (5.6m); w: up to 7 tonnes.

Tyrannosaurus ('tyrant reptile') is the most famous of all dinosaurs. At 46ft (14m) long, it was one of the biggest carnivorous dinosaurs known. It may have hunted its prey actively but there is strong evidence that it lived by scavenging as well, as did the other tyrannosaurids. *Tyrannosaurus* was so massive that it is hard to imagine that it could have run down its prey over long distances. Its skull was massively constructed, with a fearsome array of teeth.

Our knowledge of *Tyrannosaurus* dates back about a century. A partial skeleton of a very large theropod, consisting of the jaws and parts of the skull, back bones, shoulders, pelvis and the hindlimbs, was discovered in late Cretaceous rocks in Dawson County, northern Montana, in 1902. The remains were first described by Henry Fairfield Osborn in 1905 as *Tyrannosaurus*. *Tyrannosaurus* was well over 40ft (12.3m) long and may have weighed up to 7 tonnes, so its skeleton is a compromise between the need to bear this massive weight and to run around to catch food. The skull is much more massive than that of the carnosaurs, built to withstand impact. It is supported by a stout neck, which joins the compact back region. The bodies of the individual vertebrae are designed to withstand compression forces, while the stout ribs, joined by ligaments and muscles, would withstand tension. The hip girdle and back limb were extremely strong since they would take the animal's weight. As in other bipedal dinosaurs, the long tail counterbalanced the front of the body. The front legs were very small and feeble. The belly is lined with ribs – gastralia – which probably served to stiffen this area.

The skull of *Tyrannosaurus* is far more massive than that of *Allosaurus*. It too is notable for window-like openings, although they are not nearly as large as in *Allosaurus*, and the bony framework that surrounds them is thick and heavy. The enormous weight and apparent great strength of the skull must be a reflection of the feeding habits of *Tyrannosaurus*.

The massive head is supported by a very short, powerful neck, the vertebrae of which are very thick and bear stout spines for the attachment of powerful ligaments and muscles used to hold the head in position. The ribs are also very long for the attachment of more muscles used to twist the neck and swing it from side to side. The bones of the back are larger and stronger than those of the neck and acted in life like a massive girder The block-like bodies of each vertebra withstood enormous compression forces because of the great weight of the ▶

Left: **This famous dinosaur was one of the biggest carnivorous dinosaurs. It may have hunted its prey actively but there is strong evidence that, like the other tyrannosaurids, it lived by scavenging as well. *Tyannosaurus* was so massive that it is hard to imagine that was capable of running down its prey over long distances. When a dinosaur died naturally or because of an accident, its carcass would have given off a powerful smell that might have attracted the giant meat-eaters for miles around.**

body, while the roughened and ridged edges and tops of the spines projecting from the top of each vertebra were the sites for attachment of extremely powerful ligaments and muscles; these would have acted rather like hawsers holding the bones in place, while at the same time allowing them some free movement.

An indication of the enormous forces exerted on the backbone is provided by the skeleton itself. In the skeleton discovered in 1908, two pairs of vertebrae in the back have become welded together. This is a pathological condition; the great compression forces had evidently collapsed the originally flexible joints between these vertebrae, causing no doubt painful friction between the vertebrae until they finally welded themselves together.

Several vertebrae at the base of both the neck and the back possess cavities in their sides (known as pleurocoels), which undoubtedly served to reduce the weight of bone in the back wherever possible.

The pelvic bones are very large to allow for the attachment of big leg muscles and also to provide a strong socket for the hip joint itself.

The huge, blade-like upper pelvic bone (ilium) has a rather complex pattern of ridges and rough-edged patches, which mark the areas of attachment to the stout ribs (sacral ribs) of the backbone. Six bones of the back are welded together to produce a massive bar of bone; this had to be strong because the entire weight of the body – perhaps 6-7 tonnes – had to be carried across this joint to the hindlimbs. The legs are naturally very large and heavy-boned in order to support the large body. The feet are quite broad with three forward-pointing toes, which end in sharply curved talons, and a small backward-pointing, spur-like first toe.

The shoulder bones of *Tyrannosaurus* are moderately large, but the limbs are puzzlingly minute and end in small, two-clawed hands.

As with most theropods there is an array of ribs lying in the wall of the belly; in life these probably connected via ligaments (or possibly directly) to the ends of the chest ribs enclosing the chest and belly, thereby making this part of the body fairly stiff and inflexible.

Some reconstructions of *Tyrannosaurus* tend to show a very long tail dragging along the ground. However, large sections of the end of ▶

Below: **The skull of *Tyrannosaurus* is huge, and supported by a stout neck, which joins the compact back region. The individual vertebrae are designed to withstand compression forces, while the stout ribs would withstand tension. The hip girdle and back limb need to be extremely strong to take the animal's weight. As in other bipedal dinosaurs, the long tail counterbalances the front of the body. The front legs are very small and feeble. Ribs, or gastralia, lining the belly probably serve to stiffen this area.**

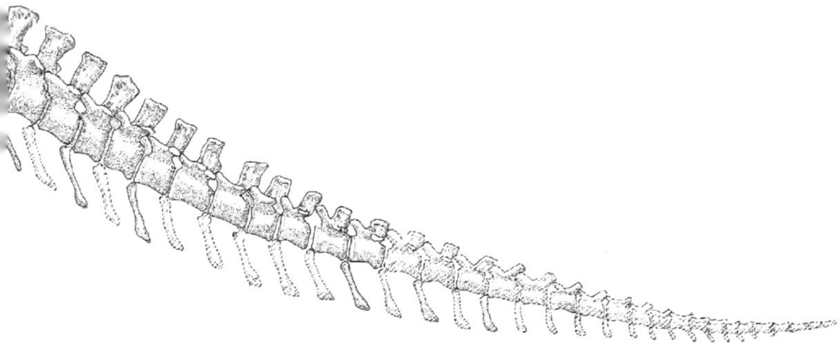

the tail are unknown. As reconstructed here, the tail is given an 'average' length for a theropod and is shown held off the ground as a counterbalance.

Tarbosaurus bataar ('alarming reptile from Bataar'), a large tyrannosaurid from the Nemegt Basin of the Gobi Desert in Mongolia, was first described in 1955. The remains of at least seven individuals were collected by the Palaeontological Institute of the Academy of Sciences of the Soviet Union. In addition, at least six more skeletons were collected during the Polish-Mongolian expeditions. The information known to date suggests that *Tarbosaurus* was practically identical with *Tyrannosaurus*, although there are a few relatively minor differences in the structure of the skull bones that serve to distinguish the two forms. Apparently fully adult specimens never attained the size of the largest *Tyrannosaurus* specimens. Despite the relatively enormous distance that separates *Tyrannosaurus* and *Tarbosaurus* geographically, it is very tempting to place them in the same genus: this would certainly have been done had the *Tarbosaurus* remains actually come from Canada.

Right: **In these views of the pelvis of *Tyrannosaurus* it is possible to see the upper pelvic bone (ilium) and the verbetrae that attach to it (sacral vertebrae). The lower pelvic bones are not shown. In the exploded view of the pelvis, middle, top and bottom) the wide, plate-like nature of the ilium is seen. This gives plenty of area for muscle attachment. The sockets for the sacral ribs (arrowed) are also visible in the middle drawing.**

Below: **These illustrations demonstrate the theory that the minute tyrannosaurid forelimbs were used as props to help the animal rise from a prone position. They would secure the front of the body while the rear legs were straightened; the upper body would then be tilted back to bring the tyrannosaurid upright.**

Pelvis (exploded view)

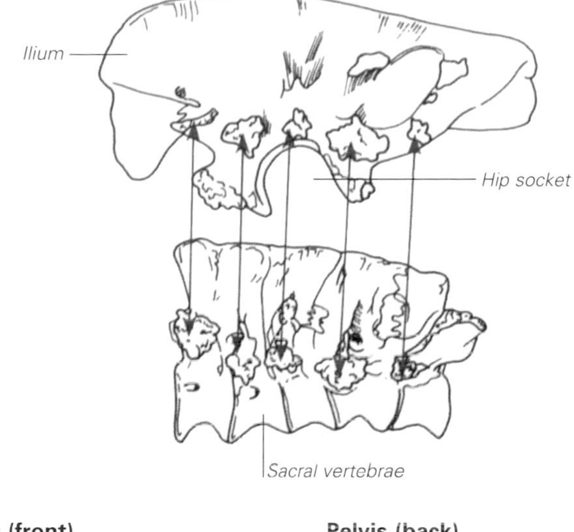

Pelvis (front)

Pelvis (back)

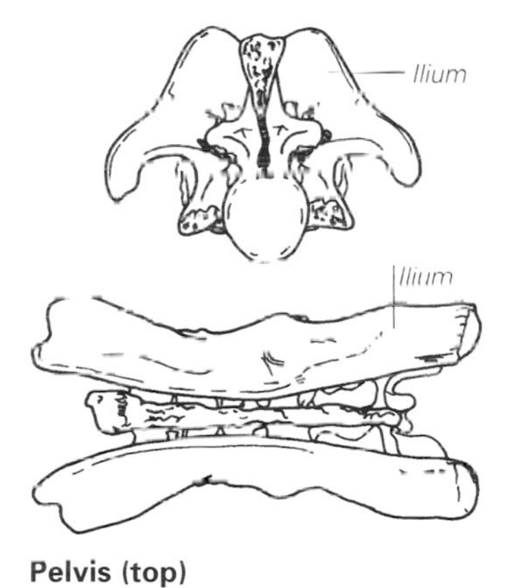

Pelvis (top)

Pelvis (bottom)

Prosauropods

Prosauropods are an interesting, but also rather puzzling group of saurischian dinosaurs. They existed in the late Triassic and early Jurassic and were distributed practically worldwide, their abundant remains having been discovered on every continent except Antarctica. They seem to represent the first major evolutionary radiation among the dinosaurs – indeed among the archosaurs (dinosaurs, crocodiles, pterosaurs, thecodontians, etc) – to exploit plant food. Until the late Triassic the world had been dominated by various herbivorous types of mammal-like reptile. During the Permian and Triassic Period the archosaurs were, with very few exceptions, exclusively carnivores of various shapes and sizes. The prosauropods, in a sense, paved the way for the evolution of the gigantic and closely related sauropod dinosaurs.

Prosauropods have now been divided into three families: anchisaurids, melanorosaurids and yunnanosaurids. The vast majority of all prosauropods known to date fall into the family of anchisaurids, which derives its name from *Anchisaurus*, a prosauropod from early Jurassic rocks of the Connecticut Valley of eastern North America. The earliest discovery of *Anchisaurus* was made in 1818. These fragmentary remains, at first thought to be human, were not confidently identified as reptilian until 1855! And it was not until 1912, when Richard Swan Lull was reviewing the fossils discovered in the Connecticut Valley, that the material was referred to the prosauropod dinosaur *Anchisaurus*.

The preponderance of prosauropod fossils at some Triassic and

Below: **Although many reconstructions show anchisaurids as bipedal animals it is probable that their long necks would make them top-heavy and give them a tendency to topple forwards. The front legs are quite robust despite being short, and so they may have been used to help stabilise the body from time to time, even if the animal did not make a habit of walking on all fours.**

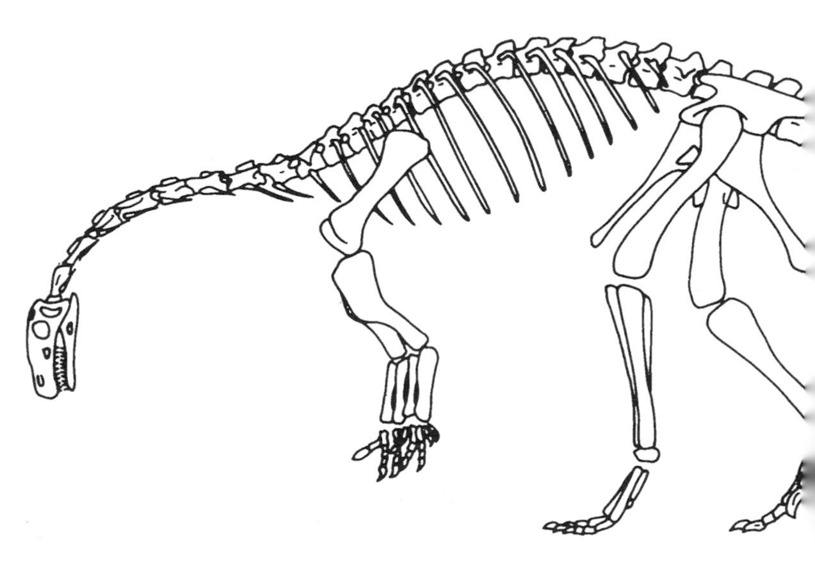

Jurassic localities has prompted the suggestion that many species lived in herds.

Another major group of prosauropods may be the melanorosaurids ('black reptiles'). These prosauropods are larger and much more heavily built than anchisaurids. Yunnanosaurids ('reptiles from Yunnan') are at present devoted to a single species, *Yunnanosaurus huangi*, from China. Apparently smaller and less heavily built than the melanorosaurids, the yunnanosaurids are notable for the structure of their teeth, which are cylindrical but somewhat flattened from side to side, presenting a somewhat chisel-like appearance. The tip of the tooth tends to be worn off at an angle, forming quite a sharp cutting edge. *Yunnanosaurus* seems therefore to have developed a full set of truly sauropod-type teeth, although the skeleton is quite typical of that of an anchisaurid prosauropod.

Below: **The skull of Coloradia bears an obvious resemblance to that of *Plateosaurus* and *Anchisaurus*, sharing the deep snout and depressed jaw joint but differing in the way that it widens at the back. Note ring of sclerotic ossicles.**

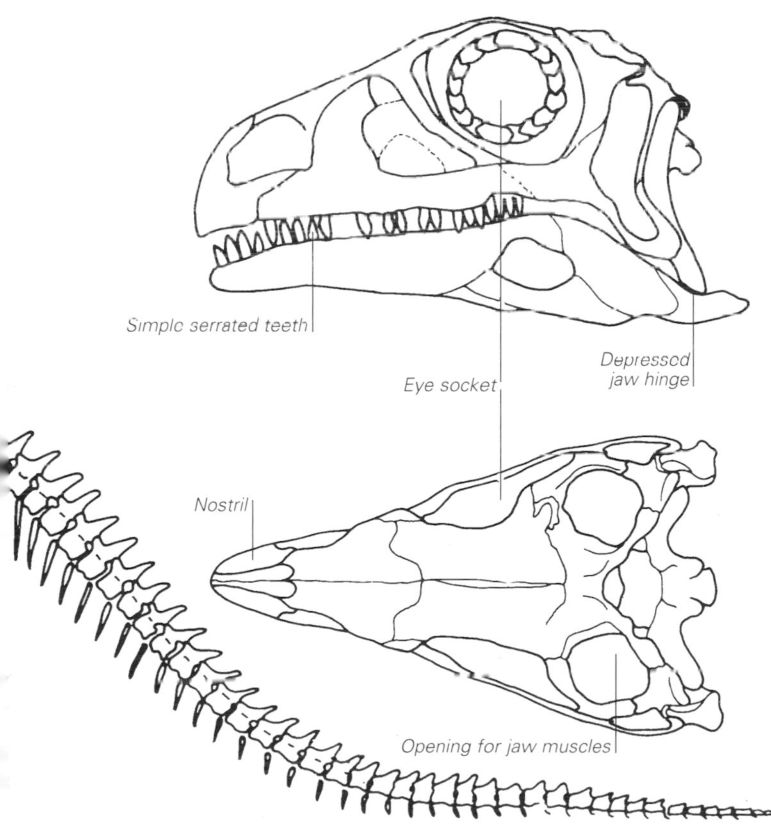

Plateosaurus

Period: Late Triassic/Early Jurassic. **Family:** Prosauropods.
Where found: Western Europe.
Estimated length: 20ft-26ft 3in (6-8m).

Another of the anchisaurid type of prosauropods, *Plateosaurus* ('flat reptile') was considerably larger (20-26ft 3in, 6-8 m body length) than other members of the family. Mass concentrations of relatively complete remains have been found in the late Triassic rocks of western Europe (Germany, France and Switzerland), notably at Trössingen and Halberstadt in Germany and La Chassagne in France. The first remains of *Plateosaurus* were described by Hermann von Meyer in 1837 from fragments of a skeleton. However, during 1911-12, 1921-23 and in 1932 extensive excavations at Trössingen were carried out by the Palaeontological Institute of the University of Tübingen. These revealed a massive accumulation of complete and partial skeletons of *Plateosaurus*. The skeletons were described in considerable detail by Friedrich Freiherr von Huene, a palaeontologist from Tübingen.

As can be seen from the skeletal reconstruction, which is taken from von Huene's work of 1926, *Plateosaurus* was larger and consequently more robustly constructed than *Anchisaurus*, although the general body proportions are remarkably similar. The skull is somewhat more heavily built, with a deeper snout region; the teeth are also more numerous. Also deserving of comment is the position of the jaw joint in *Plateosaurus*; this is sited below the level of the teeth, while in *Anchisaurus* the jaw joint is on practically the same level as the teeth. The teeth of ▶

Right: **This was the first large dinosaur, reaching a length of up to 26ft 3in (8m).** ***Plateosaurus*** **fed on plants at ground level and on leaves of tall trees.** ***Plateosaurus*** **could stand on its hind legs or on all fours, and its long neck would have allowed it to seek food over a wide area. The hands are characterised by their strong fingers and particularly the thumb, which was furnished with a broad, scythe-like claw. This thumb was probably used to rake up plants on the ground or to tear leaves down from the trees, or possibly as a defensive weapon.**

Plateosaurus have coarse serrations running down the edges of the crown, as do the teeth of almost all other prosauropods. The remainder of the skeleton is very similar to that of *Anchisaurus*.

The natural pose of these anchisaurid prosauropods has been the subject of some disagreement in the past. In the 1890s O. C. Marsh produced a skeletal restoration of *Anchisaurus*. The body in this upright bipedal pose does seem rather unbalanced; the tail looks to be too small effectively to counterbalance the front part of the body in this position. However, the arm and hand do not seem to be designed for

Below: **This large anchisaurid has been collected from over 50 localities in Europe and so its structure is pretty well known. The head is rather small and perched on a long, flexible neck. The back and tail are also long and as in other bipedal forms the tail would have helped to counterbalance the front end of the body.**

***Right:* This tooth shows the large, coarse serrations that resemble those of some modern herbivorous lizards. These teeth would shred rather than grind.**

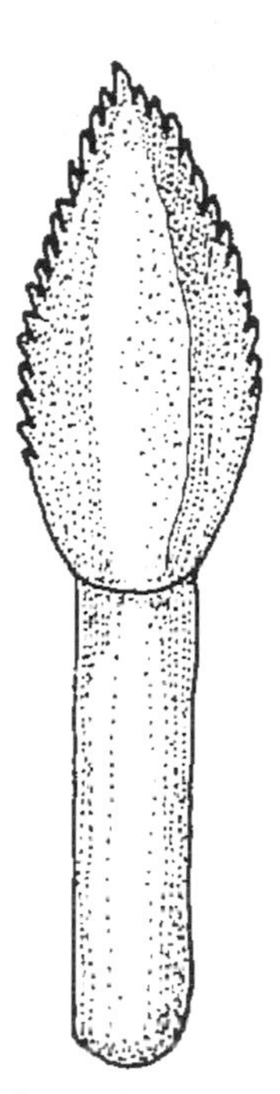

walking upon. In particular, the fingers are relatively slender and have narrow claws, which would have enabled them to be used for grasping objects. A very similar posture was used by von Huene in his 1926 reconstruction of *Plateosaurus*.

Peter Galton proposed a somewhat different posture for all prosauropods after reviewing the anatomy of the hand and the general body proportions of prosauropods. The relatively long neck and trunk of these animals does not give them a perfect balance at the hips; there is a strong tendency for the body to pitch forward on to all fours. The arms and shoulders are quite long and robustly constructed, so they could have been used for weight-bearing; and on careful investigation the hands were found to be quite sophisticated in the range of movements that they could make. Not only could the fingers be flexed to grasp objects, but they could also be hyperextended (bent backwards) so that digits 2, 3 and 4 could rest on the ground like the toes of a foot. The enlarged claw on the first finger was probably held clear of the ground in order to protect it from damage.

The preponderance of prosauropod fossils at some Triassic and Jurassic localities has prompted the suggestion that many, perhaps all, species lived in herds. In fact, the local abundance of *Plateosaurus* at Trössingen prompted von Huene to speculate vividly upon the circumstances that led to the mass accumulation. He proposed that vast herds of such creatures may have wandered through the ancient highlands of southern Germany and that, rather like the wildebeest of Africa, they underwent seasonal migrations during the dry season in search of water. Trössingen represented to von Huene a place where a large herd had perished on just such a journey.

In 1982 Dr David Weishampel (Miami) reinvestigated the Trössingen *Plateosaurus* quarry and was able to demonstrate that the *Plateosaurus* skeletons, rather than being the remains of a single vast herd, were buried over a considerable period of time. They probably represented the chance fossilisation of normal deaths of individuals of a very abundant dinosaur living in this area. However, hidden within this record there were two 'spikes', that is, narrow geological bands that seem to have unexpectedly high numbers of skeletons. Weishampel interpreted these 'spikes' as representing catastrophic deaths of large numbers of individuals. What the ▶

cause of these might have been is uncertain; one possibility is that they were animals caught in flash floods rather than members of herds that died during seasonal droughts.

Nevertheless, it is thought that many of the prosauropods were gregarious, living in herds in order to provide communal protection from some of the large predatory thecodontians of the late Triassic, such as *Sarcosuchus*, or large theropod dinosaurs of the early Jurassic, such as *Dilophosaurus*. The large claw on the hand may well have been used as a close-quarters defensive weapon.

Right: **This skull is clearly more robust than that of *Anchisaurus*. It has a deeper snout and more numerous teeth. The jaw hinge is depressed below the level of the tooth row – often considered to be a feature of a herbivore.**

Below: **The foot is large and strong for bearing the animal's weight when it stood or walked bipedally. The first four toes are well built but the fifth is rudimentary. The upper foot bones (metatarsals) are well developed and the animal probably walked on its toes, rather like modern cats and dogs.**

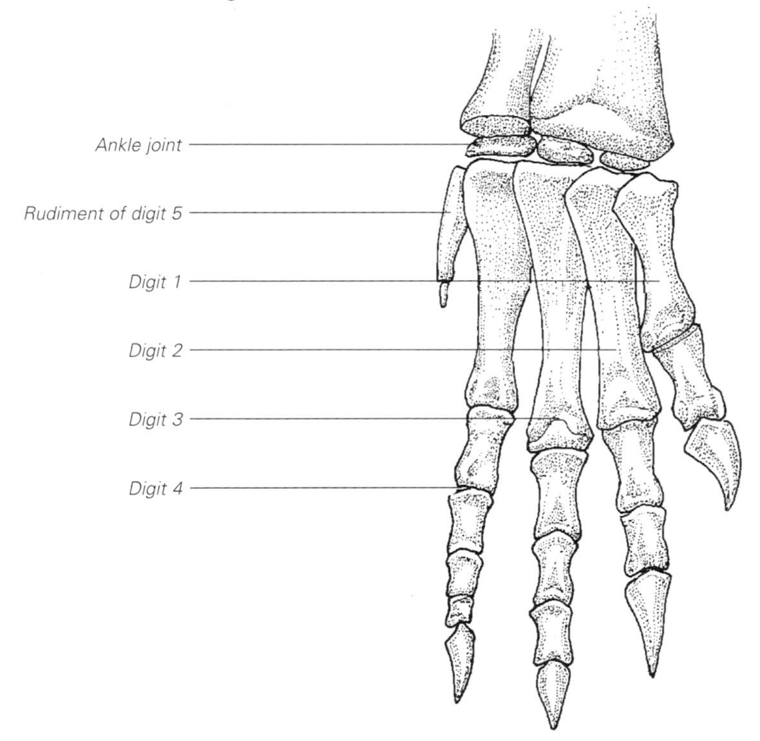

Right: **This hand is very well developed and may have been used to help support the body and in defence – note the large claw on the first finger. The hand is unusual in that fingers 4 and 5 are both poorly developed, but fingers 1 to 3 are much stronger, giving it a very asymmetrical appearance.**

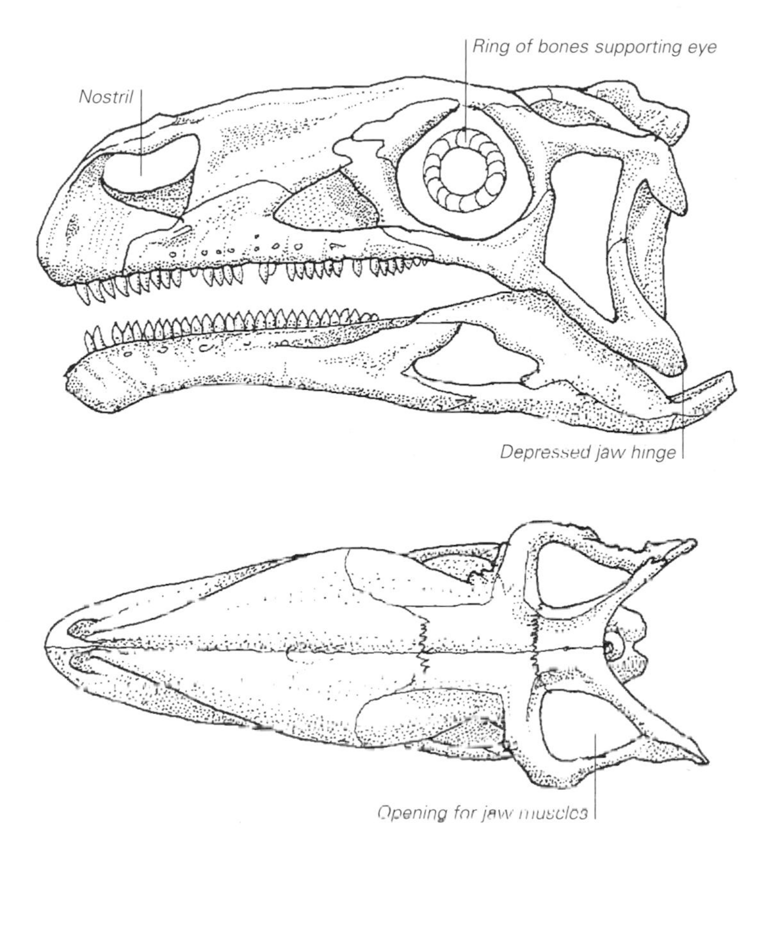
Ring of bones supporting eye
Nostril
Depressed jaw hinge
Opening for jaw muscles

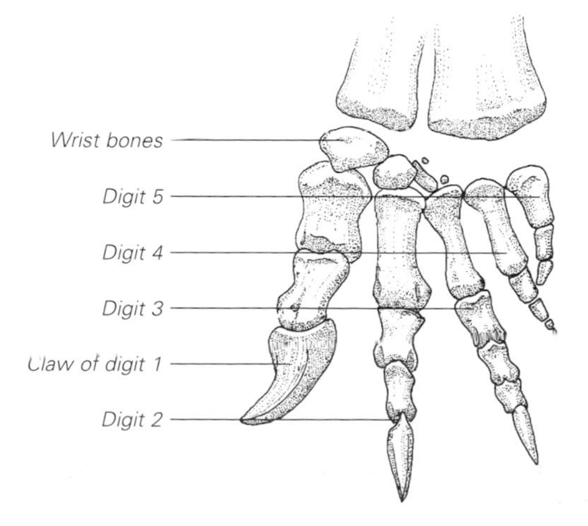
Wrist bones
Digit 5
Digit 4
Digit 3
Claw of digit 1
Digit 2

Anchisaurus

Period: Late Triassic/Early Jurassic. **Family:** Prosauropods.
Where found: Eastern North America and South Africa.
Estimated length: 8ft 2in (2.5m).

Between the time of the first discovery in 1818 and its final identification, other *Anchisaurus* ('close reptile') material was discovered in adjoining areas of the Connecticut Valley. Edward Hitchcock (who collected large numbers of fossil footprints in this area) reported bones from Springfield, Massachusetts; this skeleton was named *Megadactylus polyzelus* by his son, E. Hitchcock Jr, and subsequently renamed *Amphisaurus* by Othniel Charles Marsh in 1882 (because another animal had already been named *Megadactylus*), and then again in 1885 renamed *Anchisaurus polyzelus* by Marsh because the name Amphisaurus was also preoccupied!

The most productive site in the Connecticut Valley proved to be a quarry near Manchester, Connecticut; this produced three well-preserved prosauropod skeletons and a few other fragments. The skeletons were described in some detail by O. C. Marsh in the early 1890s as *Anchisaurus major, A. colurus* and *A. solus. A. major* was subsequently renamed *Ammosaurus major* and *A. colurus* became *Yaleosaurus colurus*, just to add to the general confusion! Other prosauropod material comes from the Navajo Sandstone of northern Arizona and consists of the partial remains of *Ammosaurus* ('sand reptile').

Anchisaurus remains have also been described from the earliest Jurassic rocks of Orange Free State, South Africa. Originally described as *Hortalotarsus, Thecodontosaurus* and *Gyposaurus*, Drs Peter Galton and Mike Culver redescribed this partial skeleton of *Gyposaurus* and noted that it was virtually indistinguishable from the North American *Anchisaurus* and so renamed it *Anchisaurus capensis*.

Palaeontologists now generally agree that *Anchisaurus*, like the other prosauropods, was a successful early vegetarian. Thanks to its

lightness and agility, *Anchisaurus* could escape the attentions of the contemporary theropod predators.

The way of life and probable diet of prosauropods have generated a lot of discussion, based mainly on the characteristics of the teeth and the body shape and size. The preferred argument seems to be that they were completely herbivorous. The teeth seem well suited for shredding up plant material. The curious low position of the jaw joint seems to be an adaptation that improves the effectiveness of the teeth along the jaw. Another important piece of evidence is that the prosauropod *Massospondylus* ('massive vertebra') had a gastric mill ('stomach stones', or gastroliths). These sizeable pebbles, which were probably lodged in the muscular walls of a 'gizzard' or an equivalent region of the stomach, could have provided an area where plant material was ground to a pulp for easier digestion. With their long necks and legs, the prosauropods were probably adept 'high-browsing' dinosaurs and may well have been the first group of reptiles to evolve the ability to feed on relatively high vegetation. Until the appearance of the prosauropods, all herbivores had been squat, short-necked creatures that would have been incapable of reaching high foliage. So, not only were they the first herbivorous dinosaurs, they were also the first high browsers as well.

The skeleton of *Anchisaurus*, based on material from the Connecticut Valley, consists of the major part of the skeleton, lacking only the tail and much of the neck. The skull of *Anchisaurus* was quite ▶

Below: One of the smaller prosauropods, the early Jurassic form *Anchisaurus* was a successful early herbivore. It had blunt, pencil-shaped teeth spaced out along its jaw, and there have been long arguments about whether it ate meat, plants or both. The balance of evidence seems to favour a vegetarian diet. *Anchisaurus* was lightly built and probably agile and thus could escape the attentions of the contemporary theropod predators.

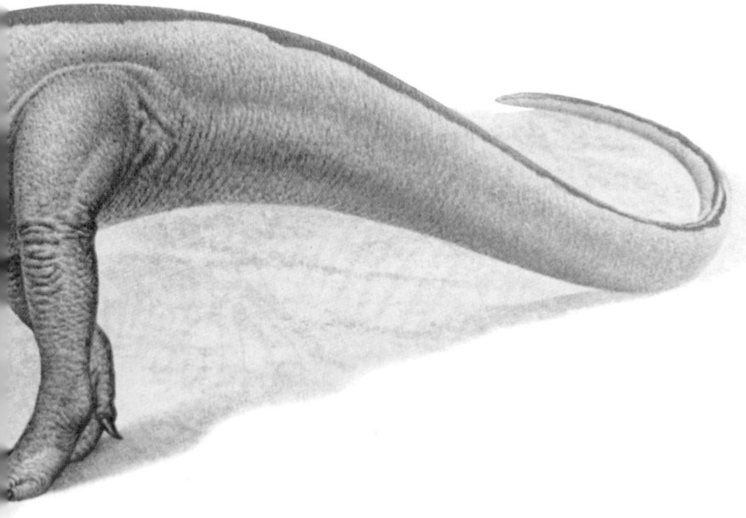

small in proportion to the body, with a relatively long and slender snout. The teeth were quite slender and pencil-shaped and may well have had rough serrations down the front and back edges, evidently suited to shredding plant fibres.

The neck and back of *Anchisaurus* are reconstructed partly by reference to other prosauropods. The neck was probably long, slender and flexible, as was the back, giving these animals a rather long-bodied look, particularly when compared with theropods. The tail was undoubtedly long and helped to counterbalance the front part of the body over the hips.

Above: **The *Anchisaurus* skeleton is comparatively small and light. With its long, flexible neck and elongated back, *Anchisaurus* may have been a high-level browser like other anchisaurids.**

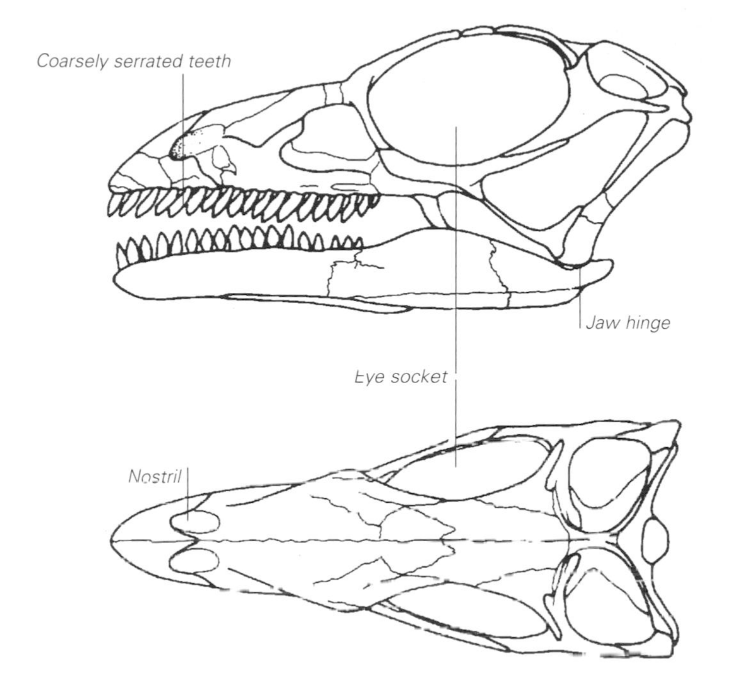

Above: This is a rather lightly built skull. The teeth are quite slender and bear coarse serrations back and front. Unlike that of *Plateosaurus*, the jaw hinge is on about the same level as the tooth row.

The limbs were of slightly unusual construction. The hindlimbs were relatively sturdy and were evidently designed to carry the bulk of the weight of the animal when walking. The foot also was quite broad, with four well-developed toes and the rudimentary remains of the fifth. The forelimbs and shoulders, however, were also remarkably well developed. The shoulders were stout and the relatively long arms were evidently capable of touching or resting on the ground with ease; this suggests that *Anchisaurus* may have walked on all fours on occasions. The hand was rather curious in that the outer fingers (fourth and fifth) are quite small and slender and may not have borne claws, while the inner fingers were well developed, particularly the first finger, which has a much-enlarged, sharply curved claw.

Diplodocids

The sauropods were undoubtedly the most spectacular of all dinosaurs. The very epitome of the popular image of the dinosaur, they were the long-necked and long-tailed giants of the Jurassic and Cretaceous Periods.

The earliest sauropods known are of early Jurassic age and very probably arose from a stock of prosauropod-like animals in the late Triassic. The diplodocids are a very closely knit group of sauropods. The relatively stout, short-necked *Dicraeosaurus* and *Apatosaurus* are followed by the longer-necked *Diplodocus, Barosaurus* and *Mamenchisaurus*. Diplodocids were notably abundant at the end of the Jurassic, although fragmentary remains from southern England and *Nemegtosaurus* from Mongolia, known from a skull alone, show that some survived to the end of the Cretaceous. Typically the diplodocids were long-necked, with long snouts, eyes set far back in the head and nostrils on top of the skull.

Scientific study of *Apatosaurus* began in an extremely confused and confusing way in 1877, largely because of the rivalry between two palaeontologists, Othniel Marsh and Edward Drinker Cope. First, Marsh described a large, incomplete section of hip bones found near Morrison, Colorado; to this he gave the name *Titanosaurus montanus*, only to discover that *Titanosaurus* ('giant reptile') had already been used for a sauropod from India. Later he coined the name *Atlantosaurus* ('Atlas reptile') for this material. Marsh also used the name *Apatosaurus ajax* for more hip and back bones found in another quarry in the Morrison area. Over the next few years more material of *Apatosaurus ajax* and of another larger skeleton named *Atlantosaurus immanis* was recovered from the second quarry. This collection included fragments of a skull. In 1879 Marsh's collectors discovered two more sauropod skeletons at Como Bluff, Wyoming, from rocks of the same age as the previous find. One of these, an almost complete skeleton lacking only the skull, was described as *'Brontosaurus' (=Apatosaurus) excelsus* by Marsh in 1879, the other was named *B. amplus* (*Brontosaurus*: 'thunder reptile'). In 1883 Marsh produced the first ever reconstruction of any sauropod, based on his *'Brontosaurus' excelsus*, but unfortunately used several limb bones as well as the feet of *Camarasaurus*. As a result, the animal was given rather graceful, slender forelimbs, not the much more stout, robust limbs that it actually had. *Camarasaurus*, or *'Morosaurus'* as it was then known, was also used as the model for the neck, which was given 12 neck vertebrae instead of the correct number, 15. Marsh was also unaware that *'Brontosaurus'* had a long, whip-like end to its tail comprising more than 80 vertebrae, almost twice the number found in the tail of *Camarasaurus*.

On the basis of better-preserved material of *Apatosaurus* and careful work on the original material, it was agreed that (i) *Apatosaurus* was the valid name for material described either as '*Atlantosaurus*' or '*Brontosaurus*'; (ii) *Camarasaurus* was the valid name for material also referred to as '*Morosaurus*'; and (iii) there were more similarities between the skeletons of *Apatosaurus* and *Diplodocus* than there were between *Apatosaurus* and *Camarasaurus*.

Right: **These skulls all show basic diplodocid features. The eyes are far back in the head and the nostrils right on top of the skull. The snout is long and broad with a cluster of rather feeble-looking teeth at the front.** ***Nemegtosaurus*** **is from the late Cretaceous rocks of Mongolia.** ***Dicraeosaurus*** **was found in late Jurassic rocks of Tanzania.** ***Antarctosaurus*** **is from the Jurassic of Argentina (not Antarctica!).**

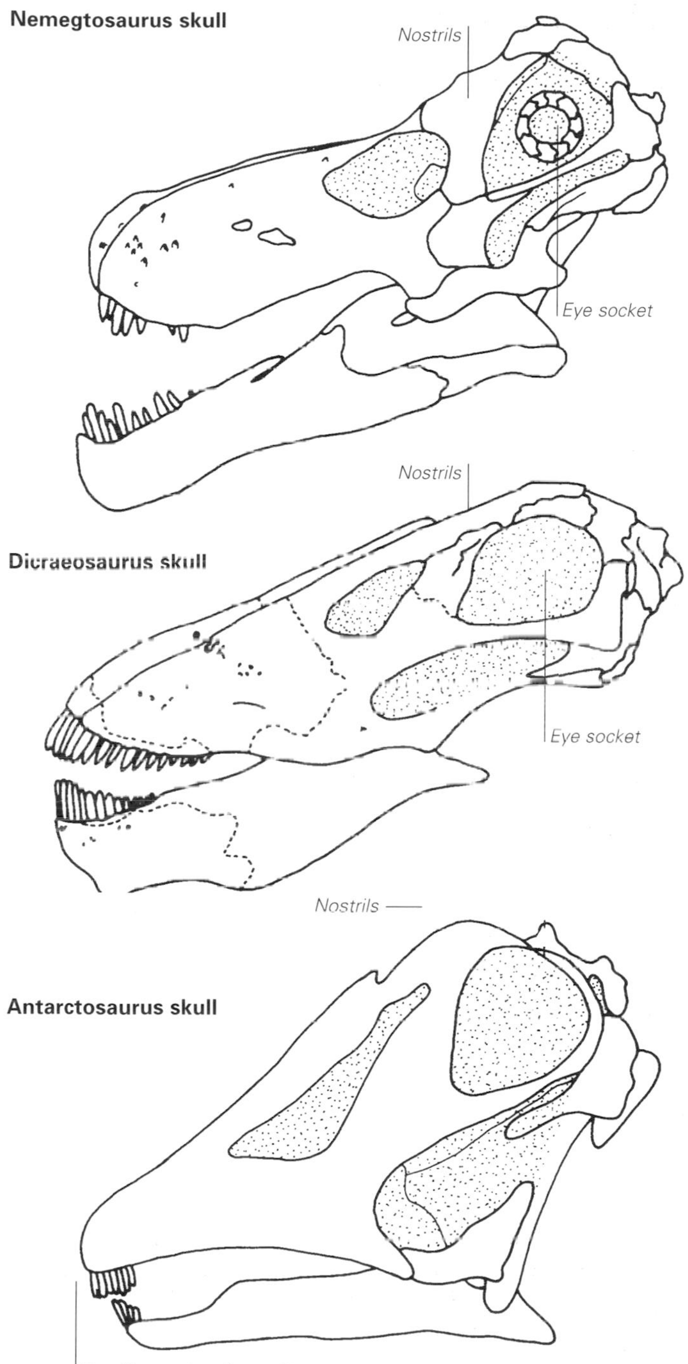
Nemegtosaurus skull
Nostrils
Eye socket
Nostrils
Dicraeosaurus skull
Eye socket
Nostrils
Antarctosaurus skull
Peg-like teeth at front of jaw

Apatosaurus

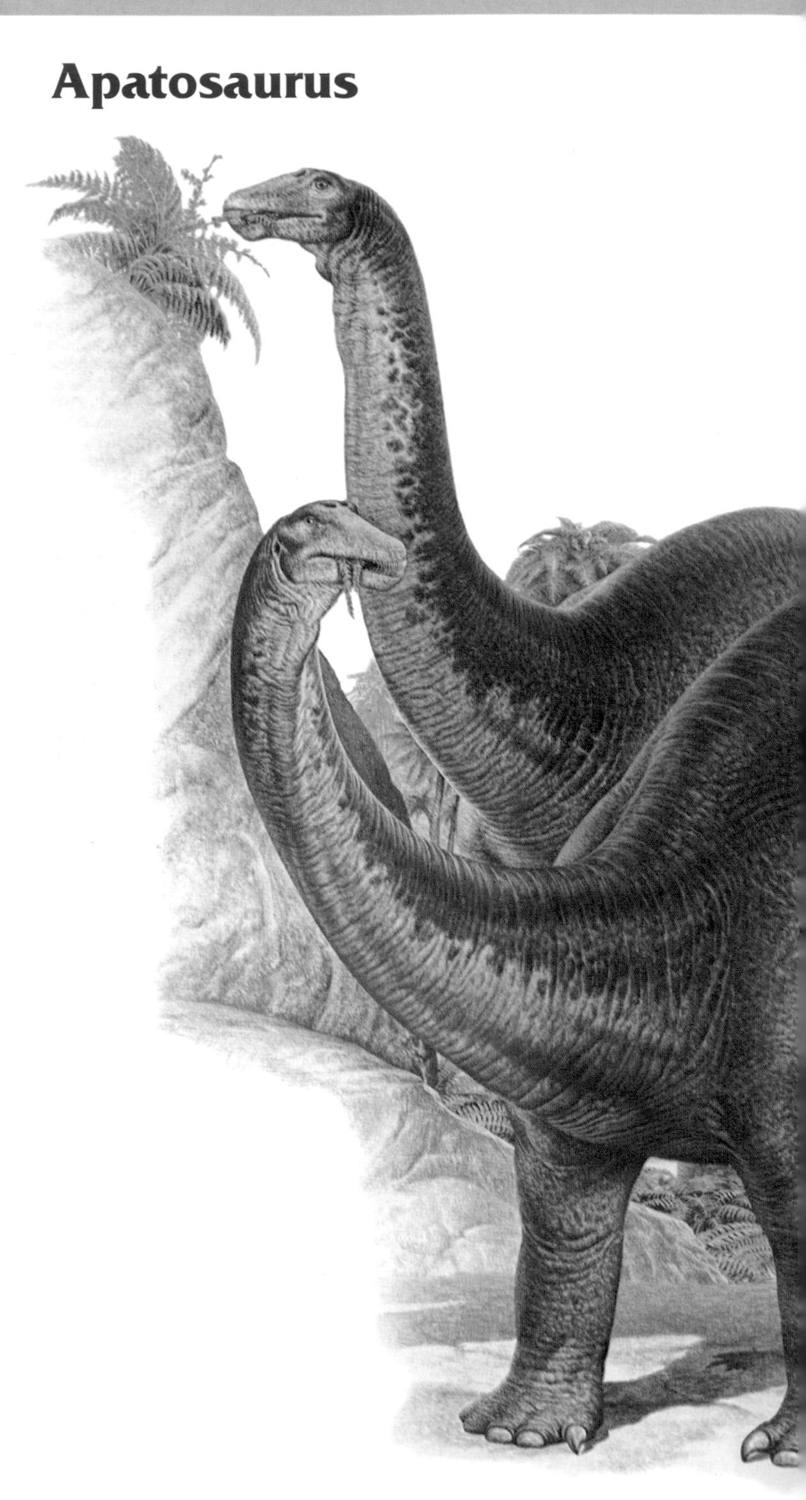

Period: Late Jurassic. **Family:** Diplodocids.
Where found: North America.
Estimated length and weight: 69ft (21m), 30 tonnes.

An obviously large sauropod, *Apatosaurus* ('deceptive reptile') weighed about 30 tonnes. The neck was relatively thick and the head was small. *Apatosaurus* must have fed nearly continuously on low-lying vegetation around lakes and on the leaves of tall trees. It snipped these off with its peg-like teeth and swallowed them whole. The plant material was ground up in the stomach, which probably contained a number of pebbles that *Apatosaurus* had swallowed for this purpose – so-called 'stomach stones', or gastroliths.

Left: **An obviously large sauropod, *Apatosaurus* weighed about 30 tonnes. The neck is relatively thick and the head is small. *Apatosaurus* must have fed nearly continuously on low-lying vegetation around lakes and on the leaves of tall trees. It snipped these off with its peg-like teeth and swallowed them whole. 'Stomach stones', or gastroliths, which *Apatosaurus* had purposely swallowed, ground the material up in the stomach of the animal. Note the short, splayed, rather elephant-like toes.**

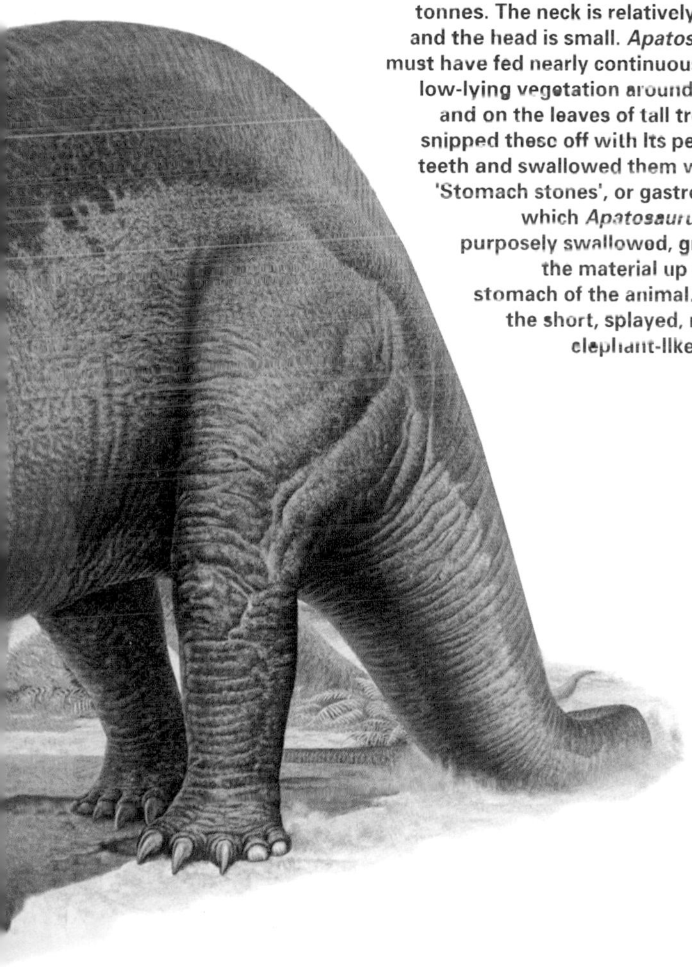

The head of *Apatosaurus* is now thought to be like that of *Diplodocus*. The neck is thicker, consisting of 15 vertebrae to which the ribs – which no doubt anchored the powerful muscles that moved the neck – are firmly fused. The sides of the neck vertebrae and those of the back are deeply excavated to form cavities (pleurocoels), which undoubtedly served to lighten the bones of the back in order to reduce the total body weight of these gigantic creatures. The spines of the neck, although apparently relatively short when compared with those of the back, are nevertheless connected to extremely powerful muscles and ligaments used for raising the neck. As in *Diplodocus*, the spines near the base of the neck are divided down the middle and probably provided a pulley-like guide for a massive ligament that ran along this groove.

The back vertebrae are less elaborately sculpted than the neck vertebrae, but have extremely tall spines, which are prominently ridged and scarred for the attachment of powerful muscles. At the hips, five of the vertebrae are fused together to form a massive support for the pelvic bones in order to transmit the enormous weight of the body into the pillar-like legs. The tail is surprisingly long for a quadrupedal animal (82 vertebrae are known in one specimen), almost half of which consists of a very slender whip-lash.

Both fore- and hindlimbs are massively built and pillar-like in order to support the weight of the animal effectively. The feet have relatively short toes, which are splayed rather like those of an elephant. The fore feet, as in the majority of sauropods, have a single clawed inner toe, the

***Below:* This is a much sturdier skeleton than that of *Diplodocus*. In particular note how much thicker the neck vertebrae are. The tail is especially long, containing perhaps 80 vertebrae and ending in a narrow whip-lash.**

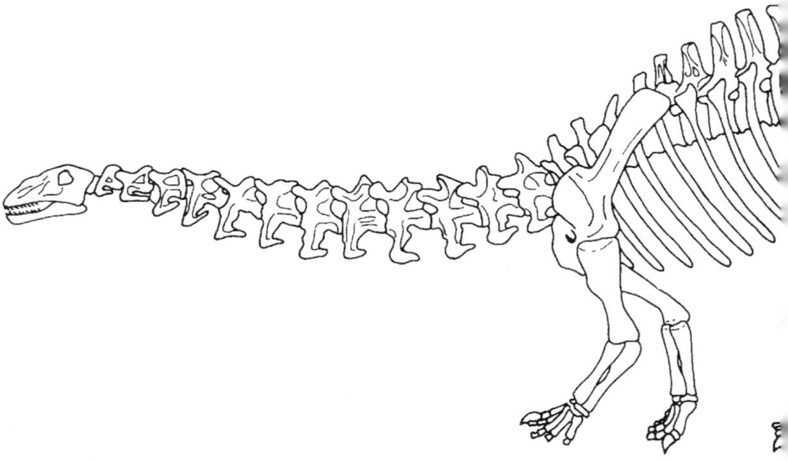

other four ending in blunt pads. The hind foot has three claws, the outer two toes again presumably ending in blunt pads.

The proportions of the toes of diplodocids bear a remarkable resemblance to those of living elephants. In elephants, the feet are supported by a thick wedge of fibrous tissue, which lies beneath the rear of the foot – rather like the heel of a modern shoe. As a result, the toes of elephants do not lie flat on the ground when they walk, but rest on the fibrous pad at an angle to the ground. By developing this wedge-heel arrangement, elephants have solved one of the 'problems' that we face when walking. Our toes lie flat along the ground and the ankle joint forms a right angle with the lower leg. Every time we take a step we have to lift our heel off the ground so that the weight of our bodies is supported on the ball of the foot. When we walk we therefore tend to bob up and down with each stride. This is in fact quite tiring, although we do not consciously realise this. It is one reason why shoes with moderate heels, which save some of the energy we would have used to lift the body up and down, are so comfortable. Elephants (being considerably heavier than humans) face this problem as well: they are heavy and therefore need broad, flat feet to bear their weight. However, they would tire very quickly if they rested the entire length of their toes on the ground when they walked and 'bobbed' in the way that we do. They therefore have developed 'built-in' heels to save energy. Sauropods must have done the same sort of thing. The broad, stubby toes were undoubtedly supported behind by a thick wedge of tissue that acted as a 'heel'.

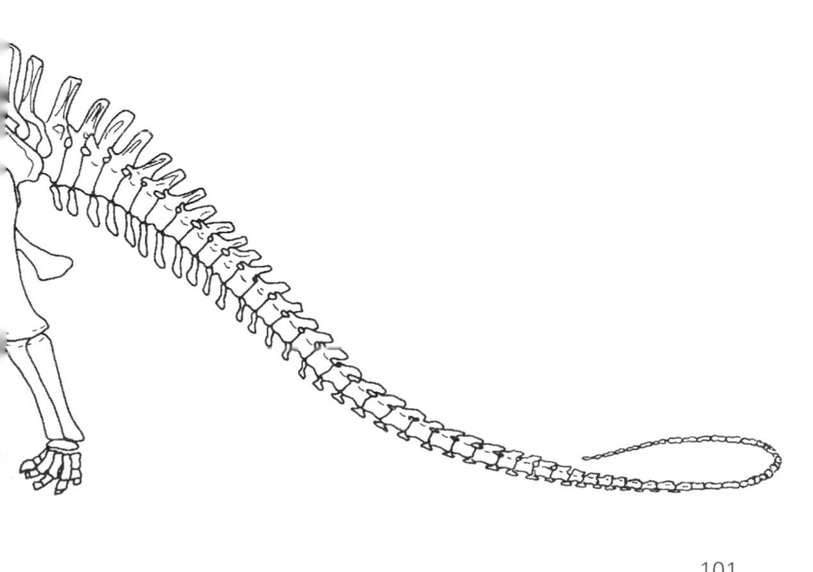

Diplodocus

Period: Late Jurassic. **Family:** Diplodocids.
Where found: North America.
Estimated length and weight: 88ft 6in (27m); 10-11 tonnes.

Diplodocus ('double beam'), another of the great and well-known sauropods from the late Jurassic of North America, was also initially described by O. C. Marsh. The first remains were found by Samuel Wendell Williston near the ranch of M. P Felch not far from Canyon City, Colorado, in 1877.

Williston managed to collect parts of a hind limb and numerous tail vertebrae. Marsh described these remains as *Diplodocus longus* in 1878. The name 'double beam' refers to the unusual form of the chevron bones that hang beneath the tail vertebrae. They are shaped like a pair of skids joined together at either end and were thought at the time to be unique to *Diplodocus*, although they have now been recognised in *Apatosaurus* and *Cetiosauriscus*. In subsequent years further fragmentary remains of sauropods, including *Diplodocus*, were recovered from Jurassic rocks in Colorado and Wyoming; however, it was not until 1899 that reasonable articulated skeletons were discovered, this time at Sheep Creek, Albany County, Wyoming. Two partial skeletons were recovered, which, together with the previously discovered remains, enabled John Bell Hatcher to provide a reasonably accurate

reconstruction of the skeleton.

The skull of *Diplodocus* is surprisingly small for an animal of such large size. The snout is quite long and broad, and the teeth, which are narrow and pencil-like, are clustered closely together to form a fringe around the front of the mouth only. The eyes are situated quite far back on the side of the head and, rather curiously, the nostrils are located right on top of the head almost between the eyes, rather than in their usual position at the tip of the snout. The positioning of the eyes and nose gives a rather 'cramped' impression to the rear portion of the skull where the brain seems to have been relatively small, as were the jaw muscles. The joint between the head and neck suggests that the head was held at a distinct angle to the neck, rather than in line with it.

As in *Apatosaurus*, there are 15 neck vertebrae; these, however, are somewhat longer, giving the neck a rather more slender appearance. The neck ribs are relatively short and fused to the vertebrae, while the vertebrae have extensive and complicated excavations in their sides to reduce their weight. The spines of the posterior neck vetebrae also have a V-shaped trough running down the centre, which undoubtedly acted as a guide for a very powerful neck ligament.

Also as in *Apatosaurus*, there are ten back vertebrae with long, complexly sculpted spines and deeply excavated pleurocoels. In the tail slightly fewer, 73 or so, tail bones are known and again the posterior portion of the tail is developed into a thin whip-lash. At the base of the tail, the sides of the vertebrae have deep, vertical plates of bone, perhaps providing areas for the insertion of massive muscles used for swinging the whip-lash end of the tail. The ribs extending from the back are very long and enclose a huge chest and belly cavity. Rather curiously, there are no good records to suggest that these animals had bony gastralia (belly ribs) as are ▶

Left: **A close relative of *Apatosaurus, Diplodocus* was lighter in build, weighing only 10-11 tonnes, even though it was longer (88ft 6in, 27m). The neck was longer and the tail was whip-like at the end. The limbs of diplodocids were pillar-like in order to support their great weight. Most of the toe nails of the front foot were small hooves, except for the inner toes, which bore long claws, possibly for self-defence.**

found extensively in prosauropods and theropods.

The shoulders and forelimbs are large and strong. The forelimb is pillar-like and ends in a rather short, broad foot. Apparently only the inner toe of the foot bore a large curved claw, the other toes ending in blunt, possibly horny pads rather like the toes of elephants. This type of fore foot seems to have been common to almost all sauropods. However, owing to the confusion that prevailed concerning the identity of these sauropods at the end of the last century, *Diplodocus* and *Apatosaurus* are often illustrated with three-clawed *Camarasaurus*-type feet!

The huge pelvis is firmly attached to the vertebral column by means of five fused vertebrae. Like the forelimb, the hindlimb is pillar-like, although it is slightly longer; as a result the back slopes down from the hips to the shoulders. The feet are again short and five-toed. In one fine skeleton of *Diplodocus carnegiei*, the five-toed hind foot is well preserved and appears to show that only two inner toes bore claws. Again, reconstructions often persist in erroneously showing a foot bearing three claws.

Below: **Diplodocids were clearly saurischian dinosaurs: the lower front bone (pubis) points forwards, not back alongside the ischium (lower rear bone) as in ornithischians. The pelvis is immensely strong and contacted five vertebrae, which were fused together for extra strength. This area of the animal had to bear enormous forces.**

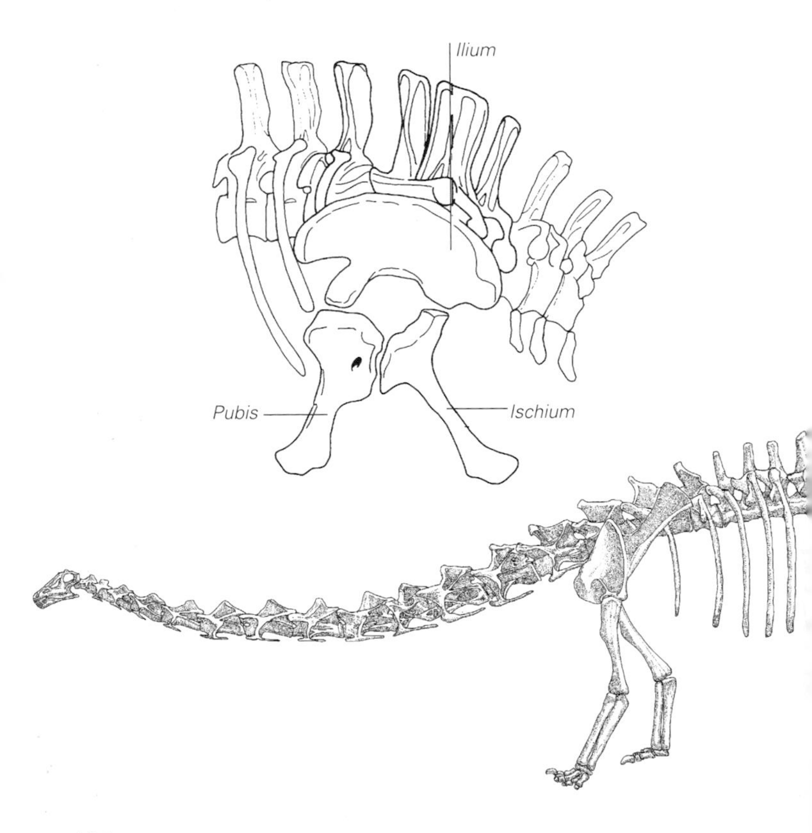

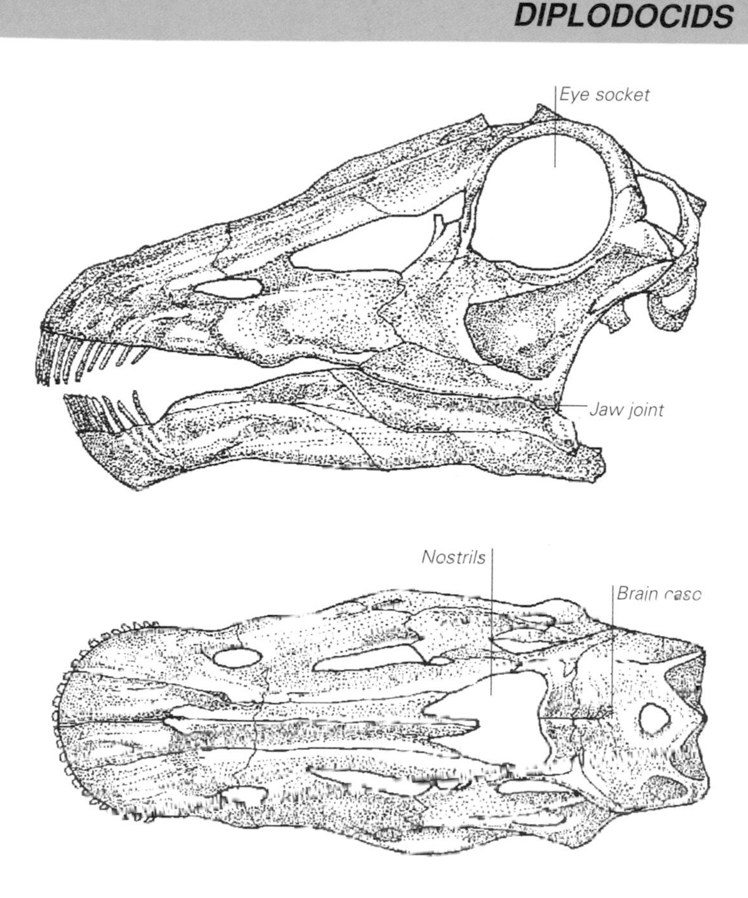

Above: **Here the features of the diplodocids are seen clearly. In the side view (top) note the large eyesocket and fine pencil-like teeth at the front of the snout. In the top view (bottom) you can see the unusual position of the nostrils.**

Below: **It has been suggested that *Diplodocus* had the body plan of a walking cantilever bridge! Both front and back legs (the pillars of the bridge) and their girdles were extremely strong, to bear the animal's weight. Despite the large belly area, there is no evidence of gastralia.**

Camarasaurids & Brachiosaurids

Another reasonably well-known group of sauropod dinosaurs are the camarasaurids, based mainly upon *Camarasaurus*. *Camarasaurus*, which was first described by E. D. Cope in August 1877, was much confused with early discoveries of *Apatosaurus* and *Diplodocus*. These dinosaurs all come from the same late Jurassic deposits of North America. Cope described *Camarasaurus supremus* on the basis of an imperfect series of vertebrae, collected from Canyon City, Colorado, in 1877. In December of that year O. C. Marsh described more sauropod material (including an imperfect skull with major parts of a skeleton of an immature sauropod) as *Apatosaurus grandis*, and another partial skeleton of a more mature sauropod, which he named *Apatosaurus ajax*; both specimens came from Como Bluff, Wyoming. In the following year more material from Como Bluff was described as *Morosaurus robustus* and *M. impar* by Marsh, while from Colorado Cope described *Caulodon leptoganus* and *C. diversidens*. Another genus, *Uintasaurus douglassi*, was described on the basis of a partial skeleton recovered from Dinosaur National Monument, Utah, in 1924. When this material was subsequently reviewed in 1958, all these species (apart from *Apatosaurus ajax*) were referred to Cope's genus *Camarasaurus*. The relationships of other possible members of the camarasaurid family are again difficult to pin down with any degree of certainty.

In Tendaguru, 40 miles (64km) inland from the east coast of Africa in Tanzania, a very dramatic dinosaur discovery was made in 1907. An engineering geologist prospecting for minerals discovered weathered fragments of enormous fossil bones. An expedition was mounted to collect the fossils and between 1908 and 1912 over 250 tonnes of fossil bone were removed from the site and shipped to Berlin. Among dinosaurian remains collected from Tendaguru was the skeleton of *Brachiosaurus*. Erected in the Natural History Museum in Berlin, this must be the most impressive skeleton of any dinosaur in the world; it stands nearly 39ft (12m) tall, and the body is some 74ft (22.5m) long.

Neck vertebra (cross section)

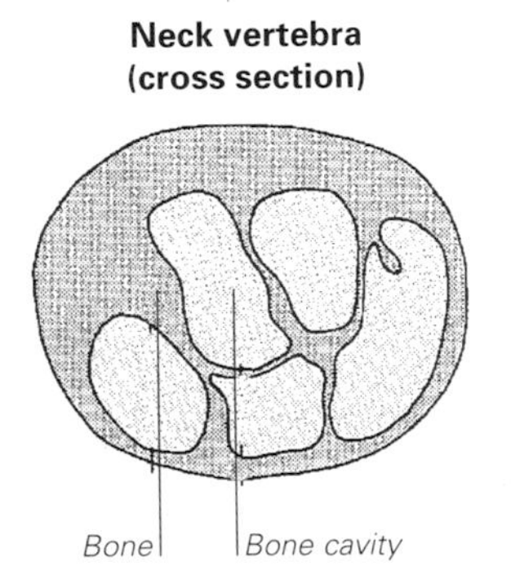

Back vertebra (cross section)

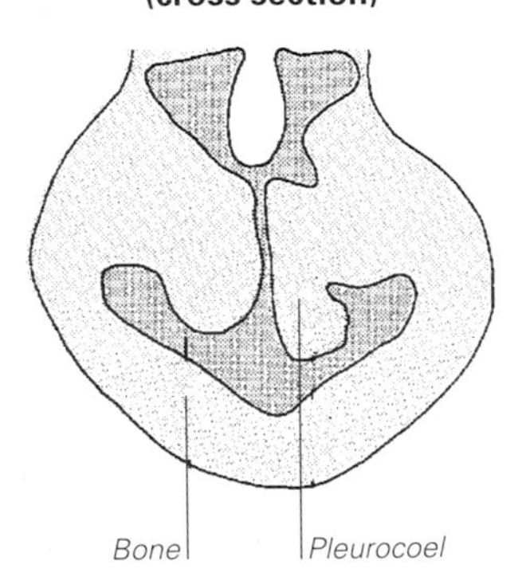

In addition to the impressive remains of *Brachiosaurus* from North America and Africa, several other *Brachiosaurus*-like sauropods are known, which constitute the brachiosaurid family, including monsters such as *Supersaurus* and *Ultrasaurus*, both even larger than *Brachiosaurus*.

For much of the 20th century sauropods were thought to have been gigantic amphibious creatures that wallowed in swampy habitats. This view has now been overturned, largely thanks to the evidence of Robert T. Bakker, who showed that the pillar-like legs and relatively narrow feet, the deep, narrow rib cage and the specially strengthened back were all features that were consistent only with land-living creatures. He argued that the long neck enabled these creatures to browse on high foliage rather like giraffes.

Below left and below: **The neck vertebrae are long, narrow, elongated structures with a low spine on which muscles attached. The front end of the neck vertebra has a rounded surface that forms a strong and flexible joint against the cup-shaped depression on the rear of the vertebra in front of it. The back vertebrae are taller and squatter to withstand supporting the weight of this animal. The tall spine is scarred for the attachment of muscles; the large 'wings' projecting from its foot support the ends of the ribs. The red lines show where the cross-sections are taken.**

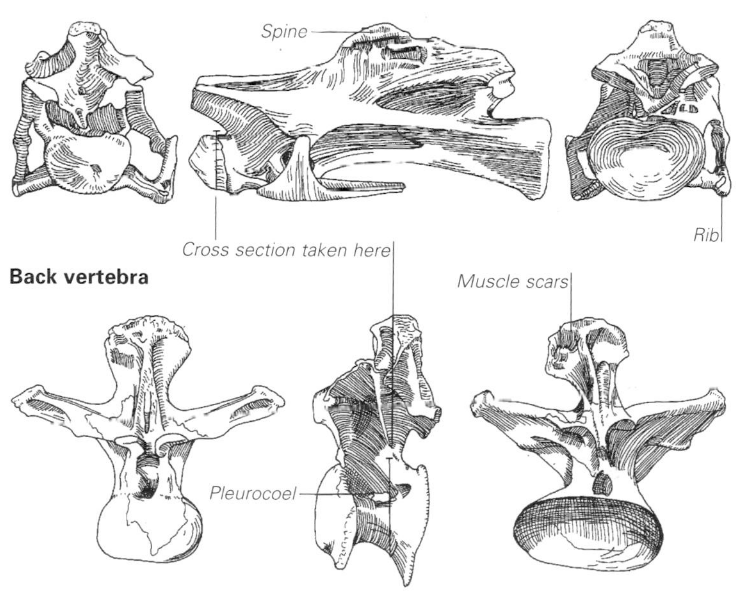

Brachiosaurus

Period: Late Jurassic/Early Cretaceous. **Family:** Brachiosaurids.
Where found: North America and East Africa.
Estimated length (l) and height (h): l. 4ft (22.5m); h. 39ft (12m).

Brachiosaurus ('arm reptile') takes its name from the prodigious length of its arms (fore legs) when compared with its hindlimbs. *Brachiosaurus* was first described by Elmer S. Riggs on the basis of a very incomplete skeleton that was discovered in 1900 at the Grand River Valley, western Colorado. The original material, which was collected by the Field Museum of Chicago, consisted of various parts of the vertebral column, the pelvis, ribs, shoulder girdle and, most importantly from the point of view of diagnosis, the humerus and femur. Judging by the way the remains were preserved on site, it appeared that the original carcass of the animal probably settled into the sediment of a lake or river system in this area but was disturbed somewhat later, perhaps by flood water. Various parts of it were washed away as the carcass disintegrated and so were lost to us for ever.

One of the most massive dinosaurs, *Brachiosaurus* was 74ft (22.5m) long and may have weighed as much as 77 tonnes. The most obvious feature of this animal is the great length of its neck and also of its forelimbs, which were longer than the hindlimbs – a very unusual characteristic of these dinosaurs. Both features seem to be adaptations for high browsing, as a present-day giraffe does.

The bones of this large sauropod dinosaur displayed several distinctive features. The vertebrae were large with the big pleurocoel cavities typical of all sauropod skeletons. Indeed, these cavities were in some cases so large that the wall of bone down the middle of the vertebrae was practically paper-thin and was even broken through in some places. A striking feature of these vertebrae compared with those of most other sauropods is the absence of forked spines to accommodate a large ▶

Below: The extremely long neck and forelimbs of *Brachiosaurus* seem to be adaptations for high browsing (there is an obvious analogy here with the giraffe), and it is probably correct to picture *Brachiosaurus* feeding from the tops of tall trees. The nostrils on top of the head are a puzzling feature.

Below: For some years it was thought that *Brachiosaurus* might have favoured an aquatic way of life, the nostrils on the top of its head acting as a snorkel. Recent analysis, however, indicates that *Brachiosaurus's* lungs would not have survived the water pressure that they would have experienced if this had been the case.

neck ligament. The vertebrae also show rather complicated joints at the foot of the neural spines, which served greatly to strengthen the joint between individual back vertebrae and also provided them with an unexpected degree of flexibility. The pelvis is supported by five vertebrae, as in other sauropods. Unusually, two tail bones, apparently coming from close to the hips, did not show any sign of pleurocoels. The dimensions of the humerus (80in, 204cm) and the femur (79.5in, 203cm) are, however, the most unusual among sauropods. In all other cases, the femur is longer than the humerus.

Below: **In this pose, *Brachiosaurus* shows a striking similarity to a giraffe, the long front legs lifting the shoulders above the hips and the neck raising the head to over 42ft (13m). The spines on the neck are heavily scarred for the attachment of muscles to raise and hold the neck in position. The ribcage is quite narrow and deep and the feet narrow and compact. The tail is relatively short.**

On the basis of this imperfect skeleton Riggs proposed (1904) that, contrary to popular opinion of the time, the gigantic sauropods were probably not amphibious marsh dwellers, but were fully terrestrial animals. He based his argument on the shape of the limbs and feet, the rather narrow and deep chest and the peculiar excavations and complexities of the vertebrae. The legs of large amphibious creatures such as hippos are relatively short and their feet are broad, the chest is barrel-shaped and their vertebrae show none of the complexity seen in the giant sauropods. Riggs even proposed that creatures such as *Diplodocus* and *Apatosaurus* were capable of rearing up on their hind legs, perhaps to browse on high foliage.

Riggs suggested that *Brachiosaurus* was a peculiarly specialised sauropod with exceptionally long front legs, a strong yet flexible back and (he guessed) a relatively short tail. His conclusions have proved to be extremely far-sighted and accurate, although it was not until the early 1970s that they found strong support.

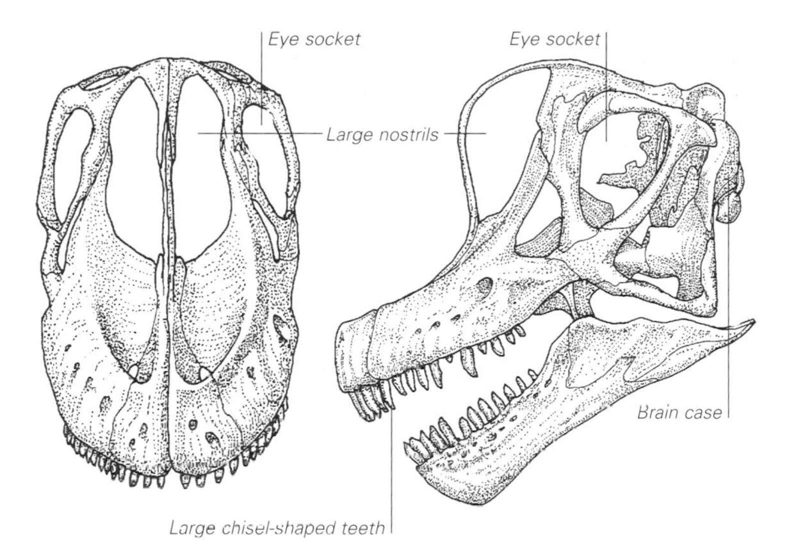

Above: In profile, this skull shows certain similarities to that of *Camarasaurus*. The jaws are stout and support large, chisel-shaped teeth. The signs of heavy wear on the teeth suggest that these animals preferred abrasive plants. The large nostrils may indicate a powerful sense of smell, a resonating device or a cooling surface for the blood.

Below: This hand is remarkably specialised, with very long metacarpals, which are clustered closely together (top). The toes (so far as they are known) have just one small bone on the end of each metacarpal except for the first toe, which bears a small claw.

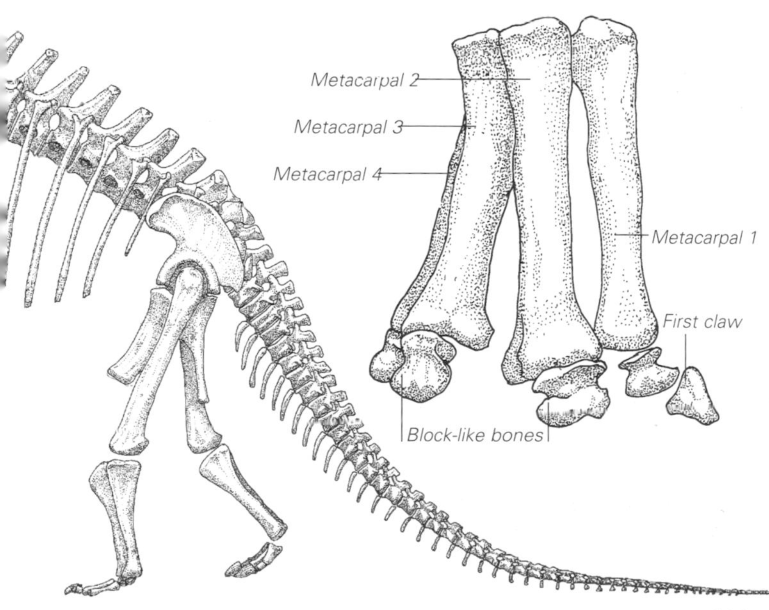

Camarasaurus

Period: Late Jurassic. **Family:** Camarasaurids.
Where found: North America.
Estimated length: 59ft (18m).

In 1925 Charles Gilmore described the beautifully preserved skeleton of a young *Camarasaurus* ('chambered reptile') that had been discovered at Dinosaur National Monument, Utah. The skeleton was almost completely intact, with just a few bones missing or lying slightly out of natural position. Presumably the carcass of this animal was buried very rapidly beneath the shifting sand bars at the mouth of a large river; if not, the rotting carcass would surely have been scavenged by carnivores or have simply fallen to pieces and its bones scattered. Around the carcass, between the ribs in particular, was found a thin layer of carbon, which probably represented remains of skin. Unfortunately, no details of the scaly surface were preserved in this layer.

The skull of this animal looks very different from that of the diplodocids. It is much deeper and the snout region is comparatively short. The jaws have large, chisel-like teeth, not only at the tip of the jaws but also spread along the sides in a much more typical reptilian arrangement. The sides of the skull are also notable for the large window-like openings cut into their surfaces. The nostrils are positioned in front of the eyes (unlike in diplodocids) and are quite enormous. The eye itself must have been situated in an enormous cavity – far larger than the area that was actually occupied by the eyeball. Immediately behind the eve cavity there are openings, which housed the major jaw muscles. The only areas of the skull with any substantial thickness of bone are the rims of the jaws, where they support the large, long-rooted teeth, and the smaller area at the rear of the skull that protected the brain.

Judging by the way the skull fits against the first of the neck vertebrae, the head was held

Right: **This sauropod is similar to *Brachiosaurus*, but smaller. *Camarasaurus* had a short skull with a blunt snout. The nostrils are high on the head, just in front of the eyes, and it was once thought that this feature indicated that the sauropods lived underwater with just the tops of their heads showing. The body is held horizontally as the fore- and hindlimbs are almost the same length.**

at an angle to the neck. The neck is somewhat shorter than that of the diplodocids, consisting of 12 relatively short, compact vertebrae. The neck ribs are quite long and slender and overlap one another considerably. The spines near the base of the neck and at the front of the trunk are, as in other sauropods, deeply cleft to accommodate large ligaments, which supported the neck. The 12 trunk vertebrae have relatively short, thick and heavily scarred spines and their sides are deeply excavated to form weight-saving pleurocoels. The trunk ribs are exceptionally long and stout, enclosing an enormous space for the chest and belly.

Five large back vertebrae are welded together in the hip region to support the massive pelvic bones. The tail is quite short, containing apparently 53 tail bones compared with 82 in *Apatosaurus* and 73 in *Diplodocus*. The tail is also appreciably shorter because it lacks the thin whip-lash end so characteristic of the diplodocids.

The limbs of *Camarasaurus* resemble those of other sauropods remarkably closely; the forelimb possessed one claw on its inner toe, while the hind foot bore claws on its three inner toes. One slightly unusual feature of *Camarasaurus's* limbs is their relative proportions. Whereas in diplodocids the humerus (upper foreleg bone) is only two-thirds the length of the femur (thigh bone), in *Camarasaurus* the humerus is four-fifths the length of the femur. In the first reconstruction of *Camarasaurus* by H. E. Osborn and C. C. Mook in 1921, this observation so strongly affected their judgement that they restored the skeleton with shoulders higher than the hips. They had in fact exaggerated the natural pose of the animal by ▶

altering the position of the shoulder girdle. In 1925 Charles Gilmore was able to correct Osborn's and Mook's first attempt on the basis of the more-or-less complete Carnegie Museum skeleton of *Camarasaurus*. Even so, the back of the animal has to be constructed practically horizontally, rather than sloping down towards the shoulders as in diplodocids. This trend towards greater length of the forelimbs in some sauropods is taken to the extreme in brachiosaurids.

It has sometimes been proposed that many sauropods were able to rear up on their hindlimbs in order to reach higher foliage. It seems unlikely that *Camarasaurus* could have done this, as it had large forelimbs and a relatively short tail. Another theory was that sauropods lived underwater with just the tops of their heads showing. Proponents of this theory pointed to the nostrils high on the head, just in front of the eyes; some even suggested that *Camarasaurus* had a trunk like that of an elephant!

Right: **The skull of *Camarasaurus* is compact compared with that of diplodocids. The jaws are stout and support a closely packed array of chisel-like teeth. Above the level of the jaws, the skull is high and spaciously designed. The large opening at the front of the skull is for extremely large nostrils. Immediately behind the nostril is the eye socket.**

Right: ***Camarasaurus's*** **right foot has five short toes, which are widely splayed to form a broad, weight-bearing arrangement. The inner toe is larger and possesses a narrow curved claw, which may have been used for self-defence. The foot of *Brachiosaurus* is known from isolated bones only.**

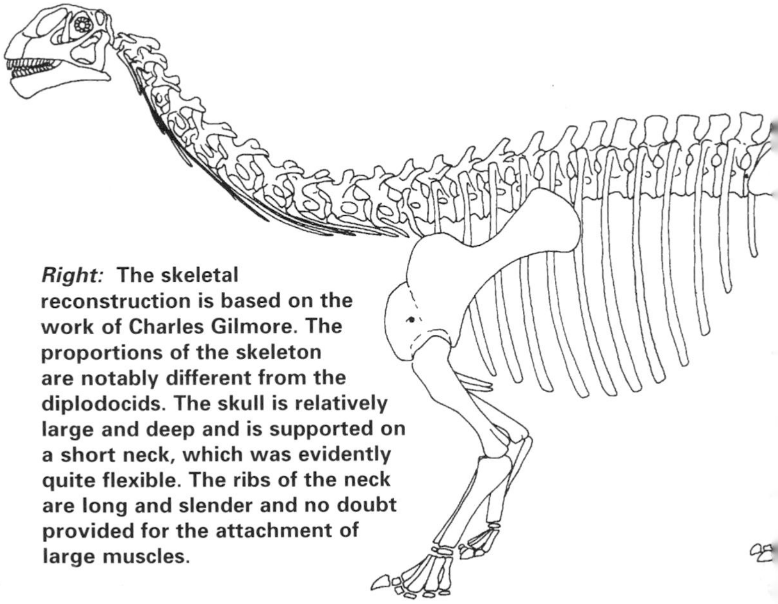

Right: **The skeletal reconstruction is based on the work of Charles Gilmore. The proportions of the skeleton are notably different from the diplodocids. The skull is relatively large and deep and is supported on a short neck, which was evidently quite flexible. The ribs of the neck are long and slender and no doubt provided for the attachment of large muscles.**

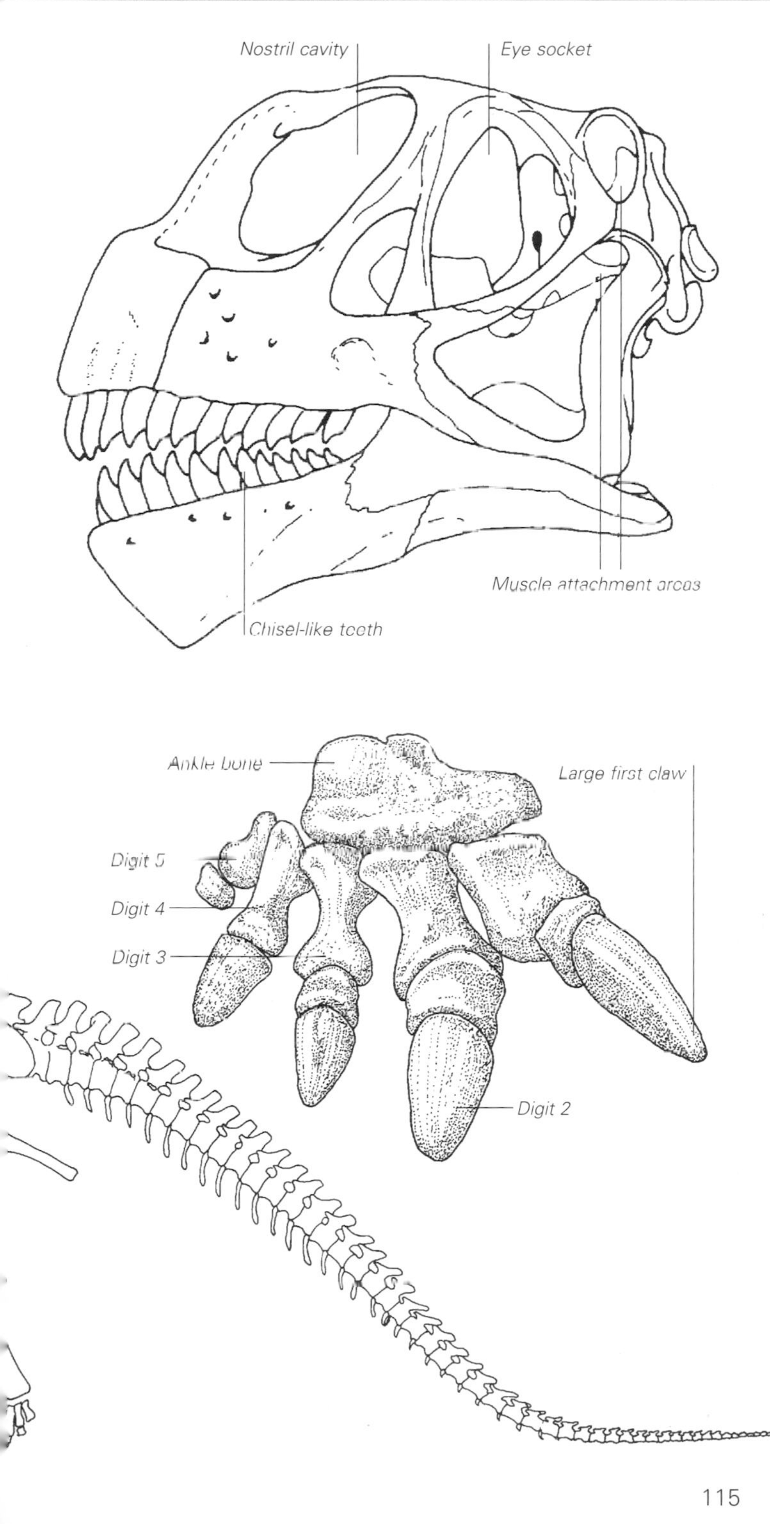
Nostril cavity
Eye socket
Muscle attachment areas
Chisel-like tooth
Ankle bone
Large first claw
Digit 5
Digit 4
Digit 3
Digit 2

Sauropods

In addition to the reasonably well-represented and distinctive sauropods such as the diplodocids, camarasaurids and brachiosaurids described earlier, a large number of less well-known sauropods are known, whose fossil remains have been reported from practically every continent.

Despite the long-held belief that sauropods were amphibious creatures, most palaeontologists now support the idea that they were primarily terrestrial creatures. The arguments in favour of this view are based on the structure of the limbs, ribcage and other characteristics.

(i) Pneumatic ducts and cavities. These lighten the skeleton and are clearly an adaptation associated with living on land where gravity is a critical factor. Large aquatic animals have equally large vertebrae but they show no weight-saving devices because their body weight is buoyed up by displacement. The particularly large sauropods such as Brachiosaurus even had pneumatic openings into the ribs – probably air-filled, as in living birds.

(ii) Energy-saving ligaments. Many non-brachiosaurid sauropods had cleft spines in the neck and back vertebrae, providing a deep trough in which probably lay a thick, rope-like ligament. This served to hold the inordinately long neck in a raised position. The neck ligament was probably connected to the tail vertebrae so that neck and tail, suspended against each other, could both be held clear of the ground. This may account for the rarity of tail-drag markings associated with sauropod footprint trackways.

Nevertheless, it is likely that sauropods may have wallowed, as elephants do. Footprints found in Texas show a sauropod apparently floating in water and moving along by kicking the bottom with its front feet, then steering with a clawed hindfoot to change direction. Footprint trackways have also shown more than 20 large sauropods moving together across an open area in the same direction; this seems to indicate herding behaviour.

Recent work in Argentina has resulted in the discovery that some sauropods had bony armour plating. A long, whip-lash tail probably served as a weapon of defence. Most non-brachiosaurid sauropods could doubtless rear up on to their hind legs and use their massive forelimbs as weapons. Brachiosaurids could not, but perhaps they were so large that they were virtually invulnerable. Curiously, all sauropods retained one enlarged, curved claw on the inner toe of the forefoot, for which the only obvious explanation is defence.

Most scientists now accept that sauropods ate terrestrial plants. Two main types of teeth have been noted among sauropods, the narrow pencil-like teeth of diplodocids and

***Right:* While the sheer size of an adult sauropod probably rendered it virtually immune from attack, it is possible that the large claw on the inner toe of each front foot could be used as a defensive weapon.**

the broader, spoon-like teeth of camarasaurids and brachiosaurids.

With regard to reproductive behaviour, it has been suggested that sauropods, unlike the majority of reptiles, gave birth to live young. It seems inconceivable that a 30- or 40-tonne female sauropod could lay a clutch of eggs without crushing them. Nevertheless, sauropod eggs are occasionally discovered – in straight lines, presumably laid while the female was on the move.

Vulcanodon

Period: Early Jurassic. **Family:** Sauropods.
Where found: East Africa.
Estimated length: 21ft (6.5m).

Described in 1972 by Mike Raath (Zimbabwe), the headless skeleton of *Vulcanodon* ('Volcano tooth') was found in early Jurassic rocks in Zimbabwe. It is of some importance because it may be one of the earliest sauropods to have been discovered to date. Unfortunately the skeleton, which was completely redescribed by Dr Mike Cooper (also of Zimbabwe) in 1984, is far from complete. Cooper was able to demonstrate that *Vulcanodon* was a very large, quadrupedal saurischian dinosaur. It shows several prosauropod features, particularly in the hips, but he claimed that in other ways (particularly in subtle changes in the structure of the vertebrae), *Vulcanodon* was very much what might be expected of an early sauropod. Obviously Cooper's arguments are based primarily on shades of opinion rather than clear and unambiguous fact. Yet again, better-preserved material may help to clear up the status of *Vulcanodon*.

Reconstructions of *Vulcanodon* draw on what is known of contemporary sauropods such as *Baraparasaurus*, giving it a bulky body, pillar-like legs and a longish neck. The animal certainly has sauropod-like limbs, but its actual nature – was it a true sauropod or simply a large prosauropod? – is still a matter of dispute. The absence of a skull among the remains of both *Vulcanodon* and *Baraparasaurus* poses an obvious difficulty. Teeth found near *Vulcanodon's* remains are those of a carnivore, but they probably belonged to a predator, not to *Vulcanodon* itself.

Below: **Another of the mysterious headless dinosaurs, this time from Zimbabwe, the skeleton as reconstructed here is based on the work of Dr Mike Cooper, who has recently redescribed the fragmentary remains. These are not as complete as shown here; *Barapasaurus* has also been used as a model for this view. The animal certainly has sauropod-like limbs, but its actual nature – was it a true sauropod or simply a large prosauropod? – is still a matter of dispute.**

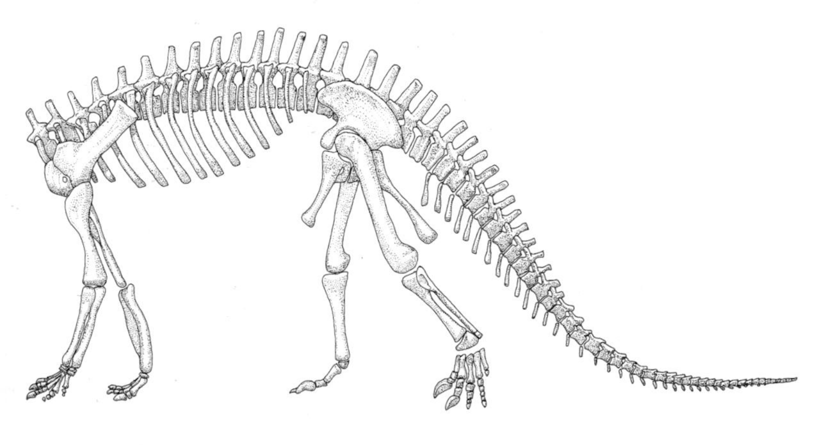

Right: This restoration shows what we think the sauropods of the early Jurassic looked like; this is *Vulcanodon*, but *Barapasaurus* probably looked very similar. The animal is shown with a bulky body and pillar-like legs. In neither case is a skull known and so the head illustrated is of necessity somewhat conjectural. Teeth found near *Vulcanodon's* remains are those of a carnivore, but they probably belonged to a predator, not *Vulcanodon*.

Saltasaurus

Period: Late Cretaceous. **Family:** Sauropods.
Where found: Argentina.
Estimated length: 39ft (12m).

Remains of an unusual sauropod, named *Saltasaurus* ('reptile from Salta Province'), were first reported by José Bonaparte and Jaime Powell in 1980. They come from late Cretaceous rocks in north-western Argentina and although incomplete provide unexpected evidence concerning the appearance of some sauropods. The remains of *Saltasaurus* appear to derive from several individuals, rather than an isolated skeleton. The general proportions and construction of the main skeletal elements (backbone and limbs) are typically sauropod-like. Points worthy of mention include spines in the neck and back region, which are not cleft, tail vertebrae that are rather stout and have a reversed ball-and-socket arrangement and chevrons that are not skid-like. However, of greatest interest was the discovery of two types of bony armour associated with these remains: fairly large, oval plates, which were perhaps rather widely scattered in the skin, and a dense layer of smaller round or angular bony studs, which were apparently widely spread across the back and sides of the animal.

This first clear record of armour-plating in sauropods may well prove to be an important one because it could lead to the re-identification of several supposed ankylosaur specimens elsewhere in the world. For example, *Titanosaurus* ('Titan reptile'), another sauropod from Argentina first described in 1893, was later redescribed in 1929 along with some fragments of bony armour found in the same area; these latter were referred to as an ankylosaur, *Loricosaurus*. The supposed ankylosaur remains almost certainly belong to the sauropod *Titanosaurus*. There are also considerable similarities between *Titanosaurus* and *Saltasaurus*, although Bonaparte and Powell were not prepared to say that these two dinosaurs belong to the same genus. Another sauropod, *Laplatasaurus*, had a type of plate with a low mid-line ridge. Sauropod armour seems to have varied in size and shape, ranging from large, ridged plates to sheets of densely packed, tiny nodular bones.

***Right: Saltasaurus*, quite a recent discovery, is of great interest because it shows that some sauropods bore bony armour. Large round plates of bone are scattered across the hide and between them lie masses of small nodules. The tail was flexible and could have supported the body when *Saltasaurus* reared on its back legs in its efforts to obtain food.**

Opisthocoelicaudia

Period: Late Cretaceous. **Family:** Sauropods.
Where found: Mongolia.
Estimated length: 39ft (12m).

The incomplete skeleton of *Opisthocoelicaudia* ('posterior cavity tail') was discovered in 1965 during a Polish-Mongolian Expedition to the Gobi Desert. The carcass of the animal had evidently been buried before it had time to disintegrate; however, neither the head nor the neck was recovered from the site. Magdalena Borsuk-Bialynicka, who described the skeleton in 1977, suggested that the carcass may have been attacked by carrion feeders (perhaps tyrannosaurids, since *Opisthocoelicaudia* comes from rocks of late Cretaceous age). Some of the fossilised bones (femur and pelvis) apparently show some evidence of gnawing, which may explain the absence of both the head and neck!

The skeleton of *Opisthocoelicaudia* is rather like that of most non-brachiosaurid sauropods in its general shape and proportions. The back vertebrae have well-developed pleurocoels and the ones near the neck have deeply cleft spines to accommodate a large neck ligament. In addition, the individual spines of more posterior vertebrae have swollen and roughened sides and tops, which indicate the areas of attachment of other powerful ligaments and muscles. Six vertebrae are fused together to form a sacrum for attachment of the pelvis. Beyond this area, the tail as preserved consists of 34 vertebrae. These bear chevrons, which are similar to those of *Camarasaurus* rather than the skid-like chevrons characteristic of diplodocids. The curious feature of the tail vertebrae, which is responsible for the tongue-twisting name of this creature, is the fact that the front end of each has a large hemispherical dome, which fits into a deep socket on the rear of the preceding vertebra. Consequently the joints between the vertebrae are remarkably strong. By contrast, the joints between the tail bones of most sauropods are much simpler, having practically flat surfaces. Borsuk-Bialynicka also noted that the spines of the tail vertebrae were exceptionally swollen and roughened for the attachment of powerful muscles and ligaments equivalent to those noted in the back. The forelimbs and hindlimbs are characteristically stout and pillar-like to carry the great weight of these creatures. The number of clawed toes on the feet of this dinosaur is unknown. ▶

***Left:* In its general body proportions *Opisthocoelicaudia* resembles *Camarasaurus* but it does have a number of peculiarities. The heavy, pillar-like legs support a bulky body, the tail is held out straight and the shoulders are quite high. Unfortunately the head and neck are unknown.**

The humerus is about three-quarters of the length of the femur This falls midway between typical diplodocid and typical camarasaurid limb proportions.

In the remains found, there was little or no evidence for the massive and powerful muscle that runs along the sides of the tail and inserts upon the hindlimb (caudi-femoralis muscle). This is a muscle that almost always provides the main source of power for the stride in dinosaurs and most other reptiles. In *Opisthocoelicaudia*, however, the posterior portion of the ilium (pelvic bone) is notably enlarged and roughened as if for the attachment of unusually powerful muscles; perhaps these were the main propulsive muscles instead?

The structure of the back vertebrae, particularly those close to the

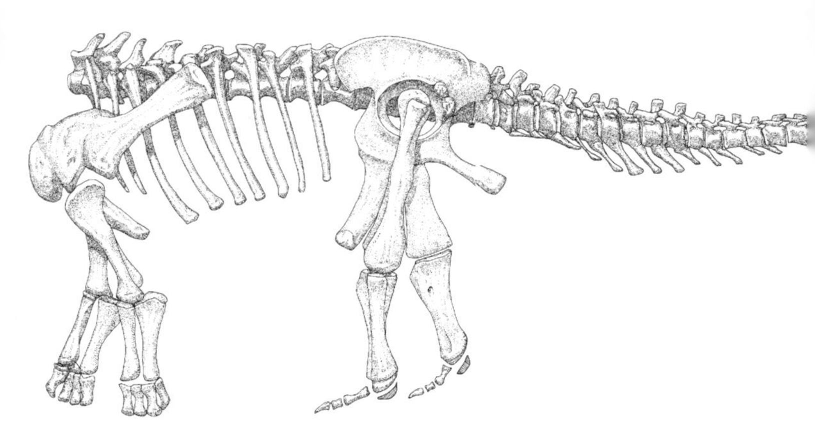

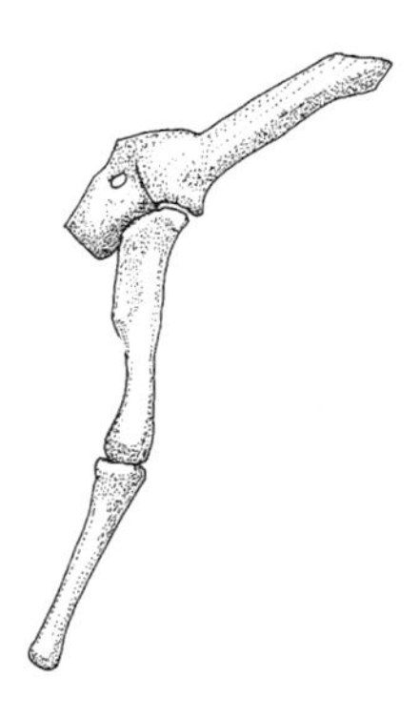

***Right:* Previously known as *Cetiosaurus*, this *Cetiosauriscus* skeleton from the late Jurassic is one of the best sauropod skeletons from Britain. The parts recovered were the forelimb and shoulder, hindlimb, pelvis and most of the tail. The tail resembles that of *Diplodocus*, particularly the chevron bones attached to the underside, and this may indicate that the fauna in Britain and North America were very similar in the late Jurassic.**

neck, led Borsuk-Bialynicka to suggest that the neck was not only flexible but that the vertebrae were relatively short. The back also seems to have been held in an essentially horizontal position or perhaps sloping very slightly down from the shoulders to the hips.

The tail appears to have created the greatest problems of interpretation. First, the tail bones when articulated naturally tend to rise slightly, passing backwards from the hips, instead of falling towards the ground as in other sauropods. Second, the ball-and-socket joint between each tail vertebra is rare. This probably allowed the tail to be used as a prop, forming a tripod arrangement with the legs. The tripodal posture was not suggested as permanent for *Opisthocoelicaudia*, merely as a favoured position for feeding.

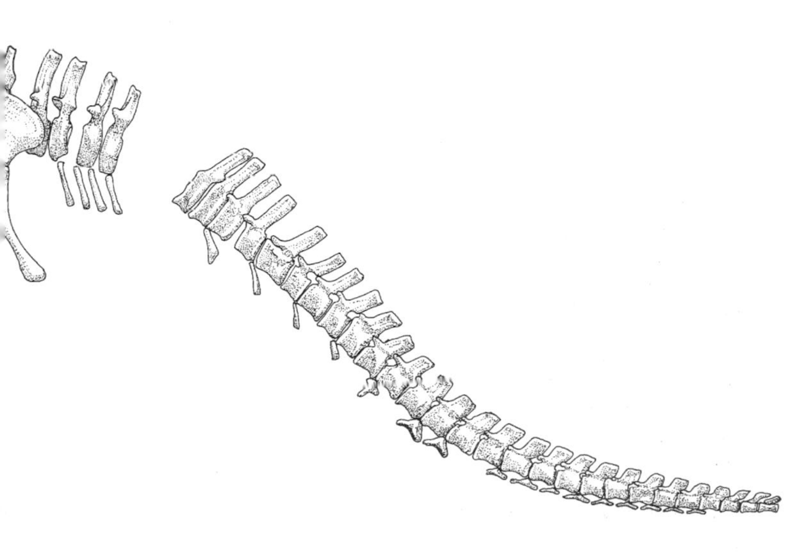

Left: *Opisthocoelicaudia* is currently known only from its headless skeleton, so its relationships with other sauropods are not precisely known. It has an extremely unusual tail: the ball-and-socket joint between vertebrae works by means of a socket in the rear of each vertebra – unlike in any other sauropod. As a result, the joints between vertebrae are remarkably strong. Note the massive pelvic region.

Fabrosaurids & Heterodontosaurids

Fabrosaurids have been known for a surprisingly long time. Well over a century ago, Sir Richard Owen described several small jaws and teeth, which had been found in quarries in Dorset, England. The jaws were small and slender and the teeth had long, narrow roots and leaf-shaped crowns, with spiky edges. Owen supposed that these belonged to a small herbivorous lizard and gave them the name *Echinodon becklesii*. Unfortunately, no more remains of *Echinodon* have been found since then. Another fragmentary piece of jaw with a few teeth was found in 1964 in southern Africa. The teeth look remarkably like those of *Echinodon*; however, this fossil came from rocks that were dated at the boundary between early and middle Jurassic, while those of *Echinodon* were from the Jurassic/Cretaceous boundary. The African fossil was named *Fabrosaurus australis* ('Fabre's southern reptile') and eventually gave its name to the family.

It was not until the early 1970s that anyone had any clear idea of the true appearance of either *Echinodon* or *Fabrosaurus*. It was now known from the evidence of its teeth that *Echinodon* was not a lizard. New information about these mysterious fabrosaurids came from the remains of the partial skeleton of a small animal from the late Triassic 'Red Beds' of Lesotho. Preparation of this fossil revealed the true appearance of a fabrosaurid. Being of the same geological age as the original Fabrosaurus, the new animal was also named Fabrosaurus australis, before undergoing a change of name – because of

uncertainties about its nature – to Lesothosaurus australis.

Heterodontosaurids are known only from the late Triassic and earliest Jurassic of southern Africa and North America. The earliest known heterodontosaurid fossil (described in 1911) was a jaw fragment with several teeth embedded in it. It came from southern Africa; this was named *Geranosaurus* ('crane reptile'). Somewhat later, another jaw was discovered, but this time was thought to belong to a mammal-like reptile and was named *Lycorhinus angustidens* ('wolf snout with sharp teeth'). This specimen lay unrecognised as a dinosaur until 1962 when yet another new dinosaur from southern Africa was described and named *Heterodontosaurus* ('mixed-tooth reptile'). The animal is apparently the same size and the same in general shape as the fabrosaurids above. However, there are several striking differences. The head and remainder of the skeleton are quite similar in shape to those of *Lesothosaurus*, except that the teeth are notably different, the hands are particularly large and strong and the bones of the lower leg are welded together.

Thus the heterodontosaurids seem to be small, agile, bipedal ornithopod dinosaurs with several features that distinguish them from their contemporaries, the fabrosaurids. They had special chisel-like cheek teeth behind the tusks, used to chew up food very finely, and large tusks probably used as defensive weapons or as social signals to establish a dominance hierarchy and to attract mates.

Below: **The fabrosaurids and heterodontosaurids seem to show a full range of strategies for survival against predators. *Lesothosaurus* was very swift and agile and would flee; *Scutellosaurus* was moderately fleet of foot but also partly armoured; *Heterodontosaurus* was speedy, but agressive in defence when cornered.**

Lesothosaurus

Period: Late Triassic-earliest Jurassic. **Family:** Fabrosaurids.
Where found: Lesotho.
Estimated length: 35in (90cm).

Lesothosaurus is the best example of a fabrosaurid dinosaur known to date and in fact establishes a very common body shape for all later ornithopod dinosaurs. *Lesothosaurus* was a small, lightly built animal with extremely slender, long hind legs and rather short forelimbs; its tail was long and counterbalanced the front part of its body so that it could stand and run on its hind legs, leaving its hands free. Unfortunately, the hand of *Lesothosaurus* is not well preserved; most probably it had five rather stubby little fingers ending in small claws, making ideal all-purpose hands.

The head of *Lesothosaurus* was rather small and triangular in outline, with a very large eye cavity and large open spaces behind for the jaw muscles. There was also a fairly large opening in front of the eye, which may have been for a salt gland. The snout was short and quite pointed, with a very slender lower jaw tipped by the horn-covered predentary bone, and the teeth were small, leaf-shaped and separate. This general shape and arrangement suggests that these animals were probably mainly herbivorous. They may well have used their narrow snout and beak to feed on small, succulent shoots of plants. Their teeth and jaws were apparently not designed to chew; instead, they simply broke the food into small pieces before swallowing it. In plant food most of the nutrients are locked inside the tough plant tissues; if the food is not chewed, it has to spend a long time in the stomach and gut being fermented and digested. *Lesothosaurus* had quite a large belly situated between its legs underneath the hips, which enabled it to maintain its balance and run unhindered on its hind legs.

The remainder of the skeleton shows a pattern common to all later ornithopods. The neck was quite long and slender and was presumably

***Below:* This small early ornithopod was a lightly built bipedal form that could probably run fast in order to avoid predators. *Lesothosaurus* had strong arms, which it might have used to help it feed.**

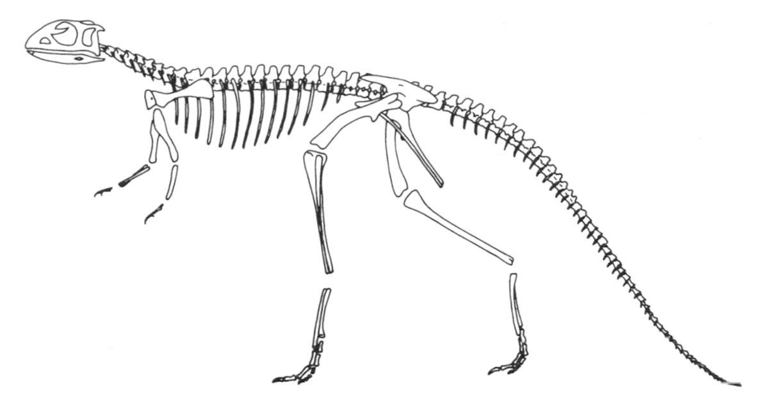

Above: **The long tail is a distinctive feature. The neck is long and flexible, perhaps useful for getting the head into vegetation to pick off shoots or buds or for keeping an eye out for predators.**

very flexible. The back, hips and tail were stiffened and supported by narrow, bony tendons and the tail was long.

Lacking both bony armour and defensive weapons such as large teeth or claws, *Lesothosaurus* would have relied heavily upon its great turn of speed and agility to avoid being caught by the thecodontians and theropods that inhabited their world.

Below: **The cheek teeth are slender, leaf-like and separated, used perhaps for shredding food but not chewing it. *Lesothosaurus* may have had a salt-gland and if so this could indicate that the animal lived in an arid environment. Conserving body water leads to a build-up of body salts, which must be disposed of by the salt-gland.**

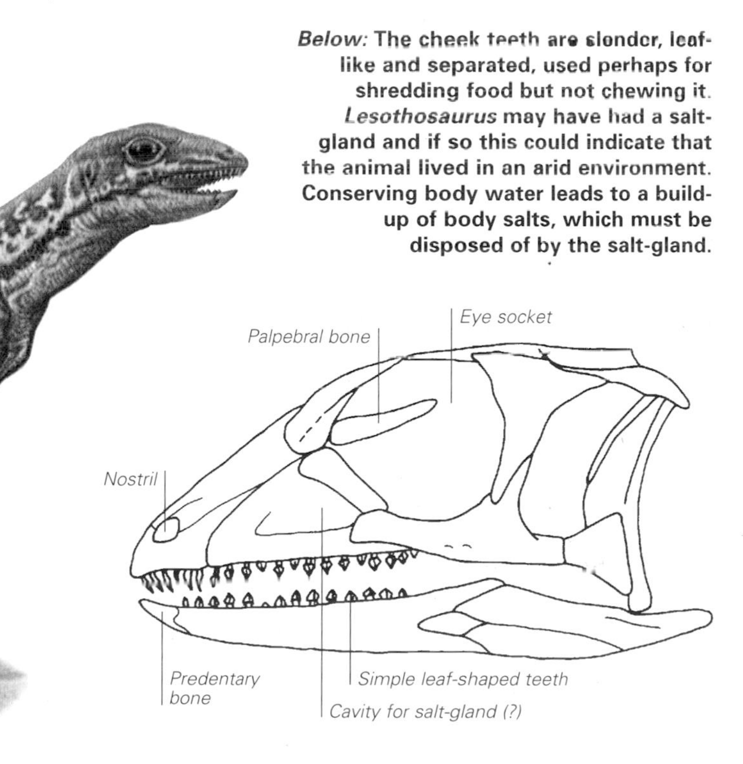

Scutellosaurus

Period: Early Jurassic. **Family:** Fabrosaurid.
Where found: North America.
Estimated length: 53in (134cm).

Another rather unusual fabrosaurid, *Scutellosaurus* ('bony-plate reptile'), was discovered and described only very recently by Professor Edwin Colbert. Discovered in Arizona, but from rocks of an age similar to those in which *Lesothosaurus* and *Fabrosaurus* were found, this animal is peculiar because it has very well-preserved bony plates (or scutes), rather like those found on the back of a crocodile. Perhaps what we are seeing here is an alternative strategy for survival to that of *Lesothosaurus*. *Scutellosaurus* was armour-plated as well as being moderately fleet of foot, judging by its limb proportions. One way of surviving predators would be to be extensively armour-plated – this makes an animal both heavier and slower and therefore more easily

***Right:* A close relative of *Lesothosaurus*, *Scutellosaurus* was distinguished by being covered with bony plates set into the skin and by the extreme length of its tail. Its hindlimbs were longer than its forelimbs, but the difference was not as great as in most other ornithopods. It seems that *Scutellosaurus* could run fast on its hindlimbs just as *Lesothosaurus* did, or it could move more slowly on all fours.**

caught, but its armour would make it unpalatable (the armadillo uses just this type of technique). Alternatively, the less armour an animal carries, the greater its agility and speed and the better its chances of avoiding capture altogether – but if it is captured it is completely unprotected. *Scutellosaurus* seems almost caught in the act of balancing these strategies.

Scutellosaurus was also distinguished by the extreme length of its tail. Its hindlimbs were longer than its forelimbs, but the difference was not as great as in most other ornithopods. It seems that *Scutellosaurus* could run fast on its hindlimbs, as *Lesothosaurus* did, or it could move more slowly on all fours.

In addition to the quite well-preserved skeletons of *Lesothosaurus* and *Scutellosaurus*, there are several other fabrosaurids known: *Echinodon*, represented by a few jaws and teeth from the late Jurassic of southern Britain; *Fabrosaurus*, a single broken jaw with some teeth from the late Triassic of southern Africa; *Nanosaurus* ('dwarf reptile'), an incomplete jaw and some skeletal fragments from the later Jurassic, Colorado; *Alocodon* ('wing tooth') and *Trimucrodon* ('three-pointed tooth'), some tooth fragments from the Jurassic of Portugal; and *Gongbusaurus* ('reptile from Gongbu') from the Jurassic of China; *Azendohsaurus* ('reptile from Azendoh'), another jaw fragment from Morocco, may even be prosauropod.

Heterodontosaurus

Period: Early Jurassic. **Family:** Heterodontosaurs.
Where found: Southern Africa.
Estimated length: 47in (120cm).

In 1962 a dinosaur from southern Africa was described and named *Heterodontosaurus* ('mixed-tooth reptile'). It was discovered by an

Right: **As the name ('mixed-tooth reptile') suggests, *Heterodontosaurus* is distinguished by its differentiated teeth, a feature uncommon in most dinosaurs.**

expedition from Britain organised by Dr Alan Charig of the British Museum (Natural History), and Dr John Attridge and Dr Barry Cox of the University of London. The animal, which was not described until the early 1980s, is apparently the same size and the same in general shape as the fabrosaurids. However, there are, if we look a little closer, several striking differences.

The head is quite similar in shape to that of *Lesothosaurus*, but the teeth are notably different. At the front of the lower jaw there is a familiar horn-covered predentary, and immediately behind this there is a very large tusk-like tooth and then a row of chisel-edged cheek teeth. The same arrangement is found in the upper jaw, except that in front of the big tusk there are two small spiky teeth and then a gap at the front end of the snout, which was probably covered by a horny pad to match the one on the predentary. Three quite distinctive kinds of teeth can be identified in each jaw: sharp cutting teeth at the front, fangs just behind these and broad, ridged teeth in the cheek region. *Heterodontosaurus* fed on tough vegetation, which it nipped off with its 'incisors', punctured with its 'canines' and ground up with its cheek teeth.

The remainder of the skeleton is similarly built to that of *Lesothosaurus* except that the hands are particularly large and strong with sharp claws, and the bones of the lower leg are welded together, a rather unusual feature that does not seem to occur in many other dinosaurs.

Heterodontosaurus was an agile, lightly built animal. In particular, it is noticeable that the foot bones (metatarsals) and lower leg bones are elongated relative to the upper leg bone (femur). These characteristics reflect the fact that the animal was small and light and a runner – the foot did not have to be specially strengthened to bear the animal's weight. The smallest toe is reversed relative to the others. This may have given the foot extra surface area for bearing the animal's weight. The metatarsal bones are particularly elongated.

This kind of long, slender hind leg is a sure sign of a fleet-footed runner, which presumably relied on speed to escape from its predators. The long, tapering tail acted as a counterbalance for the front half of the body and was probably held out almost horizontally above the ground when the animal ran.

The front limbs are very robust compared with those of *Lesothosaurus* and in particular the fingers and the small, numerous wrist bones are well developed, suggesting flexibility. The individual finger bones are long and slender and bear well-developed claws. The smallest finger does not seem to be quite so offset as in some ornithischians, so the hand appears more symmetrical. *Heterodontosaurus* was probably able to manipulate vegetation quite adeptly.

The bony rods lying along the backbone are characteristic of bipedal ornithischians; they were present in order to stiffen the back, hips and tail. ▶

Right: **There are various theories about the way the chewing action was produced in *Heterodontosaurus*: it may have been caused by back and forward movement of the lower jaw, but – perhaps more likely – the lower jaw may have rotated relative to the upper jaw as it closed. The large tusks are probably a male characteristic.**

Below: **The reconstructed skeleton of *Heterodontosaurus* shows it to be a lightly built, agile animal, typical of the early ornithopods.**

Below right: **This hand is particularly well made for a bipedal dinosaur. The individual finger bones are long and slender, and bear well-developed claws. The smallest finger does not seem to be quite so offset as in some ornithischians, so the hand appears more symmetrical. The wrist bones are small and numerous, suggesting flexibility. *Heterodontosaurus* was probably able to manipulate vegetation quite adeptly.**

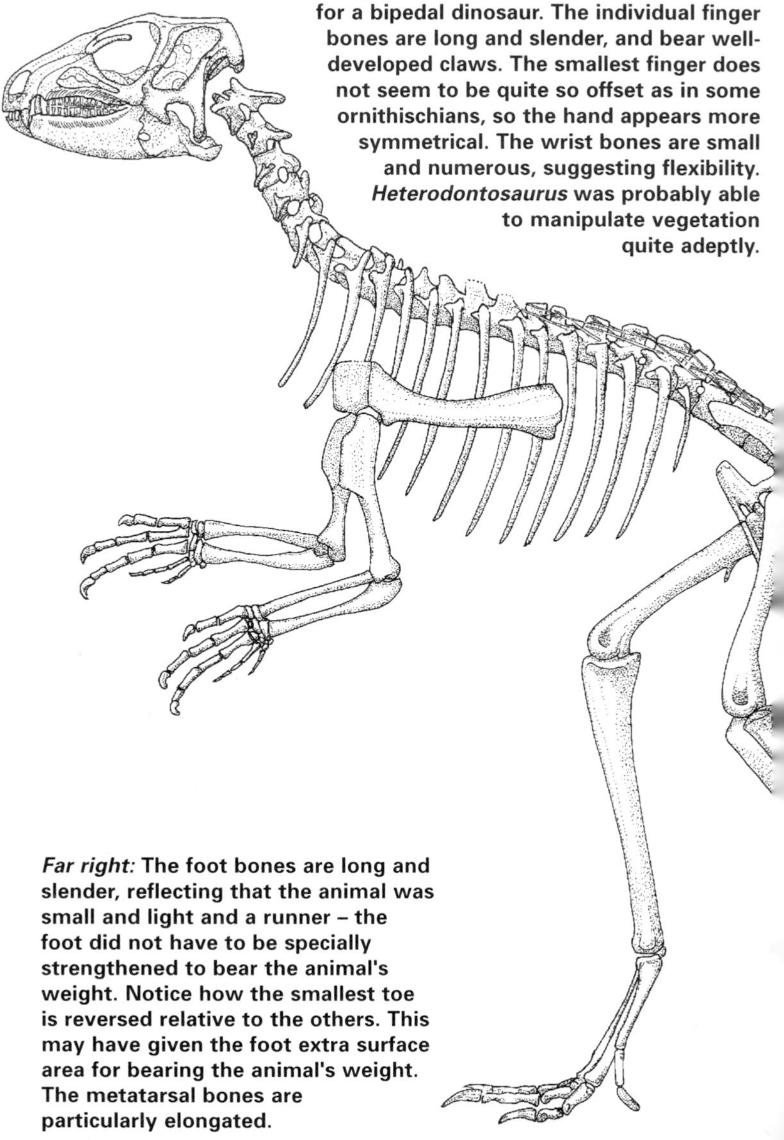

Far right: **The foot bones are long and slender, reflecting that the animal was small and light and a runner – the foot did not have to be specially strengthened to bear the animal's weight. Notice how the smallest toe is reversed relative to the others. This may have given the foot extra surface area for bearing the animal's weight. The metatarsal bones are particularly elongated.**

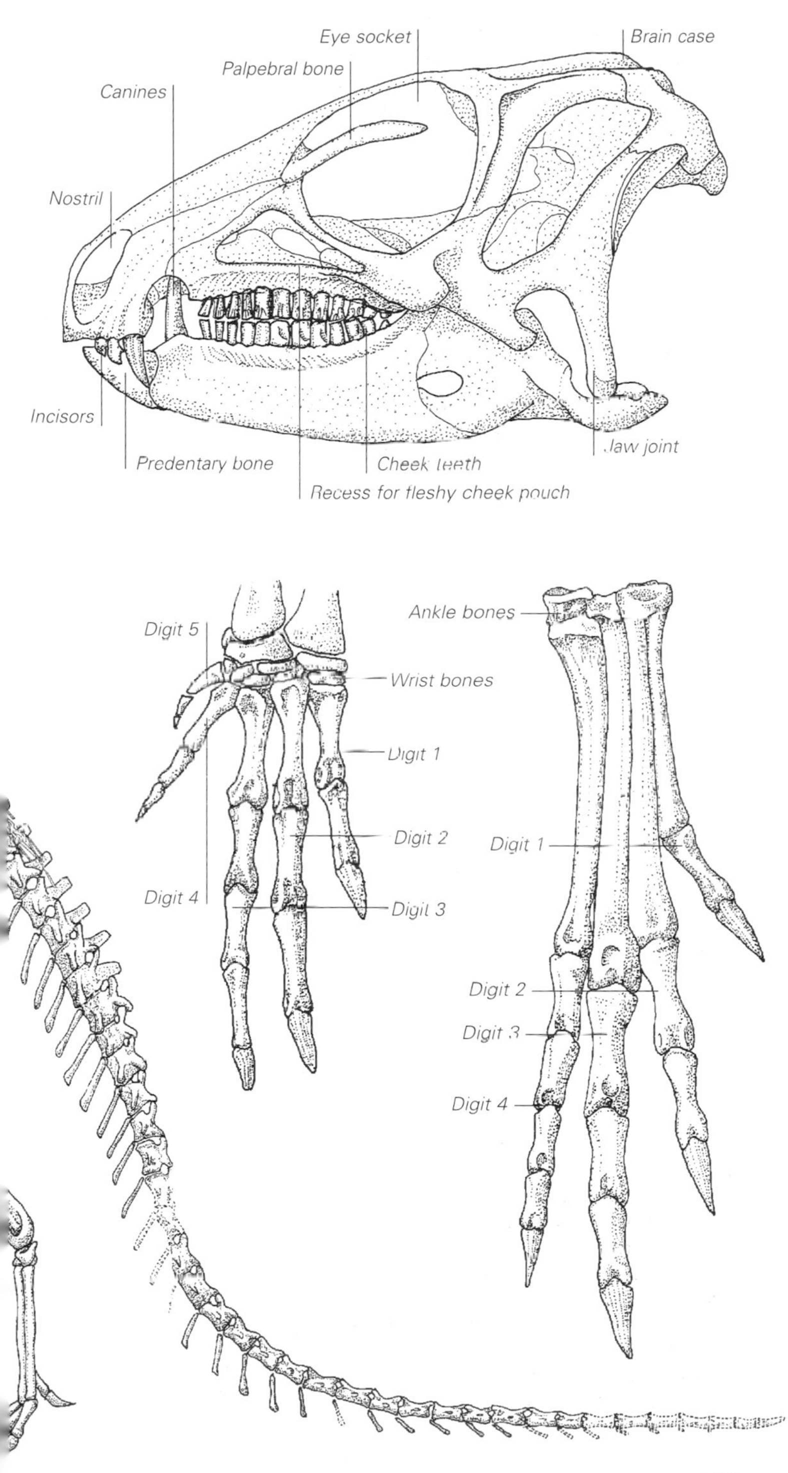
Eye socket
Brain case
Palpebral bone
Canines
Nostril
Incisors
Predentary bone
Cheek teeth
Recess for fleshy cheek pouch
Jaw joint
Ankle bones
Digit 5
Wrist bones
Digit 1
Digit 2
Digit 1
Digit 4
Digit 3
Digit 2
Digit 3
Digit 4

Hypsilophodontids

The hypsilophodontids are a family of small to medium-sized (6ft 7in-16ft 6in, 2.5-5m in length) ornithopod dinosaurs. Outwardly at least, they are not unlike the fabrosaurids, but they made their appearance considerably later, in mid-Jurassic times. The first remains are rather scrappy, consisting of tooth fragments and pieces of limb bones from Oxfordshire. Indeed, they are simply referred to as 'hypsilophodontid', being insufficiently well-preserved to be given a proper scientific name.

Several much better-preserved hypsilophodontids are known from the late Jurassic, in particular, *Dryosaurus* from North America and *Dysalotosaurus* from Tanzania in East Africa. Various types of hypsilophodontids have been found from the early Cretaceous, including *Hypsilophodon* from the Isle of Wight, England, *Valdosaurus*, a very fragmentary species from southern England, Zephyrosaurus, a partial skull from Montana, and *Tenontosaurus* represented by many skeletons from North America. From the late Cretaceous come *Parksosaurus*, an incomplete skull, and *Thescelosaurus*, known only from part skeletons and skulls.

The geographic distribution of the hypsilophodontids can be fairly easily understood. Undoubtedly these animals were present in middle Jurassic times, perhaps even a little earlier, when there were land links to all the continents, except perhaps eastern Asia. That early representatives could have spread almost worldwide is demonstrated by the presence of *Dryosaurus* in both North America and East Africa. Hypsilophodontids will probably eventually be found in late Jurassic rocks in South America, Australasia and India. In the Cretaceous, intercontinental seaways divided the land masses, leading to the evolution in isolation of distinctive hypsilophodontids on each continent.

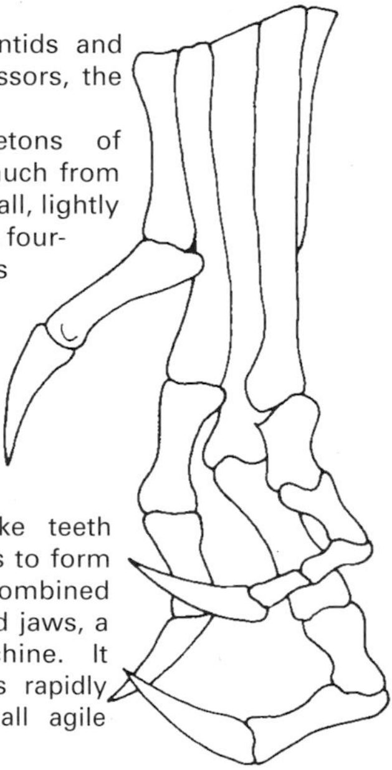

What, then, are the hypsilophodontids and how do they differ from their predecessors, the fabrosaurids?

For the most part, the skeletons of hypsilophodontids do not differ very much from those of fabrosaurids. They both are small, lightly built, bipedal animals with long, slender, four-toed hindlimbs and quite short forelimbs with stubby, five-fingered hands. The skull of *Lesothosaurus* (a fabrosaurid) is small, light and roughly triangular in shape, as is that of *Hypsilophodon*. However, whereas the teeth of Lesothosaurus are separate and leaf-shaped and set in slender jaws, *Hypsilophodon* has broader, chisel-like teeth that lock together with their neighbours to form a continuous sharp cutting edge and, combined with other differences in the cheeks and jaws, a much more efficient chewing machine. It seems likely that the hypsilophodontids rapidly replaced most fabrosaurids in the small agile herbivore niche from mid-Jurassic times.

Left and above: The drawing of the foot of *Hypsilophodon* is based on an illustration done in 1912. The reversed first toe was thought to be evidence that it was a tree-dweller and prompted restorations such as the fanciful one here. In fact the data had been misinterpreted: *Hypsilophodon's* first toe pointed in the same direction as the others.

Dryosaurus

Period: Late Jurassic. **Family:** Hypsilophodontids.
Where found: North America and East Africa.
Estimated length: 10-13ft (3-4m).

Several fairly well-preserved hypsilophodontids are known from the late Jurassic, notably *Dryosaurus* ('oak reptile') from North America and *Dysalotosaurus* ('lost wood reptile') from Tanzania in East Africa. These two dinosaurs have been compared, bone by bone, and are now considered to be so similar that they have been given the same name, *Dryosaurus*, the North American form, being called *Dryosaurus altus* and the East African form *Dryosaurus lettowvorbecki*. The similarity between the North American and the East African forms of Dryosaurus has prompted one author to speculate that Africa and North America were linked by a land route in the late Jurassic, with the result that animals could move from one area to the other unhindered. Maps that reconstruct the geography of that period, however, seem to indicate that seaways separated America from Africa. Perhaps there is no great problem here, though. In middle to late Jurassic times the northern and southern continents were linked and undoubtedly had very similar faunas. By late Jurassic times, the faunas were only recently separated, so there had been relatively little time for evolutionary divergence in the faunas to come about. This is reflected in the fact that although one or two similar genera are found in western North America and Tanzania – *Dryosaurus*, *Brachiosaurus* and (doubtfully) *Ceratosaurus* and *Allosaurus* – they are still different enough to

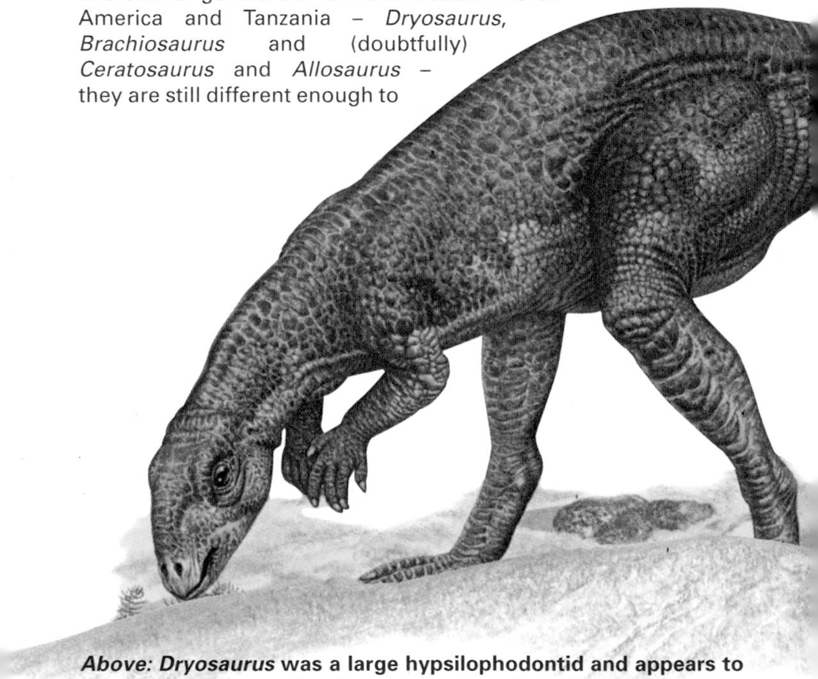

***Above: Dryosaurus* was a large hypsilophodontid and appears to have been wide-ranging: its remains have been found in North America and East Africa and it could probably migrate long distances.**

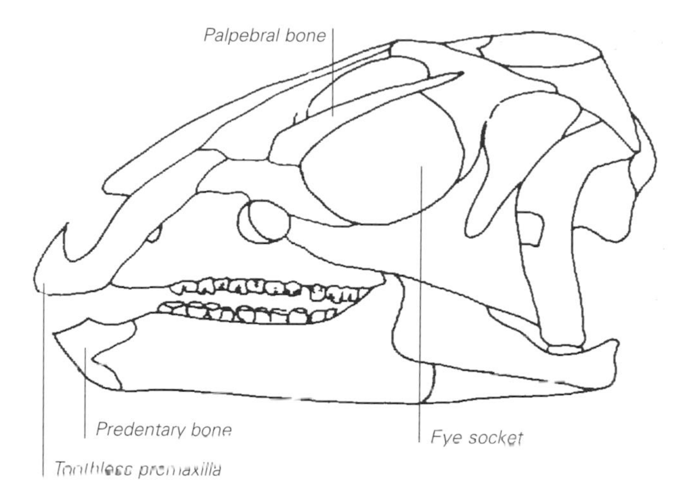

Above: **This *Dryosaurus* skull is obviously very similar to that of its relative *Hypsilophodon*, but here there are no teeth in the front part of the upper jaw (premaxilla). In this respect it resembles modern-day deer and sheep, in which a tough pad of horny tissue takes the place of upper teeth.**

be called separate species. Also, other groups, for example the stegosaurs, other sauropods and coelurosaurs, are represented by quite distinctive genera, indicating that some of the dinosaurs are not common to both continents, thereby supporting the idea of a seaway separating these two areas. As always, a balanced view, weighing all the facts pro and con, is necessary to any interpretation.

Dryosaurus was a large hypsilophodontid with long, powerful hind legs and strong arms, each with five fingers. Its tail was stiff and could have been used for balance when the animal ran. *Dryosaurus* had sharp, ridged cheek teeth but no teeth at the front of the jaw. It probably nipped vegetation off with its bony 'beak' and then chopped the leaves and shoots with its cheek teeth.

Dryosaurus is very similar to *Hypsilophodon* in size and shape, although there are consistent differences in their anatomy. For example, there are no teeth at the front of the upper jaw in *Dryosaurus*, while there are five in *Hypsilophodon*; also the arrangement of the bones of the hips is rather different, and there are only three toes on the hind foot while *Hypsilophodon* has four.

Tenontosaurus

Period: Mid-Cretaceous. **Family:** Hypsilophodontids.
Where found: North America.
Estimated length: 15ft-21ft 4in (4.5-6.5m).

From their first appearance in the mid-Jurassic until their extinction at the end of the Cretaceous, the hypsilophodontids appear to have changed very little. It seems as though these animals evolved a particularly successful structure (and way of life) and simply retained that design to the end. The only obviously aberrant form would seem to be *Tenontosaurus*, which was simply a hypsilophodontid grown rather large so that it resembles a small iguanodontid.

Tenontosaurus ('sinew reptile') was a comparatively large animal (c. 15ft, 4.5m in length) that lived in North America at about the same time as *Hypsilophodon* lived in Europe. As should be expected, its limbs are much more heavily built than those of *Hypsilophodon* to support its greater body weight. It has a sheath of tendons encasing the end of its

tail, but unlike *Hypsilophodon* it appears to have walked on all four legs, although it probably ran on its back legs alone, with its great long tail stuck straight out to counterbalance the heavy chest and belly. The relative dimensions of the hands and feet of *Tenontosaurus* and *Hypsilophodon* vary considerably, but they are basically very similar in design, suggesting close relationship.

Linked to the greater size of *Tenontosaurus*, the head is large and deeper with plenty of room for the attachment of large jaw muscles. This would permit a more considerable intake of the plants that it ate. The skull, though similar in size and shape to that of a small iguanodontid, seems to be more closely related to the smaller *Hypsilophodon*.

The skull of *Tenontosaurus* was large and robust, as would be expected in a rather big animal. Seen from above, however, it looks quite slender. The skull differs from that of *Hypsilophodon* or *Dryosaurus* in having a much deeper frontal region. This makes the skull look almost rectangular in outline when seen from the side. As the ▶

Below: *Tenontosaurus* was a much larger animal than its relative *Hypsilophodon*; it is estimated that it weighed up to 1 tonne. It has been classified as an iguanodontid, but it shows the same specialisations of the teeth as do other hypsilophodontids. *Tenontosaurus* was a strongly built ornithopod and it had a massive powerful tail, which may have been used at times to defend itself from packs of predatory *Deinonychus*.

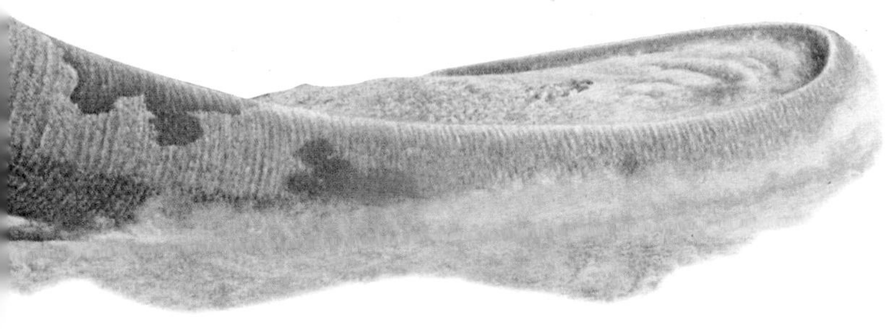

openings in the skull are much smaller than in the other hypsilophodontids, the skull would be correspondingly stronger. The premaxilla (upper jaw) was toothless.

Tenontosaurus is estimated to have weighed up to 1 tonne. Unfortunately, it had no defensive weapons, other than a massive and powerful tail, which may have been deployed for that purpose. The most numerous fossils found in the quarries in Montana that have yielded *Deinonychus* remains are those of *Tenontosaurus* tilletti, which would undoubtedly have been the main species upon which *Deinonychus* preyed. Both young and fully adult individuals of *Tenontosaurus* were likely targets, although the method of attack was probably different in each case. Small *Tenontosaurus* were lightly built, agile creatures and the stiffened tail would have acted both as a dynamic stabiliser and as an inertial beam so that they could jink from side to side when running at high speed. If alerted, the young hypsilophodontids probably stood a fair chance of escaping a predator as they perhaps had a slightly greater top speed. A fully grown *Tenontosaurus* was considerably larger than *Deinonychus*, so it is unlikely that a single *Deinonychus* could bring down a *Tenontosaurus* alone. Against a pack of *Deinonychus*, however, *Tenontosaurus* were probably doomed.

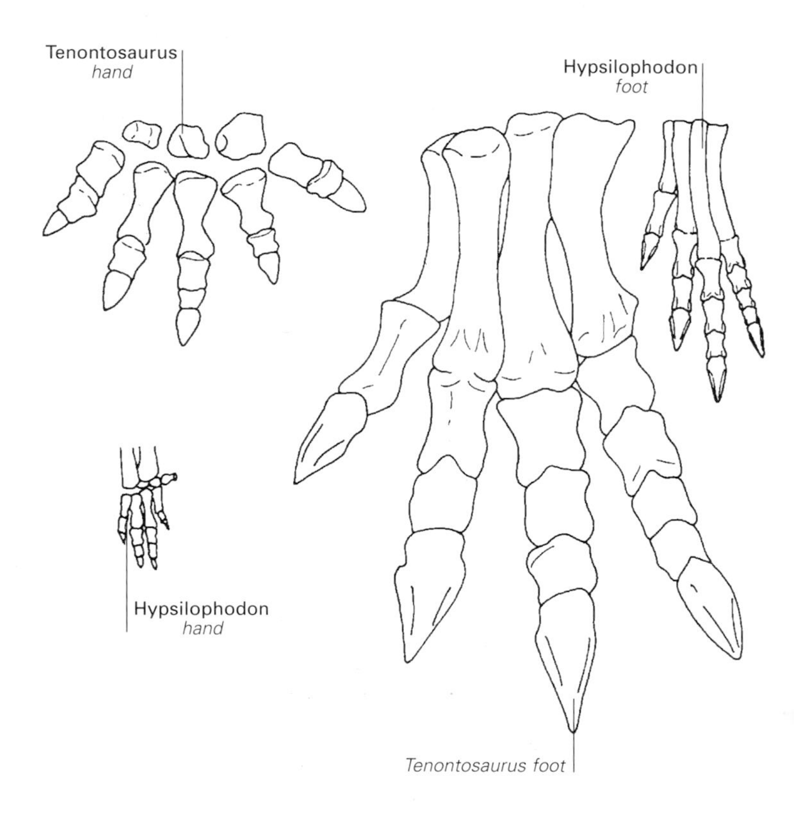

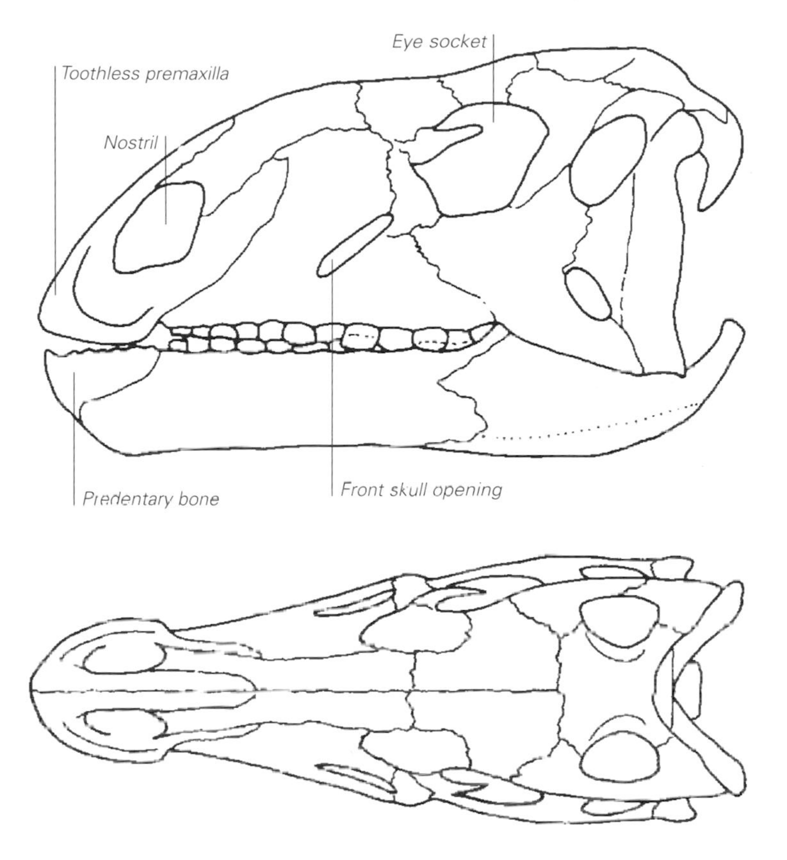

Above: The skull of this large animal is correspondingly large and robust, although quite slender when seen in plan view. In particular, the frontal region of the skull is much deeper, giving the skull a rectangular outline in side view. Also the various openings in the skull are much smaller, reducing weakness in the skull. The premaxilla is characteristically toothless.

Left: The foot of *Hypsilophodon* is typical of a fast-running creature, the upper foot bones being noticeably elongated. The toes are equipped with quite sharp claws. The hand is somewhat stubbier, and the stout claws may have been used for tearing or scratching. The hands and feet of *Tenontosaurus* and *Hypsilophodon* vary considerably in terms of relative dimensions but they are basically very similar in design, suggesting close relationship.

Hypsilophodon

Period: Mid-Cretaceous. **Family:** Hypsilophodontids.
Where found: England.
Estimated length: 6ft 6in (2m).

The first remains of any hypsilophodontid to be discovered were found in a slab of sandstone from the south-west coast of the Isle of Wight, England, in 1849. The remains, which consisted of a partial skeleton, were first described as those of a young *Iguanodon*. By 1868, several other skeletons had been recovered from the same locality by the Reverend William Fox. The new material displayed several characteristics not previously seen in *Iguanodon* and it was proposed that the animal represented a new species, *Iguanodon foxii*. It was Thomas Henry Huxley who first recognised that this dinosaur was totally unlike *Iguanodon*. Among the many differences, Huxley was struck by the shape of the teeth, which were smaller, narrower and more sharply pointed than those of *Iguanodon*. These prompted Huxley to rename the dinosaur *Hypsilophodon foxii* ('Fox's high-ridged tooth').

In 1882 James Hulke completed the first description of *Hypsilophodon* and concluded that it was adapted to climb on rocks and trees because it had long fingers and toes. From this observation, it was accepted as established fact that *Hypsilophodon* was an arboreal dinosaur and that this perhaps represented the primitive type of lifestyle of ornithopod dinosaurs. Numerous other 'facts' were adduced to support the proposal, including that the first toe of the foot was reversed so that it could grip on to branches and that the hindlimb muscles were so arranged that the animal could not run fast, but were well suited to climbing and balancing. Peter Galton reviewed these statements critically and concluded that none of them stood up to examination. In fact, many observations actually proved the reverse – that *Hypsilophodon* could not have lived in trees but was instead a rather fleet-footed ornithopod, with limb proportions typical of very fast-running animals.

About twenty-three partial or complete skeletons of *Hypsilophodon* have been discovered on the Isle of Wight, all from a small area of the cliffs, the so-called '*Hypsilophodon* bed', which has yielded virtually nothing else. Many of the skeletons are beautifully preserved with all the bones in position, and several skeletons are practically touching. Why there should be such a rich concentration of these small dinosaurs in

Right: **One of the best-known and most successful of the small ornithopods, *Hypsilophodon* was a comparatively small dinosaur. It had short arms, each with five fingers, and long legs, each with four toes. *Hypsilophodon* was probably an agile and fleet-footed creature, and it may have used its long stiff tail as a stabiliser when running. It was once thought that *Hypsilophodon* lived in trees, but there is little evidence for this.**

one place is a mystery. One suggestion is that the animals preserved there represent part of a small herd that became trapped and perished in inter-tidal quicksand. This is certainly a novel explanation, but it does have some merit. We would normally expect that the process leading to the fossilisation of any animal is quite a long and chancy one. The animal dies or is killed; its remains are left to rot and maybe scavenged so that bits are lost before it is finally destroyed or buried in sediments or washed into a river Thus we should normally expect only very incomplete or fragmentary remains to be preserved. The skeletons in the *Hypsilophodon* bed, however, must have been buried very rapidly at the time of death, allowing no time for scavenging or dipersal through rotting. Burial in quicksand is certainly one way in which this could have happened.

Like its predecessors the fabrosaurids and heterodontosaurids, this form was a lightly built, speedy biped. Here too, the hind legs show adaptations typical of cursorial (or running) animals. All segments of the leg (upper, lower, ankle, foot) are elongated, but the segment that is relatively the most elongated is the one furthest from the body – the upper part of the foot. The most robust bone, however, is that nearest the body, the upper leg. Because of these features the leg acts like a pendulum, which has a long length but a small 'bob'. Such a pendulum has a short period or swing-time, so during the stride the hind leg can swing backwards and forwards very rapidly – obviously useful for a fast runner. The characteristic bony rods are present along the backbone and in the tail. ▶

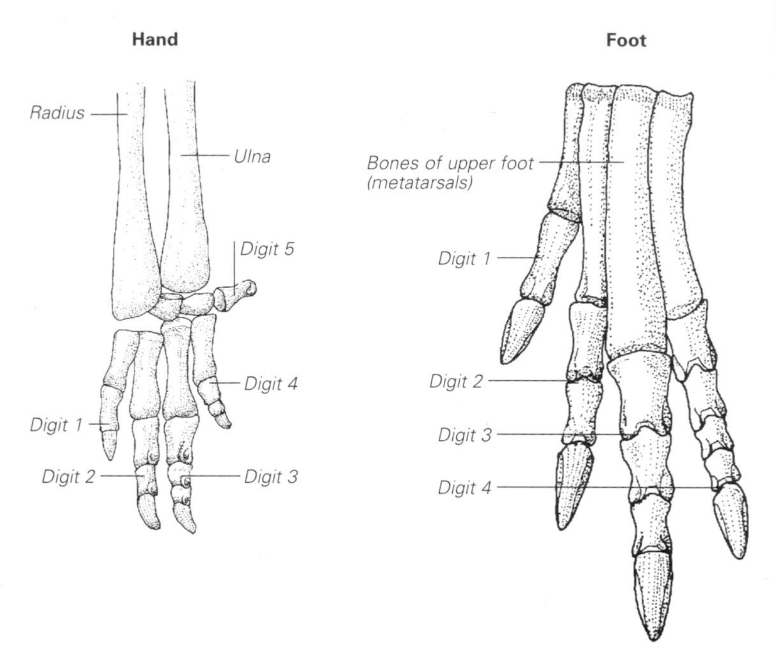

Above: **The foot of *Hypsilophodon* is typical of a fast-running creature, the upper foot bones being noticeably elongated. The toes are equipped with quite sharp claws. The hand is somewhat stubbier and the stout claws may have been used for tearing or scratching.**

Below: **The bones in all segments of the leg are elongated and show other proportions that indicate that their owner was a speedy bidped.**

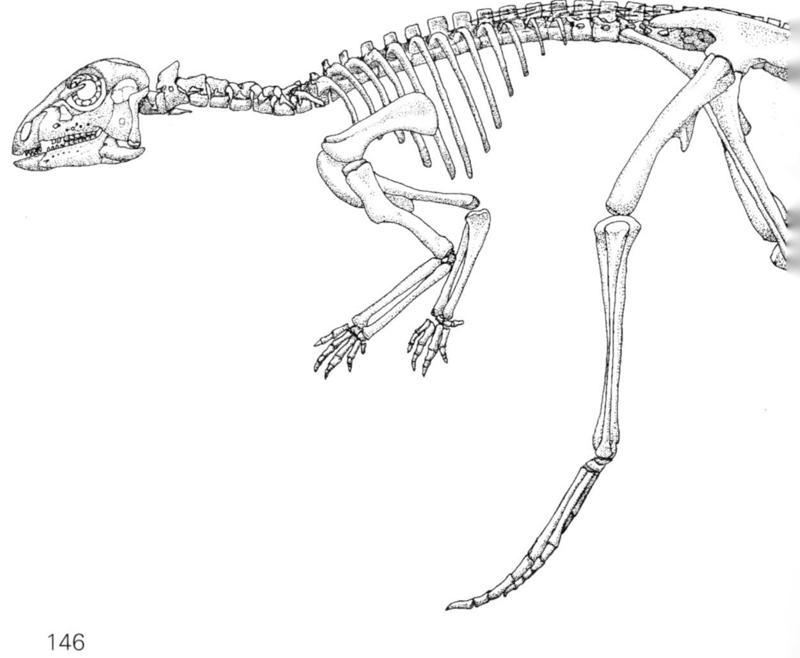

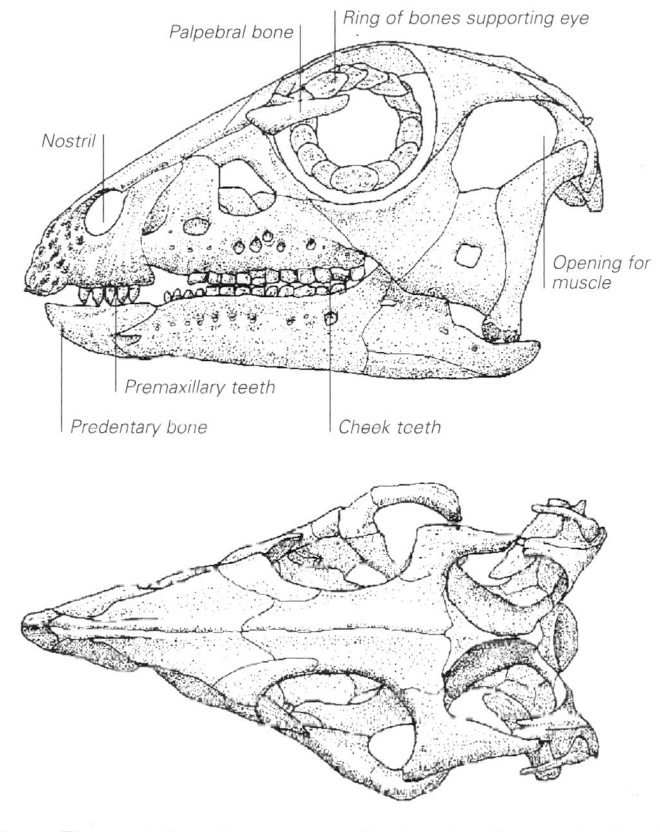

Above: **The teeth here form a very effective chewing mechanism. The pitting and roughness on the front end of the upper jaw indicate that a covering of horn was present. The ring of small bones, or ossicles, in the eye is often found in reptiles and may be part of the focussing mechanism for sharp eyesight.**

Iguanodontids

Iguanodontids are ornithopod dinosaurs of medium to large size (16ft 6in-33ft, 5-10m long), which range in time from the late Jurassic Period to the end of the Cretaceous. They appear to have co-existed quite happily with the hypsilophodontids until the early Cretaceous, when the appearance of the most advanced ornithopods, the hadrosaurids, resulted in a marked decline in their abundance and diversity – almost to the point of extinction except in western Europe.

Compared with the hypsilophodontids, the iguanodontids were rather large and clumsy animals. Many of the differences are simply size-related but iguanodontids also had a number of characteristic features, particularly in the structure of their skulls, teeth, forelimbs and hips, that set them apart as a distinct group.

Iguanodontids retained the basic ornithopod characteristics: the body was counterbalanced by the tail and they walked on their massive hindlegs, although they were also capable of walking or resting on all fours. Iguanodontids had large skulls in proportion to the body, with elongate, rather horse-like snouts, which ended in very broad, toothless, homy beaks. The long snout allowed room for much-enlarged jaws and large numbers of grinding teeth for chewing large quantities of food, while the broad beak acted as a device for effectively cropping pieces of foliage.

The earliest iguanodontid fossils come from the late Jurassic of North America and western Europe and consist of a femur of an animal named *Callovosaurus* from the late Jurassic of Northampton, England. The only record that these forms survived at all into the late Cretaceous is some teeth from western Europe and several incomplete skeletons from Romania.

The evolution of the iguanodontids in the mid-Jurassic, when the continents were in contact, meant that they could disperse practically worldwide. *Camptosaurus* was found in western North America and Europe in the late Jurassic. In the early Cretaceous, seaways had begun to separate the various continents, so each was able to evolve its own distinct iguanodontid (except East Asia, cut off by a sea barrier). Thus the continents show an interesting variety and abundance of iguanodontids: *Iguanodon* (Europe), *Ouranosaurus* (Africa), *Muttaburrasaurus* (Australia) and perhaps even Kangnasaurus (southern Africa).

While the fortunes of the iguanodontids do not seem to have been adversely affected by the hypsilophodontids, which first appear at about the same time in the fossil record, the hadrosaurids probably actively competed for the same resources with the iguanodontids, being similar in size and in the nature of their jaws and teeth.

Iguanodontids seem to have used defensive weapons to repel predators. All of them (except perhaps *Muttaburrasaurus*) had a spur-like claw on the first finger of the hand, which, used at close quarters and swung with all the weight of the massive body behind it, could cause hideous injuries to the eyes, face or neck of the predator.

Above: Muttaburrasaurus is very important because dinosaurs from Australia are still poorly known, and the find extends our knowledge of the palaeogeographic distribution of iguanodontids, which are otherwise mainly known from the northern hemisphere. *Muttaburrasaurus* was about 23ft (7m) long and had a low, broad head, with a heavy, bony lump above the snout.

Camptosaurus

Period: Late Jurassic. **Family:** Iguanodontids.
Where found: North America.
Estimated length: 16ft 6in-23ft (5-7m).

Apart from *Callovosaurus*, the earliest iguanodontids belong to the genus *Camptosaurus* ('flexible reptile'), which is known from several skeletons discovered in 1879 in the late Jurassic of Wyoming, North America. There is another genus named *Cumnoria*, which was also discovered in 1879 in late Jurassic rocks near Oxford in England. It has recently been redescribed and renamed *Camptosaurus* since it is

Right: All these skulls of iguanodontids are large compared to the body, have long snouts and end in a broad, toothless beak. But they also show considerable differences, for example ***Camptosaurus*** is lower at the back and has a comparatively narrower snout, while ***Muttaburrasaurus*** features a remarkable bump above and behind its nostrils.

Iguanodon

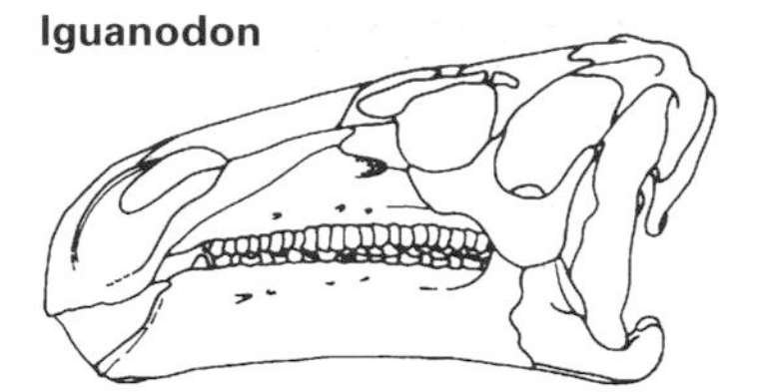

Camptosaurus

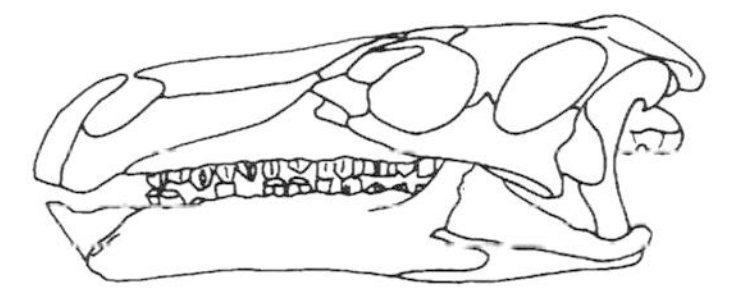

Muttaburrasaurus

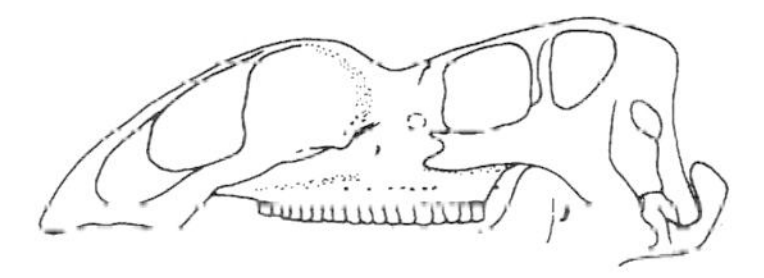

virtually identical to the North American species. The similarity between these dinosaurs from North America and Europe testifies to a land connection between these two areas well into the late Jurassic.

This ornithopod is known from a number of skeletons, which include both juvenile and adult specimens ranging in length from 4 to 23ft (1.2-7m). *Camptosaurus* resembles quite closely both *Iguanodon* and *Ouranosaurus*. The main differences are to be found in the head, hands, hips and feet. The head of *Camptosaurus* is long, but quite low when compared with *Iguanodon*, and it lacks *Ouranosaurus's* bumps on the nose and its very broad muzzle.

The backbone is much more ordinary and '*Iguanodon*-like' in its construction, with no tall spines. The forelimb differs slightly from that of *Iguanodon* in that the hand has a short, spur-like first finger, rather than a distinct spike; also, the claws on fingers two and three are more curved and less hoof-like. However, *Camptosaurus* does possess the large bony wrist and small hooves on both its fingers and toes to enable it to walk on all fours.

The pubis has a very long, narrow, posterior rod, which reaches the end of the ischium. In *Iguanodon* and *Ouranosaurus*, the posterior rod of the pubis reaches only about half-way down the ischium. Finally, its foot possesses four well-developed toes, while there are only three in *Iguanodon* and *Ouranosaurus*.

Left: *Camptosaurus* is the earliest iguanodontid that is known from skeletons. It is more primitive than the typical Cretaceous iguanodontids in being smaller, in having four toes on the foot (*Iguanodon* had three) and in lacking a fully developed spiked thumb.

Ouranosaurus

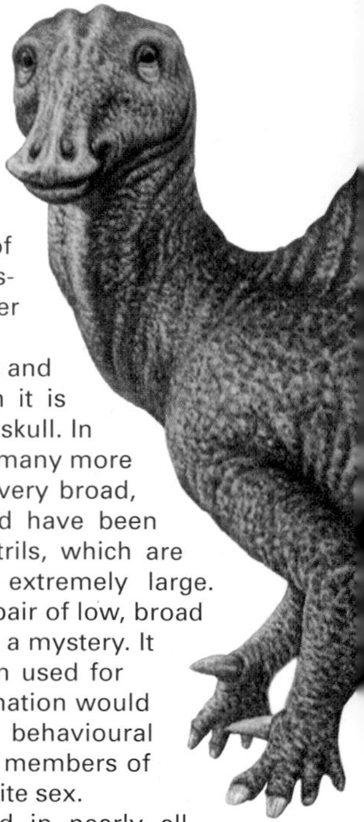

Period: Mid-Cretaceous.
Family: Iguanodontids.
Where found: West Africa.
Estimated length: 23ft (7m).

An almost complete skeleton of *Ouranosaurus* ('brave reptile') was discovered in the mid-1960s near Elrhaz in Niger (West Africa).

The head of *Ouranosaurus* is very large and long, and this is especially striking when it is compared with a typical hypsilophodontid skull. In particular, the jaws are very long and have many more large teeth, while the end of the snout is very broad, flattened and toothless; in life this would have been covered by a large horny beak. The nostrils, which are formed just above the beak, are also extremely large. Immediately behind the nostrils there is a pair of low, broad bumps. The significance of these bumps is a mystery. It seems unlikely that they would have been used for defensive purposes. The most likely explanation would seem to be that they were of some behavioural significance, perhaps to aid recognition of members of the same species or members of the opposite sex.

Another rather curious feature, found in nearly all ornithischians, is the palpebral bone, which juts out across the cavity for the eye. Again, its purpose is so far unexplained. Behind the eye, there are large openings at the back of the skull through which passed the jaw muscles; these must have been large and powerful because of the great size of the jaws that they had to move. A large bony projection sticks upwards near the back end of the lower jaw. This projection, named the coronoid process, was the point at which most of the large jaw muscles attached. In fabrosaurids there is no coronoid process and even in heterodontosaurids it is quite small. However, in the large-jawed iguanodontids (and the hadrosaurids) the coronoid process is very large. The reason for this is that it not only provides a greater attachment area for the large jaw muscles, but also greatly improves the leverage of the muscles on the jaws, so that they can close the jaws more powerfully and therefore chew food more efficiently.

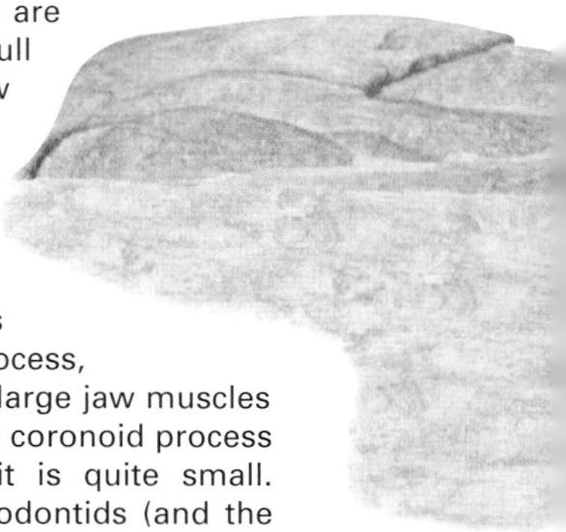

The back, hips and tail of *Ouranosaurus* have the most enormous spines, which form a high, almost sail-like ridge down the back of the animal. The skin in the 'sail' was probably richly supplied with blood vessels but the purpose of the sail is unknown. *Ouranosaurus* has been found in sediments that indicate dry equatorial conditions. The midday

Above: Ouranosaurus was one of the more spectacular ornithopods. It had a remarkable 'sail' on its back, which was made from skin stretched over elongated spines along the backbone. It may have served as a heat-exchanger.

sun was undoubtedly hot, while nights may have been very cold. Thus the skin covering the 'sail' on the back could have been used rather like a solar panel. Blood in the skin could be warmed by the sun's rays so that these animals might warm up their bodies quickly – perhaps after enduring a cold night. Equally, the sail could be used as a radiator to cool the animal down in the heat of the day or after very strenuous activity. This sort of function has recently been proposed for the plates of *Stegosaurus*, where it is supported by a lot of additional evidence. In the case of *Ouranosaurus* it is not quite so clear-cut, although a heat-regulating function is quite possible. It is also interesting to note that the carnivorous dinosaur *Spinosaurus*, which appears to have lived at the same time and in the same area as *Ouranosaurus*, had similar tall spines on its back. Presumably both dinosaurs grew spines for a similar reason, although the actual cause, whether physiological, behavioural or ecological, is not yet clear.

In most respects the forelimb of *Ouranosaurus* is very similar to that of *Iguanodon*. It is fairly long in comparison with the hindlimb and could have reached the ground quite easily. The claws on its second and third fingers are also very broad and hoof-like for use when walking or resting

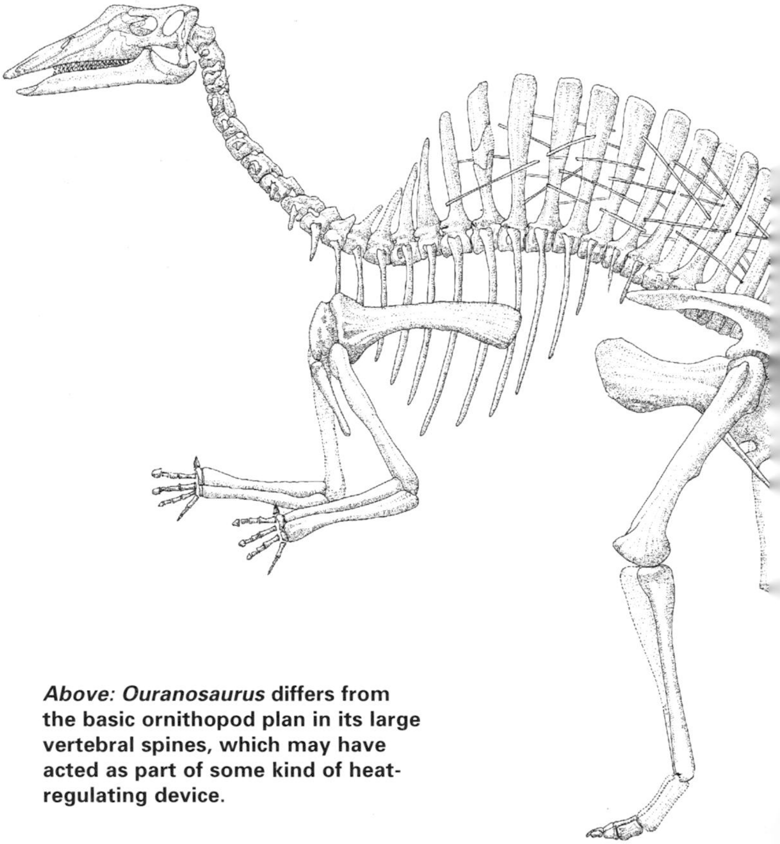

***Above: Ouranosaurus* differs from the basic ornithopod plan in its large vertebral spines, which may have acted as part of some kind of heat-regulating device.**

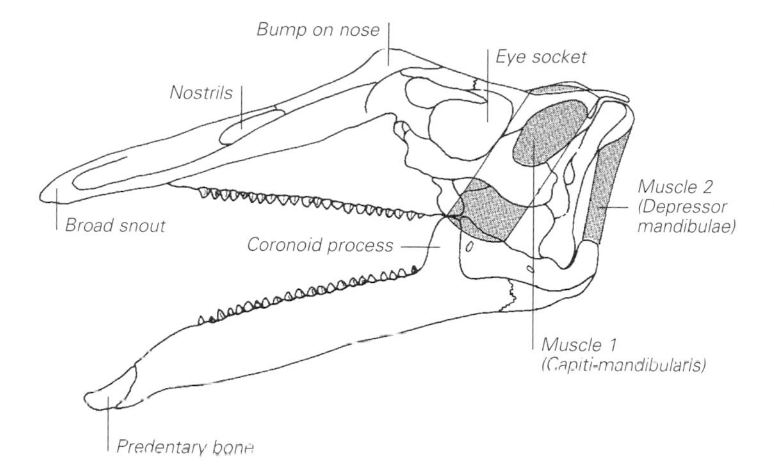

***Above:* The jaw muscles of *Ouranosaurus* are large and powerful as expected in a large ornithopod. Muscle 1 arises from a large opening in the skull and it has a firm insertion on to a projection of the lower jaw (coronoid process). This insertion increases the moment arm of the muscle, a measure of the force that it can produce.**

on all fours. In addition, the wrist bones are very large and welded together so that the weight of the body would not dislocate them when the hands were used for walking. As in *Iguanodon*, the hand is equipped with a very large thumb-spike that would have made a formidable defensive weapon. The fifth finger is quite long and flexible and may well have been used for holding or plucking plant stems or twigs.

The hindlimb of *Ouranosaurus* is much more heavily built than that of *Hypsilophodon*. The individual bones are much more massive to support the great weight of the body, while the proportions of the bones are rather different. The femur (upper leg bone) is longer while the tibia (lower leg) is shorter and the foot is much shorter, more compact and has only three toes. All these changes indicate that the legs were designed primarily to act as pillars, rather than to move the animal quickly as was the case with hypsilophodontids.

Iguanodon

Period: Early Cretaceous. **Family:** Iguanodontids.
Where found: North America, Europe and western Asia.
Estimated length: 33ft (10m).

In early Cretaceous times a variety of iguanodontids appeared in various parts of the world. *Iguanodon* ('iguana tooth'), which has given its name to the family, is found abundantly right across western Europe, from Spain, Portugal and Britain in the west to the Urals in the east. Large accumulations of skeletons of *Iguanodon* in Belgium and Germany and tracks of footprints from England provide circumstantial evidence of the social behaviour of this type of dinosaur. Large numbers of fossil skeletons suggest that they were very numerous and by implication quite successful for their time.

Footprint trackways, particularly in southern England, seem to show several dinosaurs moving about in the same direction at the same time – perhaps as a herd. Herding, if it did take place, is an important method of gaining protection from predators. The largest fully grown *Iguanodon* individuals were 33ft (10m) or more in length and probably sufficiently large to be practically invulnerable to attack. The prime subjects for

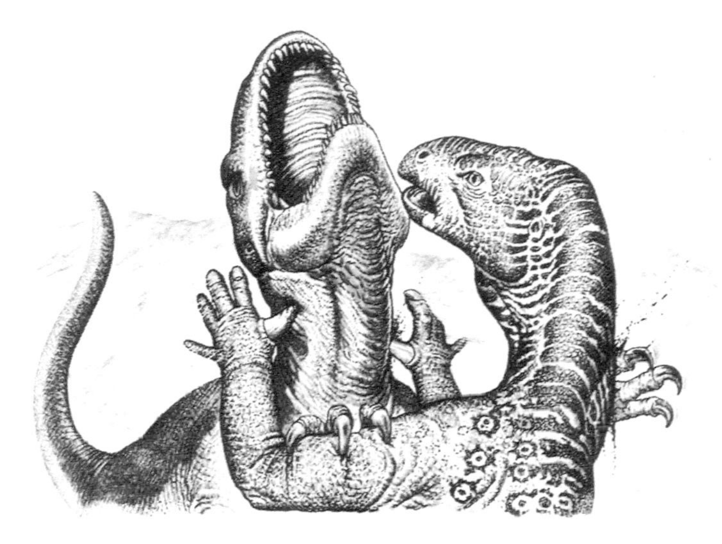

Above: **A fully grown iguanodontid must have posed a formidable challenge to any potential predator. Here we see a carnosaur being viciously stabbed by an *Iguanodon* using its thumb spike to good effect. At close quarters, *Iguanodon* was probably more than a match for most attackers.**

attack would undoubtedly have been old or infirm individuals or the smaller, less powerful, young ones. Herding allows animals to protect themselves, particularly the more vulnerable individuals, by structuring the herd so that the young (and perhaps pregnant females) stay near the centre, while the larger adults (perhaps exclusively the males if they are the larger) patrol the edges as 'look-outs' in order to give the alarm and defend the herd from predators.

The remains of *Iguanodon* are frequently found in lowland, marshy or estuarine areas in Britain and Europe and it seems quite possible that these animals lived in herds in such areas, feeding on the rich vegetation that would be expected to grow in such conditions. The plants growing in these areas were probably primarily horsetails (*Equisetum*), ferns, cyads, bennettitaleans and various conifers; many of these, although we do not know exactly which, would have formed the diet of these animals.

The skeleton of *Iguanodon* was fairly ▶

Left: Iguanodon **was a very common inhabitant of early Cretaceous lowland habitats in much of Europe. Large accumulations of *Iguanodon* skeletons have been discovered in England, Belgium and West Germany; these may indicate that *Iguanodon* lived in herds.**

typical for an ornithopod, athough more powerfully built than some. It was bipedal, with front legs reduced in length but particularly strong. These may have been used in walking or resting on all fours, rather in the manner of modern-day kangaroos. This use of the front legs is quite different from that seen in the earlier ornithopods, and in fact iguanodontids are much more robust, less agile animals all round.

The hand of *Iguanodon* was typically robust. The middle fingers were strong and hoof-like for supporting the body weight during four-footed locomotion or when the animal was at rest. The wrist bones were fused together for extra strength during weight-bearing. The sharp, off-set thumb with its large spike could have been used as a formidable stabbing weapon or to rake branches of trees down to its mouth. The fifth finger was probably quite flexible – perhaps to manipulate food. *Iguanodon* had small 'hooves' on its hands and feet, and both could be used for locomotion.

***Below: Iguanodon* had a fairly typical ornithopod skeleton. It was a large, bipedal animal, powerfully built compared with some ornithopods, and with particularly strong but shorter front legs. These may have been used in walking or resting on all fours, rather in the manner of modern-day kangaroos. This use of the front legs is quite different from that seen in the earlier ornithopods, and in fact iguanodontids are much more robust, less agile animals all round.**

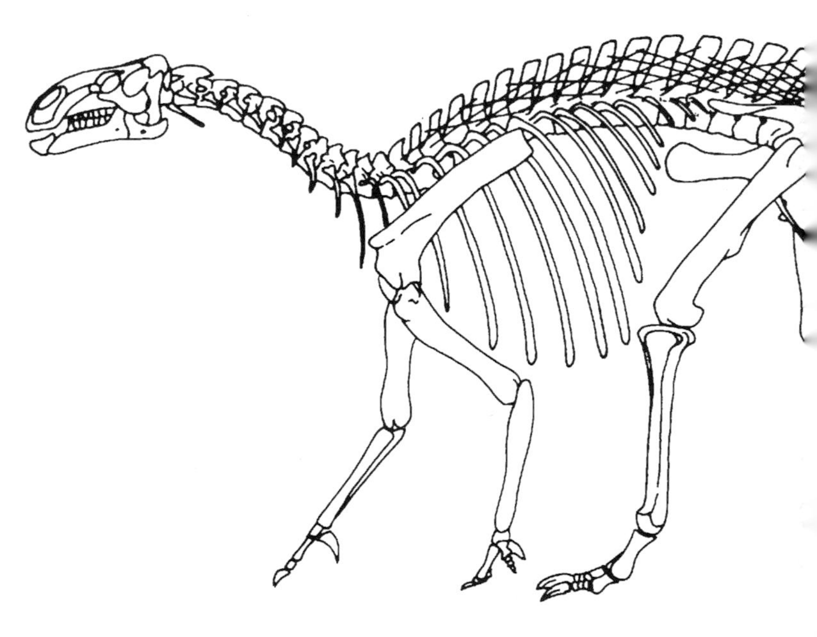

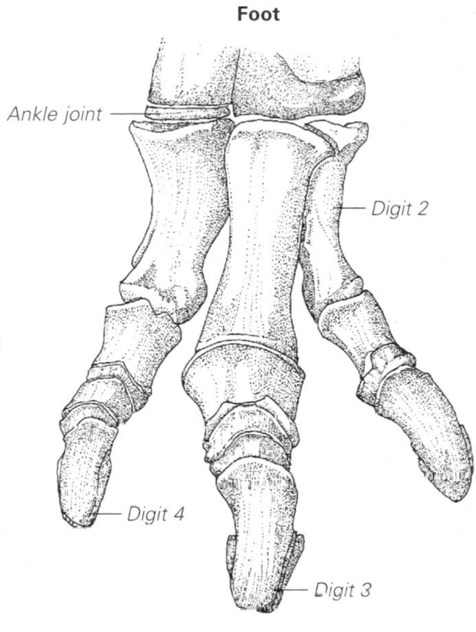

Right and below right: **The hand of *Iguanodon* was typically robust and the strong, three-toed foot would have been necessary to support the weight of this large beast. Some of the individual toe bones have been much reduced in size, while the upper foot bones are fairly elongate and strong. *Iguanodon* probably walked on its toes like modern-day cats and dogs.**

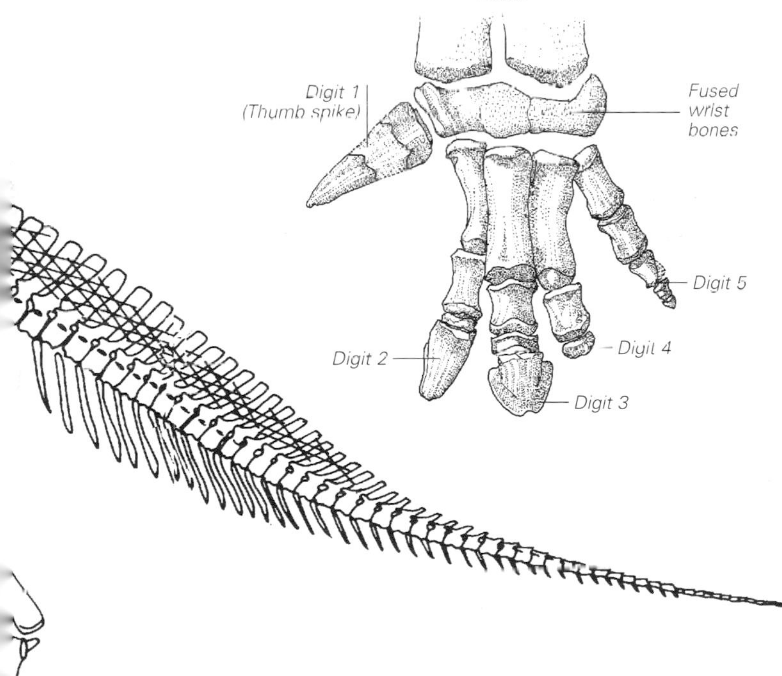

Hadrosaurids I

Hadrosaurids were the last group of ornithopods to evolve, appearing in the mid-Cretaceous Period. The bodies of virtually all the hadrosaurids are remarkably similar – resembling also the iguanodontids apart from a few changes, for example, the absence of a thumb in hadrosaurids. The main differences are in the head shapes, which exhibit remarkable variety.

The first hadrosaur remains were excavated from a marl pit at Haddonfield, New Jersey, and described in 1858 by Joseph Leidy.

Hadrosaurids had horny beaks like ducks' bills (hence their common name, 'duck-billed dinosaurs'). Ducks, however, have no teeth, whereas the teeth of hadrosaurids were arranged in dental batteries, each with hundreds of teeth in each jaw. The teeth were cemented together by bony tissue and formed a long grinding surface, which could have been used to pound up tough plants, even woody twigs. Analysis of the fossilised stomach contents of a hadrosaur shows that it contained conifer needles and twigs, seeds and other land plants.

The hadrosaurid body was balanced at the hips and the long hindlimbs were arranged to act as pillars supporting the weight of the body. The three toes of the foot splayed outwards, forming a broad contact with the ground for good grip and balance. The ankle region was very powerfully built. Another curious feature is a trellis-like arrangement of bony rods (ossified tendons or ligaments) alongside the spines on the back, in front of and behind the hip region. The rods probably acted like hawsers supporting the backbone. These features confirm a land-based lifestyle, although hadrosaurids were certainly capable of swimming.

It has been claimed that the extraordinary tubes and crests on the heads of some hadrosaurids served as 'snorkels' for underwater breathing, reserve 'air tanks' or 'air traps' to prevent water flooding the lungs. None of these suggestions is tenable; for example, the 'snorkel' idea relied on the presence of holes in the tops of the crests – there were none!

In 1978 the fossilised remains of fifteen baby *Maiasaura* ('good mother reptile') hadrosaurids, along with fragments of eggshell, were found in and around a mound-shaped structure in western Montana – a hadrosaur nest. The young dinosaurs had well-worn teeth and were considerably larger than newly hatched individuals. This indicated that the young dinosaurs had stayed together for some time. Perhaps adults brought food to them or the young went out in search of food and subsequently returned to parental supervision. Thus it looks as though hadrosaurids took care of their young. Further excavation revealed other nests – suggesting the existence of a nesting colony. Other remains show that the animals returned to the same nest year after year and also reveal the way in which their eggs were laid, with the pointed end directed into the soil.

***Right:* Evidently some hadrosaurs looked after their young in a nesting colony. Here a female *Maiasaura* digs out a nest (front right) while the central dinosaur defends her territory. At the back the mother covers newly laid eggs with sand. The fourth *Maiasaura* sleeps on the nest.**

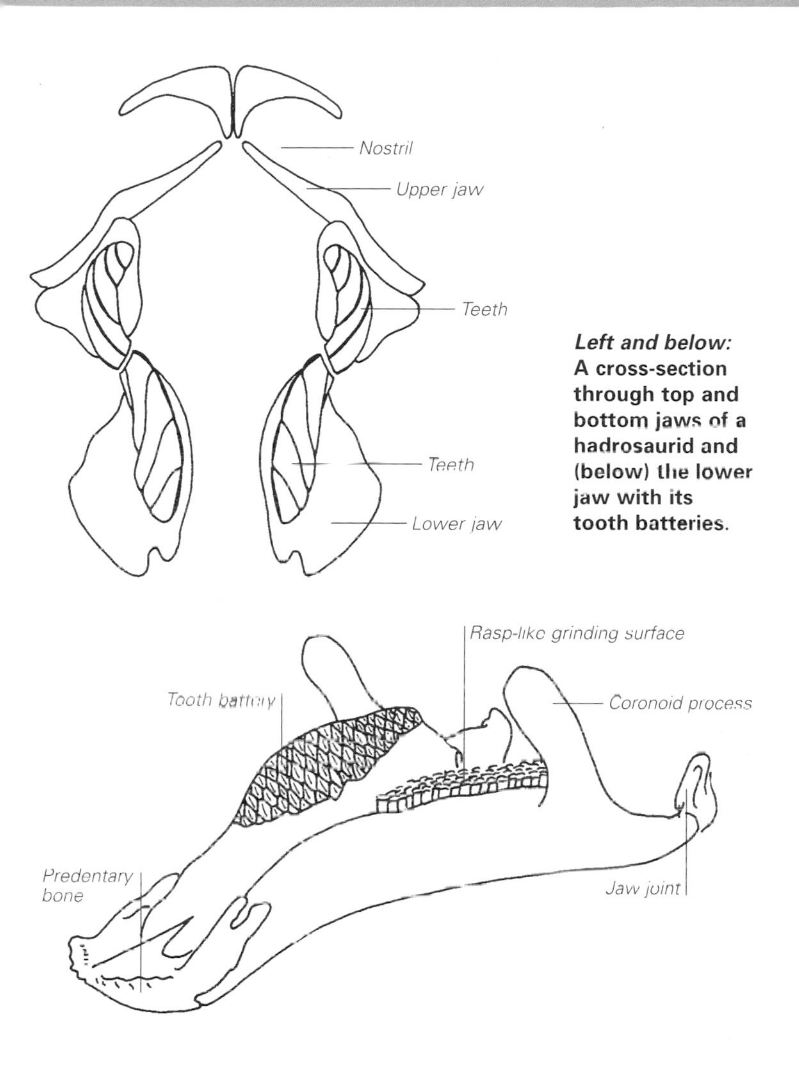

Left and below: **A cross-section through top and bottom jaws of a hadrosaurid and (below) the lower jaw with its tooth batteries.**

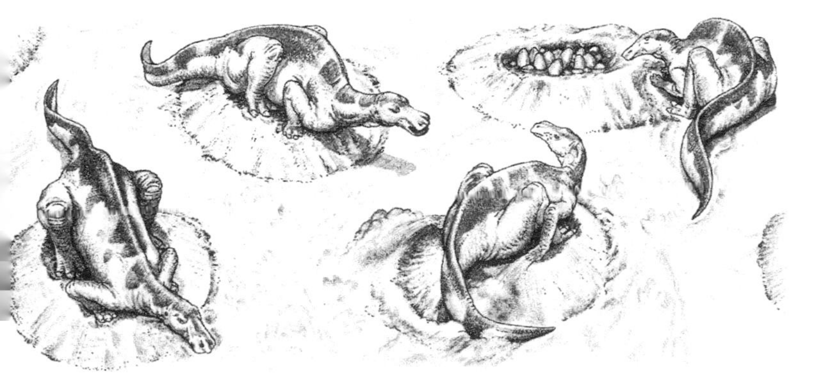

Anatosaurus

Period: Late Cretaceous. **Family:** Hadrosaurids.
Where found: North America.
Estimated length: 33-42ft (10-13m).

Anatosaurus ('duck reptile') was a common hadrosaur and it is one of the best-known 'crestless' forms. It was a large animal, normally around 33ft (10m) long, and weighing about 3 tonnes. The massive limbs and the broad 'duck bill' were distinctive features. Like the other hadrosaurids, *Anatosaurus* had a broad and capacious mouth with batteries of strong cheek teeth, with which it could have gathered up large amounts of vegetation.

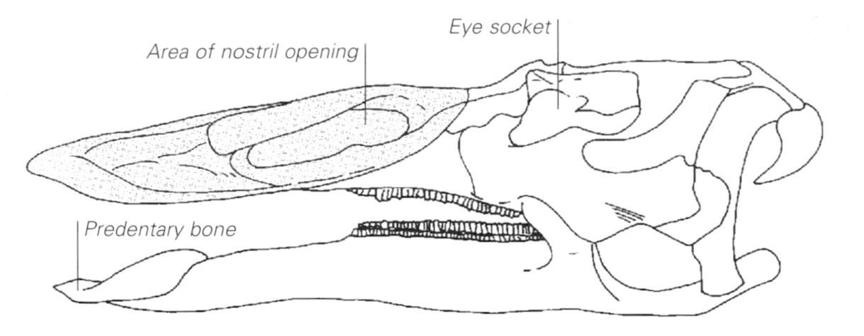

Above: *Anatosaurus* had an extremely long, broad snout, which gave rise to the description 'duck-billed'. The area of the nasal passages is coloured red.

It was originally thought that a duck-billed animal must have led an aquatic lifestyle. The claim was first made by Joseph Leidy in the 1850s and seemed to have been reinforced by the discovery in 1908 of 'mummified' remains of *Anatosaurus* by C. H. and C. M. Sternberg, which showed evidence of a mitten-like covering of skin over the hand, giving it the form of a paddle. Indeed, many books on dinosaurs featured (and still feature) hadrosaurs wallowing in lakes or on the banks of rivers, chewing water plants. However, there is much evidence that they were in fact land-based creatures, although it seems quite plausible that they may have retreated into deep water to escape from predators such as the large tyrannosaurids. Hadrosaurid remains have been found in rocks near coasts, swamps and rivers, which may suggest an aquatic or amphibious lifestyle but equally the likelihood that their carcasses were swept away and deposited by water. Few aquatic plant fossils have been discovered from the time of the hadrosaurids. And the animals preserved as fossils with hadrosaurids were largely terrestrial.

Hadrosaurids had no notable defensive weapons; they had no large teeth, claws or spikes to fight with and had lost the large thumb spike so characteristic of the earlier iguanodontids. They were also probably far too large and heavy-footed to be able to outrun predators, so an ability to escape into deep swamps may have been very useful.

Left: *Anatosaurus* was a common hadrosaur and it is one of the larger and best-known of the 'crestless' forms, with an unusually distinctive 'duck bill' and massive limbs.

Bactrosaurus

Period: Mid-Cretaceous. **Family:** Hadrosaurids.
Where found: Mongolia.
Estimated length: 13-20ft (4-6m).

One of the earliest hadrosaurids known is *Bactrosaurus* ('reptile from Bactria') from Mongolia. It comes from rocks dated around the middle of the Cretaceous Period. In its general appearance this animal resembled iguanodontids very strongly. It did, however, show, in the structure of its teeth in particular, the development of a grinding battery. Unfortunately the fossilized remains so far discovered do not include its hands, so it is uncertain whether this dinosaur possessed an iguanodontid thumb spike or whether it was like all other hadrosaurids and had only four fingers on its hand. *Bactrosaurus* was fairly small, being only 20ft (6m) long.

Although *Bactrosaurus* lacked a crest, it seems to be related to later 'lambeosaurine' hadrosaurs such as *Corythosaurus* and *Parasaurolophus*, which are discussed on the next pages. Like all other hadrosaurs, *Bactrosaurus* had batteries of cheek teeth set well back in the mouth forming a long grinding surface (rather like a rasp, a carpenter's coarse file), which could have ground up very tough plant material. The original suggestion that hadrosaurs lived an aquatic life and generally were the prehistoric equivalents of ducks has been discounted. A duck-like existence does seem a little improbable for a 2-3-tonne hadrosaurid! A far better comparison, particularly with regard

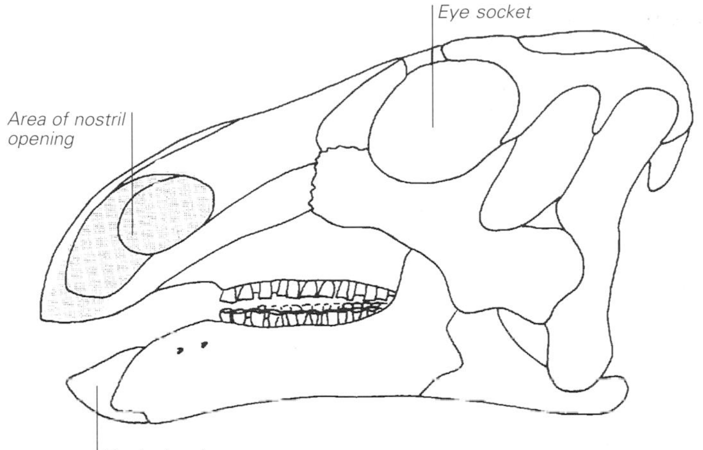

Above: **The snout of *Bactrosaurus* is very generalised, rather like an iguanodontid. The area of the nasal passages is coloured red.**

to the beak, would be with the turtles and tortoises, which have sharp, horny beaks. Such a tough, sharp and continuously growing beak would have been well suited to nipping off twigs and stripping leaves from branches.

At least two types of early hadrosaurid are known from Mongolia. The other is known as *Gilmoreosaurus* (named after Charles Witney Gilmore, the palaeontologist who first described this fossil in the 1930s). As with *Bactrosaurus*, *Gilmoreosaurus* is not at all well preserved, so its detailed anatomy is very unclear. After these early first appearances, hadrosaurids seem to have evolved very rapidly, producing a considerable variety of different species (including *Anatosaurus*, 'duck reptile', and *Edmontosaurus*, 'reptile from Edmonton'), which are found quite widely distributed.

Left: **This is one of the earliest hadrosaurs. Although *Bactrosaurus* lacked a crest, it seems to be related to later 'lambeosaurine' hadrosaurs such as *Corythosaurus* and *Parasaurolophus*. Like all other hadrosaurs, *Bactrosaurus* had batteries of cheek teeth set well back in the mouth, which could have ground up very tough plant material. *Bactrosaurus* was a fairly small hadrosaur, being only 20ft (6m) long.**

Edmontosaurus

Period: Late Cretaceous. **Family:** Hadrosaurids.
Where found: North America.
Estimated length: 33-42ft (10-13m).

Edmontosaurus ('reptile from Edmonton') was a large hadrosaur, up to 42ft (3m) long, and closely related to *Anatosaurus*. *Edmontosaurus* had about a thousand strong teeth in the cheek region. The low area on top of the skull near the front might have been covered with loose skin, which could have been inflated to make a loud bellowing call.

Early palaeontologists expressed the view that *Edmontosaurus*, like the other hadrosaurids, was a creature that liked to wade in deep water on its long legs, rather like a gigantic flamingo. The geological evidence suggests that hadrosaurids in North America lived in areas that were coastal plains, close to sea-level with swamps and large meandering rivers. The finding of their carcasses in swampy or lake areas may not, however, indicate that the animals in life inhabited wet areas, rather that they had been washed down and deposited there when they died.

One of the main pieces of evidence concerning the environment in which hadrosaurs lived comes from the plants preserved with these dinosaurs. An analysis of these plant fossils has suggested that they grew in warm temperate or subtropical conditions in humid, lowland areas. The plants themselves, however, are represented by very few aquatic or marginal pond weeds but by abundant remains of lowland forest trees and shrubs, dominated by conifers, poplars, willows and oaks. Thus most plant food seems to have been on land.

The animals living (or rather preserved as fossils) with the hadrosaurids include hypsilophodontids, ankylosaurids, ceratopians, sauropods, tyrannosaurids and other smaller theropods. Very few of these types of dinosaur have ever been thought of as being aquatic or amphibious – only the sauropods, but there is quite convincing evidence that these animals probably only ventured into water occasionally. Finally, anatomical evidence of hadrosaurids' diet and of their physiology demonstrates that these animals were principally terrestrial.

The skeleton of this hadrosaurid is similar to that of an iguanodontid. It had an enlarged hind leg, a long tail balancing the front end of the body, a flexible neck and small front legs. The trellis of bony tendons attached to the vertebral spines of the back tied the vertebrae ▶

***Above: Edmontosaurus* was one of the larger hadrosaurids, up to 42ft (1m) long. Perhaps its most distinctive feature was the low area on top of the skull near the front, which may have been covered with loose skin that could be inflated. This sac on its nose could perhaps have been used as a resonator to produce distinctive calls to attract or warn members of its group, rather in the manner that elephant seals do today.**

together so that the body did not sag either side of the pelvic girdle. Although early workers thought that hadrosaurids were aquatic animals we can see that the skeleton is designed to support weight on land – the strong back legs acting as weight-bearing pillars and trellis-strengthened vertebral column both demonstrate this. However, the deep tail shows that hadrosaurids also ventured into water. The long spines below the tail vertebrae (haemal spines) would increase the surface area of the tail, making it more effective for lashing through the water and providing room for muscle attachment.

The hadrosaurid hand has been described as 'paddle-like' and this is probably easier to appreciate if you imagine a mitten of skin covering the bones. Some of the finger bones have been reduced but the claws of the first two fingers are large and hoof-like. The foot was very similar to that of iguanodontids except that the toe bones tended to be a little shorter. It exhibits the same adaptations to support the weight of a large animal – compact, robust toe bones, spreading toes to support the weight over a larger area and a powerfully built ankle.

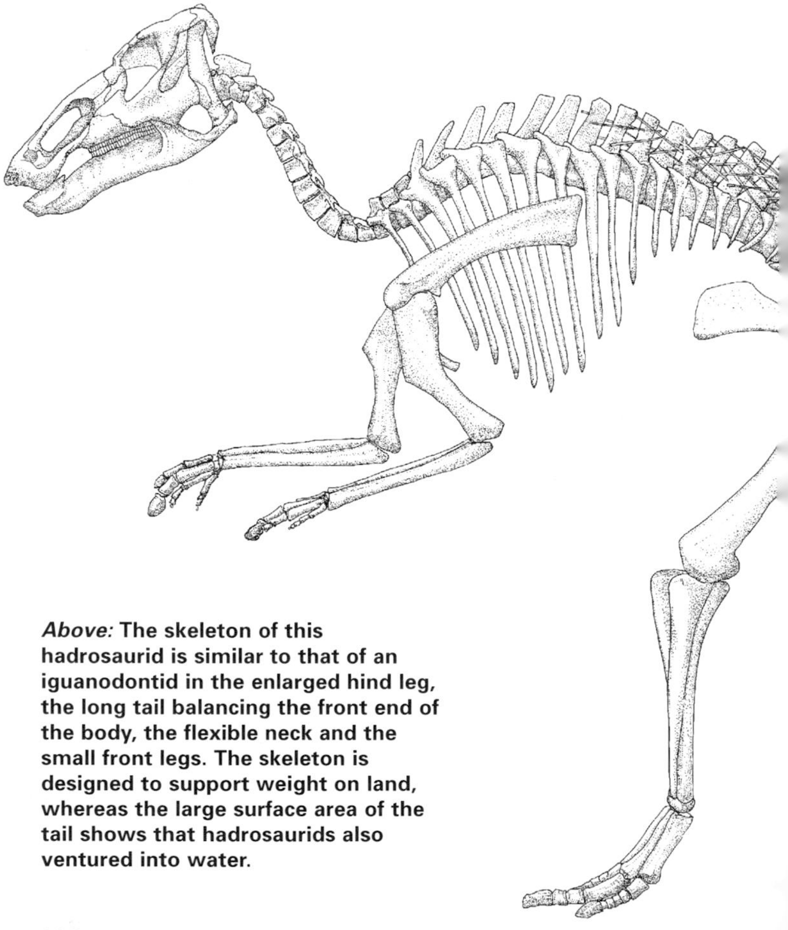

Above: **The skeleton of this hadrosaurid is similar to that of an iguanodontid in the enlarged hind leg, the long tail balancing the front end of the body, the flexible neck and the small front legs. The skeleton is designed to support weight on land, whereas the large surface area of the tail shows that hadrosaurids also ventured into water.**

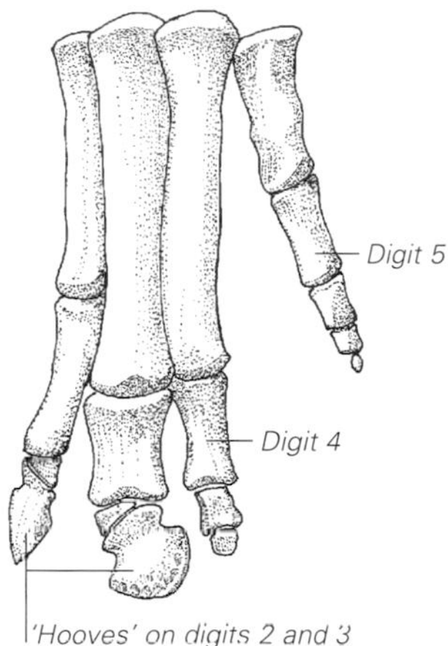

Above: **The drawing illustrates the so-called 'paddle-like' hand of *Edmontosaurus*.**

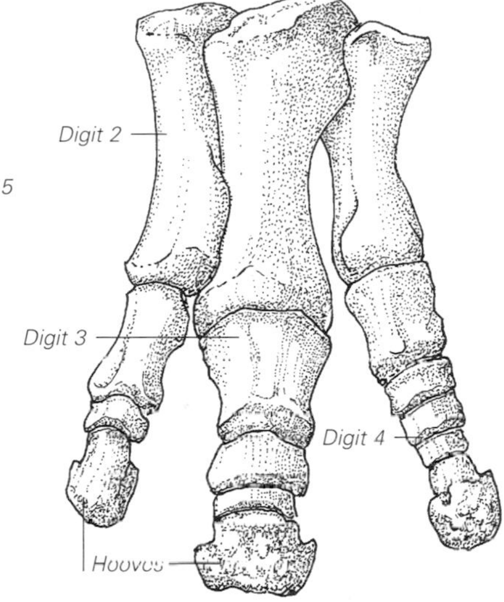

Above: **The foot is very similar to that of iguanodontids except that the toe bones tend to be a little shorter. We see the same adaptations to support the weight of a large animal – compact, robust toe bones, spreading toes to support the weight over a larger area and a powerfully built ankle.**

Kritosaurus

Period: Middle to late Cretaceous. **Family:** Hadrosaurids.
Where found: North America.
Estimated length: 30ft (9m).

The remains of the first hadrosaur were excavated by William Parker Foulke in New Jersey. Apparently Foulke had heard that many large reptile bones, probably vertebrae, had been excavated from the pit about twenty years earlier, but these remains had been scattered and lost. So in 1858 Foulke relocated the pit, which had been filled in and was overgrown again, and reexcavated it in the hope of finding more of the same animal. At a depth of about 10 feet (3m) he discovered a pile of

fossil bones , including twenty-eight vertebrae, teeth and bones of the forelimb, hindlimb and pelvis. These remains were described by Joseph Leidy in 1858 and if complete would probably have resembled *Kritosaurus*. Leidy immediately recognized similarities between the shape of the teeth of this new animal and the British dinosaur *Iguanodon*. However, *Iguanodon* was at this time rather poorly known, having been described from fragmentary remains only, and was ▶

Below: **A medium-sized crestless hadrosaur, Kritosaurus had a deep, narrow face with a rounded hump in front of the eyes, which may have been a sexual recognition signal.**

believed to look rather like a giant reptilian rhinoceros. Leidy quickly recognized that although *Hadrosaurus* had teeth like those of *Iguanodon*, it did not look at all like a reptilian rhinoceros because its front legs were much shorter than its back ones.

So it was that Leidy was able to provide a much more accurate picture of the shape and proportions of ornithopod dinosaurs from the fortunate discovery of a single incomplete skeleton.

A medium-sized crestless hadrosaur, *Kritosaurus* ('chosen reptile') was very similar to *Hadrosaurus* in many respects. *Kritosaurus* had a deep narrow face with a rounded hump above the nostrils in front of the eyes, which was probably covered with thick skin in life. Both of these hadrosaurids also had a mass of reinforcing bony rods along the spines of the back. *Hadrosaurus* probably grew to about the same length as *Kritosaurus*. It has been suggested that the female *Kritosaurus* did not have the bump on the nose. It may therefore have been a sexual recognition characteristic.

The way in which hadrosaurids fed has been the subject of much fascination, specifically how they moved their jaws while chewing. At first it was thought that hadrosaurids were able to slide their lower jaw backwards and forwards to produce a grinding action on the food trapped between the teeth. This was supposed to be possible because the jaw hinge was quite loose to allow the jaw to slide, and because they had special muscles that were able to pull the jaw backwards and forwards. This model indicated that these animals chewed their food in the same way as rats and elephants do today. However, further detailed study of hadrosaurid teeth and jaws proved that their jaws could not have worked in this way. The arguments are quite detailed, but put very simply can be expressed in this way. The grinding ability of teeth depends on their roughness. The example of the carpenter's rasp is a very good one. Teeth can create this 'roughness' by being made of different materials (enamel, which is very hard and covers human teeth, and dentine, which is slightly softer). As teeth are worn down with use, they develop ridges of resistant enamel separated by grooves of softer dentine. In hadrosaurids the ridges of enamel are found arranged along the length of the jaw. If the jaws moved only backwards and forwards the enamel ridges on the teeth in one jaw would wear against the softer dentine of the teeth in the other jaw, producing huge grooves; such grooves are never seen in hadrosaurid teeth. However, if the jaws moved in the normal way – up and down rather than backwards and forwards – the ridges of enamel in the jaws would rub past one another, crushing and slicing the food trapped between them and also maintaining even wear across the grinding surface.

Very powerful jaw muscles and abrasive batteries of teeth seem to have been important developments in later omithopods such as the iguanodontids and hadrosaurids and in fact may be largely responsible for the dramatic evolution of these animals in the Cretaceous Period, both these groups becoming very abundant (hadrosaurid fossils are extremely common in late Cretaceous rocks in North America and Asia). It is possible that the proliferation of hadrosaurids (with their very efficient jaws) mirrors changes that took place in the type of plants living in the world during the Cretaceous Period. This time marks the arrival of the first flowering plants and it is tempting to propose that the apparent success of the ornithopods was a reflection of their greater ability to feed upon these newly evolved plants.

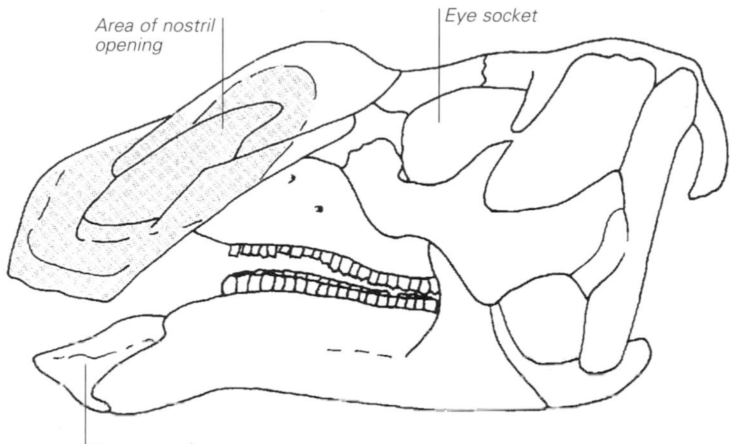

Above: **'Hadrosaurids' had duck-like beaks but little development of the crest, as can be seen from the size of the regions coloured red, which delineates the area of the nasal passages. The back of the skull in all forms does not change very much but even the crestless forms show some variation in their snouts. Unlike *Bactrosaurus* and *Anatosaurus, Kritosaurus* has an unusual bump on its nose.**

Below: **The pelvis of crested hadrosaurs is quite distinct from that of non-crested types. The front pelvic bone (pubis) in the crested hadrosaurs has a large, plate-like extension and the rear pelvic bone (ischium) is wide and has quite a large, hook-like process on the lower end. *Kritosaurus* was a non-crested hadrosaur.**

Non-crested hadrosaurid pelvis **Crested hadrosaurid pelvis**

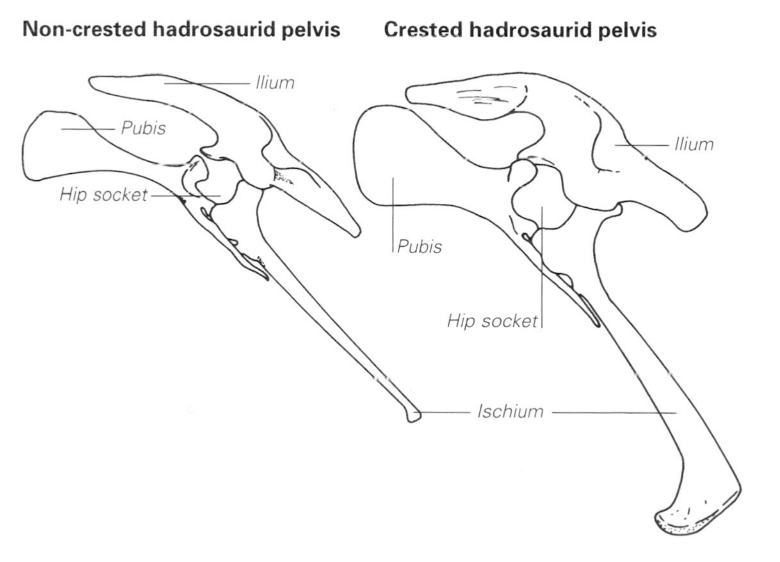

Hadrosaurids II

Hadrosaurid fossils are known in western and eastern North America, Central and South America, Europe and Asia (Mongolia, China and Japan). The most likely reason for the distribution of hadrosaurids across the northern continents and their virtual absence from the southern continents would seem to be the relative position of the various continents at the time when they first evolved. In the mid-Cretaceous the southern continent, Gondwanaland (present-day South America, Africa, India, Australia and Antarctica), was separated from the northern continent, Laurasia, by a large sea composed of Tethys to the east and the beginnings of the Atlantic Ocean to the west. That the north-south barrier was not absolute is, however, proven by the recent discovery of hadrosaurids in South America, which were probably able to migrate to South America across an island chain.

The hadrosaurids themselves continue the typical anatomical plan seen in the iguanodontids with relatively few changes. There are subtle differences between them too. *Edmontosaurus* is rather more lightly built than Parasaurolophus and has lower spines along the backbone, while the bones of the pelvis have a strikingly different shape. The really obvious differences between the various species of hadrosaur, however, are to be found in their heads. Some hadrosaurs, such as *Edmontosaurus, Anatosaurus, Bactrosaurus* and *Kritosaurus* – so-called 'hadrosaurines' – have very broad, duck-like beaks but generally lack elaborate ridges or crests of bone on the head. By contrast, 'saurolophines' such as *Saurolophus, Maiasaura* and *Tsintaosaurus*

show the development of a spine-like outgrowth from the top of the head. The other variety of hadrosaurids is the so-called 'lambeosaurines', which have much larger hollow or tubular crests of bone on their heads – *Parasaurolophus* and *Corythosaurus* are quite typical examples.

The earliest known types of hadrosaurids seem to be the 'hadrosaurines'; these are found on all continents and appear to rise in abundance until the very end of the Cretaceous. The 'saurolophines' seem never to have been particularly abundant at any time in their history in North America, apparently going extinct before the end of the period, but they may have been more successful in Asia. Finally, the 'lambeosaurines' seem to have been particularly abundant, outnumbering all other hadrosaurids in the middle part of the late Cretaceous of western North America but declining rapidly towards the end of the period. Curiously, to date there are no reliable fossils of any 'lambeosaurines' from Asia.

If the curious waxing and waning of these groups of hadrosaurid is not simply an accident of collecting but a reflection of their natural numbers, then some interesting questions come to mind. Why were the crested 'lambeosaurine' hadrosaurids so successful earlier than the flat-headed types? Why were the 'saurolophines' never particularly abundant in North America and why do 'lambeosaurines' appear not to have inhabited Asia? Renewed collecting should provide the answers to some of these questions.

Left: **Although the general consensus now is that hadrosaurids were not primarily aquatic animals, their characteristic deep tails and paddle-like hands are evidence that they were certainly capable of swimming. It is possible that when threatened by a tyrannosaurid predator they would retreat to the safety of deep water, as these *Parasaurolophus* are doing.**

Tsintaosaurus

Period: Late Cretaceous. **Family:** Hadrosaurids.
Where found: China.
Estimated length: 25ft (7m).

'Saurolophines' such as *Saurolophus* ('ridged reptile'), *Maiasaura* ('good mother reptile') and *Tsintaosaurus* ('reptile from Tsintao') show the development of a spine-like outgrowth from the top of the head. The spine of *Tsintaosaurus* is particularly odd because, unlike the others of this general type, it is a hollow tube that projects forward from the top of the head, just like the horn of the legendary unicorn.

One extremely novel suggestion concerning crest function in hadrosaurids, specifically the 'lambeosaurines', was that it may form an ideal deflector of low branches. Perhaps such animals lived in quite heavily wooded areas and used the 'deflector' arrangement in order to crash through heavy foliage to escape from predators, without damaging their heads. At the moment it is impossible to tell whether 'lambeosaurines' were indeed confined to heavily forested areas. Also, it is not possible in all cases to reconcile the crest shape of hadrosaurids with the proposed function. The long, slender, unicorn-like spike of

Tsintaosaurus is an obvious case in point: it would certainly not survive impacts against branches.

Saurolophus and *Tsintaosaurus* and the other 'saurolophines' probably possessed inflatable flaps of skin over their nostrils, which may not only have served as resonators to produce loud snorts (perhaps ather like the roars produced by elephant seals, which have very bulbous noses), but also have formed inflatable (perhaps highly coloured) display structures. Such visual signals play a prominent part in the lives of present-day reptiles; many have highly colourful dewlaps that are used as flash signals for courtship and various other behaviours.

A superb specimen of *Tsintaosaurus spinorhinus* stands re-onstructed in the Institute of Vertebrate Palaeontology in Beijing. It omes from late Cretaceous rocks of Laiyang County, Shandong, China.

Left. ***Tsintaosaurus*** **was one of the most unusual crested hadrosaurs since its crest pointed forwards. It took the form of a hollow tube, which stood straight up between the eyes. Despite its unique crest the remainder of the skull and skeleton seem to indicate that** ***Tsintaosaurus*** **is related to** ***Saurolophus*****.**

Saurolophus

Period: Late Cretaceous. **Family:** Hadrosaurids.
Where found: North America and Asia.
Estimated length: 30-40ft (9-12m).

Saurolophus ('ridged reptile') had a prominent bony ridge on the top of its skull, which ran back into a small spike. The exact shape and size of the spike varied considerably between the several species of *Saurolophus* that have been described from North America and Asia. For example, the Asian species had a relatively long spike. Like *Tsintaosaurus* and the other 'saurolophines', *Saurolophus* probably had an inflatable flap of skin over its nostrils, with which it may have produced a loud snort and which may have served also for display. These spaces may also have allowed for a greater area of sensitive skin and thus an improved sense of smell.

Variations in the size and shape of the head crest may indicate differences between males and females (sexual dimorphism) or between adults and juveniles of the same species.

There were three types of hadrosaurids. The 'hadrosaurines' had very broad, duck-like beaks and quite large nostrils but very little development of elaborate ridges or crests of bone on the head. 'Saurolophines' showed the development of a spine-like outgrowth from the top of the head. The third variety, the 'lambeosaurines', had much larger hollow or tubular crests of bones on their heads. 'Lambeosaurine' hadrosaurs were abundant in the middle of the late Cretaceous, while 'saurolophines' persisted into the very latest Cretaceous alongside the 'hadrosaurine' forms, lasting right up to the time of the mass extinction of all dinosaurs.

***Right: Saurolophus* had no large crest, rather a prominent bony ridge that ran back into a small spike at the back of the head. The spike varied in shape and size from one species to another. It was longer in Asian varieties.**

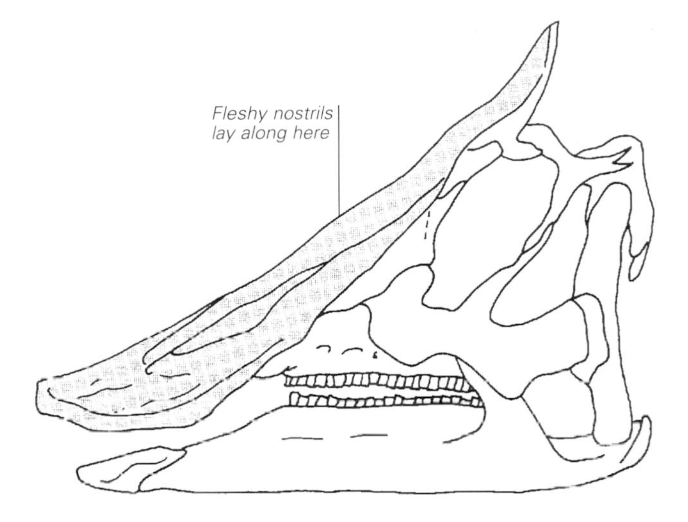

***Above: Saurolophus* had a spine-like outgrowth on the top of its head. The great variations in crest size and shape may be attributable to sexual dimorphism or differences between adults and juveniles.**

Parasaurolophus

Period: Mid- to late Cretaceous. **Family:** Hadrosaurids.
Where found: North America.
Estimated length: 33ft (10m).

Parasaurolophus ('beside ridged reptile') had probably the most striking crest of all. It was a long tube that extended back for a distance of up to 3.3ft (1m) behind the skull. *Parasaurolophus* was one of the 'lambeosaurine' hadrosaurids, having large, hollow crests.

The crests of hadrosaurids provide clues to the growth stages in their lives and the differences between the sexes. However, we do not know why some hadrosaurids had crests while others did not, nor what the crests were used for. The question has generated many theories, for example:

(i) Underwater feeding. The long, curved, tubular crest of *Parasaurolophus* was thought to act as a snorkel so that the animal could breathe while feeding underwater. It was supposed that the tip of the crest had a small air hole. Unfortunately no such hole exists in any of the crests of *Parasaurolophus* so far discovered. An alternative theory was that the crests served as air-storage 'tanks', so that these animals could stay submerged for long periods. However, the amount of air that could have been stored in the crests was really very small. A third proposal suggested that the loop in the air passages inside the crests acted as 'air locks' to prevent water from flooding into the lungs when the head was underwater. This would not have worked, and in any case most aquatic animals have special muscular valves around their nostrils for this purpose.

(ii) Salt-glands. The theory is that the crests were occupied by salt-glands that regulated the salt balance in their bodies. But if so, why were the crests so variable in

Right: **This hadrosaur probably had the most striking crest of all. It was a long tube that extended back for a distance of up to 3ft 4in (1m) behind the skull. It cannot have been a snorkel as there was no opening at the end.**

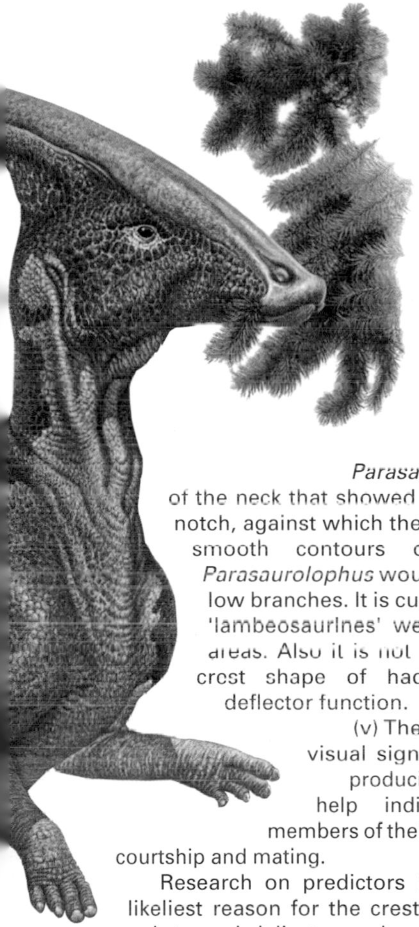

shape and how did the crestless hadrosaurs survive?

(iii) Sense of smell. The tubular cavities inside the crests may have provided space for a much-enlarged sensory area that endowed these animals with a very acute sense of smell. But again, why were the crests so varied if they were simply providing more area for nasal lining and why did some 'hadrosaurines' lack crests altogether and yet others have solid crests?

(iv) Foliage deflectors. *Parasaurolophus* had spines at the base of the neck that showed a peculiar flattened structure, or notch, against which the crest could be made to rest. The smooth contours of the head and back of *Parasaurolophus* would thus form an ideal deflector of low branches. It is currently impossible to tell whether 'lambeosaurines' were confined to heavily forested areas. Also it is not always possible to reconcile the crest shape of hadrosaurids with the proposed deflector function.

(v) The last theory is that the crests were visual signal structures and resonators for producing distinctive calls, which would help individual hadrosaurids recognise members of their own species – especially useful in courtship and mating.

Research on predictors has shown that this last is the likeliest reason for the crests. For one thing, very large eye sockets and delicate ear bones indicate that hadrosaurs had good eyesight and hearing. Second, if the external shape of the crest was the vital characteristic for distinguishing the animal, then the internal passages need not be the same shape as the crest. This prediction is borne out by *Corythosaurus*. Third, the crests would be expected to be specific to each species, that is, they should be visually very distinct, and males and females should be indentifiable. The evidence also strongly supports this prediction. Fourth, if several species are found in the same area then they should exhibit great differences in head shape – to prevent any confusion when animals were trying to meet members of the same species, at mating time for example. This prediction seems to be amply confirmed by remains in the Old Man Formation, where there are known to be at least six hadrosaurid species. The fifth prediction postulated that the crests should become much more prominent as time passed. This, however, is certainly not supported in the case of ▶

'lambeosaurines', although it may be so among the 'saurolophines'. This idea has been further elaborated in order to explain likely behavioural differences between crestless and crested dinosaurs. It is thought that the 'lambeosaurines' and 'saurolophines' used their distinctive cranial crests as visual signals to establish a dominance hierarchy. In the 'lambeosaurines' this was probably accompanied by noisy honking or bellows. The tubular crest of *Parasaurolophus* probably served as a resonator for producing distinctive calls.

Below: Parasaurolophus **would probably have made a good deal of use of its front legs in walking or wading. This form shows the special pelvic structure of the crested hadrosaurids with the enlarged front pelvic bone (pubis) and back pelvic bone (ischium). These expanded bones would have probably provided more area for hip muscle attachment. The tail here shows the flattening typical of hadrosaurids.**

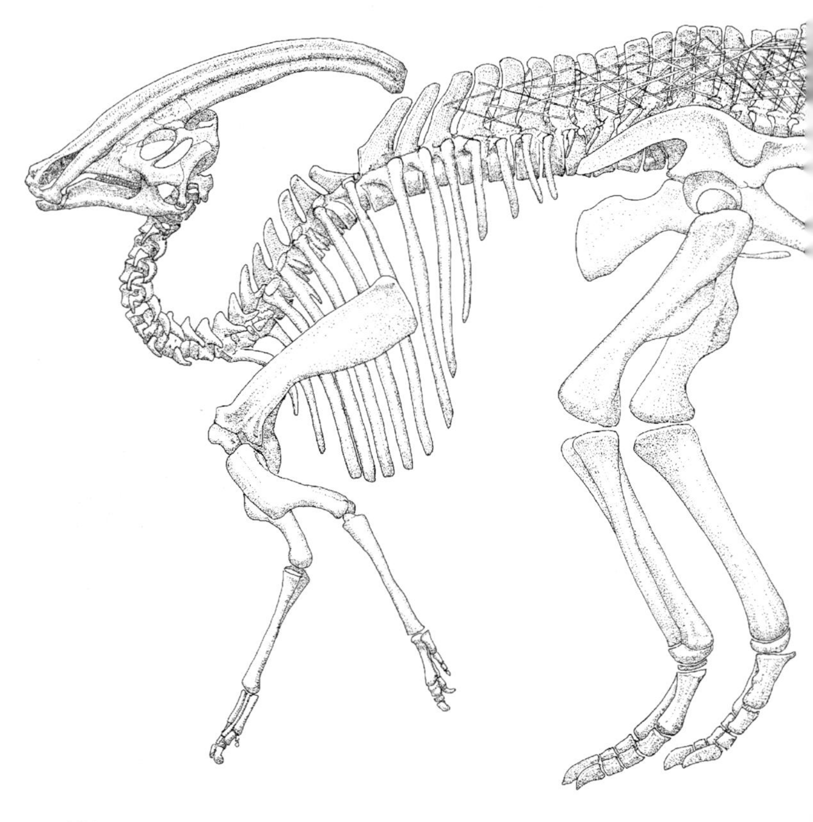

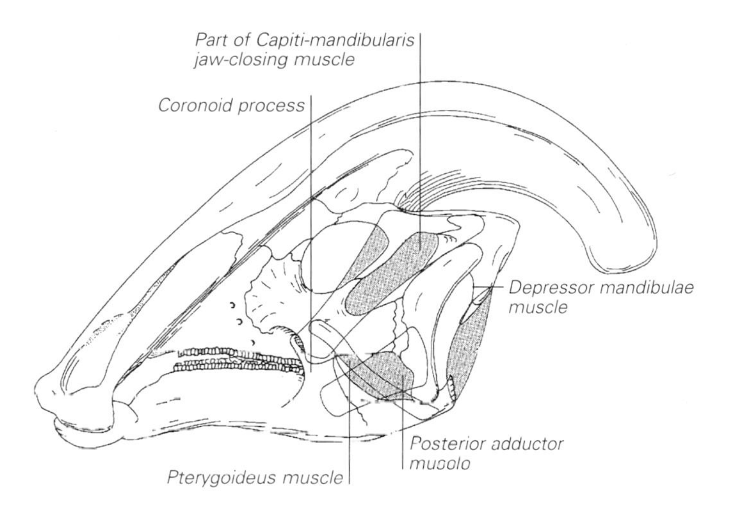

Above: This drawing shows a female _Parasaurolophus skull._ The crest is much less developed than the male's. An efficient muscle set-up is present here to make full use of the powerful tooth batteries. The capiti-mandibularis muscle runs from a prominent lower jaw process to a crest along the top of the skull. The adductor muscle is short and close to the jaw hinge and so probably acted as a 'tie' to stabilise the hinge.

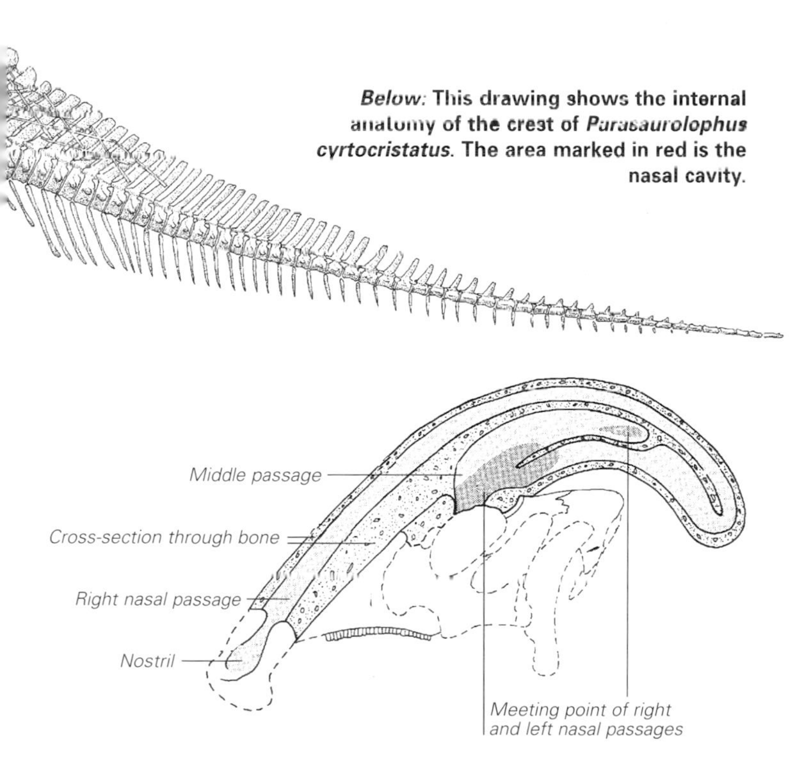

Below: This drawing shows the internal anatomy of the crest of _Parasaurolophus cyrtocristatus_. The area marked in red is the nasal cavity.

Psittacosaurs & Protoceratopids

The ceratopian ('horned-face') dinosaurs became particularly abundant during the last 35 million years or so of the late Cretaceous. Some areas of North America have yielded literally hundreds of their remains (including complete skeletons). The great majority of ceratopians were quadrupedal. Their distinctive characteristics are the facial horns, the distinctive parrot-like, hooked beak and the large frill, a bony ruff projecting from the back and sides of the head. Some of the earliest ceratopians were the psittacosaurs from Mongolia. After this, the protoceratopids appeared and they persisted until the mass extinction.

Together, the psittacosaurids and protoceratopids seem to represent an interesting intermediate step in the evolutionary line that led to the large and very powerful horned dinosaurs. Psittacosaurids retained many of the features of ornithopod dinosaurs such as the hysilophodontids as well as the very beginnings of the ceratopian features, notably the parrot-like beak. The protoceratopids in many ways seemed to continue this 'trend'; some of them became essentially slower-moving, four-footed animals with well-developed bony frills and the first rudiments of horns – very much smaller versions of the later ceratopids. Others, such as *Microceratops* and possibly *Leptoceratops*, seem to have persisted with the more active lifestyle of the psittacosaurids. These latter, however, seem never to have become as successful as the larger four-footed forms.

Ceratopians had strong, bulky jaw muscles, which must have given them an immensely powerful bite. The muscles ran forward and downward from the edge of the frill into long, slit-shaped holes on either side of the back of the skull. From there they ran straight down to attach to the raised bone on the lower jaw behind the teeth. The teeth of

***Below:* The teeth are arranged in concentrated batteries forming vertical shearing blades, which would have cut up food like a pair of scissors.**

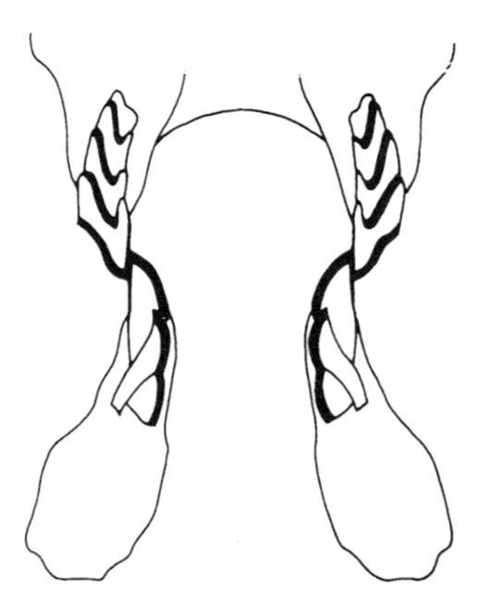

ceratopians are rather similar to those of the hadrosaurids, at least insofar as there are many replacement teeth stacked together to form a tooth battery. One notable difference is that instead of forming sloping wear surfaces, ceratopians' teeth formed vertical shearing blades – just like an enormous pair of scissors. Ceratopians would presumably have chopped their food into short, uncrushed lengths of twig or leaf. Like most other ornithischians, ceratopians seem to have had muscular or fleshy cheeks, which would have prevented the food from spilling out of the sides of the mouth.

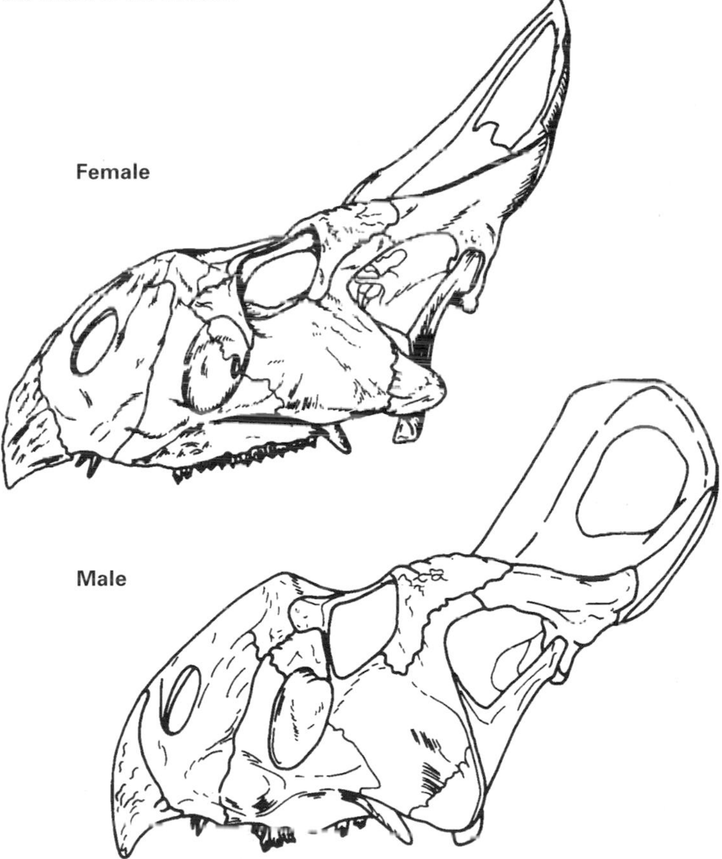

***Above:* Adult male Protoceratops have more erect frills and a more prominently humped snout than females. These differences may be related to social and sexual behaviour – the larger the frill, the more sexually attractive the male might appear to the female.**

Protoceratops

Period: Mid- to late Cretaceous. **Family:** Protoceratopids.
Where found: Mongolia.
Estimated length: 6ft (1.8m).

Protoceratops ('first horned face') was one of the earliest horned dinosaurs, and it has long been regarded as an ancestral form. The skull had a well-developed neck shield, but there were no horns on the face. Nevertheless, there were thickened areas of bone just above the eye sockets and on the top of the snout in the positions in which horns appeared in later ceratopians.

While *Psittacosaurus* has so far been discovered only in Asia, *Protoceratops* and its close relatives (together known as protoceratopids) are known from the late Cretaceous of Asia and North America. Protoceratopids are typically small ceratopians (maximum length about 6ft 6in, 2m) that have the characteristic parrot-like beak seen in *Psittacosaurus* and also a well-developed bony frill, which overhangs the neck. Although the areas over the eyes and the snout tend to be rather raised and roughened there is no strong development of the brow or nose horns as there is in later ceratopians.

Protoceratops was the first protoceratopid to be discovered. Its remains were found in the Djadochta Formation in the Gobi Desert in the 1920s and included dozens of complete skulls and skeletons of individuals that ranged from newly emerged hatchlings right through the age range to elderly specimens. in addition to this, the first nests of dinosaur eggs were discovered with these skeletons. Many of the nests were very well preserved and showed clearly that the eggs had been laid in ring-shaped clutches in shallow depressions scooped out of the sand. It is assumed that this was a nesting site, like that of the hadrosaurid *Maiasaura*. It seems that at least towards the end of the Cretaceous some dinosaurs were notably gregarious creatures, indulging in a variety of group activities such as using colonial nesting sites. These patterns of behaviour are more reminiscent of the birds of today than of most reptiles, and give us a rather different perspective on dinosaur lifestyles.

Detailed analysis has been carried out of the skulls of twenty-four of the best-preserved *Protoceratops*. Measurements of various parts of the skull were taken, for example, the height of the nose, the diameter of the eye, the length and width of the frill, etc. The results made possible the identification of seven adult females and eight adult males. The study also revealed something rather unexpected. For a long time it was thought that the purpose of the frill at the back of the skull was solely to provide a large area for attachment of powerful jaw muscles. The main jaw-closing muscles seem to have run forward and downward from an area of attachment around the margins of the frill. The edge of the frill is thickened to withstand the stresses and strains of muscular attachment. The area immediately in front of the back edge of the frill has a large, window-like opening on either side, which at first sight seems rather strange if large muscles are attached to the frill. However, the muscle would almost certainly have been firmly attached only to the edges of the frill and the edges of the 'windows', and in fact these 'extra' edges make the attachment stronger rather than weaker. There is another advantage to these openings in the frill that is slightly more obvious: they make the head and frill lighter and more easy to carry than it would be if it were a solid sheet of bone.

While it is not seriously doubted that the frill served as a site for jaw muscle attachment, nevertheless ▶

Left: *Protoceratops* is probably the most famous Mongolian dinosaur because many nests of eggs were discovered. Young *Protoceratops* were also found and even some babies that had not yet hatched from their eggs. It seems that female *Protoceratops* would lay their clutches of eggs in concentric rings in hollowed-out depressions in the ground.

careful study of the shape of the frill in *Protoceratops* has shown that its shape was not in all circumstances controlled by the need for powerful jaw muscles. After all, if this had been the only requirement then both males and females would surely have had frills of exactly the same shape – which they do not!

Right: **The upper drawing shows the skull from above, the lower drawing gives a side view. Typical ceratopian features are the narrow, parrot-like beak and the bony frill at the back of the skull. The frill provides an attachment area for the immensely strong jaw muscles and it is made lighter by the window just inside the back edge. The brow ridges characteristic of later ceratopians are not present in this form.**

Below: Protoceratops **moved around fairly slowly on all fours. The hind legs are still much the bigger, being the source of power during locomotion, whereas the fore leg acts much more as a shock absorber as the body is forced forwards. Even though the front leg now supports the front of the body, there are still trellis-like bones spanning the vertebrae, helping to prevent the body from sagging. The long tail and rotated pubic bones, typical of all ornithischians, are seen here too. The feet and hands are well built and the fingers and toes rather splayed out, helping to support the weight of this fairly bulky animal on land. The head is quite low.**

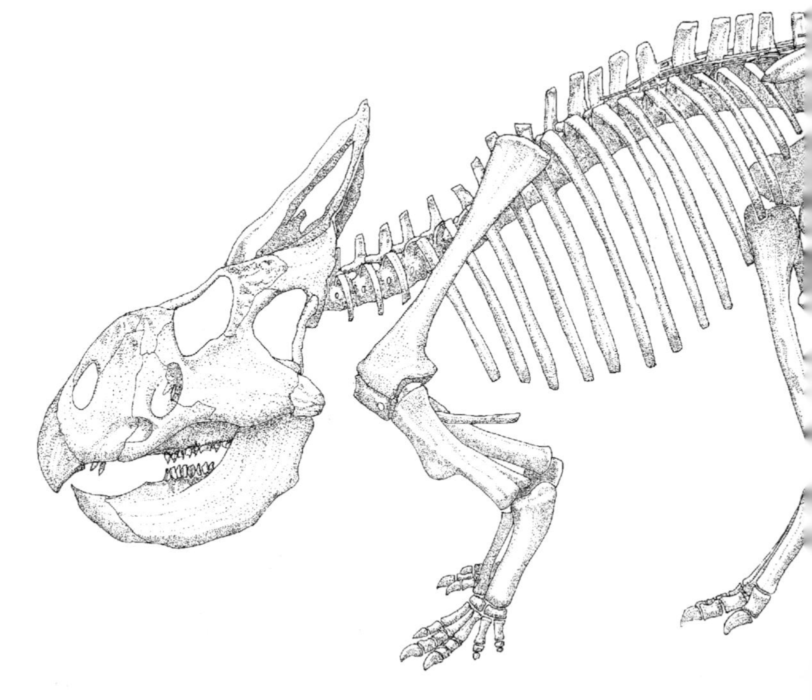

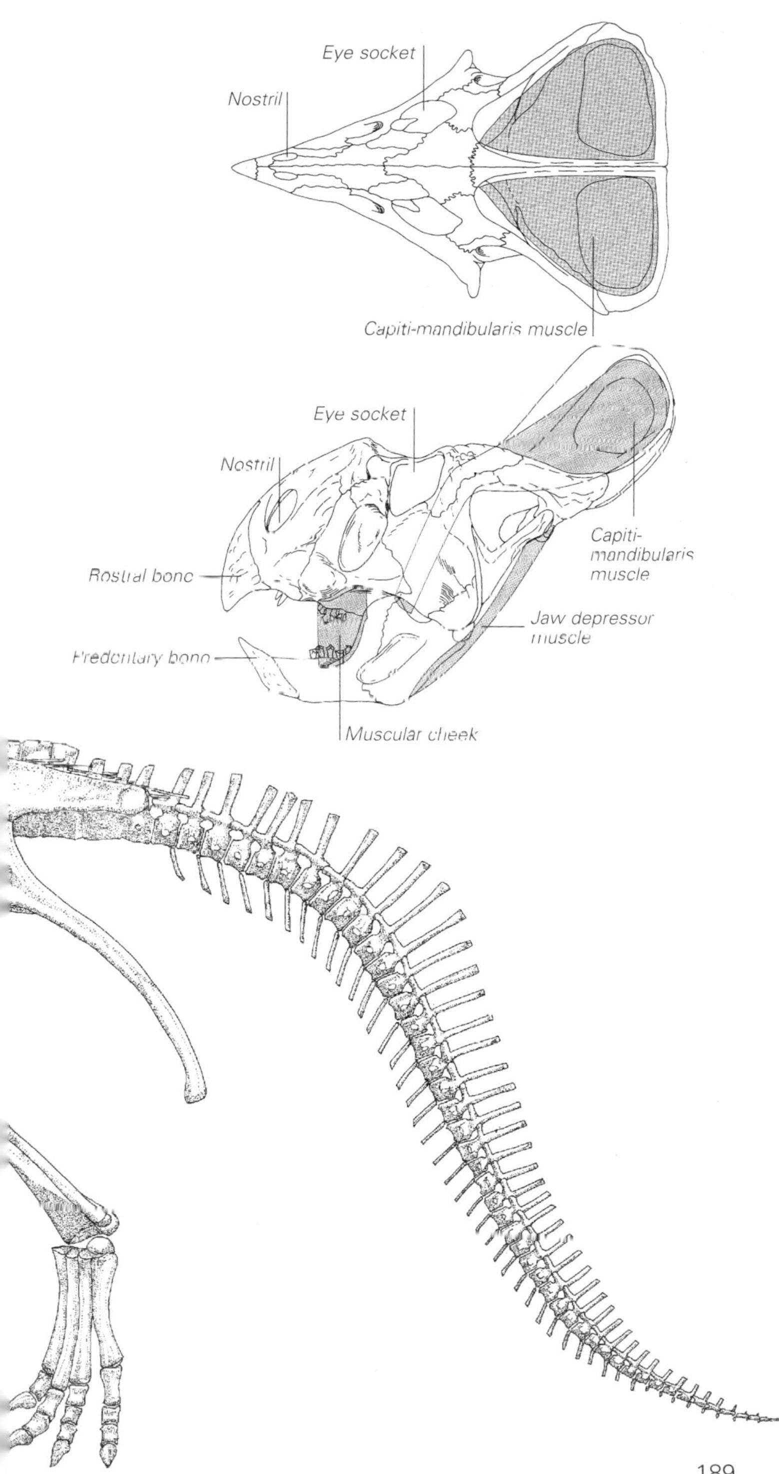

Eye socket
Nostril
Capiti-mandibularis muscle
Eye socket
Nostril
Capiti-mandibularis muscle
Rostral bone
Jaw depressor muscle
Predentary bone
Muscular cheek

Psittacosaurus

Period: Mid-Cretaceous. **Family:** Psittacosaurs.
Where found: Central Asia.
Estimated length: 6ft 7in (2m).

Psittacosaurus ('parrot reptile') does not really resemble the general description of ceratopian dinosaurs. The remains of *Psittacosaurus* were first discovered during an expedition to the Mongolian Peoples' Republic organised by the American Museum of Natural History between 1922 and 1925. During this expedition, two quite well-preserved skeletons were discovered in the Oshih Formation (early Cretaceous) of Mongolia. They were first described as different animals and named *Psittacosaurus* and *Protiguanodon*. The fact that neither of the skeletons was complete nor completely cleared of matrix caused a certain amount of confusion; they are now both recognised as specimens of *Psittacosaurus*.

For many years *Psittacosaurus* was thought to be a member of the ornithopod group of dinosaurs (hence the name *Protiguanodon*) as a fairly close relative of *Hypsilophodon*. Just like Hypsilophodon and its relatives, *Psittacosaurus* was a small (6ft 7in, 2m long) bipedal, fairly lightly built creature, with a long tail counterbalancing its body over the hips; its front legs were also equipped with blunt-clawed hands which seem to have been 'multi-purpose', serving both to walk upon and to grasp foliage for feeding. The head, supported on the long flexible neck, was apparently unadorned by the horns or frills so characteristic of ceratopians generally. The key to the affinities of *Psittacosaurus*, however, does lie in the head – in the beak to be exact! As the name suggests, these animals had a sharp, narrow, parrot-like beak typical of all other ceratopians.

More important than the shape of the beak was the fact that beneath the horn-covered part of the upper beak there is found a characteristic bone known as the rostral bone, which is found only in ceratopian dinosaurs. The remarkable overall similarity between *Psittacosaurus* and hypsilophodontids and the fact that *Psittacosaurus* predates all other ceratopians seem to suggest quite strongly that ceratopians evolved ▶

Left: An early ceratopian, *Psittacosaurus* has been considered particularly significant because it seems to show characteristics that are intermediate between the ornithopods and the ceratopians. The long hindlimbs, short forelimbs with grasping hands and the powerful skull all seem to be ornithopod characteristics. However, *Psittacosaurus* has a curved, parrot-like beak, which is a ceratopian characteristic, although it lacks the neck frill that is seen in *Protoceratops*.

from hypsilophodontid types of dinosaur. Precisely why ceratopians should have appeared when they did and why the peculiar rostral bone appeared in the upper beak is not at all clear. Perhaps a new type of plant had evolved that required this type of beak to crop it, or perhaps the parrot-beak was a new 'invention', which allowed the ceratopians to feed on plants that had previously been inedible to most dinosaurs. The appearance of the ceratopian dinosaurs coincides very roughly with the

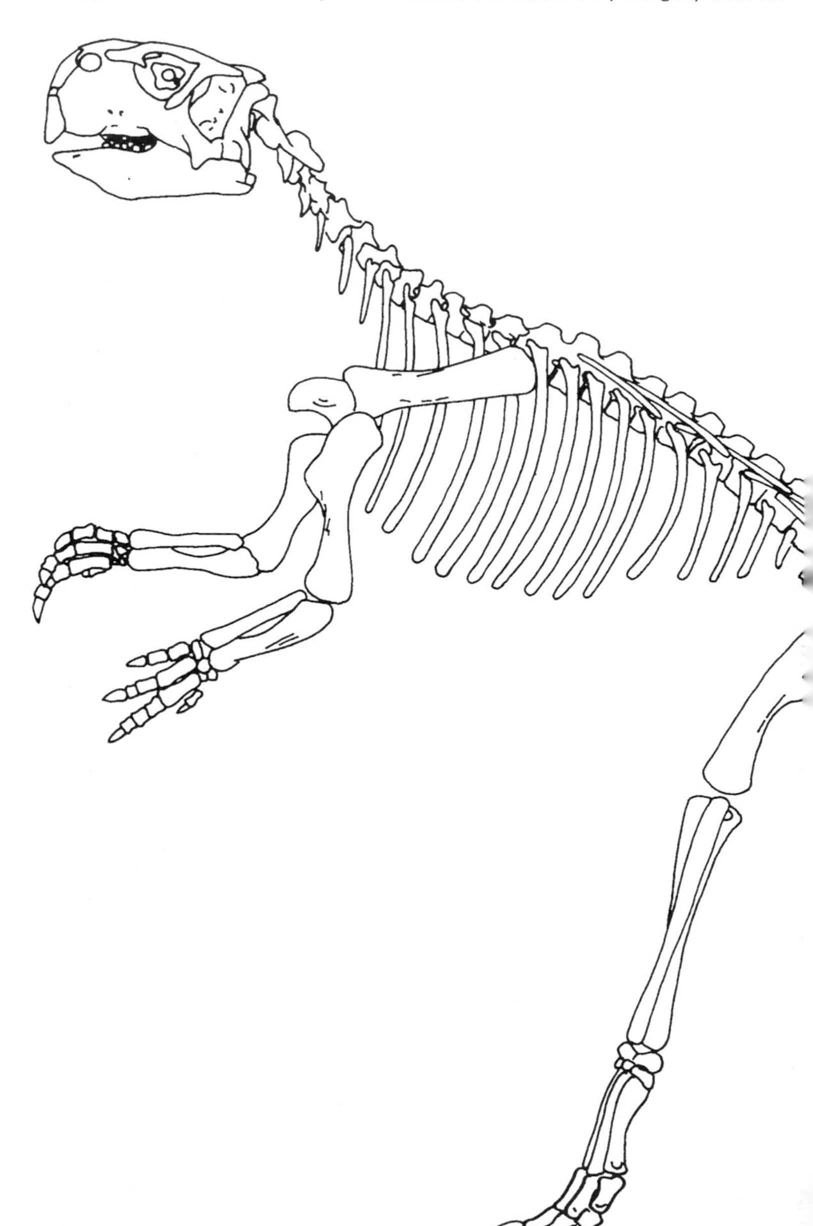

time of appearance of the first angiosperms, or flowering plants: is this the key to the problem? At the moment we have no positive evidence of the true diet of ceratopians, so this suggestion can be neither supported nor denied.

In 1980 some more *Psittacosaurus* material was found among the collections from the Asiatic expeditions of 1922-1925. This comprised the skull of one individual and the skull with several parts of the skeleton of another individual. The remarkable thing about these specimens was their size. The skulls of the two individuals were tiny: 1.6in (42mm) and 1.1in (28mm) long respectively. A simple size-for-size comparison between the original skeletons of *Psittacosaurus* and these tiny ones suggests that they could only have been about 16in (40cm) and 10in (25cm) in total length when complete. These are some of the smallest dinosaur remains so far discovered. Various features of the two specimens, such as the very large size of their eyes and the incomplete way in which the bones of the back are arranged, tell us that they were hatchling dinosaurs. Even at this tiny size, these young dinosaurs were evidently quite independent: their teeth show signs of wear, which indicates that they were already feeding on abrasive plant food. It was claimed that the minute size of these hatchlings and the fact that they already had worn teeth indicated that there was unlikely to be parental care of the young among this species. Attempts to feed such small young would most likely result in their being stepped on. However, this type of argument does not seem very convincing, because we already know that adult crocodiles (which are considerably larger than their hatchlings) show considerable parental care – even ferrying them to favoured nursery pools between their jaws. As was suggested in the case of the hadrosaurid *Maiasaura*, *Psittacosaurus* parents may well have brought plant food to the nest for the young hatchlings.

Since *Psittacosaurus* was a herbivore it probably relied upon its fleetness of foot to escape from predatory dinosaurs, in the same way as hypsilophodontids did.

Left: **This form is still very like the earlier bipedal and lightly built ornithopods. The front legs are quite robust, however, and may well have been used for walking as well as for other tasks. The parrot-like beak shows that *Psittacosaurus* is a ceratopian.**

Ceratopids I

The ceratopids or ceratopians were a very successful group of dinosaurs in the late Cretaceous Period. The short-frilled forms were particularly abundant in the Red Deer River area of Alberta, Canada.

The larger and more typical ceratopian or horned dinosaurs were first found in 1855 around the mouth of the Judith River in Montana. Among the rather broken and fragmentary remains collected were several double-rooted teeth, which were later to be referred to the genus *Monoclonius* ('single horn'). Further significant discoveries of ceratopids were made in 1872 about 80km from Green River in Wyoming and in the 1920s in Central Asia, where a systematic collection was made of dinosaurs of many types of small early mammals. Most of these were completely new to science. Of the dinosaurs, the most notable were the remains of *Protoceratops*. More than one hundred specimens were collected, many of complete animals. Not only that, but they also showed a complete age range, from tiny hatchlings up to fully grown adults. Further expeditions that went to Mongolia and the Gobi Desert shortly after the Second World War and in the 1960s and 1970s also proved very successful.

The more spectacular ceratopid dinosaurs were both numerous and varied in appearance. However, they did share a considerable number of features in common. They were all large, four-footed creatures with tails

***Below:* The finger bones in this strong, stubby hand are short but wide and capped with strong hoof-like claws, particularly on the middle fingers.**

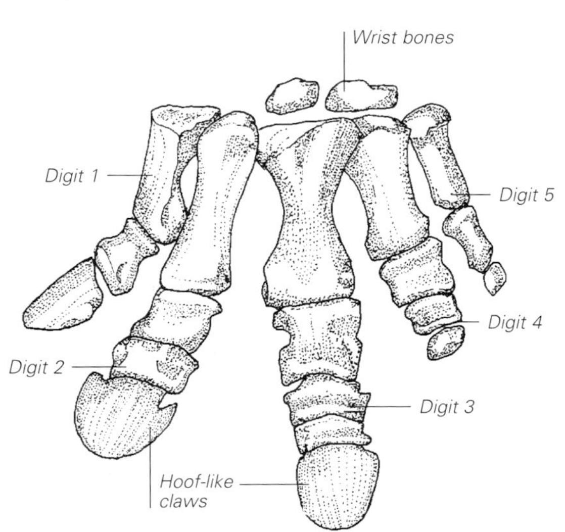

that were relatively short because they were no longer used as a counterbalance as in *Psittacosaurus*. The back legs were stout, pillar-like and considerably longer than the front legs. In fact, the extreme difference in length between front and back legs seems to support the idea that the large ceratopids evolved from originally bipedal ancestors not unlike *Psittacosaurus* or *Microceratops*. The forelimbs may have been short but the shoulder and arm muscles were powerful enough to leave distinctive patterns of large roughened areas and ridges on the shoulder and arm bones. These animals must have had extremely heavy heads, which they swung around to browse on plants and also used for fighting, hence the need for such strong front legs.

The full set of ceratopid features included the sharp beak, large neck-frill and large horns. The first three vertebrae immediately behind the head were fused together into a solid piece of bone. All ceratopids (and some protoceratopids) show this modification, which was undoubtedly a means of strengthening the top of the neck in order to be able to bear the great weight of the head.

Ceratopids may be divided into short-frilled and long-frilled types. The skeletons of all these are virtually indistinguishable, the differences being found in the skulls.

Below: **The four toes are all strong but fairly short and like the fingers they are splayed out to form a wide surface area. *Centrosaurus* probably walked up on its toes, rather than on its whole foot.**

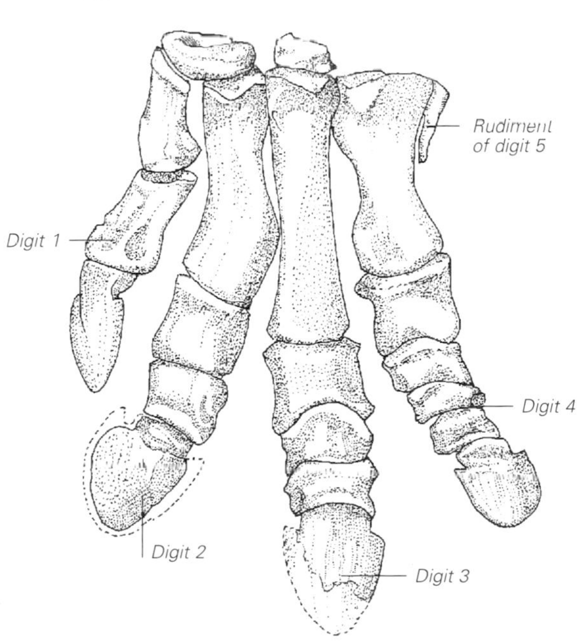

Styracosaurus

Period: Mid-Cretaceous. **Family:** Ceratopids.
Where found: North America.
Estimated length: 18ft (5.5m).

Styracosaurus ('spiked reptile'), *Centrosaurus* (sometimes referred to as *Monoclonius* instead) and *Triceratops* were representatives of the short-frilled type of ceratopid, of which there are at least two other well-known species: *Pachyrhinosaurus* ('thick-nosed reptile') and *Brachyceratops* ('short-horned face').

Styracosaurus from the Belly River of Alberta has a rather extraordinary skull; it is long and low with a very prominent nose horn like that of Centrosaurus. At first sight this seems to be a long-frilled ceratopid. However, a closer look shows that the frill is actually short with large windows in it – just as in *Centrosaurus*. The frill is surrounded with the usual nodules of bone at the sides, but these become progressively longer round the back. The six most posterior pieces of bone are very long, pointed spines, which must have formed a very prominent visual display to threaten rivals or attract mates. The horn on its nose was, no doubt, a formidable weapon. The visual effect of the spikes on the edge of the frill is quite striking. Rather than being purely

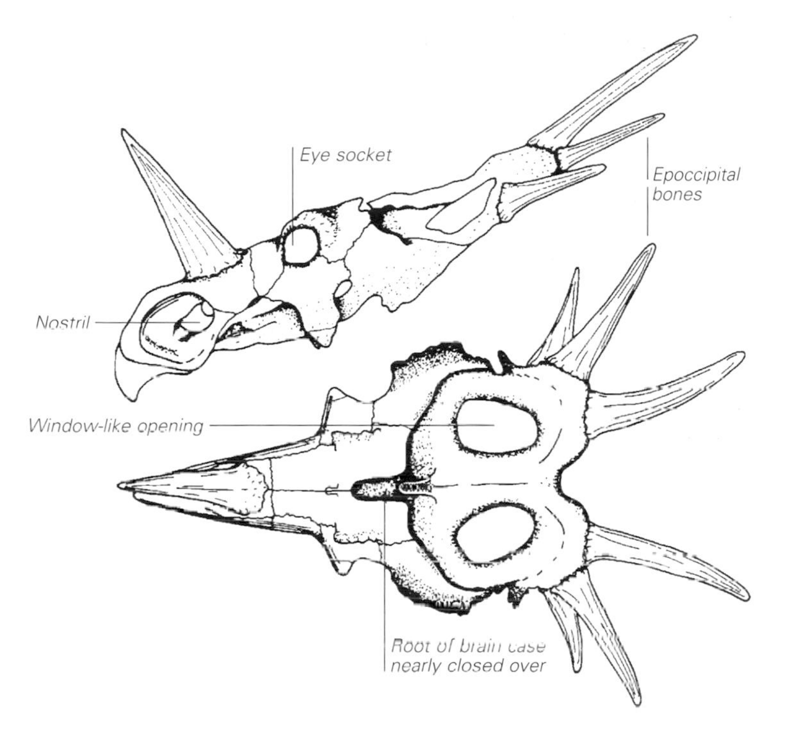

defensive, the spikes may have served as behavioural signals to rivals or to attract mates. Unfortunately, all that is known of *Styracosaurus* is this single skull, from which the lower jaw is missing, and a few other smaller skull fragments.

The heads of all ceratopids are considerably larger in proportion to body size than is the case in the protoceratopids. Some idea of the great weight of the head in the dinosaurs can be gained by looking at the structure of the neck vertebrae. The first three vertebrae immediately behind the head are fused together into a solid piece of bone, a modification found in all ceratopids (and some protoceratopids), the purpose of which was undoubtedly to strengthen the top of the neck so that it could bear the great weight of the head.

***Above:* In *Styracosaurus* the epoccipital bones have been drawn out into long spikes. Rather than being purely defensive these may have provided behavioural signals for rivals or to attract mates.**

***Left:* This interesting ceratopid had one of the most remarkable and characteristic neck-frills. The epoccipital bones – bones around the perimeter of the spike – which are small nubbins in *Centrosaurus*, are developed into great long spikes pointing backwards.**

Triceratops

Period: Late Cretaceous. **Family:** Ceratopids.
Where found: North America.
Estimated length: 29ft 6in (9m).

Triceratops ('three-horned face') must be one of the best-known of all dinosaurs. The first specimens of this ceratopian were first found in 1889. In the next three years, more than thirty complete or partial skulls and skeletons of ceratopian dinosaurs were found in Niobrara County, Wyoming, by John Bell Hatcher. Almost all of them belonged to the genus *Triceratops*. Between 1909 and 1916 some equally remarkable dinosaur collections were made along the Red Deer River in Canada.

There are ten species of *Triceratops* currently recognised from these collections. They are distinguished by their size and general proportions, but it does seem very unlikely that there were in fact ten distinct species living within a relatively short time period. It is more

likely that this number would be reduced if we were able to establish with some confidence young individuals, the normal range of variations within any single species population of *Triceratops* and the differences between males and females. A study of the type done on Protoceratops may be one way of resolving this problem.

Nevertheless, all *Triceratops* share a number of common features. They have relatively short, but solid frills (there are no window-like openings as in *Centrosaurus* and indeed most other ceratopids). Around the fringe of the frill is an even row of conical epoccipital bones. In contrast to *Centrosaurus*, the eyebrow horns are very large and the nasal horn tends to be somewhat shorter. In fact, the length of the nose horn may vary from individual to individual. The snout of *Triceratops* is also lower and longer than that of *Centrosaurus*. However, apart from these differences, the remainder of the skeleton is very similar in these two animals. Some *Triceratops* species were enormous. The head alone of *Triceratops horridus* ('horrible three-horned face') was 6ft 7in (2m) long and the whole animal was probably 29ft 6in (9m) long, even though its tail was very short. It may have weighed as much as 6 tonnes.

The division of the ceratopids into long-frilled and short-frilled types is rather an arbitrary one, but it serves as a convenient way of dividing up a very varied group of animals into two more manageable groups. By doing this, we can learn about them more easily. ▶

***Left:* The best-known horned dinosaur, *Triceratops* was one of the largest members of the group. It might weigh up to 5.4 tonnes and reach a length of 30ft (9m). The neck frill was short and rimmed by bony lumps. There were three sharp horns on the face, one on the snout and one above each eye. The bony horn cores measure 3ft (90cm) long. With the addition of the horn covering, they must have been considerably longer in life.**

However, the assumption that all the short-frilled ceratopids are more closely related to one another than to the long-frilled types, and vice versa, may not be correct. As an example of the problems that can be created by this kind of classification, let us look at the position of *Triceratops*, the best-known of all ceratopids. Although *Triceratops* does indeed have a relatively short frill, it does not share some of the other characteristics normally seen in the short-frilled forms. In particular, it has long pointed brow horns and a short nose horn: a combination typical of the long-frilled types. The question then arises: is *Triceratops* really a long-frilled type of ceratopid with an unusually short frill, or is it a short-frilled type that is mimicking the horn arrangement usually found in long-frilled types? Or does *Triceratops* prove that dividing the ceratopids into long- and short-frilled types is a complete waste of time?

One solution to the 'problem' of *Triceratops* was provided by Charles M. Sternberg. He decided that, instead of looking at the overall length of the frill, it was more useful to study the individual bones from which it was made. Using this method he was able to divide the ceratopids into so-called 'long-squamosaled' and 'short-squamosaled' forms. (The squamosal is the bone that forms each side of the frill.) By doing this, Sternberg was able to include *Triceratops* with all the other 'long-frilled' forms. However, it is very difficult to be sure that this means of classifification is better or more natural, rather than one that merely satisfies our sense of order.

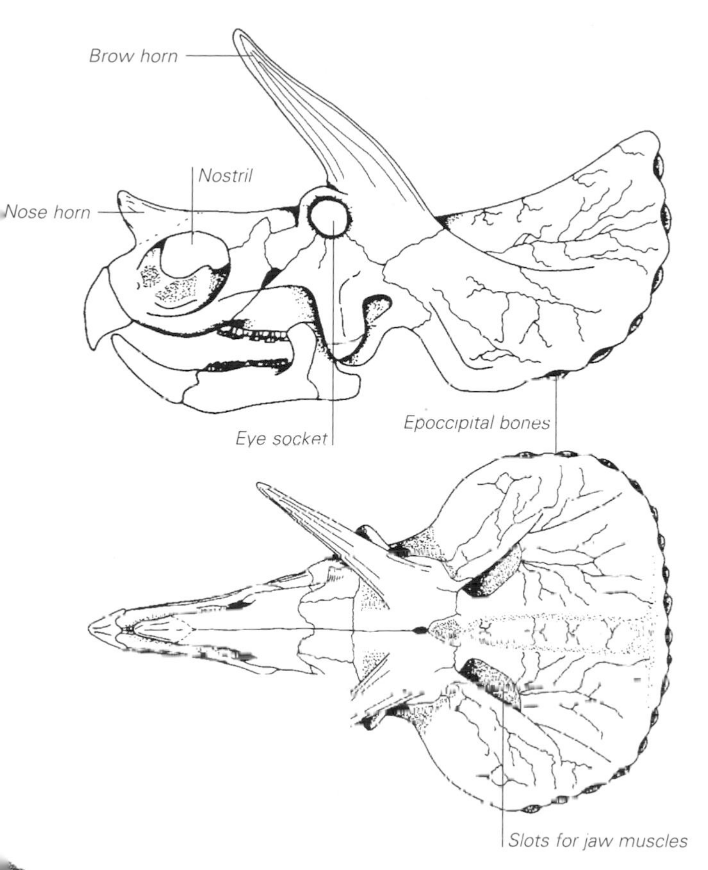

Above: **The skull of *Triceratops* has a short, solid frill encircled by a series of epoccipital bones, giving the frill its characteristic wavy edge. The brow horns are large and the nose horn small.**

Left: **An aggressive 5-tonne adult *Triceratops* charges a fully grown tyrannosaurid predator. The combination of its long facial horns and powerful build would have made it a formidable opponent for even the largest carnosaur.**

Centrosaurus

Period: Mid-Cretaceous. **Family:** Ceratopids.
Where found: North America.
Estimated length: 20ft (6m).

Centrosaurus ('sharp point reptile'), sometimes still described as *Monoclonius*, is distinguished by the rather curious tongue-shaped pieces of bone that point down into the window-like openings of the frill. These do not appear in any other known ceratopid. *Centrosaurus* has, further, a very prominent nasal horn and small eyebrow horns. Most of the features of the skull are similar to those seen in protoceratopids: a pronounced, parrot-like, toothless beak at the tip of the jaws and the teeth forming powerful cutting blades. The jaws are operated by very powerful muscles, which run down from the frill and attach to a large bar of bone that sticks up from the back end of the lower jaw. This process, termed the coronoid process, provides extra leverage for the jaw-closing muscles.

Two other features not found in the protoceratopids are the epoccipital bones and a secondary skull roof. In the case of *Centrosaurus* the epoccipitals are smallish. They were probably decorative and covered in life by horny layers of skin, being perhaps aids to individual recognition. In the area of the skull roof, just in front of the frill and between the raised ridges over the eyes, there is a deep U-shaped notch. This represents the ingrown edges of the top of the skull roof, which have grown up and over the original roof of the braincase. This secondary skull roof was probably an essential reinforcement.

Centrosaurus was fully quadrupedal. The tail is quite short and slender, being of no use for counterbalancing the body, and only its tip rests on the ground. The bony rods that ran along much of the length of the back and tail in most ornithischians and stiffened the backbone are now simply concentrated across the spines immediately above the hip. The connection between the backbone and hips is greatly strengthened by an increase in the number of vertebrae attaching to the pelvic bones. The back legs are large and powerful with broad, hooved, four-toed feet. The neck, shoulders and forelimbs show evidence of great strengthening. The front feet are broad, the inner of the (five) toes having well-developed hooves.

***Right:* Centrosaurus had a single horn on its snout and small spines round the back of its neck frill. There were two forward-pointing horns on the posterior edge of the frill.**

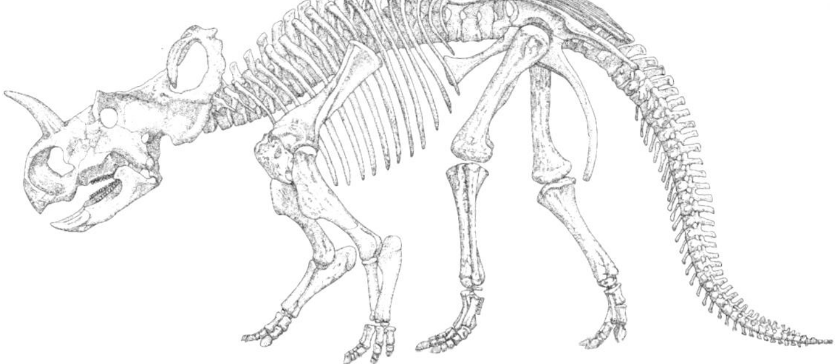

Above: Centrosaurus was definitely quadrupedal and its tail is reduced, no longer being required to balance the body. Also the trellis-like bones are now confined just to the hip region, which has been strengthened, along with the neck and shoulders, to bear the animal's weight. The tongue of bone hanging down into the frill window distinguishes *Centrosaurus* from other ceratopids in this group.

Ceratopids II

The long-frilled ceratopids were practically identical in body shape to the short-frilled forms: they were, without exception, large, lumbering, quadrupedal dinosaurs. The general pattern was for the frill to be greatly lengthened and somewhat lower than the short-frilled types, when seen in profile. As a result, the frill seems to have lain like a shield over the shoulder region of the animal, completely covering its neck. The faces of these ceratopids were typically not as deep as those of the short-frilled forms but were long and low with a tapering muzzle. The nose horns were very short and blunt and the brow horns long and pointed.

A study of the structure and function of ceratopian frills concluded that the combination of variable horn arrangement and frill shape was most likely explained in terms of behavioural functions.

(i) Protoceratopids probably used their low nasal horn to deliver sideways blows to the flanks of opponents. The moderately large frill may have been deployed as a visual display signal.

(ii) Short-frilled ceratopids tended to have large, unpaired nose horns, which would have been formidable weapons if used for fighting, but it is

likely that these animals relied heavily on bluff displays and evasive manoeuvring. They may even have been rather solitary animals, thereby reducing the need for combat. The frills may have acted as shields to deflect the horns of opponents and protect the neck and shoulder muscles.
(iii) Long-frilled ceratopids would have been able to produce an impressive frontal threat display simply by nodding the head forward and swinging it from side to side. Such displays may have reduced the need for direct combat. However, when combat did occur, the brow horns may have locked together in pushing and wrestling contests.

The front legs of these ceratopids could be held directly beneath the body like pillars or held slightly apart with the feet more widely spaced. In the latter position these animals would be very stable and they may well have adopted this posture in combat.

The best-known long-frilled ceratopids are *Chasmosaurus, Pentaceratops, Torosaurus, Anchiceratops* ('close horned face') and *Arrhinoceratops* ('no nose horned face'), all from the late Cretaceous of western North America.

Left: **Apart from their display function, ceratopian horns were also probably very powerful defensive weapons. Evidence of herding behaviour indicates that ceratopids may have formed defensive circles in order to protect their young as these *Chasmosaurus* are doing.**

Pentaceratops

Period: Late Cretaceous. **Family:** Ceratopids.
Where found: North America.
Estimated length: 23ft (7m).

Pentaceratops ('five-horned face') was first described in 1923 by Henry Fairfield Osborn. The name was suggested to recognise the existence of five horns, two more than is usual in ceratopids. The extra 'horns' were supposedly beneath and behind the eye. In fact, as was the case in *Arrhinoceratops,* the name *Pentaceratops* turned out to be rather fanciful. The additional 'horns' are in fact pointed cheek bones, which are found in the skulls of nearly all ceratopians. The cheek bones are not even particularly horn-like in some specimens and other ceratopids have equally large cheek bones. Nevertheless, we are again stuck with this rather misleading name.

All the remains of *Pentaceratops* come from late Cretaceous rocks in the San Juan Basin of New Mexico and are of a very large-frilled ceratopid. The bony frill was massive and the border was set with low, triangular epoccipitals – pointed bony nodules – which were both decorative and an added defence against predators that might have tried to sink their teeth into the fleshy neck area. The openings in the frill were large and rather like those of *Chasmosaurus. Pentaceratops* had a long, low face and a tapering muzzle. The brow horns were very long and pointed and the nose horn was of moderate size.

Other ceratopians include *Eoceratops* ('dawn horned face'), of which a partial skull was found in the Red Deer River area. It was a young individual with long brow horns and a short nose horn and a relatively short frill without any obvious epoccipitals. From the same area comes

Arrhinoceratops, named for its supposed absence of horns. In fact, this ceratopod did indeed have a nose horn, or at least a clear lump on the nose where a horn should be – but the inappropiate name has stuck.

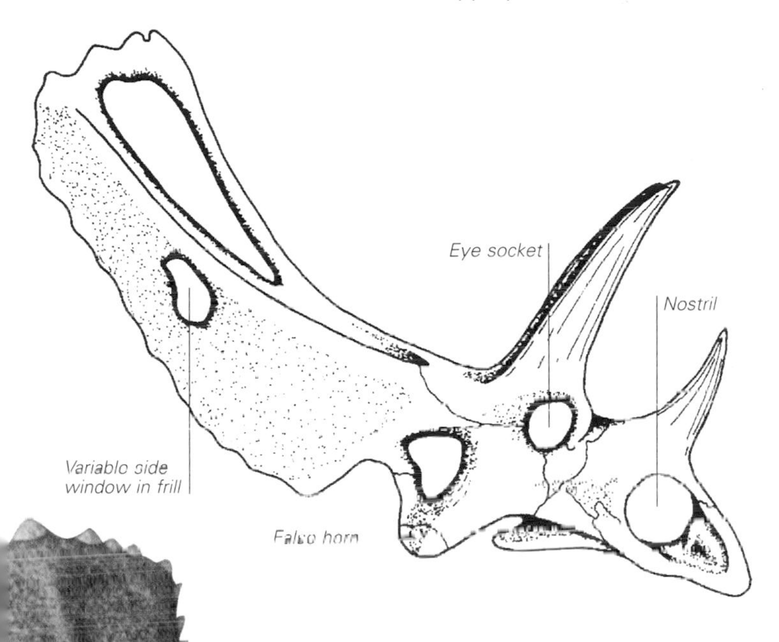

Above: **To live up to its name this form should have five horns, but in fact the so-called cheek horns are really just elongated bones and they can also be seen in other species. As in all the long-frilled forms, *Pentaceratops* has a long, low face and a tapering muzzle.**

Left: Pentaceratops **was supposed to have five horns, two more than is usual in ceratopids. The additional 'horns' are in fact pointed cheek bones and they are found in the skulls of nearly all ceratopians. It has a massive bony frill, its border set with pointed bony nodules.**

Torosaurus

Period: Late Cretaceous. **Family:** Ceratopids.
Where found: North America.
Estimated length: 25ft (7.6m).

Torosaurus ('bull reptile') was, along with Triceratops, one of the last of the dinosaurs, appearing in the latest part of the Cretaceous Period. *Torosaurus* is known only from the character of its skull; none of the remainder of the skeleton has so far been identified. The genus is represented by two species, *Torosaurus gladius* and *Torosaurus latus*, both collected in Niobrara County, Wyoming; and both represented by incomplete single skulls.

Torosaurus latus had a skull that was probably almost 8ft (2.4m) long when complete. Unfortunately the muzzle of the skull is not preserved, so it is not possible to give an exact measure of the length of the skull or the shape of the snout. The frill is distinctive; it is very long and low, with very smooth edges exhibiting no sign of the epoccipitals seen in all other ceratopids. The frill also has moderately sized circular openings, unlike most other ceratopids. The smooth contours and smoothness of the frill contrast quite strongly with the features of the only other very late ceratopian genus, *Triceratops*, which has a scalloped edge to its frill and no openings at all.

The inner surface of parts of the frill in this specimen of *Torosaurus* reveals signs of a bone disease. The bone had a series of irregular holes and dimples in its surface. On examination these lesions were found to be identical to some found in the skeletons of prehistoric Native Americans. The disease in humans is known as multiple myeloma, the pockmarking having been caused by the growth of small cancerous tumours within the bone. This is rather a chilling example of the existence of cancer since prehistory among all kinds of living species.

The other species of *Torosaurus, T. gladius*, is represented by another incomplete skull, which may have reached a total length of 8ft 6in (2.6m); this is the largest skull known of any land-living animal. The skull differs slightly in its general shape from that of *T. latus*, but whether the differences really represent different species is an open question. It seems quite probable that both of these individuals belong to the same species and represent normal variations attributable to age or sex.

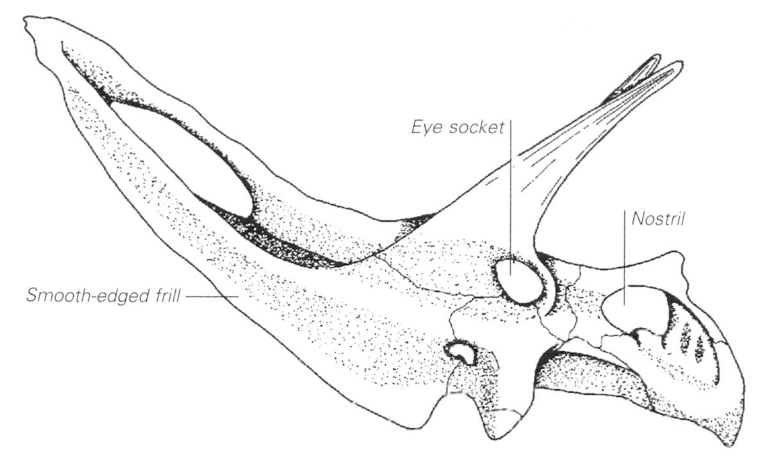

Above: Typical long-frilled ceratopid features can be seen here: the extensive frill, large brow horns and smaller nasal horn. But we also see the specialised features of *Torosaurus* – the frill is rather low and lacks epoccipital bones, giving it a very smooth outline, and its windows are rather small.

Left: The largest of the long-frilled ceratopians, at least judged from its skull, which is the only part of the animal known, *Torosaurus* has been restored here by reference to other typical ceratopian skeletons. The frill was longer than the skull itself. One specimen of *Torosaurus* had a skull that was about 8ft 6in (2.6m) long – the size of a small car.

Chasmosaurus

Period: Late Cretaceous. **Family:** Ceratopids.
Where found: North America.
Estimated length: 17ft (5.2m).

Chasmosaurus ('ravine reptile') is known from several well-preserved skulls and skeletons, which were discovered along the Red Deer River in Alberta by Lawrence Lambe and the Sternberg family. It is the earliest known long-frilled ceratopian. About 17ft (5.2m) in overall length, *Chasmosaurus* was smaller than its later relatives.

The skull of this ceratopid is very long and low. Its frill is large, indeed longer than the skull itself. The frill's thick edges are fringed by low, rounded epoccipitals (lumps of bone edging the frill), which get progressively larger and more pointed towards each of the posterior corners. When viewed from above, the enormous size of the frill's window-like openings is very noticeable. Its back edge is formed by quite a thin bar of bone supported by a thin spar projecting back from the middle of the head. Presumably all the strength of the frill lay in the thick bones lying along either side of it. The enormous size of the openings immediately casts doubt on the idea that it was used as a defensive shield. The space between the thickened edges of the frill is scooped out on either side of the ridge that runs down its middle. These two trough-shaped depressions almost certainly contained the enlarged jaw-closing muscles of these dinosaurs, which plunge deep into spaces in the head just behind the eye, before attaching to the lower jaw. This arrangement is like that seen in *Protoceratops*, but on a much larger scale.

As well as the frill, the face deserves mention. It was stated earlier that most long-frilled ceratopids have long, pointed eyebrow horns and short blunt nose horns. *Chasmosaurus* already shows a variation on that theme: the eyebrow horns of the individual illustrated (skeleton) are really quite short and blunt, as is the nose horn.

This combination of horn sizes characterises a particular species of *Chasmosaurus* – *Chasmosaurus belli*. Another species, known as *Chasmosaurus kaiseni*, is also known from the Red Deer River. In most respects the skulls of these two species are similar: The horns, however, differ strikingly: *Chasmosaurus kaiseni* has very long, pointed eyebrow horns, as seen in the reconstruction. The discovery of two such similar dinosaurs in the same geological deposit seems to point quite strongly to the possibility that the difference in brow horn size may in fact be an indicator of their sexes. We saw earlier in the case of *Protoceratops* how the shape of the nose and frill was associated with the sex of individuals.

Right: **The earliest long-frilled ceratopian, *Chasmosaurus* was 17ft (5.2m) long and thus smaller than its later relatives. In *Chasmosaurus*, as in several other ceratopids, the bony frill at the back of the skull was longer than the skull itself. The frill had large openings in its bony skeleton, but they were probably filled with muscle and covered over with skin, as is shown here. The frill was square in shape at the back and the edges were lined with small pointed bones. This species, *Chasmosaurus kaiseni*, had a short nose horn but long, pointed eyebrow horns.**

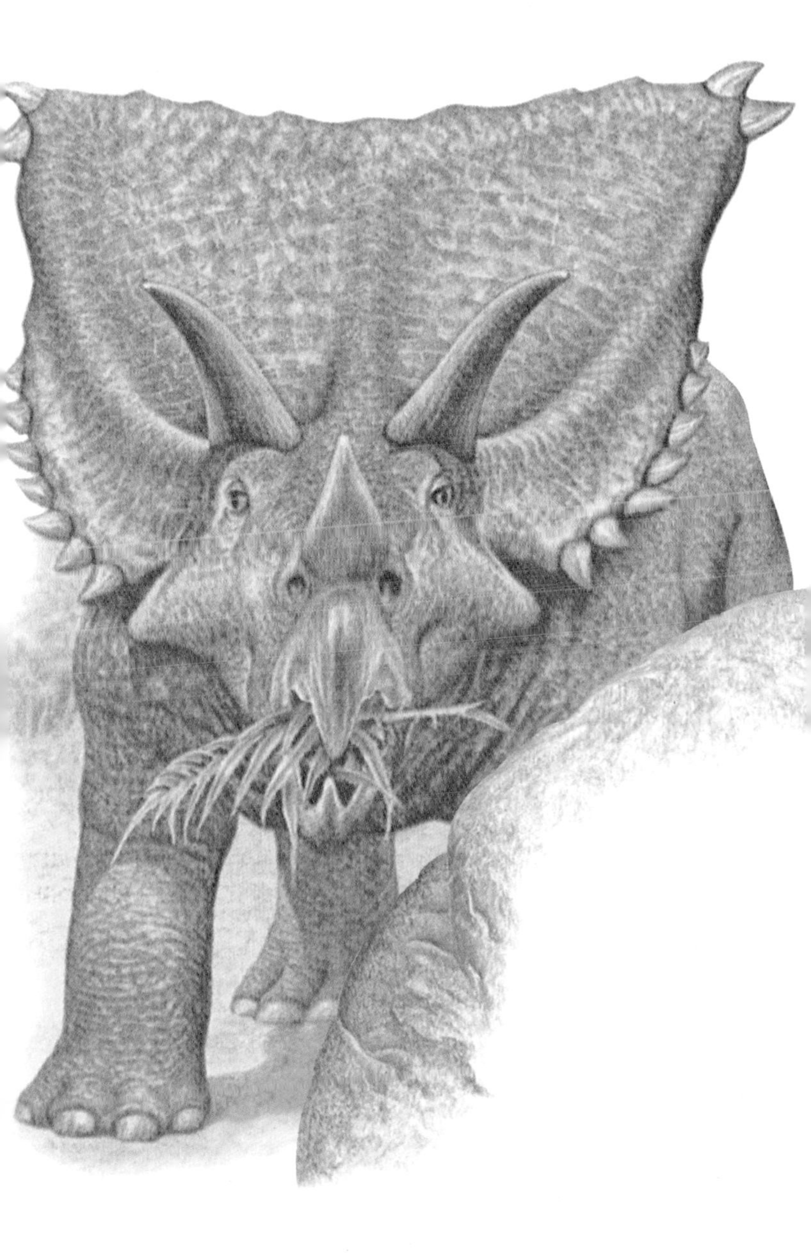

It seems equally possible that *Chasmosaurus kaiseni* (with the large brown horns) was a male individual, while the short-horned species, the so-called *C. belli*, may have been the female. Unfortunately a detailed analysis to identify sexual characteristics in *Chasmosaurus* is not possible, because there are simply not enough skulls known to get sufficient scientific data for such an exercise.

The skeleton is typical of a large, lumbering reptile. Both the hip and shoulder girdles, as well as their respective legs, are very solidly built – designed for weight-bearing, not speed. The vertebrae are also very large and strong, especially in the neck and back regions. They have extensive spines to which head-supporting muscles attach. In the pelvic area at least eight vertebrae contact each upper pelvic bone (ilium) – obviously a very strong arrangement for transmitting locomotory

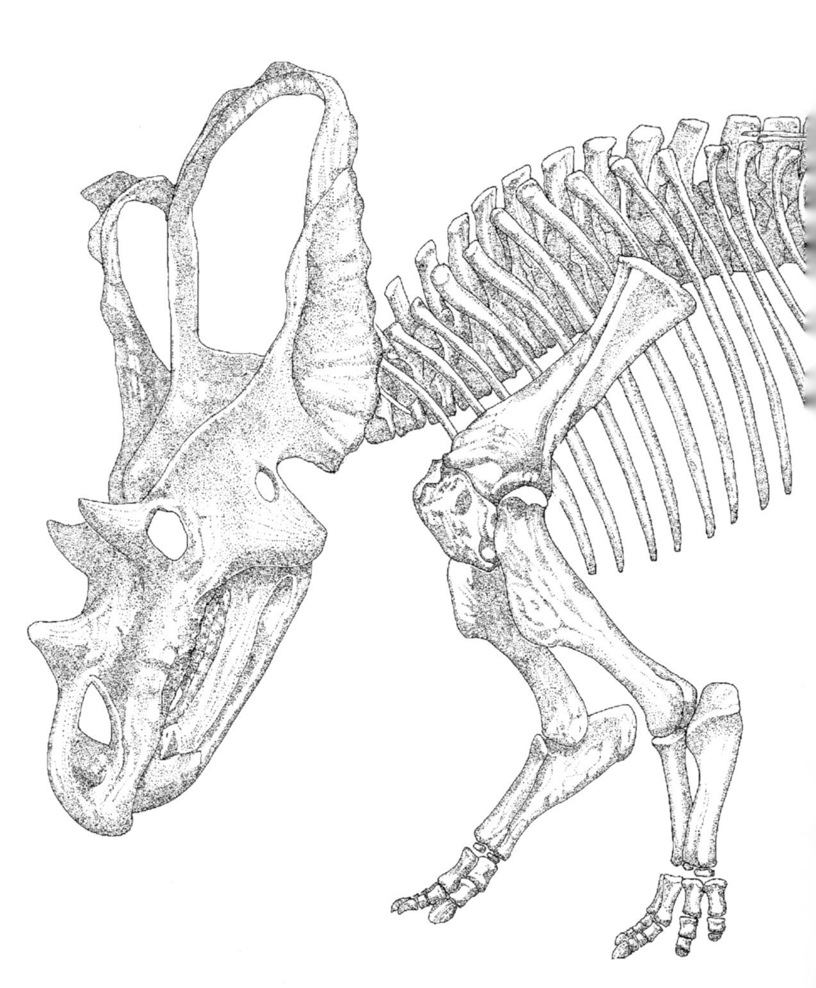

forces. Extra strength is provided in this region by the fusion of the vertebrae. The ribs are also stout. These would have helped to support the bulky gut that such a hefty animal would have needed to process large amounts of food.

Below: **This skeleton is typical of a large, lumbering reptile, built very solidly for weight-bearing, not speed. The vertebrae are also very large and strong and have extensive spines to which head-supporting muscles are attached. The ribs are also stout. In the skull notice the small, blunt brow horns – they are typical of *Chasmosaurus belli*.**

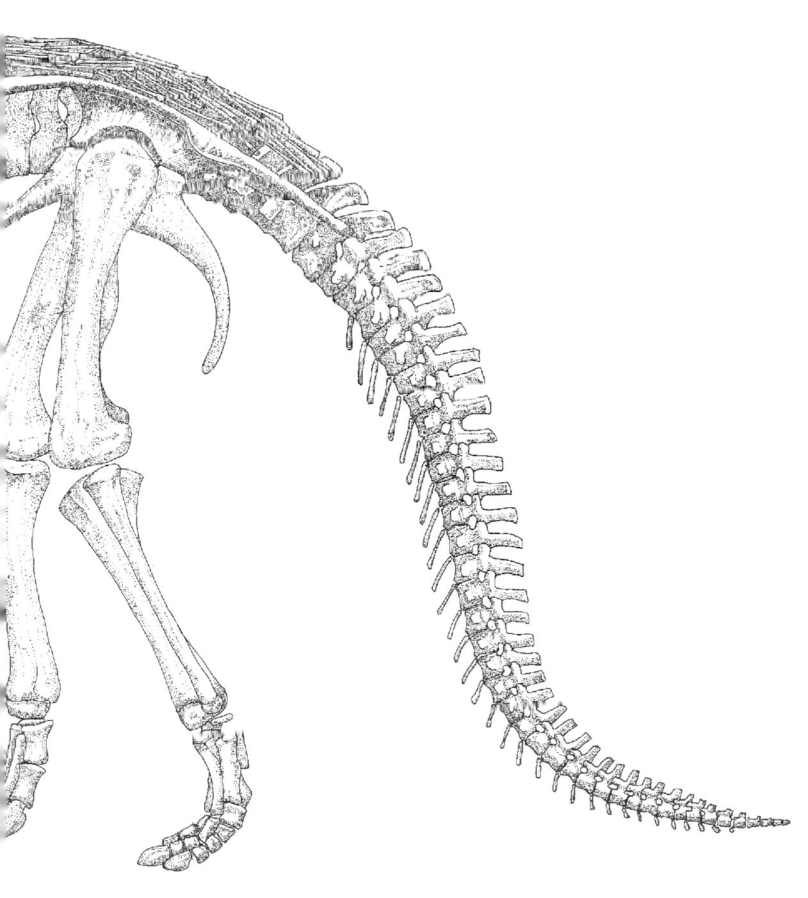

Pachycephalosaurs

Pachycephalosaurs ('thick-headed reptiles') are a relatively rare and puzzling group of dinosaurs, which lived towards the end of the Cretaceous Period. The first possible pachycephalosaur remains to be discovered consisted of a single tooth from the Judith River Beds of Montana. It was flattened and slightly curved and had serrations along its edges. This tooth was described by Joseph Leidy in 1856 and named *Troödon formosus* (*Troödon*: 'wounding tooth'). Leidy suggested that the tooth may have belonged to a large monitor lizard or some other extinct meat-eating reptile.

In 1902 Lawrence Lambe described two skull fragments from the Belly River Formation of Alberta, to which he gave the name *Stegoceras* ('horny roof'). These were shortly recognised as fragments from the back part of the skull, and so different were they from any other known dinosaur that they belonged in an entirely new family. This animal was named *Stegoceras*. With the discovery of more fragments in later years Lambe proposed that *Stegoceras* was a distant relative of the stegosaurids.

Things became a little clearer in 1924 when Charles Gilmore was able to describe a skull and partial skeleton of a new dinosaur discovered on the Red Deer River, Alberta. The material, although incomplete, gave a much clearer idea of the nature of the animals previously named *Troödon* and *Stegoceras*; the teeth near the front of the upper jaw were very similar to *Troödon*, while the head showed the great thickening of the skull roof found in *Stegoceras*.

In the 1930s and 1940s more material of these thick- or bone-headed dinosaurs was discovered in geologically younger deposits in Montana,

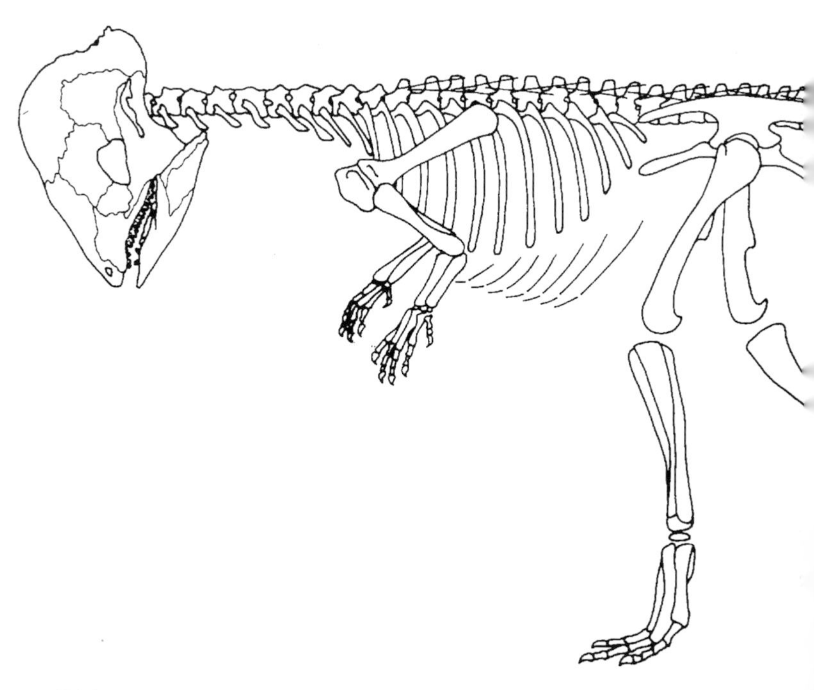

South Dakota and Wyoming. This consisted of skull fragments of much larger individuals, which were again at first referred to the genus *Troödon*. Finally in 1940 William Winkley discovered in Montana the almost complete, beautifully well-preserved skull of another thick-headed dinosaur. This new specimen was so obviously different from *Stegoceras* ('*Troödon*') that it was given a different generic name, *Pachycephalosaurus* ('thick-headed reptile'). The large size of the skull of this creature indicated that it probably had a body length of about 26ft (8m). Unfortunately, although several partial skulls are known, there is very little skeletal information, so any body restorations are based largely upon guesswork and comparison with the little that is known about *Stegoceras*. Until *Pachycephalosaurus* was discovered, *Stegoceras* and its allies were known as Troödontids. However, since *Troödon* is a dubious name (based only on non-diagnostic teeth), a new family name was chosen in 1945: the Pachycephalosauridae. This name has stuck with us to the present day.

Since those early days a considerable number of remains of pachycephalosaurs have been discovered from many parts of the world.

Below: **This diagram shows how the body would have been held as the animal attempted to butt another with its head. The skull is held face-down, so that the ramming surface of the head and the neck joint are in a straight line with the horizontally held vertebral column. The battering force is transmitted through the skull and absorbed by the backbone.**

Stegoceras & Pachycephalosaurus

Period: Late Cretaceous. **Family:** Pachycephalosaurs.
Where found: North America.
Estimated length: *Stegoceras* 6ft 6in (2m); *Pachycephalosaurus* 26ft (8m).

Because the remains of the pachycephalosaurs, or 'bone-heads', are so scarce and mostly consist of just skulls or skull fragments, it has proved very difficult to decide how they relate to other dinosaurs generally. They are clearly ornithischians because they have the tell-tale horn-covered predentary beak in the lower jaw. However, their skulls are so highly modified by the great dome of bone that they show no overwhelming similarities to any of the other omithischian groups. Ankylosaurids have thickened skulls, but these are created by the plastering of new bone on to the skull, while in pachycephalosaurids it is the actual bones of the skull roof that become thicker.

In 1974 Polish researchers noticed that remains discovered in Mongolia had an extraordinary pelvis, vaguely similar to that of ankylosaurids. On the basis of this and several other characteristics, the researchers proposed that the pachycephalosaurs should be raised to the same level of importance as the ornithopods, stegosaurs, ceratopians and ankylosaurs, and classed as a major group of ornithischians. This view is not accepted by all palaeontologists, some of whom prefer to consider them as rather unusual ornithopods.

Within the pachycephalosaur group, the animals may, perhaps, be divided into high-domed and low-domed types: *Stegoceras* and *Pachycephalosaurus* are among the high-domed 'pachycephalosaurids'; while *Homalocephale, Goyocephale, Ornatotholus, Yaverlandia* and *Micropachycephalosaurus* were low-domed 'homalocephalids'.

The largest known pachycephalosaur, *Pachycephalosaurus* ('thick-headed reptile'), was up to 26ft (8m) long. Other pachycephalosaur genera were probably only 3ft 4in-10ft (1-3m) long. *Pachycephalosaurus* had a massively thickened skull roof, which gave its head a domed appearance. The effect was enhanced by the presence of additional pointed and flattened nodules of bone arranged round the back and sides of the skull and on the snout.

Stegoceras ('horny roof') was a medium-sized pachycephalosaur, possibly 6ft 6 in (2m) long. The high dome on the skull was not so large in juveniles, becoming ▶

***Right: Stegoceras validus* was a medium-sized pachycephalosaur. The skulls are well known. The high dome was not so large in juveniles but thickened in older animals. Adult female *Stegoceras* seem to have had thinner, lighter domes than males.**

Left: Pachycephalosaurus was the largest known pachycephalosaur. Its massively thickened skull gave its head a domed appearamce. Nodules of bone around the back and sides of the skull and on the snout added to the effect of the extremely thick bones of the skull roof.

relatively thick only in older animals. One group of adult *Stegoceras* had thicker, heavier domes than another group – perhaps males and females of the same species.

The enormously thickened dome of bone on the skulls of pachycephalosaurs has long attracted attention. In 1955 it was proposed that it may have served as a protective zone for the head if it were used as a battering ram. Like most ornithopods, the pachycephalosaur's backbone may well have been held horizontally balanced at the hips. In addition, the head, instead of being held in line with the bones of the neck, is offset from it at a sharp angle. So, the 'natural' position of the

Right and below: **The skeleton of *Stegoceras* is poorly known and the reconstruction is based on comparison with other ornithischians and some guesswork! The head is offset at an angle to the neck vertebrae, the back vertebrae are held tightly together by ossified tendons, and there is a special anti-twist articulation between individual vertebrae (right). The tail was probably long and as in all bipedal dinosaurs served to counterbalance the front end of the body. Note the presence of belly ribs.**

Right: Stegoceras's **teeth were typically compressed, slightly curved and serrated. Such teeth would have belonged to a herbivorous animal and would have been used to shred plants.**

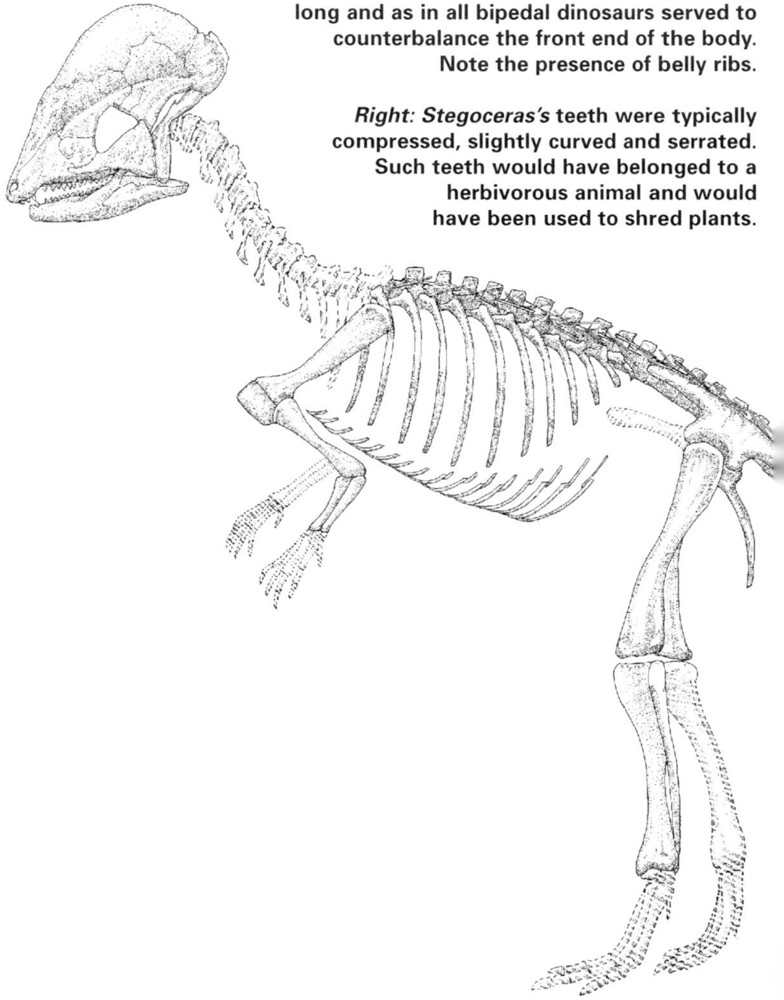

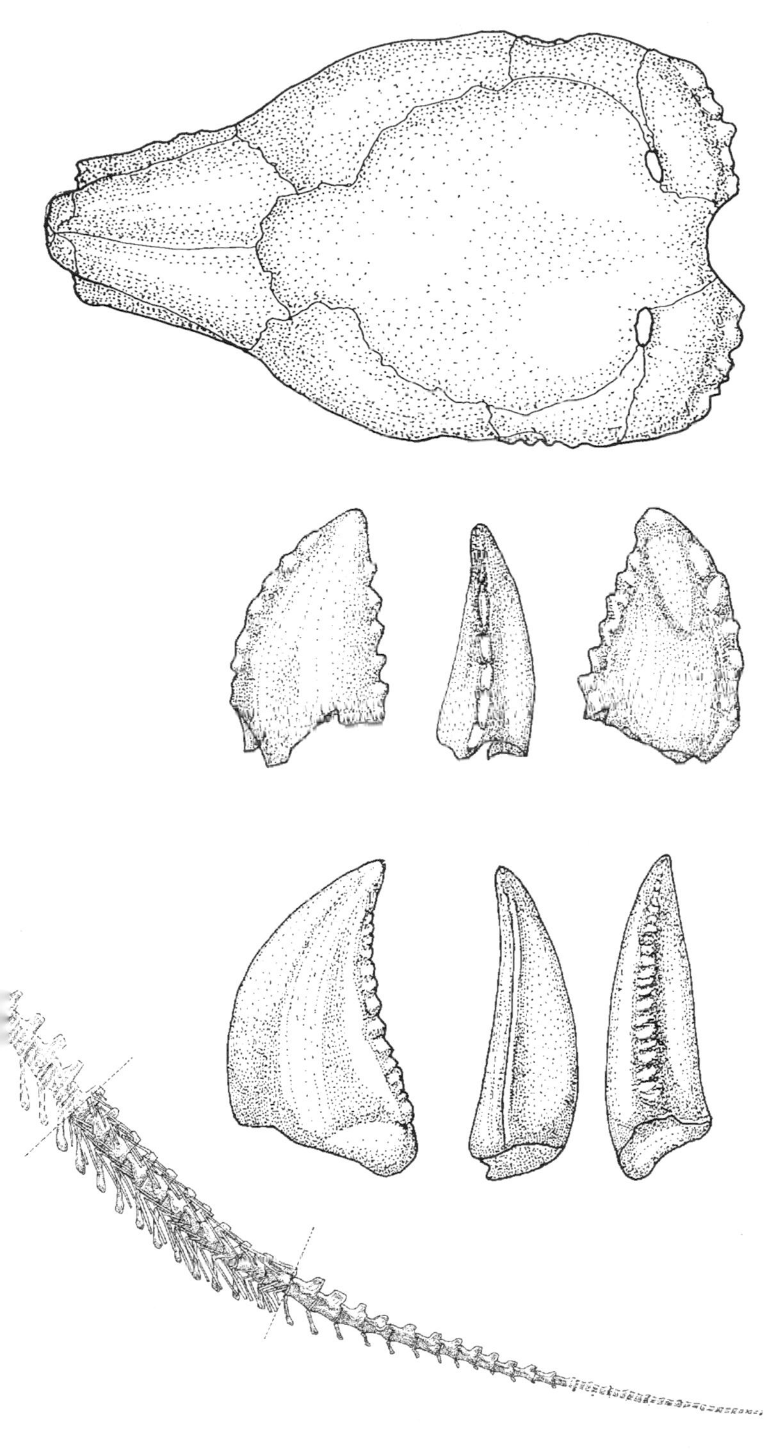

head would be pointing nose-downward while the animals walked or ran. Equally, the neck was flexible and could be bent upwards sharply to hold the head upright. However, the arrangement of the neck-head joint, which is unlike that of all other dinosaurs, did allow the dome to be held forward in a 'battering' position. Moreover, the backbones fitted together in an especially stiffened arrangement, tendons in the back were ossified and the joints between individual bones of the back had special grooved surfaces to stop them from twisting too much. It certainly seems possible therefore that pachycephalosaurs were able to use the head as a battering device.

But why would they do this? It has been proposed that pachycephalosaurs did not just employ head-down charging to fend off predators, but also as a part of their social life! As in living sheep and goats, butting behaviour is part of a way of creating an ordered society. Especially among the males, the horns serve as visual signals of dominance: the larger the horns, the more dominant the male. However, when competing males have very similar-sized horns, then head-butting is resorted to as a test of strength or endurance.

Pachycephalosaurs differed from sheep and goats in the structure of their heads. First, they did not have well-developed horns. There were small lumps and ridges around the dome on the skull roof of most pachycephalosaurs but these were clearly ornamental rather than functional. Second, there were no special air spaces in the skull roof of pachycephalosaurs: the skull dome was solid bone right through to the brain cavity. These differences suggest that the impacts of head-butting were carried straight through the skull roof across the brain cavity, giving it quite a severe shock, and then into the specially strengthened backbone. The brains of these dinosaurs were, however, much smaller than those found in sheep and goats, and quite probably there were spaces around the brain itself that cushioned it from too severe a shock.

Pachycephalosaurs may well have lived rather like sheep and goats do today, in small groups in upland areas. Their social life was dependent upon the use of the head as a means of signalling the status of individuals. In most cases the visual signal would have been sufficient. However, when similarly sized individuals met, the seniority of each would have to be decided by head-to-head pushing or butting contests. The low-domed 'homalocephalids' probably used head-to-

***Right:* Here we see two pachycephalosaurs indulging in the sort of violent head-butting contest for which their extraordinary skulls made them uniquely qualified. It is thought that such behaviour was a way of establishing a social hierarchy, allowing males in particular to achieve dominance over one another within the group.**

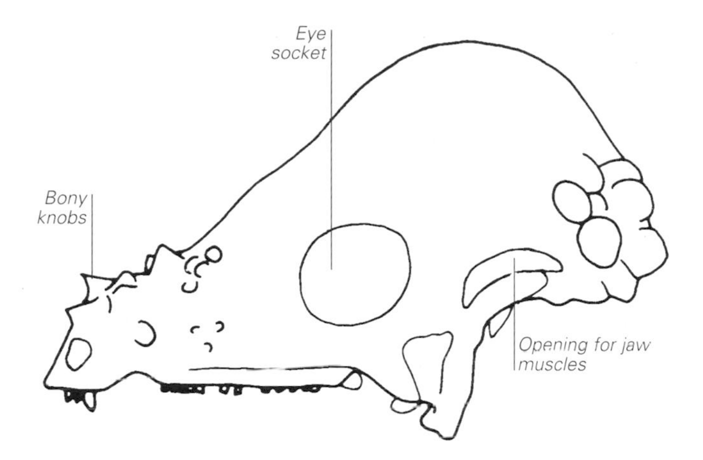

Above: **The skull of *Pachycephalosaurus* is a high-domed form with very distinctive bony spikes on its snout and knobs on the back of the head.**

head pushing contests rather than violent head-banging struggles because their skulls were not very strongly built. The high-domed forms undoubtedly indulged in violent head-butting contests. *Stygimoloch,* unusual among the high-domed pachycephalosaurids, may not have indulged in head-butting at all, relying instead upon the visual effect of the tall bony spikes around its domed head.

Homalocephale ('even head'), from which the 'homalocephalids' are named, is remarkable since parts of its skeleton are known in addition to the skull. As its name suggests, it had a flat head and it lacked the massively thickened cranial roof that most of its relatives had. Nevertheless, *Homalocephale* did have a thickened skull roof lined with nodules of bone at the sides. The hip bones of *Homalocephale* are very wide, and it has been suggested that it gave birth to live young rather than laying eggs in typical dinosaurian fashion.

Stegosaurids

The stegosaurids are a group of quite large, four-footed ornithischians characterised by a double row of tall spines running down their backs. By far the best known of these dinosaurs is *Stegosaurus* ('roofed reptile'). The first stegosaurid remains to be described were those of an incomplete skeleton found in England and illustrated by Richard Owen in 1875. It was recognised as an armour-plated dinosaur, because among the remains were found large, shield-like plates of bone. These early reports were eclipsed by the discoveries made in North America in the late 1870s by teams of excavators in two quarries: 'Quarry 13' in Albany County, Wyoming, and 'Quarry 1' in Fremont County, Colorado. Since then, several other stegosaurids have been discovered in places reasonably widely spread across the world. Their presence in North America, Africa and Europe is easily explained by the fact that these continents had all been in contact with one another up to this time. The discovery of stegosaurid remains in China suggests that they spread there quite early on in the Jurassic by means of some sort of short-lived land connection between Europe and Asia. The earliest stegosaurid remains identified so far are some odd plates and bones (*Lexovisaurus*) from the middle Jurassic of England, and the latest come from the late Cretaceous of India.

The late Jurassic was probably the most successful time for the stegosaurids; they seem to have become extinct in North America at the end of the Jurassic. Fragmentary remains of stegosaurids are, however, known from the early Cretaceous of Europe (*Craterosaurus*), Africa (*Paranthodon*) and China (*Wuerhosarus*). By the later Cretaceous stegosaurids seem to be absent everywhere except for India. The survival of stegosaurids such as *Dravidosaurus* in India is interesting, because from the middle of the Cretaceous onwards, India was isolated from the rest of the world. Right up until the early part of the Cretaceous, India nestled against the southern end of Africa and presumably shared its fauna with those of Africa. Once India began to drift away from Africa, it may perhaps have acted as a haven for the stegosaurids and other species.

It has often been suggested that the cause of the widespread waning and extinction of stegosaurids in the Cretaceous was the appearance of the ankylosaurs. The intriguing fact is that ankylosaurs are not found in India at all. Perhaps stegosaurids were able to survive in India because, through freakish geological conditions, India became isolated from the rest of the world in the early Cretaceous just at the time when the ankylosaurs were diversifying.

***Right:* It has been suggested that the plates on *Stegosaurus's* back actually fulfilled the role of armour-plating, protecting these slow-moving creatures from predators. In fact, as the drawing shows, even if the plates had lain flat on its back (which is improbable physiologically), the belly and flanks of *Stegosaurus* would still have been vulnerable to attack.**

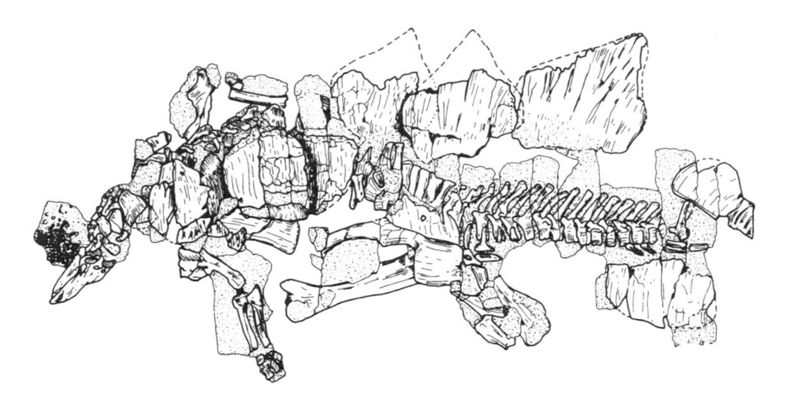

Above: This drawing shows the disposition of the skeleton of *Stegosaurus* stenops as it was found. The plates seem to lie in an alternating pattern but arguments persist as to whether this was how they were arranged in life.

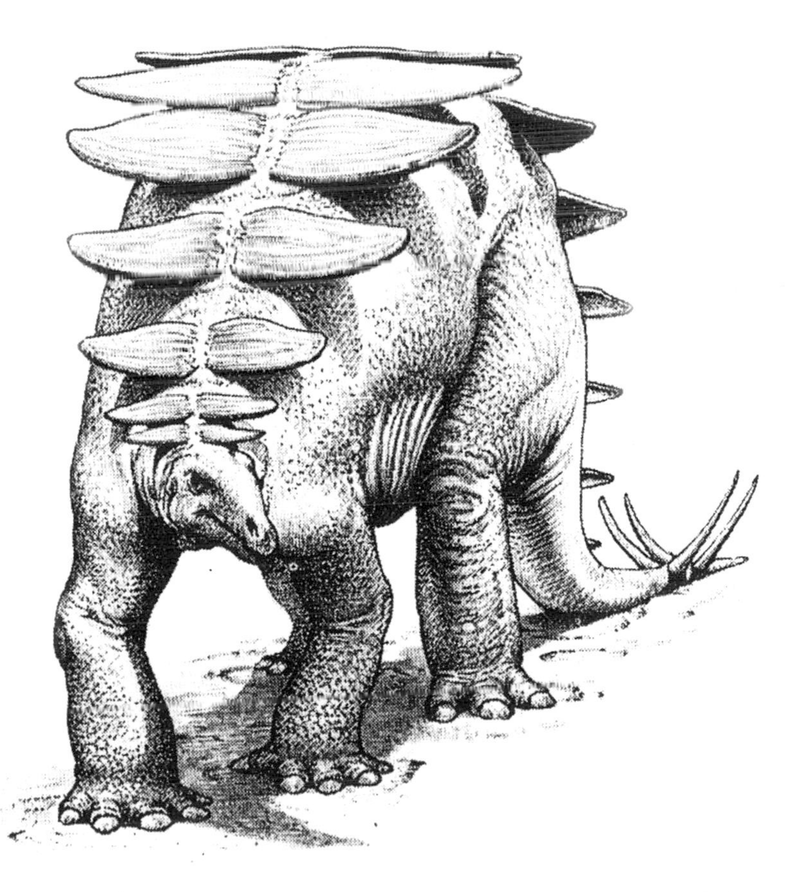

Tuojiangosaurus

Period: Late Jurassic. **Family:** Stegosaurids.
Where found: China.
Estimated length: 20ft (6m).

Tuojiangosaurus ('Tuojiang reptile') is by far the best preserved of the known stegosaurids from China. Coming from the late Jurassic, it was a contemporary of both *Stegosaurus* and *Kentrosaurus*. It was similar in size to *Stegosaurus* and boasted an array of plates running down its back that were more conical in shape and somewhat narrower over the hips than those of *Stegosaurus*. It had no para-sacral spines.

The structure of stegosaurid legs indicates that they were rather slow, lumbering creatures. The low position of the head was probably well suited to a habit of browsing on ferns, cycads and other low ground cover, rather than higher up in the trees where the ornithopods and sauropods presumably fed. The rather feeble jaws and teeth simply served as cutting devices and the plants (once swallowed) were probably stored for several days in a very large stomach, which acted as a fermenting tank.

As slow-moving herbivores, these stegosaurids must have been preyed upon by the large carnosaurs of the time: *Allosaurus* and *Ceratosaurus*. It used to be assumed that the spines were a defensive armour or that the large plates of stegosaurids such as *Stegosaurus* lay flat against the sides of its body as a protective shield. Neither of these proposals seems particularly convincing. Most of the plates across the back are broad and not particularly sharp. And if the plates were laid flat, they would scarcely form a complete bony covering to the flanks of the animal – great areas of belly and neck would still be very vulnerable.

It was suggested in 1977 that the plates acted both as radiators and solar panels for regulating the body temperature of the animal. The first clue was that the plates (of *Stegosaurus*) were seen to be covered with lots of fine grooves, which are usually associated with numerous small blood vessels running across the surface of the plates: hardly what you would expect of bony armour-plating! A thin section cut across one of these plates revealed that it was a honeycomb of spaces. This implied that the plates were very richly supplied with blood. Why? The answer seems now quite obvious: like most living reptiles, *Stegosaurus* was using its blood rather like the water in the central-heating system of a house to regulate its body temperature. Tested in a wind tunnel, the plates turned out to be the ideal shape for dissipating heat in a breeze and so cooling the animals. However, they may also have been used like solar panels to absorb heat from the sun to warm the animal should it become chilled.

A stegosaurid's actual defence against predators would undoubtedly have been the spike-bearing tail.

Below: *Tuojiangosaurus* is seen in a typically stegosaurid pose, using its low-slung head in order to browse on plants on the ground. The fine array of plates running down its back are more conical than those of the similarly sized *Stegosaurus*. Large defensive spikes are found on the tail.

Kentrosaurus

Period: Late Jurassic. **Family:** Stegosaurids.
Where found: East Africa.
Estimated length: 8ft 2in (2.5m).

Kentrosaurus ('prickly reptile') is a much smaller stegosaurid than *Stegosaurus*, reaching a length of about 8ft 2in (2.5m). Many remains of *Kentrosaurus* were found in rocks of the later Jurassic in Tendaguru, Tanzania, East Africa, between 1909 and 1912. Unfortunately, the great majority of these fossils, which were preserved at the Humboldt Museum in Berlin, cannot now be found, and it seems likely that they were lost during the Second World War.

Kentrosaurus has a clearly different plate and spine pattern from the better-known *Stegosaurus*. The anterior plates are like those of *Stegosaurus*, being quite narrow and flattened, and these become slightly larger and more triangular towards the rear of the animal. However, instead of resembling the huge triangular plates above the hips of *Stegosaurus*, those of *Kentrosaurus* become taller and narrower and continue down the length of the tail as pairs of long, very sharp spines. In addition to this double row of spines there is another pair of 'para-sacral' spines attached to the hips on either side, which points obliquely down and back. They were more like the quills of a porcupine, protecting the rump, hips and tail. Clearly these spines were primarily defensive in nature and were intended to deter larger predators, which risked impalement upon them. Whether *Kentrosaurus* could rush backwards at predators in the way that porcupines can do today is uncertain. The tail spines certainly look defensive in nature.

Near the shoulders and on the neck the plates were broader and flatter. These may have served as a slightly less sophisticated temperature-regulation arrangement. The little that is known of the head of *Kentrosaurus* indicates a shape rather similar to that of *Stegosaurus*.

Below: **The front plates of both *Kentrosaurus* and *Stegosaurus* are similar in shape, but over the hip region and down the tail they become compressed into long, narrow spikes in *Kentrosaurus* which also has an extra spike pointing down and outwards from the hip.**

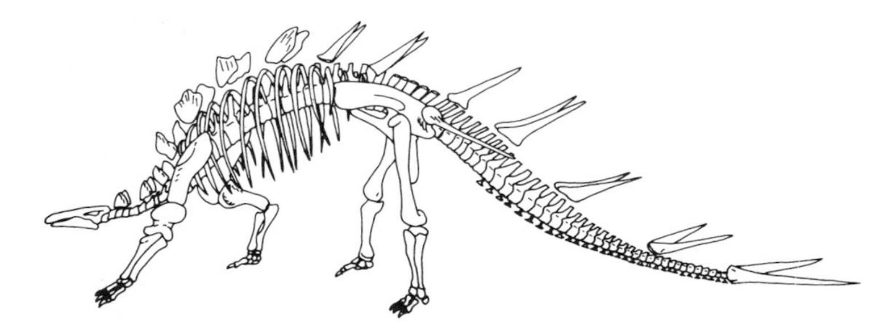

Below: **The pattern of spikes in *Kentrosaurus,* one of the smaller stegosaurids, so far known only from Tendaguru in Tanzania, is very distinctive. Those near the front of the body are flat and plate-like. However, by the middle of the back they have changed into narrow spines, which continue to the end of the tail. in addition there is another pair of spines, which point diagonally backwards from their attachment to the pelvis.**

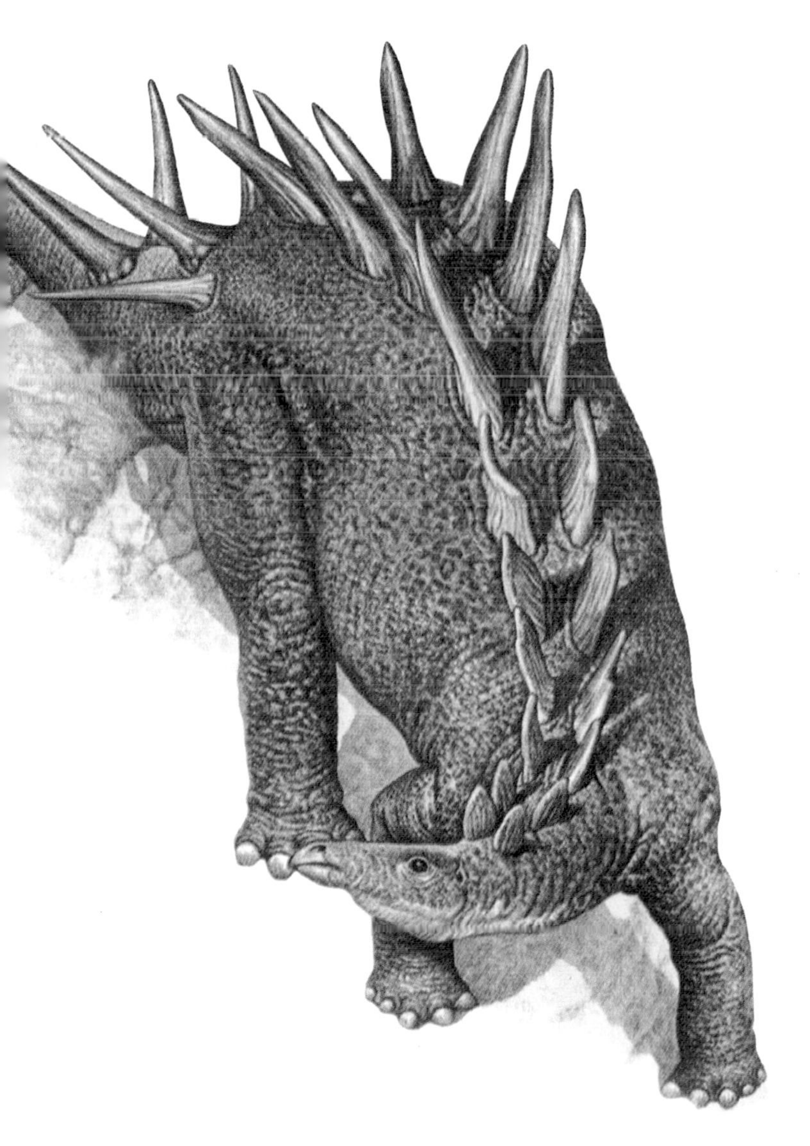

Stegosaurus

Period: Late Jurassic. **Family:** Stegosaurids.
Where found: North America.
Estimated length: 20ft-24ft 7in (6-7.5m).

Stegosaurus gets its name – 'roofed reptile' – from the large bony plates along its back; these were long thought to form some sort of protective shield ('roof') over its back. *Stegosaurus* is one of the best-known stegosaurids, its remains having been well preserved and well described.

The plates found in two rows down the back of *Stegosaurus* are unique to the stegosaurids, although they do vary a bit in shape between different genera. In *Stegosaurus* the plates are quite small and flat, with irregular edges in the region immediately behind the head, becoming progressively taller and broader across the back. The largest plates of all are found just behind the hip region. Beyond this there seem to be a few smaller plates (six pairs) before the end of the tail. The end of the tail also possesses bony plates but these are shaped as two pairs of long, thin pointed spikes. The precise arrangement of these bony plates along the back has been the subject of some debate over the years. It was postulated that they formed a single line right down the middle of the back, that they were arranged in a double row of pairs of plates on either side of the backbone or that they were arranged in a staggered series of alternating pairs with only two pairs of tail spines.

The source of this disagreement is the very well-preserved skeleton of *Stegosaurus* in the Smithsonian Institution in Washington, DC. A drawing of this skeleton as it was originally discovered is shown here. The large bone plates are shown in a definite alternating pattern along the back of the skeleton, but whether this was their natural arrangement or the plates simply slipped past one another as the flesh of the carcass rotted is not known.

Stegosaurus also had quite a well-developed layer of bony knobs and bumps over other parts of its body. Again, some of these can be seen in the drawing of the skeleton as it was found; these small bones were found in clusters around the throat area and were very probably widely spread in the skin all over the animal.

Another noteworthy feature of *Stegosaurus* is the remarkable difference in length between the fore- and hindlimbs. The forelimb is stout and powerful to support the weight of the animal, and the feet are broad, with five stubby toes, clearly designed for walking upon rather than grasping. The hindlimb is considerably longer than the forelimb

Below: This North American form is by far the best known of the stegosaurids. Several fine skeletons have been recovered but disagreement still prevails relating to the arrangement of the plates and the pose of the forelimbs: were they bent or straight? As can be seen, we have adopted a straight-legged pose and an array of upright plates staggered alternately along the back. They were probably used as heat-transfer surfaces, while the sharp tail spikes were for defence.

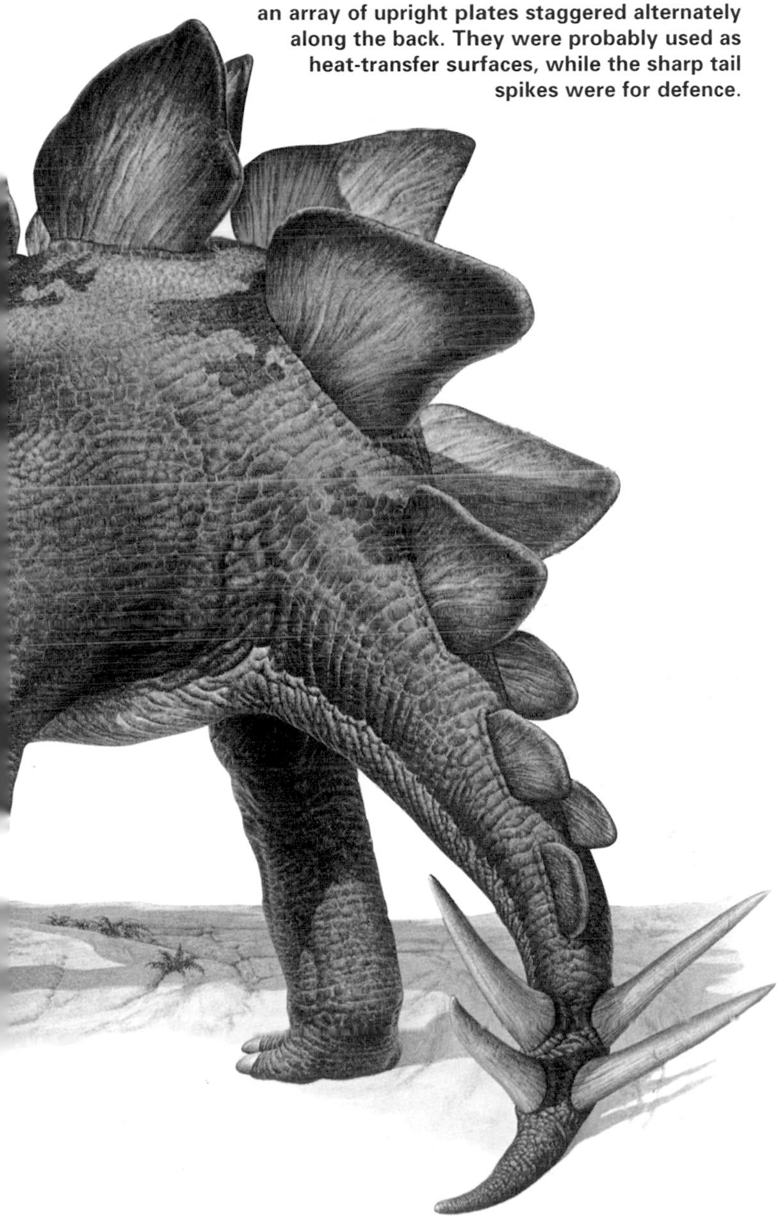

and is designed to be a pillar-like support for these slow-moving animals. In a fast runner the thigh is short, the shin is longer and the toes are slender and long. *Stegosaurus*'s legs show the exact opposite of these proportions, with a long thigh, short shin and broad, short-toed feet.

The head of *Stegosaurus* is rather low and slender for such a large animal, with a narrow, toothless, horn-covered beak at the tip of its snout. Behind the beak the teeth are quite numerous, but are not arranged into a special cutting battery. Therefore it seems that the stegosaurids were not capable of grinding up plant food in their mouths

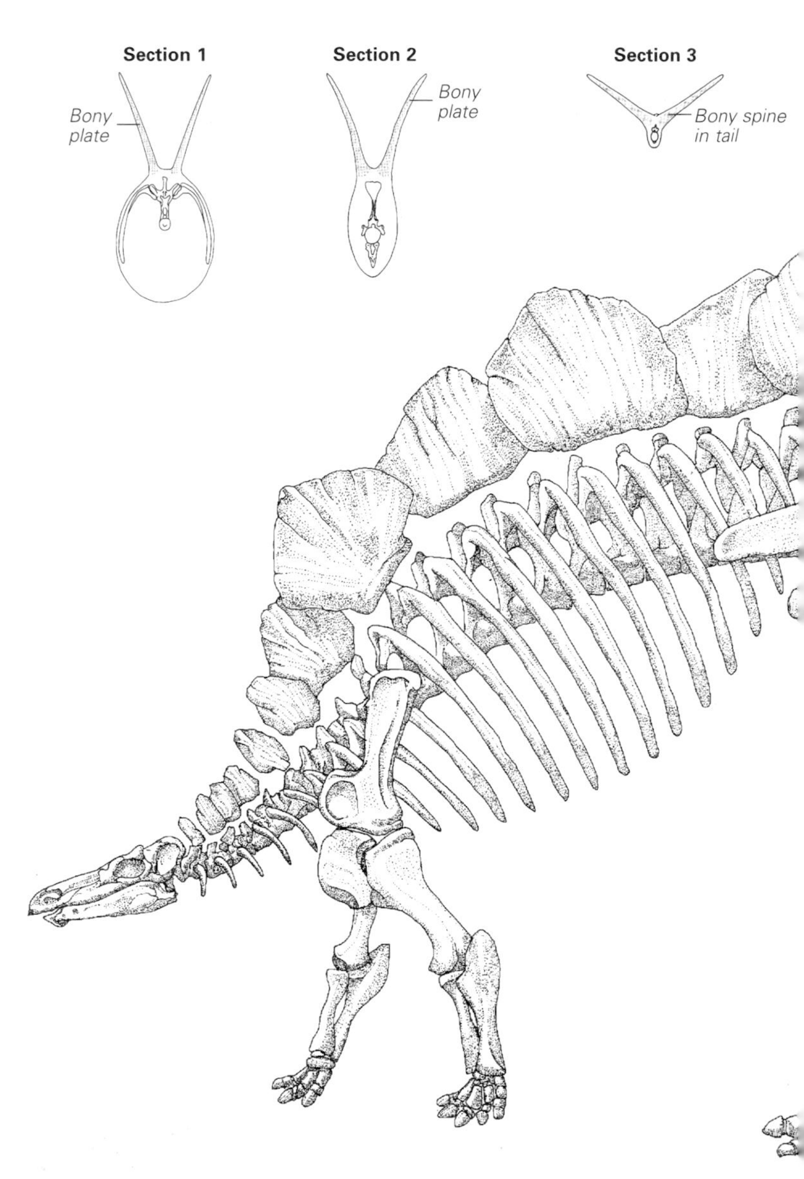

as some ornithopods and ceratopids could. The jaw muscles were also apparently quite simple, without the special mechanical devices for improving the efficiency of the jaw-closing muscles such as are seen in ceratopids. Despite this, the great size of these animals suggests that they had to consume large quantities of plant food to sustain themselves. These ornithischians probably used their jaws to chop up ▶

Left and below: **This genus shows basic stegosaurid features well: the relatively small head, the short front legs compared with the back ones, the large bony plates along the back and the tail spines. You can see clearly the variation in shape of the plates along the body, and by looking at the sections through the body at certain points along the animal you can see how the angle of attachment of the plates varies – it is very wide in the lower tail region. The tail spikes were used for defence, being swung from side to side by powerful tail muscles. The marked difference in length of fore- and hindlimbs is readily apparent.**

crudely large quantities of plant food and then swallowed it quickly, passing it to a very large stomach where it was left slowly to ferment. Stomach stones may also have been used to help pulverise some of the tougher plant tissues.

One of the skulls found of *Stegosaurus* was sufficiently well preserved for O. C. Marsh to be able to obtain a cast of the cavity in which the brain lay. This showed that the brain must have been very small, perhaps the smallest of any dinosaur. For an animal that grew to a length of 20ft (6m) and may have weighed 1.5 tonnes or more, to possess a brain that could have weighed no more than 2.5-2.8 oz (70-80 grams) seems extraordinary. This observation more than any other must be responsible for the persistent and very widely held belief that all dinosaurs were dull and extremely stupid animals. Quite why *Stegosaurus* should possess such a small brain is not obvious. Many dinosaurs have quite respectably sized brains, particularly the carnivorous theropods. All we seem able to say at the moment is that the brain of *Stegosaurus*, although small, was evidently large enough for its needs! Associated with the very small brain of this animal is the fact that the spinal cord in the region of the hips was enormously enlarged. Again, casts were made of this area, which seemed to show that this part of the spine was over 20 times the size of the brain. This gave rise to the belief, again still widely held, that dinosaurs had a second brain in their tail. This rather curious enlargement of the spinal cord almost certainly does not form a second brain. The enlargement of the spine at the hips probably marks the area where all the nerves of the back legs and tail met, forming a large relay station for messages or signals on their way to and from the brain. In addition to this, most land animals seem to store fat around this area of the spinal cord.

Below: **The back foot has three toes (with only the rudiments of a fourth, not shown here), which are short and wide with large oval claws.**

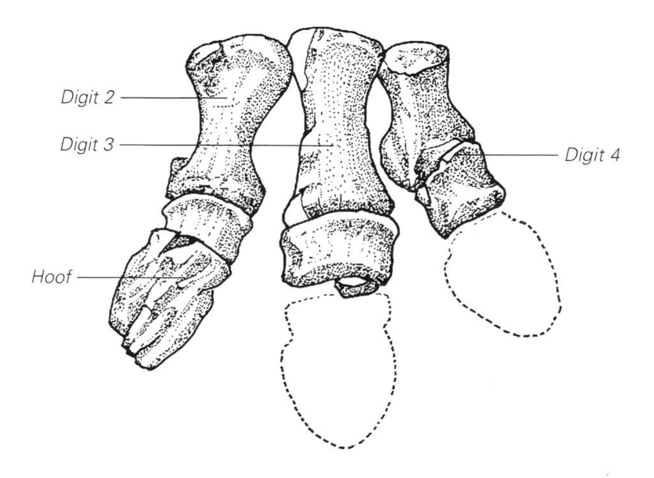

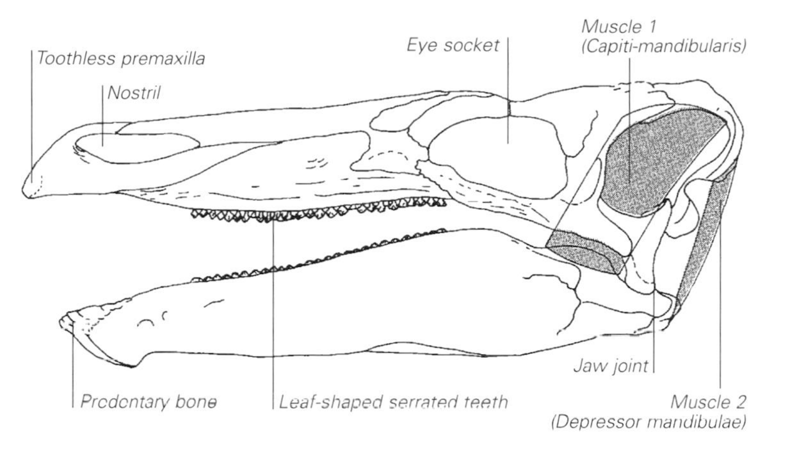

Above and right: **The skull of *Stegosaurus* seems rather small and the jaws quite weak for such a large animal. The jaw muscles are fairly simple and there is no obvious lower jaw projection to which they can attach. There is some evidence of a muscular cheek. The teeth are numerous, leaf-shaped and serrated, but not organised into a grinding battery of any sort. At the front of the skull there is a narrow, toothless beak. This would suggest that *Stegosaurus* used stomach stones rather than teeth to grind up its food.**

Leaf-shaped serrated teeth

Below: **The front foot has five short, strong toes and looks a little like that of an elephant. The claws are short and rounded.**

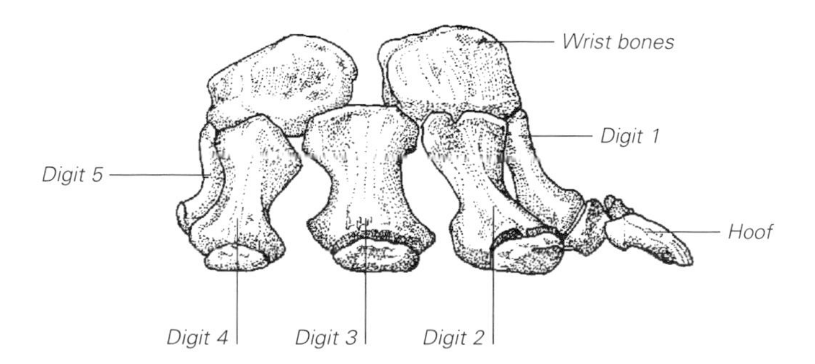

Scelidosaurids

Until the discovery of *Heterodontosaurus* in 1962, *Scelidosaurus* ('limb-reptile') was the earliest known ornithischian dinosaur. It was first referred to by Richard Owen in 1859, who described remains recovered from early Jurassic rocks of Charmouth (Dorset) in southern England. Owen went on to describe and illustrate an assortment of bones under the name *Scelidosaurus* in 1861. A little later, in 1863, Owen described an almost complete skeleton of this animal. Fragmentary remains of another possible scelidosaurid – *Lusitanosaurus* ('Lusitania reptile') – have also been found in Portugal.

It has since been shown that the odd bones that were described in 1861 were in fact a mixture of theropod (*Megalosaurus*) and ornithopod bones. Technically the name *Scelidosaurus* should apply to these bones alone, rather than the complete skeleton described in 1863, but this would clearly be absurd, and thus it was proposed that the rules governing the use of fossils' names should be suspended in this case so that the skeleton could 'adopt' the name *Scelidosaurus*.

The thyreophorans (armoured and plated dinosaurs) were a subgroup of one of the two great groups of dinosaurs, the Ornithischia, or 'bird-hips'. In ornithischian dinosaurs the distinguishing feature is that the pubic bone is angled down and back, lying alongside the ischium just above it. (In the saurischian, or lizard-hipped, dinosaurs the

***Below:* For many years the large *Scelidosaurus* skeleton described by Richard Owen was displayed like this. In recent years the skeleton has been dipped in acid baths in order to dissolve away the limestone. The result is that *Scelidosaurus* is now one of the best-known of all early ornithischians.**

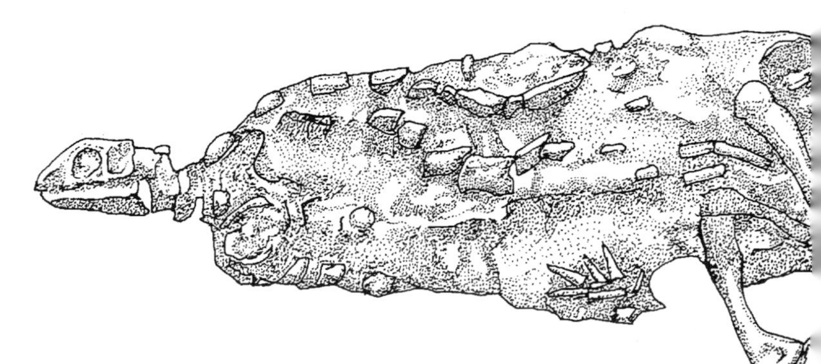

pubis is angled down and forward.)

The most ancient group of thyreophorans was the scelidosaurids. Compared with their later cousins, they were small and only lightly protected. Part-armoured plant-eaters, they included *Scelidosaurus* from the early Jurassic and other types such as *Tatisaurus* and *Echinodon*, which are known only vaguely from scarce remains. The scelidosaurids may have evolved from small ornithischian dinosaurs, similar to fabrosaurids. The fabrosaurids were probably able to walk on their two rear legs alone. But as the thyreophorans began to develop bony armour, they became too heavy to get about on two legs and instead had to use four.

Being one of the early ornithischians, *Scelidosaurus* is primitive in many of its characters. Its feet, legs and tail are rather similar in shape to those of many ornithopods, but it has teeth and body armour like that of many ankylosaurs and a skull and hips reminiscent of stegosaurs. The stegosaurs and ankylosaurs were ancestors of later members of the thyreophoran group. In other features, the scelidosaurids resemble the nodosaurids. The most likely relationship for the scelidosaurids is with the ankylosaurs, with which they share the development of body armour and of extra bone welded on to the roof of the skull and the jaws, along with the arrangement of the teeth.

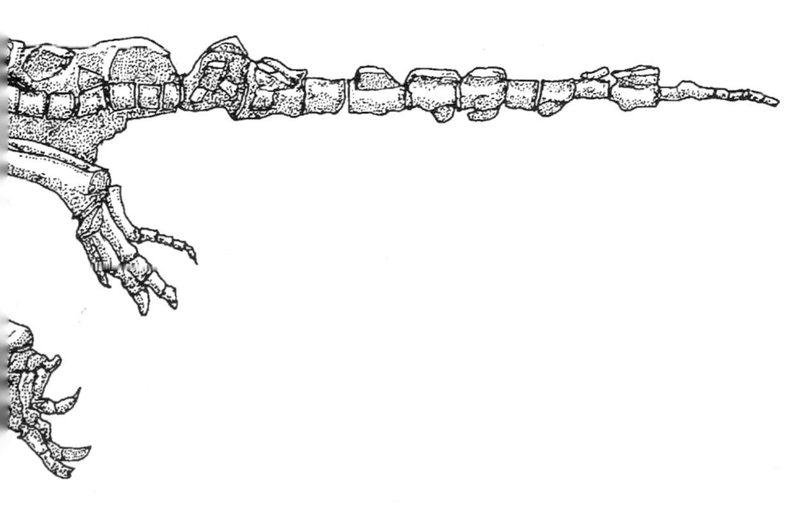

Scelidosaurus

Period: Early Jurassic. **Family:** Scelidosaurids.
Where found: UK.
Estimated length: 13ft (4m).

Scelidosaurus ('limb reptile') grew to at least 13ft (4m) in length and is now well known not only from the original skeleton, but also from a very small partial skeleton found in a nodule of rock early in the 20th century, some imperfect fragments discovered in 1980 and a very exciting new skeleton from Charmouth, Dorset, southern England, discovered and excavated by amateur collectors in 1985.

As with the stegosaurs and the ankylosaurs, *Scelidosaurus* had many bony plates embedded in its skin across its back and sides; these did not form the high, thin plates seen in stegosaurs but more closely resemble the low, bony studs seen on the backs of most ankylosaurs. The bony plates on either side are arranged in clusters of three, a curious pattern not seen anywhere else in the skeleton.

The skull of *Scelidosaurus* is deeper and shorter than that of *Stegosaurus* and not so heavily armoured as that of a typical ankylosaur. However, as with ankylosaurs, there is evidence of extra bony tissue welded on to the surface of the skull and the sides of the lower jaw. The teeth are simple and leaf-shaped, extending right down towards the tip of the snout so that the horny beak, if it was present, must have been extremely small.

***Below:* The back of *Scelidosaurus* is studded with low conical bones and just behind the head these are modified into peculiar tricorn arrays, perhaps for extra protection.**

The skeleton of *Scelidosaurus* is quite heavily built, with pillar-like hind legs and broad, four-toed feet. The form of the front legs is a bit of a mystery since none is presently known. An upper arm bone preserved with the recently discovered skeleton is quite large and heavy; this suggests that *Scelidosaurus* was a quadruped, rather than a biped. The tail, however, is long judged by the standard of most ornithischians and may have at least partly counterbalanced the front part of the animal. As a result, most of the weight was probably carried by the hind legs, and the animal may have been able to run for short distances on the hind legs alone.

Scelidosaurus remains have been found in rocks deposited at the bottom of a sea, but it is probable that their carcasses were carried there by rivers. *Scelidosaurus* seems to have been a fairly slow-moving, terrestrial plant-eater, which relied upon its armoured skin to protect it from attackers. It is possible that *Scelidosaurus* was capable of short bursts of speed to evade the larger theropods.

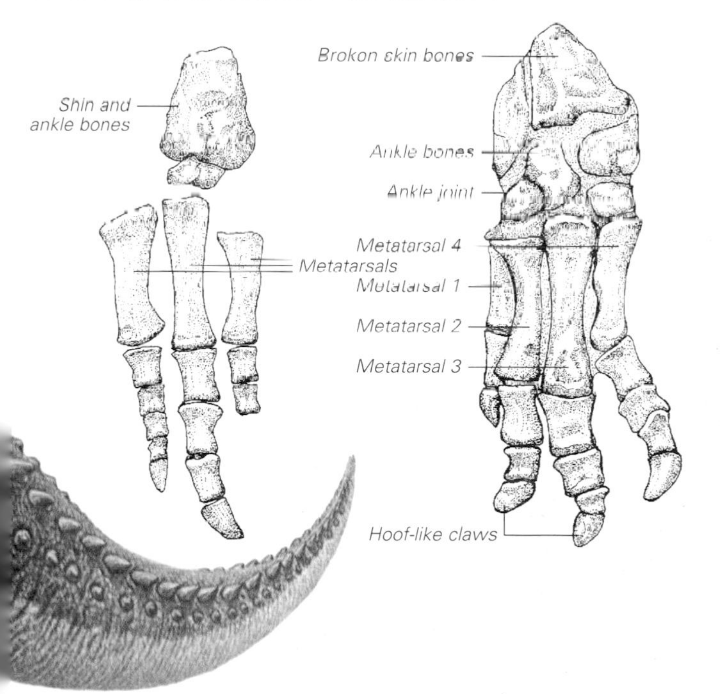

Above: **The hind feet (right) of the large *Scelidosaurus* described by Owen are well preserved. These broad, but fairly elongated feet would carry the animal by spreading its weight evenly between the toes. The best pieces from the Charmouth specimen are shown (at left).**

Nodosaurids

The other major group of armoured dinosaurs and the last of the major groups of dinosaurs to be considered are the ankylosaurs ('fused' or 'joined-together reptiles'). Ankylosaurs are known from Jurassic and Cretaceous rocks worldwide. The unusal name refers to the fact that the bones in the skin of these animals tend to be fused together into great shield-like pieces of armour-plating. In fact, this armour-plating was so extensive that large slabs of bone were even welded on to the head, giving them quite a grotesque appearance. These were the tanks of the dinosaur era.

In general ankylosaurs are medium-sized (6ft 6in-26ft 2in, 2-8m long), heavily built, quadrupedal ornithischian dinosaurs; they all tend to have low, broad, heavily armoured heads. Their bodies are low and broad, the legs being short and powerful rather than long and graceful. Their backs and legs also tend to be covered in various patterns of bony plates and studs or spikes. The tail is relatively short and in some cases bears a very large bony club.

Below: **This shoulder blade belongs to *Sauropelta* and is typical of the type seen in nodosaurids. Its most outstanding feature, and one in which it differs from that of ankylosaurids, is the large pseudo-acromion process which overhangs the shoulder joint and which may have improved the mechanical advantage of some of the shoulder muscles. It is possible that this allowed nodosaurids to crouch against the ground for protection against predators, relying on their armour to withstand any attack.**

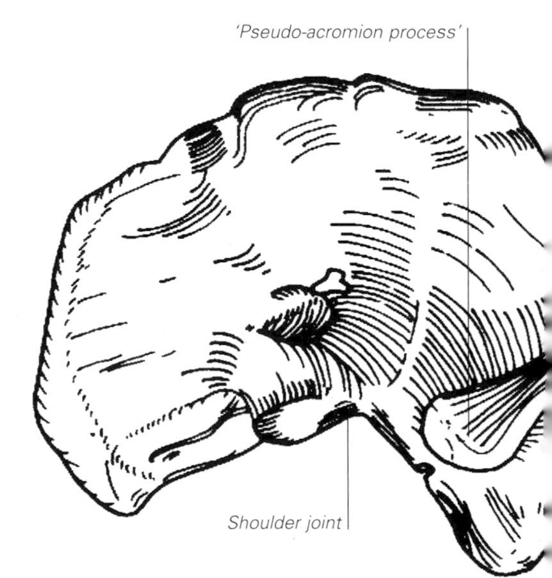

Ankylosaurs can be divided into two quite distinct families: the nodosaurids ('nodular reptiles') and the ankylosaurids. One of the most obvious differences between the two families is the presence or absence of a tail club.

The skull of a late Cretaceous North American nodosaurid, *Panoplosaurus* ('fully plated reptile'), is fortunately very well preserved and as far as we know the skull of all nodosaurids seems to resemble that of *Panoplosaurus*. Unlike the ankylosaurids, the nodosaurid skull is rather narrow, with a more pointed snout, and lacks the horn-like projections from the rear corners of the skull. There is also an opening on the side of the skull behind the eye, which is not seen in ankylosaurids. The teeth are quite simple, leaf-shaped and rather similar to those of stegosaurs. Indeed, although the jaws are massive, they are not specially modified for grinding in the way that the jaws and teeth of ceratopids and hadrosaurids were. The front of both upper and lower jaws ends in a toothless, horn-covered beak.

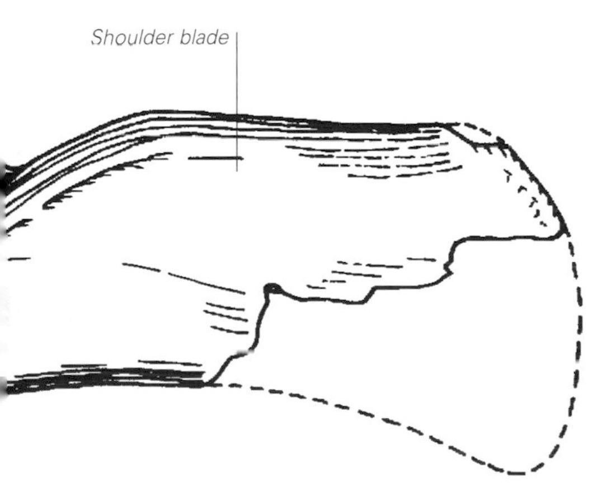

Hylaeosaurus

Period: Early Cretaceous. **Family:** Nodosaurids.
Where found: UK.
Estimated length: 13ft (4m).

The first nodosaurid to be discovered was *Hylaeosaurus* ('woodland reptile'), which was found in 1833 in the Tilgate Forest area of Sussex in southern England. The fossil remains of *Hylaeosaurus* consisted of the front half of the skeleton embedded in a large piece of limestone. This fossil was first described by Gideon Mantell and somewhat later by Richard Owen. It was Owen who coined the term Dinosauria, or dinosaurs, and *Hylaeosaurus*, *Megalosaurus* and *Iguanodon* were the 'founder members' of the group. This fossil has unfortunately never been prepared out of the stone in which it is embedded. Nevertheless, the parts that are exposed seem to show an animal with rows of large, curved plates running down its back. Few other remains of *Hylaeosaurus* have been discovered to date, with the result that not a great deal is known about either its appearance or its relations with other ankylosaurs.

Another nodosaurid dinosaur, *Polacanthus*, which also comes from early Cretaceous rocks in southern England, is similar to *Hylaeosaurus*, and some palaeontologists have even suggested that the two are in fact one and the same species. The fragmentary nature of their remains –

***Above:* Hylaeosaurus may have defended itself against predators by passive resistance, clutching the ground with its strong limbs and relying on its body armour to deter the attacker.**

and the fact that they do not overlap – makes it impossible to be sure either way at present. Other nodosaurids include *Panoplosaurus* ('fully plated reptile'), *Saltisaurus* ('forest reptile'), both from North America, and *Sauropelta* ('shielded reptile'). *Minmi* (named after the Minmi Crossing where it was discovered) was the first Australian ankylosaur to be found; known only from a small portion of the back and parts of a foot, *Minmi* comes from early Cretaceous rocks near Roma, Queensland.

***Left:* This early Cretaceous dinosaur is frustratingly incomplete. At present the skeleton, consisting of the front half of the animal, is embedded in a block of limestone in the Natural History Museum, London. The reconstruction seen here is based on the work of George Olshevsky; its proportions and the detailed arrangement of its armour are speculative. In recent years it has been suggested that *Hylaeosaurus* and *Polacanthus*, which are both from the early Cretaceous of southern England, are one and the same.**

Polacanthus

Period: Early Cretaceous. **Family:** Nodosaurids.
Where found: UK.
Estimated length: 13ft (4m).

Another early British nodosaurid is *Polacanthus* ('many spikes'), which was discovered in 1865 by the Rev. William Fox. The skeleton, which consisted of the hind part of the animal including many spines, various back and tail vertebrae, the hips and hind legs, had evidently weathered out of the cliffs on the coast of the Isle of Wight. It seems quite likely that much of the skeleton was present originally but that, once exposed by a cliff fall, much was lost by being washed out to sea. The frustrating thing about this specimen is that, although it must have lived at about the same time as *Hylaeosaurus*, the parts of both skeletons do not overlap (one being the front half, the other the back half). It is therefore impossible to compare the two skeletons directly to prove that they belonged either to the same or to different animals. The skeleton of *Polacanthus* lacks the head and much of the front half of the body before

the pelvis – apart from the spines, which were found scattered near by. So even their position is a matter of guesswork. The long dorsal spines may have formed a frill around the sides of the body to guard the flanks and legs of *Polacanthus* when under attack. The hips were covered by a mosaic of small bony nodules.

In 1979 William T. Blows, an amateur collector of fossils continuing in the footsteps of the Rev. Fox in working on the Isle of Wight, discovered some more *Polacanthus* material. Again, this is far from complete, but it does include some very nice pieces of its armour-plated ▶

Below: **As in the case of the other nodosaurids, much of this reconstruction is conjectural. The skeleton of *Polacanthus* lacks the head and much of the front half of the body before the pelvis – apart from the spines, which were found scattered near the remainder of the fossil. So even their position is a matter of guesswork. The long dorsal spines may have formed a protective frill around the sides of the body to guard the flanks and legs of *Polacanthus* when under attack.**

hide and various bones from the back of the animal. Some of these latter may help to solve the problem of the *Polacanthus-Hylaeosaurus* relationship.

The story of frustration revealed in the *Polacanthus-Hylaeosaurus* issue is by now a familiar one. The fossil remains are not well enough preserved to give precise information about these interesting animals and indeed this problem applies very strongly to nearly all ankylosaurs. In some geological formations ankylosaur-type bony plates can be very abundant, but these always seem to be isolated bones, presumably scattered from rotting carcasses. Very few nodosaurids are known at all well and many of the reconstructions of these animals seen in books are based on little more than guesswork.

Below: **Though lacking a head and much of the front part of the body, the spikes and rear part of *Polacanthus*, found in early Cretaceous rocks in the Isle of Wight, are quite well preserved. The hips were covered by a mosaic of small bony nodules. The reconstruction seen here is based on the work of Francis Nopsca. The pattern of bony spikes shown is speculative.**

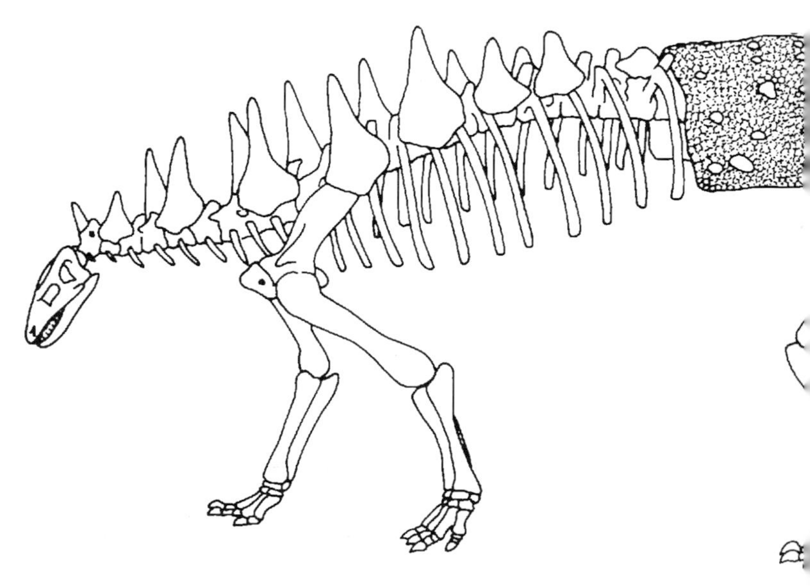

Panoplosaurus skull

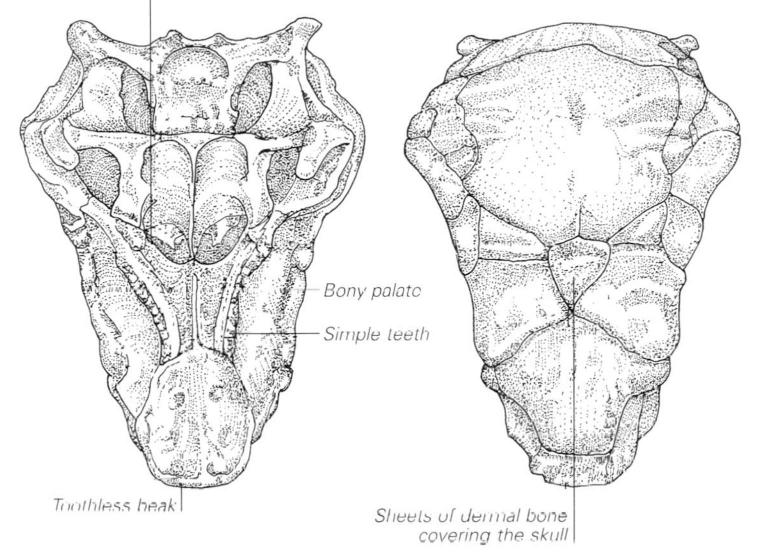

Above: **From above (right) the details of the armour-plating on the skull of *Panoplosaurus* are clear; the grooves show where the slabs of bone join. From below (left) one can see the toothless beak on the snout, the teeth, the internal nostrils and the brain case behind. The skull of the *Panoplosaurus* is well known and appears to be typical of all nodosaurids.**

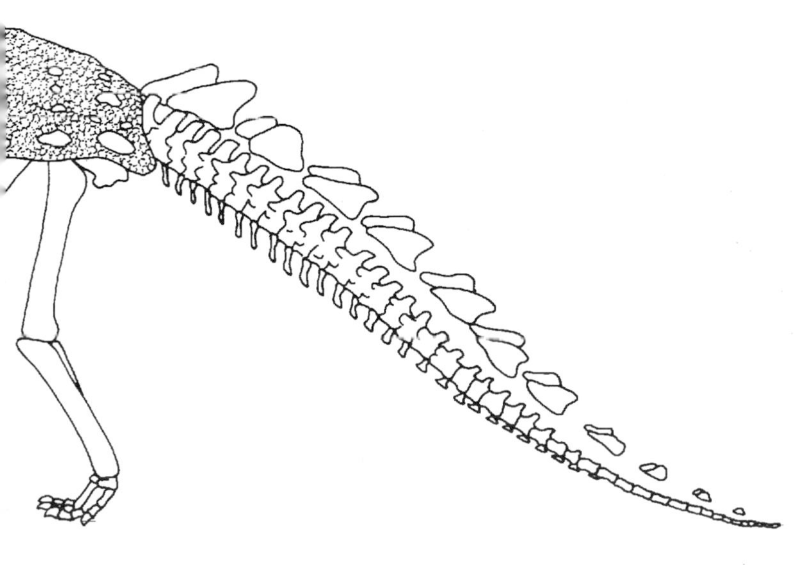

Nodosaurus

Period: Mid-Cretaceous. **Family:** Nodosaurids.
Where found: North America.
Estimated length: 18ft (5.5m).

Nodosaurus ('nodular [lumpy] reptile') was first mentioned by Othniel Charles Marsh in 1889, but was only described in some detail in 1921 by Richard Lull on the basis of partial remains of the skeleton. *Nodosaurus* remains come from the late Cretaceous of Wyoming and Kansas. *Nodosaurus* gives us a fair idea of how most nodosaurids must have looked. The skeleton is about 18ft (5.5m) long and the whole of its upper surface is studded with bony plates in regular bands of larger and smaller plates, forming a very thick and heavy protective coat. The pattern of armour-plating seen in *Nodosaurus* is the animal's most distinctive feature and it would have undoubtedly conferred upon the animal both considerable strength and a certain amount of flexibility. It is possible that the margins of the armour were fringed with tall spines, as seems to have been the case with *Hylaeosaurus* and *Polacanthus*.

The hind legs of *Nodosaurus* were pillar-like in order to support the heavy body and the feet were naturally short and broad. The pelvis was ▶

Below: **From what is known of the skeleton found in Albany County, Wyoming, the armour is the most distinctive feature of Nodosaurus. It seems to have consisted of broad bands of alternating large and small nodules (hence the name). The margins of the armour may have been fringed with spines. The head is conjectural and is based on that of Panoplosaurus, as no head was found with the skeleton.**

rather a different shape from that of other ornithischians because the ilium at the top of the hip was greatly enlarged and overhung the legs, while the lower hip bones (pubis and ischium) were very much reduced. Large leg muscles attached to the underside of the ilium, while its upper surface was covered by extensive armour-plating. The front legs of *Nodosaurus* are not very well preserved but were undoubtedly, as shown here, short and powerfully built to support the great weight of the body.

The shoulders were similarly very strong and in many cases scarred by powerful muscles. Nodosaurids differed from ankylosaurids in the structure of the shoulder blade, specifically in having a feature called a 'pseudo-acromion process', which overhung the shoulder joint and may have improved the mechanical advantage of some of the shoulder muscles. It is possible that this allowed nodosaurids to crouch against the ground for protection against predators, relying on their armour to withstand any attack.

Below: **It is a sad fact that nodosaurids are very poorly known at present. This reconstruction of *Nodosaurus textilis* is based on Richard Swann Lull's work and has been given additional material from other nodosaurids. The specimen is badly preserved and so the skull is 'borrowed' from *Panoplosaurus*, while the shoulders are those of *Sauropelta*. The armour-plating is distinctive, consisting of bands of rounded nodules. It is not known whether this animal had a fringe of longer spikes, as other nodosaurids did.**

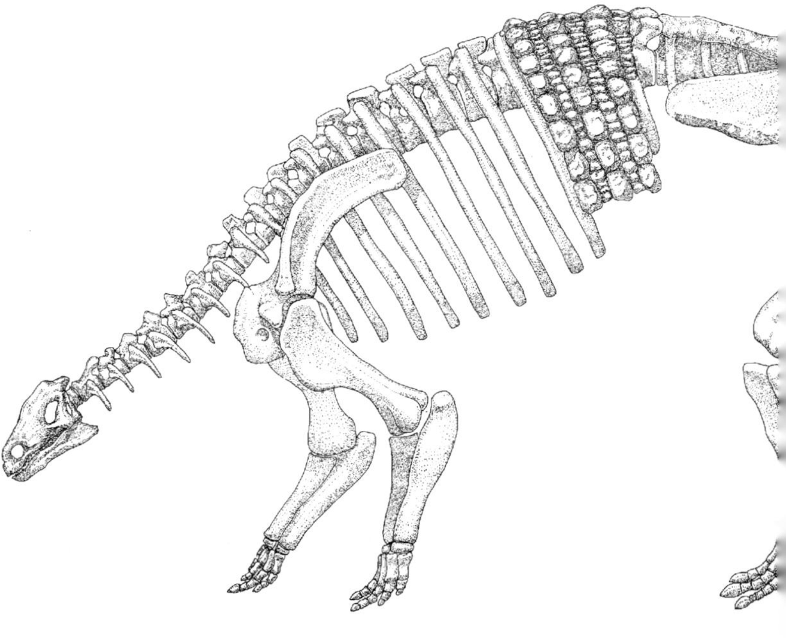

Nodosaurid skulls were massively constructed, with large bones plastered all over the skull. The skull of *Nodosaurus* itself is unfortunately not known to date. The head of the colour reconstruction shown here is conjectural, based upon that of *Panoplosaurus*, as no head was found with the skeleton in Albany County, Wyoming.

An oddity in the realm of nodosaurids was *Struthiosaurus*, a poorly known species from the latest Cretaceous of southern Europe (France, Hungary, Austria) and especially from localities in an area originally known as Transylvania in Romania. These remains are particularly interesting because all the dinosaurs from this area (including a sauropod, a hadrosaurid and an iguanodontid) are dwarf species. *Struthiosaurus* was the smallest of all known nodosaurids, measuring no more than 6ft 6in (2m) in length. Why these dinosaurs should be so small is a mystery. One explanation is that they lived on small islands, whereon there has been shown to be a surprisingly common tendency towards miniaturisation.

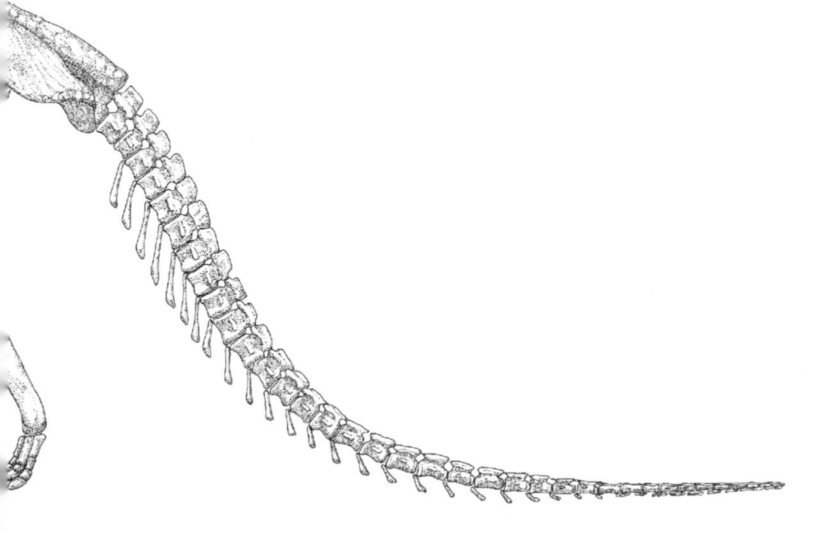

Ankylosaurids

Ankylosaurids had broad, armoured heads that were about as wide as they were long. There were large triangular horns at the rear corners of the skull, and the sides of the head were completely closed in by bone. The bony armour-plating covering the body tended to have very few tall spines and the tail was highly modified to form a heavy bony club.

Ankylosaurids appeared in rocks of the early to late Cretaceous and appear to have been much less widespread geographically than nodosaurids, having been recovered with certainty only from western North America and eastern Asia (Mongolia and China). Remains of ankylosaurid-type dinosaurs are quite abundant but they tend to be isolated pieces of armour-plating or other skeletal fragments.

Nodosaurid nasal passages were relatively simple paired tubes, which ran from the nostrils directly to the back of the throat. By contrast, ankylosaurid nasal tubes followed an S-shaped course through the head and on either side of these were additional passages (sinuses). These elaborate sinuses may have had several purposes, such as to filter, warm and moisten the air that the animals breathed.

The ankylosaurid brain cavity was fairly typical, except for one unusual characteristic – a large, divergent pair of olfactory stalks, which

ran towards the complex nasal passages. The relatively small size of the parts of the brain concerned with co-ordination and general activity tends to confirm the notion that these animals were slower-moving than their agile, bipedal contemporaries. Further evidence comes from the arrangement and likely size of the muscles of both fore- and hindlimbs, which were designed to generate great power rather than speed.

For defence, ankylosaurids would have relied first and foremost on their well-developed bony armour-plating, which would have acted as a deterrent to all but the largest and most powerful of the theropods. Ankylosaurids also possessed the unique tail-club. Several of the bones embedded in the skin at the end of the tail were greatly enlarged and had become fused to one another and to the last few tail bones, to form a very heavy club. The long tail muscles could swing the club from side to side with enough force to fell an assailant such as one of the large, agile tyrannosaurid theropods.

Below: **The ankylosaurid *Euoplocephalus* is active in its self-defence, swinging its big tail-club in order to topple and so disable a tyrannosaurid predator.**

Euoplocephalus

Period: Late Cretaceous. **Family:** Ankylosaurids.
Where found: North America.
Estimated length: 20ft (6m).

The first remains of the animal later to be known as *Euoplocephalus* ('true plated head') were recovered from the Red Deer River of Alberta in 1902; they consisted of a partial head and incomplete skeleton. Other remains of armoured dinosaurs were found in the same general area in subsequent years and given various names including *Dyoplosaurus* ('doubly armoured reptile') and *Scolosaurus* ('thorn reptile'). Careful study revealed that these separate 'species' were all parts of the same type of animal and they were renamed *Euoplocephalus*.

The material recovered includes skulls, several partial skeletons and fairly complete armour. In common with all the quadrupedal ornithischians, the neck of *Euoplocephalus* is quite short and the forelimbs are shorter than the hindlimbs. It has long been supposed that the legs of heavily built animals such as this (especially the front ones) were held out sideways from the body, in the sprawling position of a lizard, so that they would have crawled very slowly along the ground. Current opinion, however, does not agree with this view, neither in the arrangement of the bones in the shoulder, hip and legs, nor with the evidence of a footprint trackway. One such trackway shows a four-footed creature moving with both front and back legs tucked in beneath

Right: **One of the largest ankylosaurs, *Euoplocephalus* probably weighed about two tonnes. Most of the back was armoured with heavy nodules of bone set into the leathery skin. There were pointed spines at the back of the head, over the shoulders and down the middle of the back and tail. In addition, the skull itself was protected by additional sheets of surface bone. Its tail-club was probably a formidable weapon.**

the body. This almost certainly indicates the normal walking posture of ankylosaurs generally.

The backs of these animals were at least partly stiffened by bony tendons running down either side of the spine. However, these are not developed into the large lattice-like arrangements seen across the hips of hadrosaurids, but appear much more sporadically. The region where they are best developed is towards the end of the tail – near the tail-club. The tendons probably served two purposes. First, they provided firm anchorage for the tail-swinging muscles; second, they stiffened the end of the tail in order to prevent 'whip-lash' effects from damaging the bones near the tail-club. The main part of the tail had no ossified tendons and could therefore be swung freely from side to side.

The dominant characteristic of this animal is, however, the bony armour-plating. The ground plan for the arrangement of the armour lies in the skin, practically all of which is embedded with small, bony studs. On the back and tail the studded skin is divided up into bands of much larger bony plates of various shapes running across the body. Over the neck there are two bands; the first appears to consist of two large, slightly ridged plates, followed by a second ring with a whorl of very large, oblique, blunt spikes. These are arranged so as to give not only protection but also a great deal of flexibility to the neck. Behind this area, the back is covered by four bands ▶

of armour studded with rows of large but quite low, keeled plates. Across the hips there are three further bands, which are covered by a mosaic of disc-shaped studs. The front part of the tail is also banded, with four rows of keeled spikes that get progressively smaller, except for the middle two spikes on the last band. Beyond this region the tail lacks the bands of bone, but is studded with small bony nodules. The shoulders, arms and thighs were probably also covered with variously sized bony plates.

Large slabs of bone are plastered all over the exposed surfaces of the skull and jaws of ankylosaurids, forming an almost impregnable covering; these must have given them almost complete immunity to attacks by the large theropods of the time. Two rather exceptional skulls of *Euoplocephalus* show that these dinosaurs even went so far as to develop bony eyelids! Both skulls are preserved with curved bony plates inside the eye socket, which undoubtedly closed rather like steel shutters to protect the delicate eye from the talons of theropods. Although such bony eyelids have been found in *Euoplocephalus* only to date, it seems quite likely that other ankylosaurids possessed them.

Euoplocephalus, then, was a large animal weighing something like two tonnes. Rather than being an enormous, very slow-moving creature somewhat like a gigantic tortoise, it is here pictured as a surprisingly agile animal, perhaps more like a modern rhinoceros, which, although large and heavy, is by no means slow-moving.

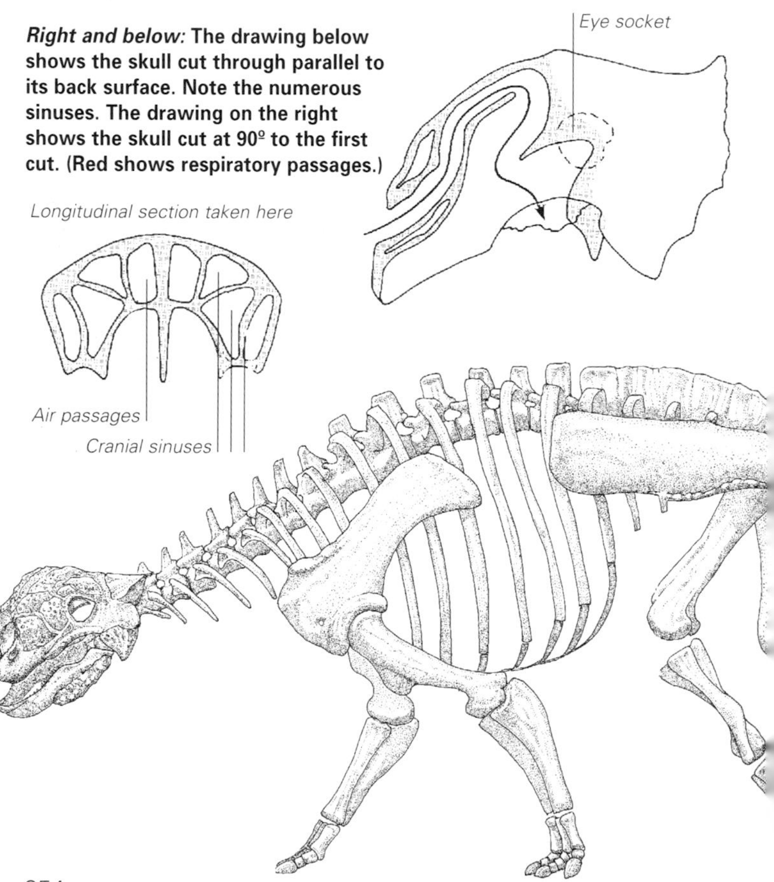

Right and below: **The drawing below shows the skull cut through parallel to its back surface. Note the numerous sinuses. The drawing on the right shows the skull cut at 90º to the first cut. (Red shows respiratory passages.)**

Right: **The skulls here show basic ankylosaurid features: broad and long; armoured, with the sides completely closed in; a slightly downturned beak at the front of the jaws; and large horns at the back corners. Euoplocephalus even has bony eyelids! The skull looks compact and immensely strong.**

Below: **In this ankylosaurid skeleton you can see the characteristic armoured head with its toothless beak, the shortish neck, the strongly built legs and the tail-club. The legs are tucked in underneath the body, a posture adopted more by mammals than by reptiles. The vertebral spines in the hip region are welded together, giving extra attachment area for hip muscles and also extra strength to transmit the powerful locomotory thrust of the leg. The relative size of the tail-club can be fully appreciated in the plan view (bottom).**

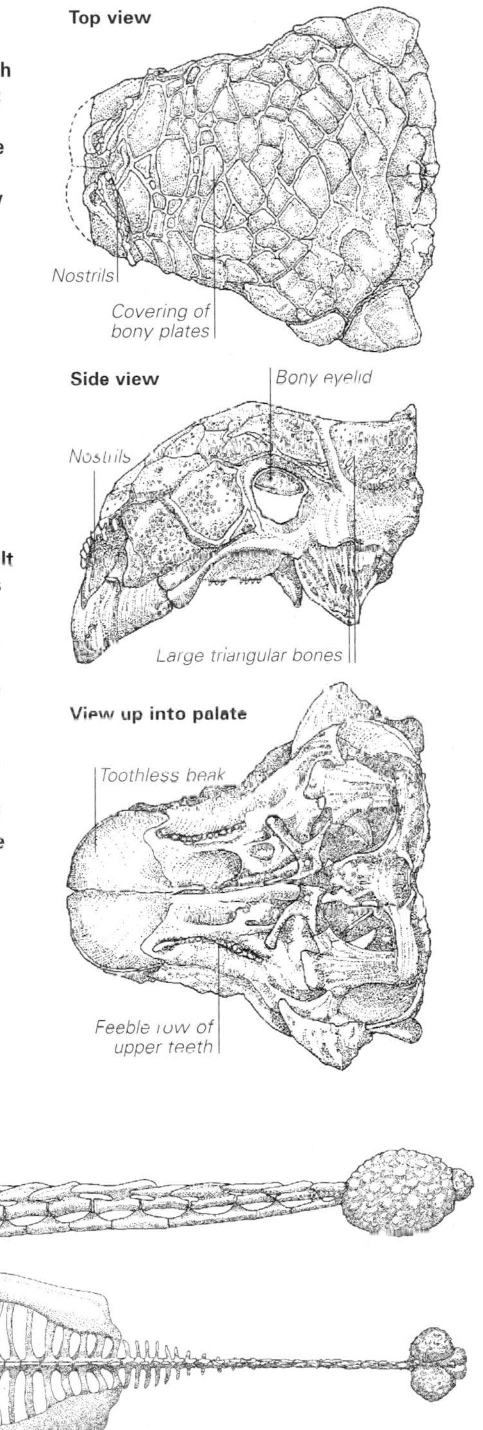

Pinacosaurus

Period: Late Cretaceous. **Family:** Ankylosaurids.
Where found: Mongolia.
Estimated length: 16ft 5in (5m).

Pinacosaurus ('plank reptile') was smaller than some of its relatives and of slender build. Its back and tail were covered with bony spines, and the end of the tail bore a heavy bony club. This was probably used as a defensive weapon: it could have been swung with some force to inflict a crippling blow to the legs or the stooped head of an attacker. *Pinacosaurus* had small, weak teeth and must have fed on relatively soft vegetation. The nasal passages in *Pinacosaurus* are interesting. Inside them, there are thin curved bones, which look strikingly similar to the turbinal, or scroll, bones found in the noses of mammals. These bones are covered by membranes, which filter, warm and moisten the air we breathe. It seems reasonable to assume they performed a similar function in ankylosaurids.

Pinacosaurus, also incorrectly referred to as *Syrmosaurus, Ninghsiaisaurus* and *Virminicaudus,* was first described by Charles Gilmore from material collected in the Gobi Desert during the American Museum Mongolian expedition of 1922-25.

A fairly recently discovered skull of a young *Pinacosaurus* is a rare example in which the bones that normally form a solid covering to the skull have not yet firmly attached themselves, with the result that the pattern of true skull bones is revealed for the first time. This is of great help when trying to discover the relationships of ankylosaurs to other ornithischians. Reaching a maximum body length of 16ft 5in (5m), *Pinacosaurus* was a relatively slender ankylosaurid.

Right: The tail-club is unique to ankylosaurids. It is formed from bones embedded in the skin, which have become greatly enlarged and fused to each other and to the tail vertebrae.

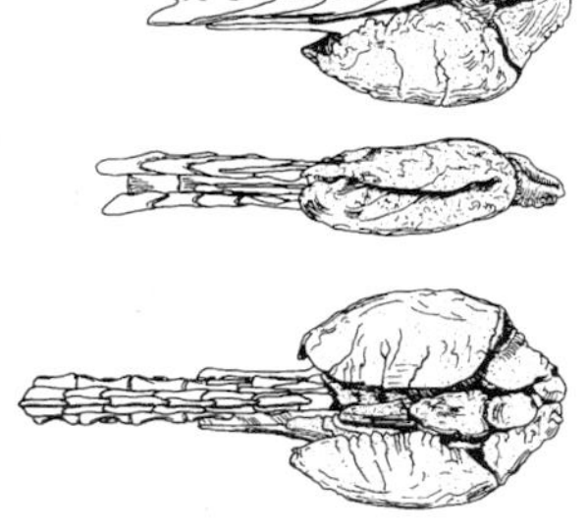

***Right:* *Pinacosaurus* ('plank reptile') was smaller than some of its relatives and of relatively slender build. Its back and tail were covered with bony spines, and the end of the tail bore a heavy bony club, which was probably used as a defensive weapon. The animal could have swung it with some force to inflict a crippling blow to the legs or the stooped head of an attacker. *Pinacosaurus* had small, weak teeth and must have fed on relatively soft vegetation.**

Left and above: The skull of *Pinacosaurus* shown here is a juvenile and the individual bones of the skull can still be seen – in adults they are welded together.

Dinosaur contemporaries

The following section of the book is devoted to a few of the other groups of animals that were contemporaries of the dinosaurs during the Mesozoic Era. It is not intended to be a completely comprehensive review, but it serves to highlight some of the more interesting non-dinosaurian types.

The **crocodiles** are a remarkable group of reptiles, which are quite close relatives of the dinosaurs. They appear to have evolved from archosaurian ancestors during the late Triassic. So successful were their form and lifestyle that they have remained almost unchanged since then, surviving even the mass extinction at the end of the Cretaceous.

In addition to the various archosaurian types of reptile (pterosaurs and crocodiles), a number of other groups of reptiles co-existed with the dinosaurs during the Mesozoic Era. Many of these were **marine reptiles** of considerable variety. They included the ichthyosaurs ('fish reptiles'), plesiosaurs ('ribbon reptiles'), placodonts ('flat teeth'), mosasaurs ('reptiles from the Meuse') and turtles. Generally these date from the Triassic Period.

The **lizards and snakes** are by far the most successful of modern reptiles, There are some 6,000 species alive today. The first lizards seem to have appeared in the late Triassic Period and, like the crocodilians, they have remained virtually unchanged to the present day - apart from some relatively short-lived variants. They are typically relatively small, agile, insectivorous creatures.

The **mammal-like reptiles and mammals** represent a very important group of animals in the fossil record. The mammal-like reptiles were particularly abundant in the Permian Period and the early part of the Triassic but their numbers declined rapidly towards the close of the Triassic. They included pelycosaurs ('sail reptiles'), therapsids ('beast arch') and cynodonts ('dog teeth'). The descendants of the mammal-like reptiles were the mammals, which today are quite distinct from the reptiles in a number of important ways.

The **pterosaurs**, or 'wing reptiles', were contemporaries of the dinosaurs throughout the Triassic, Jurassic and Cretaceous Periods; they also appear to be quite close relatives of the dinosaurs. Both dinosaurs and pterosaurs evolved from small, agile archosaurs in the late Triassic. However, while the dinosaurs rose to dominance on land, the pterosaurs became the first specialist flying vertebrates.

Because of the constraints imposed upon flying animals, their bodies were of necessity extremely light and delicate; this factor, allied to the fact that they lived in the air, militates very strongly against the preservation as fossils or their remains. Nevertheless numerous, sometimes spectacularly well-preserved fossils of pterosaurs have been discovered over the last two centuries, which provide ample evidence of pterosaurian biology. The vast majority of fossil remains of pterosaurs come from marine deposits; this has led to the widespread belief that they lived lives similar to those of modern sea-birds such as terns and albatrosses. However, it is also probable that there were a considerable number of inland forms.

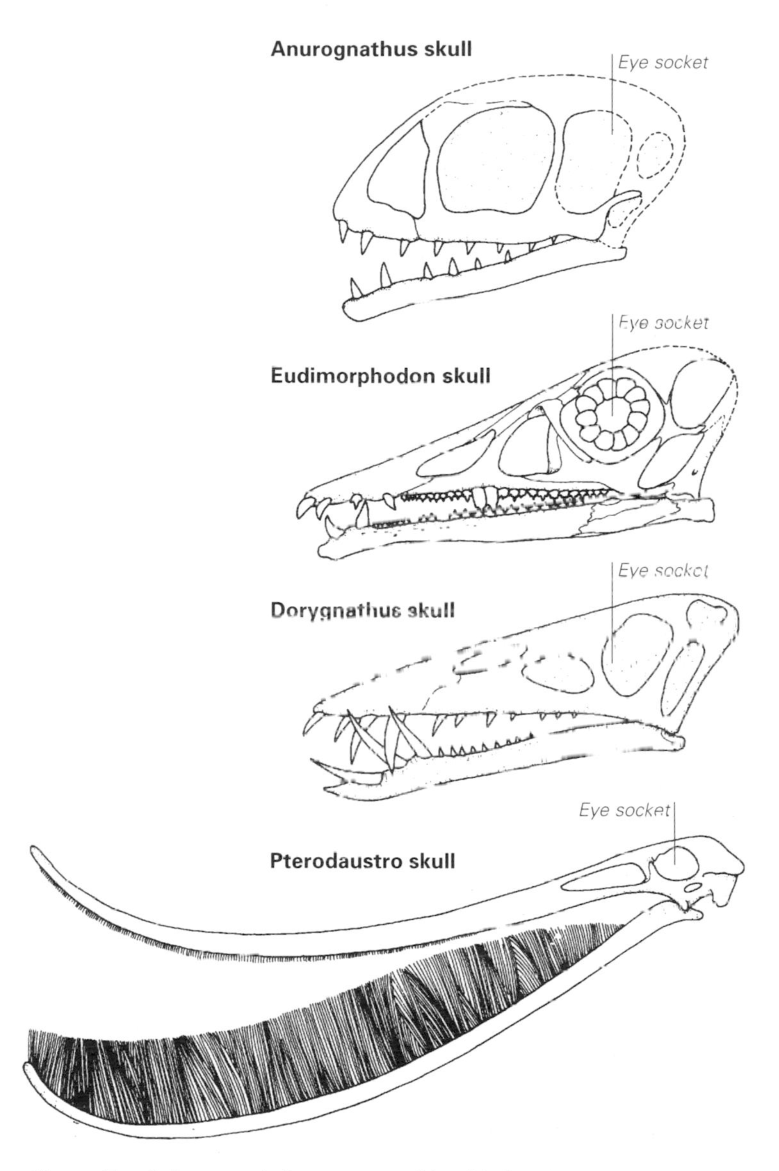

Above: **Head shape and size vary considerably in pterosaurs. *Anurognathus* (top) has a 'primitive' shape with a deep skull, while *Eudimorphodon* and *Dorygnathus* show the more typical long-snouted head. *Pterodaustro* has a comb-like array of teeth, possibly for sieving plankton.**

Crocodiles

The crocodiles are a remarkable group of reptiles, which are quite close relatives of the dinosaurs; they appear to have evolved from archosaurian ancestors during the late Triassic. However, for some reason they avoided the mass extinction at the end of the Cretaceous. The group is enormously conservative: once crocodiles appeared, as medium- to large-sized semi-aquatic predators, their fate was sealed, and they have changed relatively little in body form since then.

Modern crocodilians are found in tropical and subtropical environments and are of two major types. One group, the crocodylids, consists of the crocodiles and alligators of almost worldwide distribution; the gavialids comprise the slender-snouted fish-eating gavials (gharials) of India.

Crocodilians are long-bodied reptiles with a long and extremely powerful tail, which is used for swimming and as a defensive lash on land. They are perfectly equipped to catch their prey in or near water by stealth. The limbs are relatively short and are used for manoeuvring and steering in water.

Crocodiles can adopt an unusually high gait when they walk (i.e. holding the belly very high off the ground). The legs are drawn in very nearly underneath the body. This 'semi-erect' position is a more efficient method of walking than the sprawling posture used by most other reptiles, in which the belly is close to the ground and legs splay outward. Crocodiles have developed ankle joints with a swivel section in the middle that permits powerful twisting movements to occur at the ankle during the 'high walk'. The animals are capable of short bursts of fast running.

The eyes are positioned on top of the skull and the nostrils are right at the tip of the snout, containing special valves to close them off when the animals are submerged. The jaws are long and lined with large, deeply rooted conical teeth. Another notable feature of crocodilians is the heavy bony armour-plating of their backs, which affords protection

***Below and right:* This late Triassic animal was small, with a slender build, short trunk and long legs that lifted the belly quite high off the ground. Its back was extensively armour-plated.**

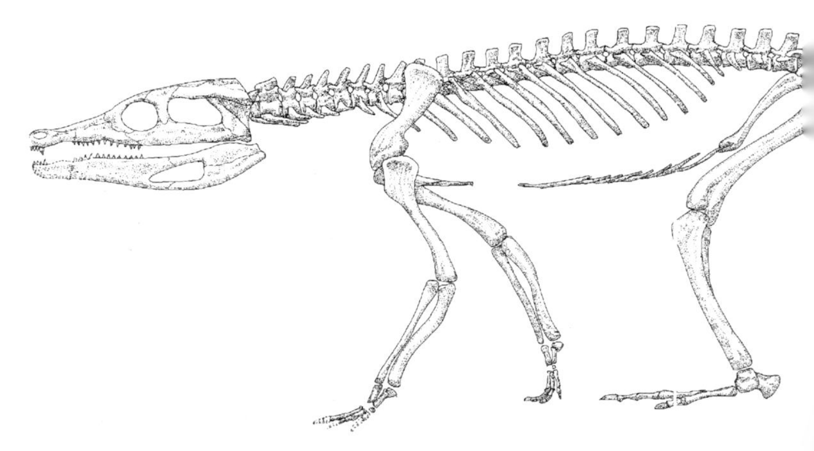

for young ones and lends support during locomotion on land. It may even be that the development of body armour down the back was a crucial step in the evolutionary line that led to the appearance of the dinosaurs on land.

Crocodiles are capable of very complex behaviour. One of the best examples is the exhibition of parental care in the Nile crocodile. In this species the hatchling crocodiles call to their parents from the next mound. This stimulates the parent crocodiles to break open the nest and release the young; these are then carried in the jaws of the parents to special 'nurseries' where they are watched over and protected. They are finally released when they are large enough to defend themselves against potential predators. In the Mesozoic, crocodilians of various sorts are known, some from very well-preserved fossil material. *Protosuchus* ('first crocodile') is a small (3ft 4in, 1m, long) primitive crocodilian from the late Triassic or possibly early Jurassic of Arizona. In its proportions, *Protosuchus* is generally more compact than modern crocodiles. As in all archosaurs, the hindlimbs are longer than the forelimbs. *Protosuchus* was evidently primarily terrestrial, as is suggested by not only the proportions of the body and limbs but also the position of the eyes and nostrils on the side of the head rather than on top.

Orthosuchus ('straight crocodile') is from the late Triassic of Lesotho. *Orthosuchus* closely resembles *Protosuchus* in its general proportions, notably a short body, but its limbs appear somewhat shorter and there is less disparity between fore- and hindlimbs. The narrow snout and relatively feeble teeth may indicate that *Orthosuchus* ▶

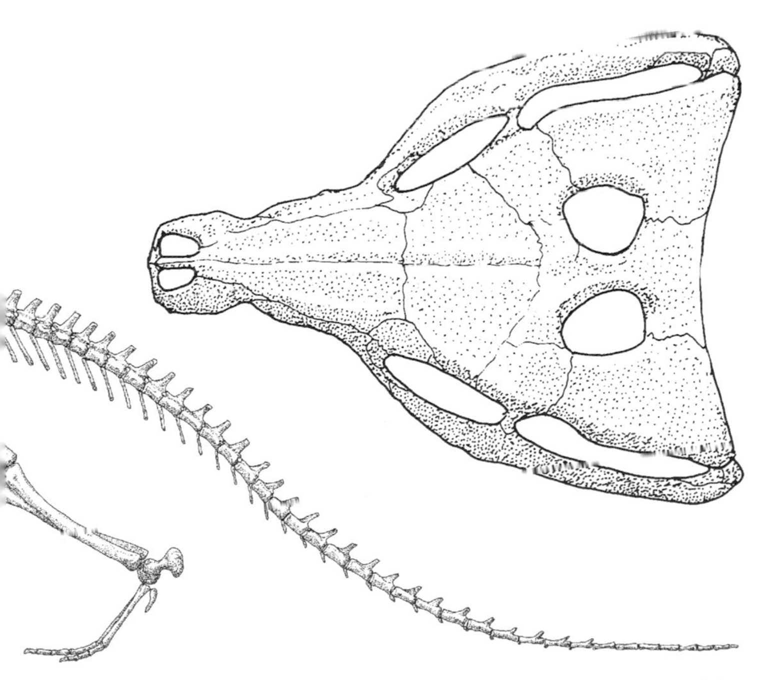

preyed upon fish rather than larger terrestrial vertebrates; thus the animal may have inhabited swampy areas.

More typical crocodilians are found in the Jurassic Period. *Teleosaurus* ('end reptile') and Steneosaurus ('narrow reptile') appear to have been marine or possibly estuarine inhabitants. They have long bodies and notably elongate snouts lined with thin, sharp teeth, indicating that they were primarily fish-eaters. Although generally aquatic, these forms retained the typical heavily armoured body and well-developed limbs and feet.

Metriorhynchus ('long snout') and *Geosaurus* ('rock reptile') are members of a very distinctive group of Jurassic crocodilians, the thallatosuchians ('sea crocodiles'). These long-snouted, presumably fish-eating crocodilians were completely unarmoured and their limbs were modified into flippers or paddles. For propulsion, however, they relied on the tail, which was modified by the development of a tail fin. For some reason these 'sea crocodiles' were not particularly successful: they seem to have become extinct in late Jurassic times.

Modern types of crocodile begin to appear towards the end of the Jurassic Period. *Goniopholis* (6ft 6in-10ft, 2-3m, long), a reasonably typical crocodile, is found fairly widespread across Europe. Two rather fine *Goniopholis* skeletons were found at Bernissart among the many *Iguanodon* carcasses, as was another specimen, a tiny crocodilian, less than 3ft (1m) long. Though small, *Bernissartia* was well-armoured and had rather teeth evidently made for crushing (cracking open clam shells?) rather than for piercing.

During the Cretaceous Period, the crocodilians were far more abundant and widespread than today. This probably reflects the fact that the conditions were much milder then. Records of warmth-loving plants from the Mesozoic Era indicate that tropical or subtropical conditions extended into the temperate and subarctic regions of today.

One of the most remarkable of the Cretaceous crocodiles comes from the Rio Grande in Texas. Named *Deinosuchus* ('terrible crocodile') or *Phobosuchus* ('fearsome crocodile'), this is the largest crocodile so far found. The skull is 6ft (1.8m) long, indicating that the animal may have attained a total length of 40-50ft (12-15m). *Deinosuchus* was either a typical amphibious crocodile preying upon occasional wading sauropods or hadrosaurs, or a short-bodied, longer-legged terrestrial predator.

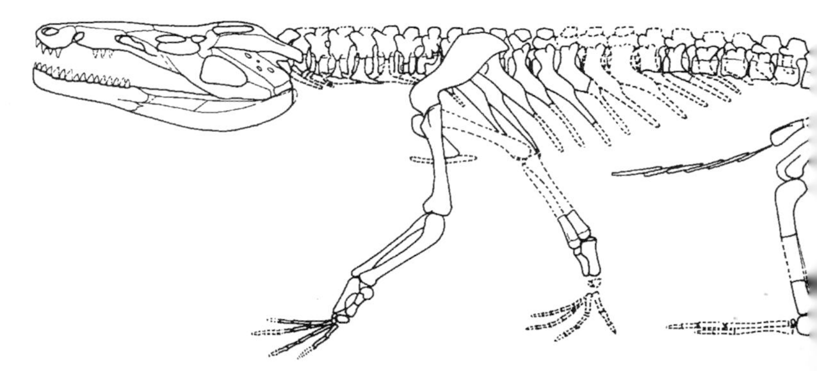

Right: Orthosuchus and *Protosuchus* skulls are broad and short-snouted. *Metriorhynchus* and *Pelagosaurus* show an extreme elongation of the snout that suggests a fish diet, while *Crocodylus* is a broad and powerful general predator.

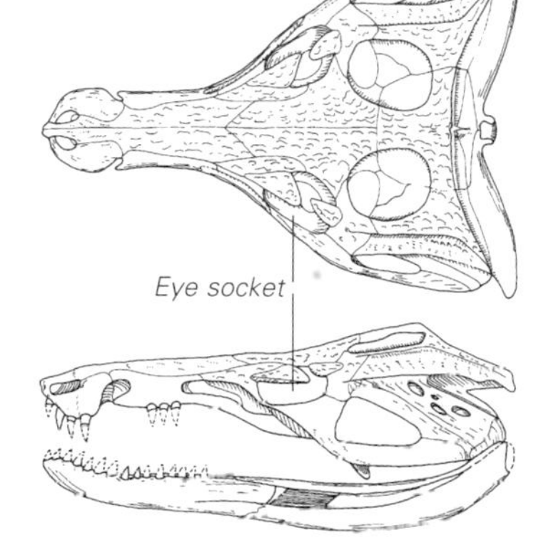

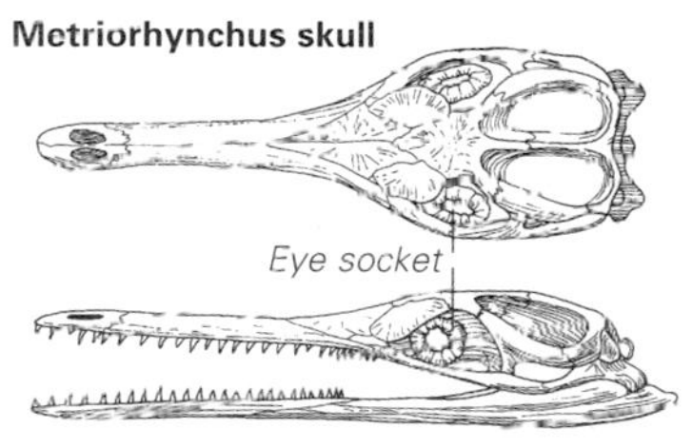

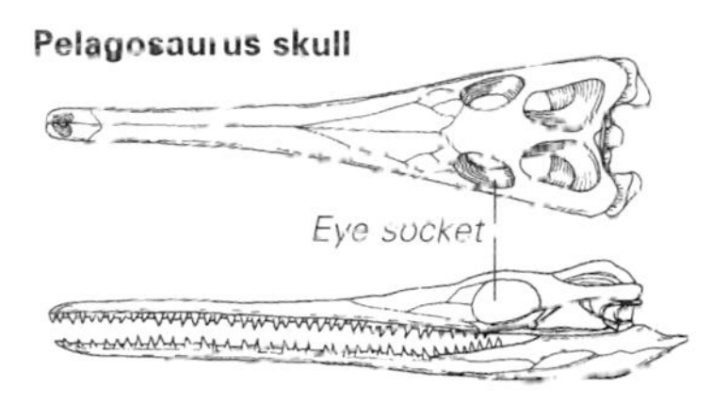

Below: To judge by its jaws and rather feeble teeth, *Orthosuchus* was a fish-eating swamp-dweller, rather than a land-living predator.

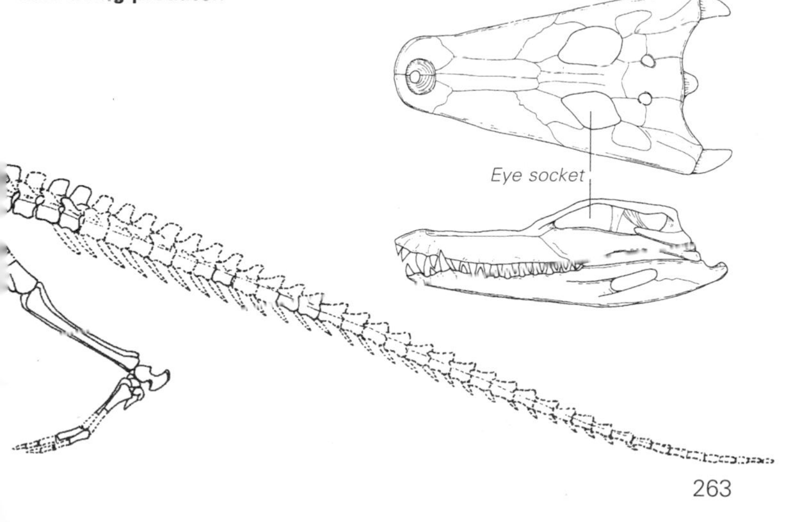

Marine reptiles

Of all the varied reptilian types that co-existed with the dinosaurs during the Mesozoic Era, the ichthyosaurs ('fish reptiles') are by far the most highly adapted to an aquatic lifestyle. The earliest ichthyosaurs date back to the late Triassic. Ichthyosaurs were particularly abundant in the Jurassic Period, although their remains extend into the late Cretaceous too.

Mixosaurus ('mixed reptile') from the late Triassic is an early example with a full range of ichthyosaur characteristics. The head is drawn out into a long, thin snout fringed with small spiky teeth; the eyes are unusually large and supported by a circular array of bones, presumably for focusing. The body is smooth and streamlined and the neck is absent, thanks to great compression of the neck vertebrae. The limbs are modified into paddles for steering. The tail is long and tapering, but the elongate spines near its base suggest the presence of an auxiliary fin to assist propulsion.

Temnodontosaurus ('cutting toothed reptile') from the early Jurassic was one of the largest of all ichthyosaurs, reaching lengths of 30ft (9m). *Temnodontosaurus* has its tail bones curved down near their tip to support a broad paddle-like fin. Skin impressions of ichthyosaurs found at several localities in southern Germany reveal that the tail 'fluke' also extended upwards.

Ophthalmosaurus ('eye reptile'), also from the Jurassic, was named for its particularly large eyes. Although typically ichthyosaurian,

Right: **The skull of *Ophthalmosaurus* (top), a Jurassic ichthyosaur, has a very long, slender, toothless snout and a large eye socket with a ring of bony plates. Below is a typical plesiosaur skull with a broad, flat snout armed with large teeth.**

Below: **The ichthyosaur's streamlined body shape is very similar to that of a porpoise.**

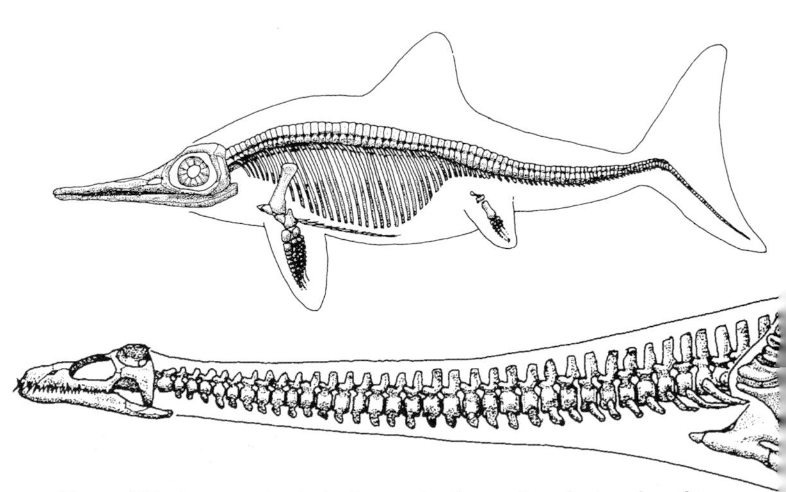

Above: **This long-necked plesiosaur is shown in a fast swimming position with front flippers fully raised ready to be swept downwards powerfully.**

Ichthyosaur skull

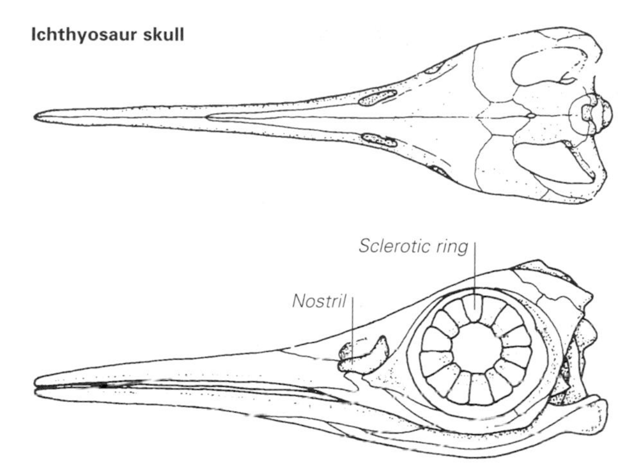

Plesiosaur skull

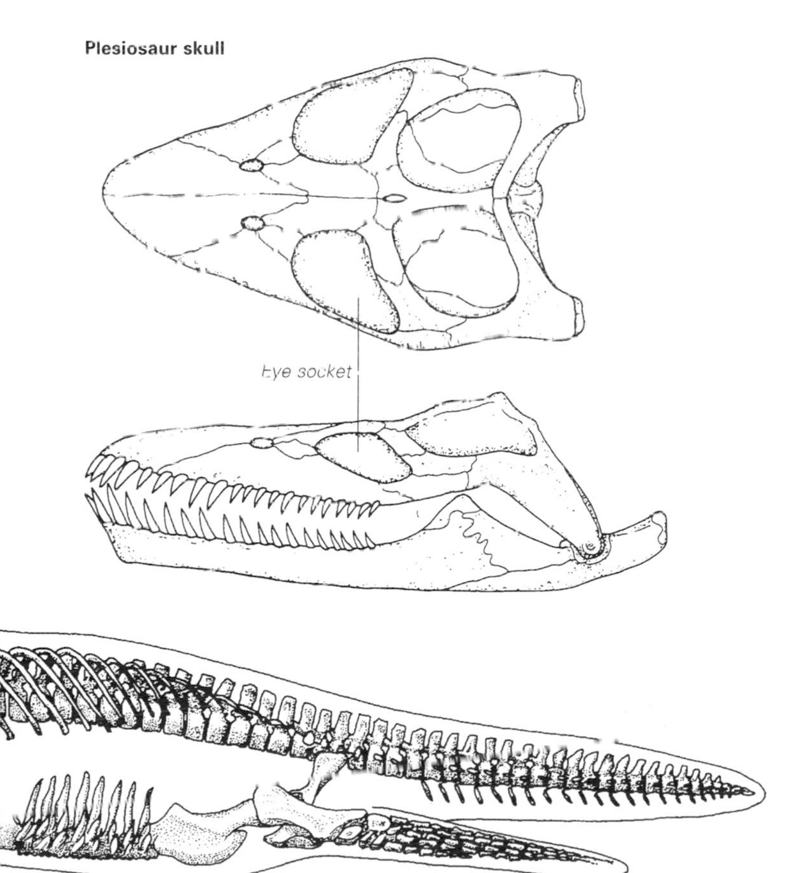

Ophthalmosaurus apparently lacked any teeth.

The discovery of some beautifully preserved ichthyosaur skeletons, including fossilised soft tissues within the ribcage, has provided information about the feeding and reproductive habits of ichthyosaurs. Ichthyosaurs fed upon cephalopods, fish and occasionally pterosaurs. Several skeletons reveal the presence of embryos within the body cavity of a mother ichthyosaur; one appears to have been preserved at the moment of birth (tail first) of the baby! The necessity of bearing live young, rather than laying eggs as many reptiles do, reflects the fact that ichthyosaurs were so highly adapted to aquatic life that they were unable even to crawl on to land to lay their eggs.

Plesiosaurs ('ribbon reptiles'), another important group of reptiles of the Mesozoic, were less obviously fish-like than the ichthyosaurs but nevertheless well adapted for marine existence. Many plesiosaurs have relatively short tails and long necks. The body is broad and quite compact with closely set strong ribs and well-developed gastralia lining the belly area. The limbs are also large and bear well-developed paddles, which were flapped up and down for propulsion like the paddles of a turtle.

The long-necked or 'plesiosauroid' plesiosaurs, such as *Elasmosaurus* ('plated reptile') and *Plesiosaurus* ('ribbon reptile'), had relatively small heads and sharply pointed teeth. Probably these were fish-eaters using the neck like a sling to 'throw' the head at the prey.

Short-necked or 'pliosauroid' plesiosaurs were powerfully built with enormous heads - *Kronosaurus* ('time reptile') from Australia had a head nearly 8ft (2.4m) long - and must have been formidable predators. Placodonts ('flat teeth') are a rather odd group of Triassic reptiles. The neck and trunk is relatively short and generally covered in well-developed bony armour. The tail is fairly short and apparently not always used for swimming. The limbs are short and powerful. Evidently these animals walked across the sea floor and used their claws to prise

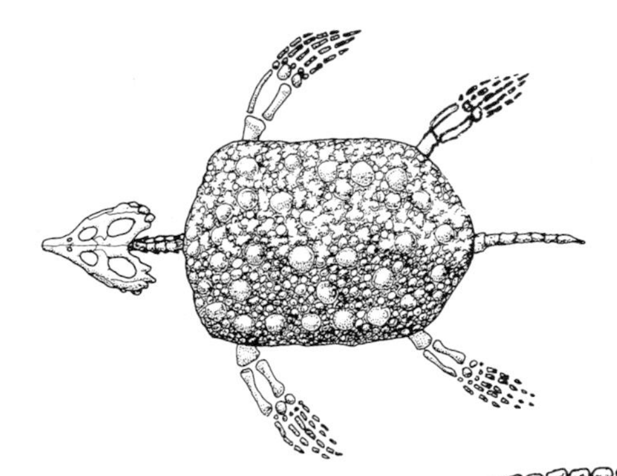

Left: **Placodonts resembled turtles, with heavily armoured backs and flipper-like legs.**

Below: **With its armour-plating removed, *Placodus* looks much like other reptiles. Its body is quite short and is supported by powerful legs that splay outwards.**

clams and suchlike from rocky ledges or crevices.

The front teeth are blunt and forward-pointing in order to grasp potential food, the sides and roof of the mouth covered by large, flat crushing plates. Powerful muscles operate the jaws. These features all point to a diet of hard-shelled molluscs. The extraordinary degree of armour-plating found in these animals presumably reflects the fact that they were slow-moving and therefore open to attack from various aquatic predators.

Mosasaurs ('reptiles from the Meuse') were very large (15-30ft, 4.5-9m, long) marine lizards that evolved in the late Cretaceous. They are especially abundant in the Cretaceous rocks of northern Europe (Maastricht, Netherlands) and Kansas (USA). The head is long and the jaws armed with long, sharp fangs - a standard pattern for most aquatic predators. The neck is quite short and the body behind particularly long and slender. The tail was the main swimming organ, while the paddle-like limbs were used for steering. The feet and hands have long, delicate toes which were probably webbed. The lower jaw has an extra joint half-way long its length, a feature it shares with living monitor lizards, to which it is probably closely related. Mosasaurs were sufficiently large to take a whole range of large vertebrate prey.

The earliest turtles are Triassic *Proganochelys* ('first turtle') had a well-developed bony carapace and a horny beak covering its jaws, like modern turtles and tortoises. However, it probably could not withdraw head, tail or legs inside the shell. Unlike modern forms it retained some teeth on the roof of its mouth, possibly to hold slippery fish in the mouth before they were swallowed.

One of the most impressive turtles was *Archelon* ('ancient turtle'). This Cretaceous turtle grew to over 12ft (3.6m) in length. Its carapace was well developed and its flipper-like limbs were very large.

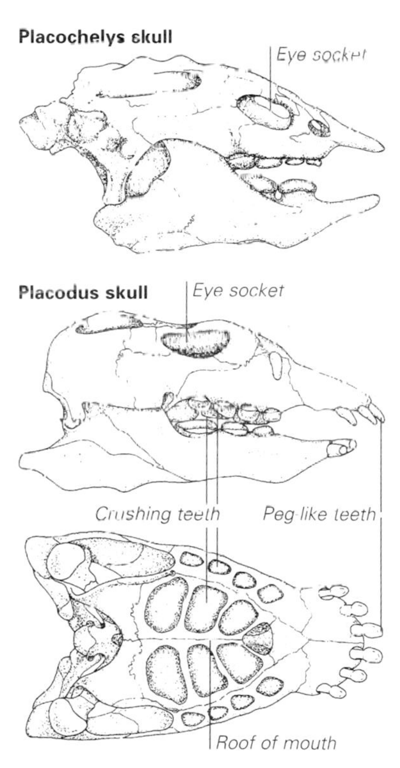

Above: The head of _Placochelys_ is very short-jawed and powerful. The short, block-like teeth are absent from the front of the jaws, which was perhaps covered by a horny beak. The skull of _Placodus_ is seen in side view and looking into the roof of the mouth with the lower jaw removed. The jaws contain peg-like teeth at the front and massive crushing teeth at the back.

Lizards and snakes

The lizards and snakes are easily the most successful of modern reptiles, with about 6,000 species alive today. The first lizards appear in late Triassic rocks. These relatively small, agile, insectivorous creatures have, with few exceptions, remained virtually unchanged to the present day.

One 'secret' of their success may be that their structure ideally suits them to particular ecological niches, specifically, the way in which the skull and jaw bones are linked together in a moveable chain of bones.

Non-lizard reptiles possess an arch of bone, marked (J). In lizards, however, this bone has disappeared. As a result, the bone Q in lizards (a bone that forms the joint with the lower jaw) is permitted to swing backwards and forwards. This means, first, that the lower jaw can be slid fore and aft. Second, movement of Q also operates a series of joints within the skull. Thus the snout can be raised and lowered. This mobility in the jaws of lizards was undoubtedly important, perhaps allowing them to feed more effectively on insects, thanks to greater precision of jaw closure. The unusual hingeing system may also have acted as a 'shock-absorber' in the skull, cushioning the brain against the jarring effect caused by snapping the jaws shut.

The fossil record of lizards is poor, largely because lizards tend to live in dry uplands away from the areas that are most likely to produce fossils, and because their skeletons are so small and easily destroyed. Nevertheless, several fossil lizards are known. *Kuehneosaurus* ('Kühne's reptile') from the late Triassic of Britain was already highly specialised; its ribs were enormously elongate and formed membranes that allowed the animal to glide from tree to tree.

Snakes have an even worse fossil record than lizards. The first remains of snakes are known from the late Cretaceous of North America (*Coniophis*, 'Coniacian snake') and Patagonia (*Dinilysia*, 'terrible destroyer').

A key difference between lizards and snakes is that in a snake skull, not only J but also the arch of bone above it (U) has been lost. The bone (Q) that supports the lower jaw has therefore only the flimsiest attachment to the skull - giving great mobility to the lower jaw. Further, both sides of the lower jaw are separate, and the skull bones are extremely loosely connected. As a result, the whole head has amazing

Below left: **The ability of bone Q to move to and fro is used by lizards to tilt the snout up and down.**

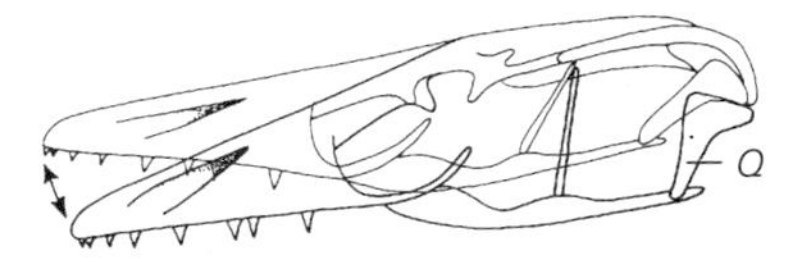

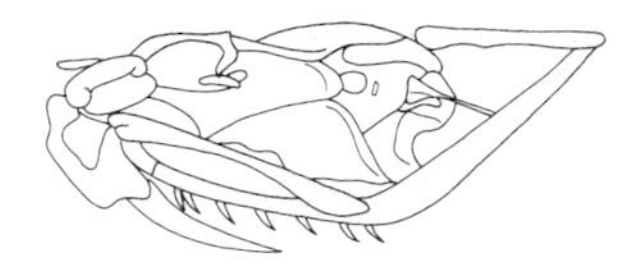

Right: Seen here is the mechanism of fang erection in venomous snakes (red). With jaws closed the fangs are folded back, but when the jaws open they swing forward ready to strike.

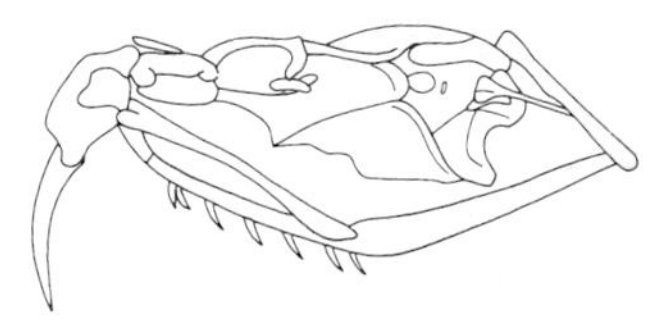

flexibility, allowing it to swallow very large animal prey.

Snakes use a variety of methods for killing their prey. The large boas, pythons and anacondas use constriction to suffocate their prey. Other types of snakes (notably the viper family) are able to inject deadly venoms. Whether vipers had evolved in late Cretaceous times is uncertain.

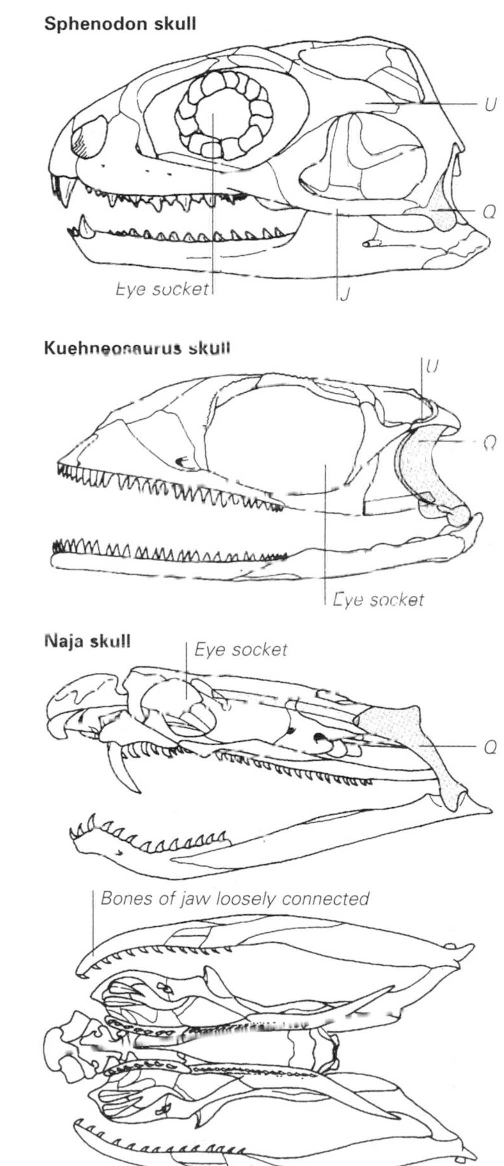

Right: *Sphenodon* (top) is a typical early lizard. Note the positions of the bony arches J (jugal) and U (upper temporal) and the bone Q (quadrate), which forms part of the jaw joint. *Kuehneosaurus* is an early true lizard. J has been lost leaving bone Q free to swing backwards and forwards. In the snake skull (bottom) arches J and U have both been lost. Both sides of the lower jaw are separate.

Mammal-like reptiles and mammals

The mammal-like reptiles were particularly abundant in the Permian and early Triassic, at the end of which their disappearance heralded the arrival of two new groups: the dinosaurs, which rose rapidly to dominate the land for the next 140 million years or so, and the first true mammals. Rather than being large, dominant creatures as they are today, these early mammals were small, shrew-like insectivores, which remained in the shadow of the dinosaurs throughout the remainder of the Mesozoic Era. Things might have continued like this had it not been for the mysterious and sudden mass extinction of the dinosaurs and many other creatures at the end of the Cretaceous Period 64 million years ago. Within the space of a few million years thereafter, the mammals that had survived the extinction event underwent a spectacular evolutionary radiation. They evolved not only into large, land-living animals of all shapes and sizes, but also into sea creatures - whales, dolphins, seals, sea cows - and flying animals, in the form of bats. Part of the wide radiation of mammals in the early Tertiary included some fairly small, almost rat-like creatures, the first primates, from which the human species was eventually to arise only 2-3 million years ago.

The earliest known mammal-like reptiles are called pelycosaurs ('sail reptiles') and are first found in rocks of late Carboniferous age. *Archaeothyris* ('ancient opening') from Nova Scotia is small and lizard-like - but with one particular distinguishing feature, the small single opening on the side of the skull just behind the eye. This one character is found only in the synapsids, or mammal-like reptiles, and, in a highly modified form, in mammals.

From these small beginnings, the pelycosaurs evolved into some of the dominant terrestrial animals of the early Permian. There were apparently three main types of pelycosaur, the large long-bodied and long-snouted ophiacodonts (named after *Ophiacodon*, or 'snake tooth'); the sphenacodonts (*Dimetrodon*); and the edaphosaurs (*Edaphosaurus*).

Dimetrodon ('two long teeth') was a large predator with enormously long dorsal spines that looked like a large fan perched on the back. The spines were undoubtedly covered by thin skin and the 'sail' could have

***Below:* This reconstruction shows the large head, sprawling limbs and tall 'sail' of spines of *Dimetrodon*.**

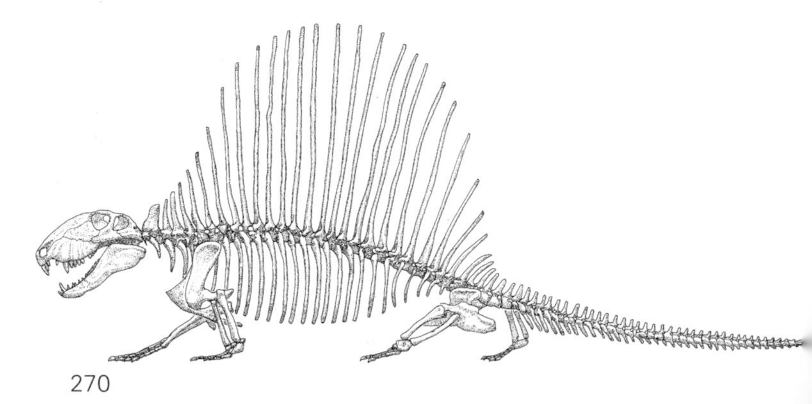

***Right top and middle: Archaeothyris* is the earliest well-described pelycosaur, a small lizard-like creature of the late Carboniferous. *Ophiacodon* from the Permian is a larger form that was clearly a predator. It may have been aquatic.**

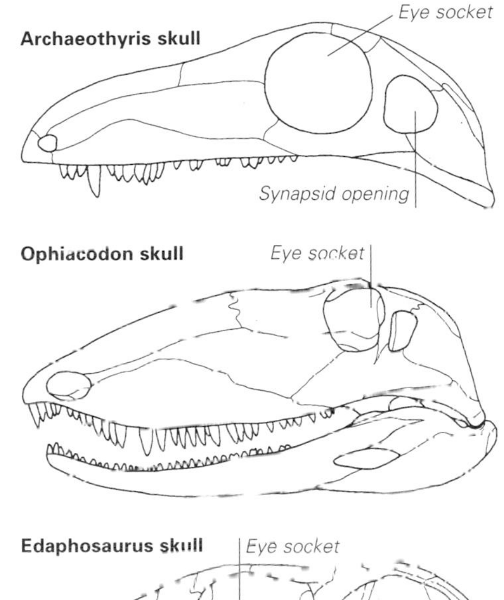

***Right: Edaphosaurus's* teeth are blunt and modified to form large grinding plates for crushing plants.**

***Below: Lycaenops* was a therapsid mammal-like reptile of the late Permian with the large stabbing teeth of a carnivorous predator.**

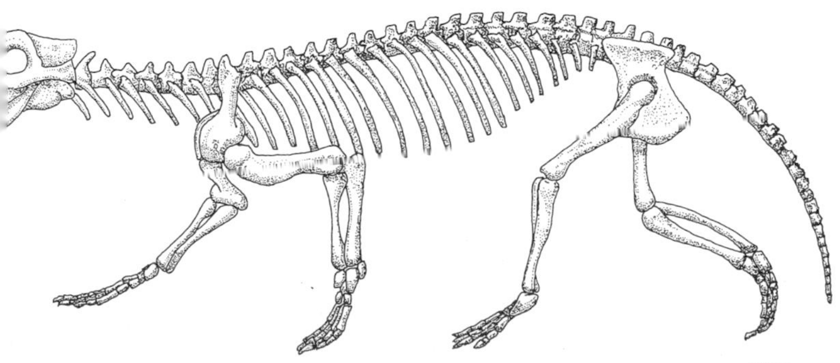

regulated temperature, acting as either a solar panel or as a radiator, depending on the amount of blood flowing through it.

Edaphosaurus ('earth reptile'), a Permian herbivorous pelycosaur, had a sail made up of knobbly spines (unlike the smooth spines of *Dimetrodon*), which may have increased surface area and therefore temperature-regulating efficiency.

At the very beginning of the late Permian, the pelycosaurs dwindled in numbers and rapidly became extinct. Their place seems to have been taken by another mammal-like reptile group known as the therapsids ('beast arch'). *Cynognathus* was an advanced carnivore with a striking similarity to a modern dog. The teeth are highly differentiated for different purposes.

Morganucodon skull

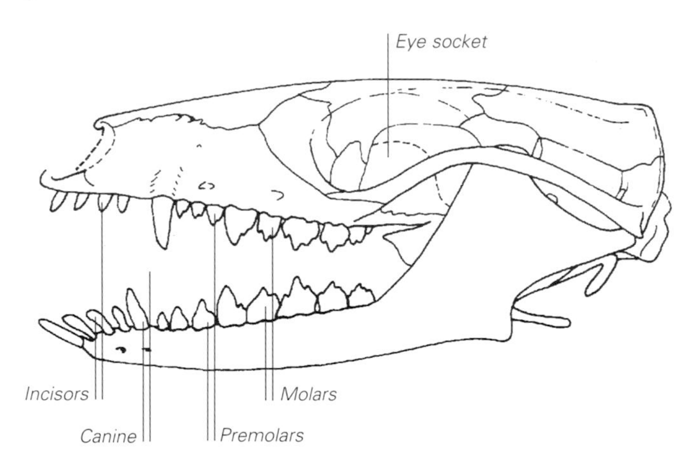

***Above:* A close relative of *Megazostrodon, Morganucodon* is an early mammal from south Wales. It had four types of teeth.**

***Below:* One of the more advanced types of cynodont, *Probelesodon* from South America was a small, nimble predator. It had large spaces behind the eyes for the jaw muscles.**

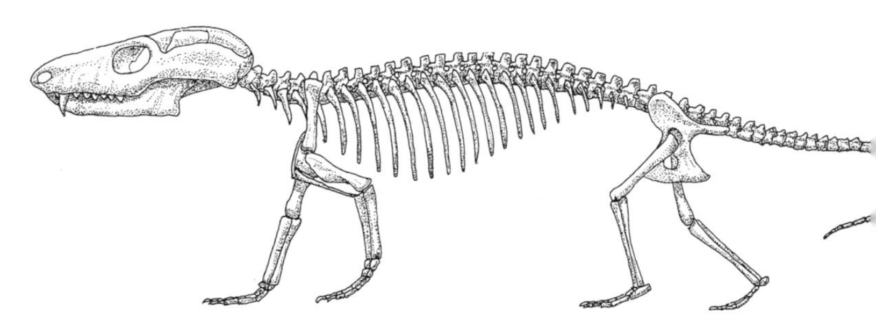

***Right:* Delphinognathus was typical of an early Permian therapsid, *Dicynodon* of dicynodont therapsids of the late Permian and Triassic. The creatures were about the size of modern sheep. *Cynognathus* was an advanced carnivore with a striking similarity to a modern dog. The teeth are highly differentiated for different purposes.**

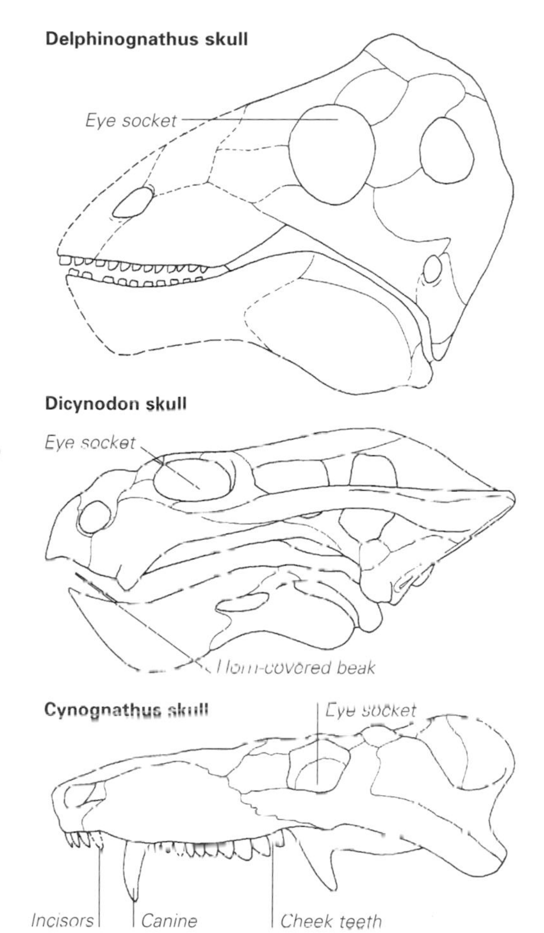

***Below:* The discovery in 1966 of the partial skeleton and skull of this tiny, agile insectivore, *Megazostrodon*, marked a breakthrough in our understanding of mammal-like reptiles.**

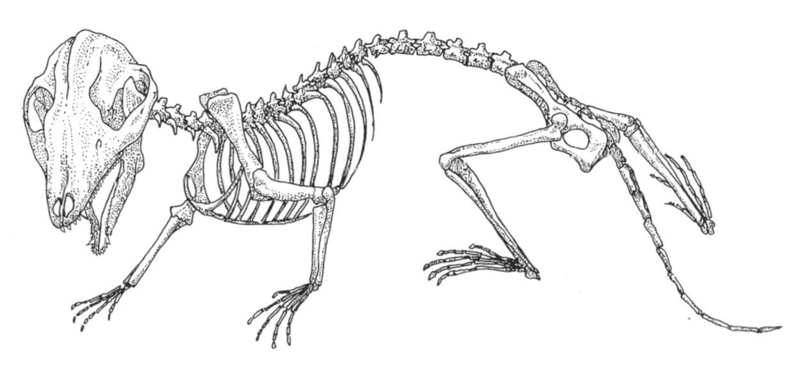

Pterosaurs

The first pterosaur find was a small fossil on a slab of Solnhofen lithographic limestone from Eichstätt in Bavaria. In 1801 the great Parisian anatomist Georges Cuvier recognised that it was a reptile that could fly - a hitherto entirely unknown type of creature that he called *Pterodactylus* ('flight finger'). Many other pterosaur finds followed, at Solnhofen and in many other geological formations as well, from the late Triassic (220 million years ago) to the late Cretaceous (65 million years ago). Pterosaurs lived on all continents except Antarctica and appeared in an extraordinary variety of forms, including genera from the size of a sparrow up to the largest flying creatures of all time. Nevertheless, pterosaurs maintained their special characteristics to the end: a unique wing structure and extreme lightness of skeleton. The most important finds have been made in the region of Solnhofen and Eichstätt but pterosaur fossils have also been found in France, England, Portugal, Russia, East Africa, Cuba, the USA and China.

Reptiles flourished for the first time in the Triassic Period. Reptiles lay their eggs on dry land. The eggs are large, with big yolks, and protected by a hard shell. Unlike amphibians, they do not have to go through a larval stage in water. This 'invention' about 300 million years ago was the essential step that enables the reptiles to conquer dry land and to evolve in the astonishing way they did. Their descendants, birds, mammals and human beings, owe their existence to this crucial development.

Evolution grabbed this opportunity with great suddenness, and in the Triassic all orders of reptiles, including pterosaurs, plesiosaurs, dinosaurs, placodonts and others were established.

There is evidence of the earliest pterosaurs in the late Triassic. Pterosaurs were the first vertebrates to adapt to a life of active flight. They dominated the air without competition until the late Jurassic, for ▶

Below: **The earliest known diapsid is *Petrolacosaurus kansensis*. This lizard-like reptile, about 23in (58cm) long, lived about 300 million years ago.**

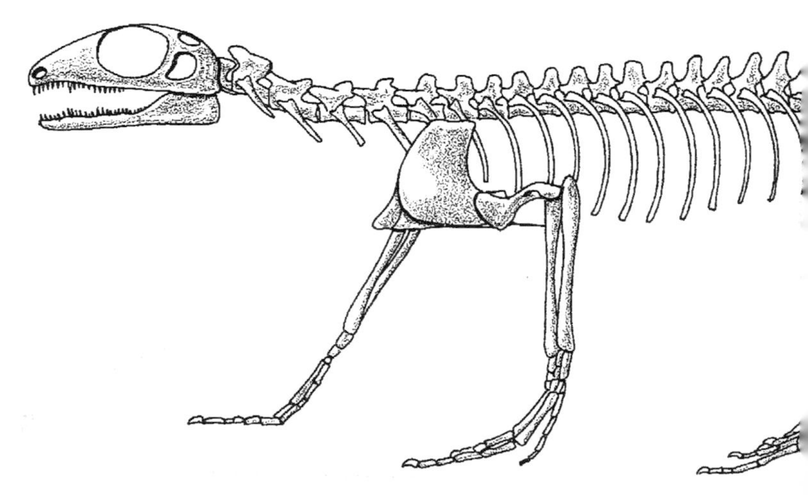

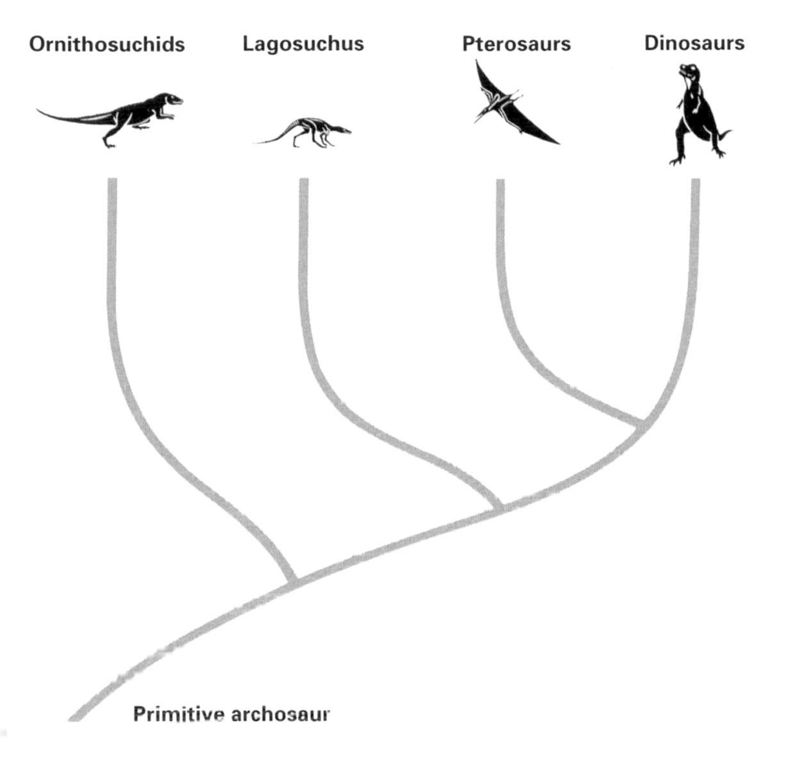

Above: This cladogram shows the hypothetical phylogenetic relationships between the pterosaurs, dinosaurs, *Lagosuchus* and ornithosuchids, all sharing a common ancestor.

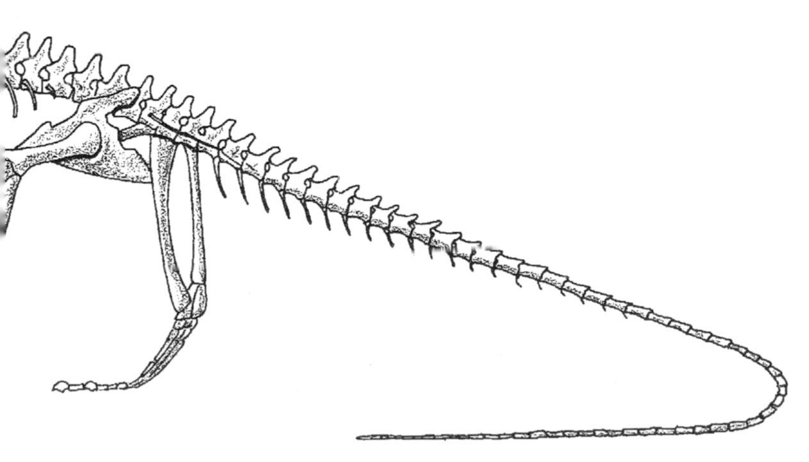

almost 70 million years. After the long-tailed pterosaurs, the Rhamphorhynchoidea, became extinct in the late Jurassic, short-tailed pterosaurs, the Pterodactyloidea, developed considerably in the Cretaceous. The largest known pterosaur, *Quetzalcoatlus*, lived in what is now Texas towards the end of the Cretaceous, about 65 million years ago. At the end of the Cretaceous most reptiles became extinct, among them the pterosaurs. Latterly these reached enormous dimensions, with wing spans of 39ft (12m).

If the history of the earth is imagined as one 24-hour day, the beginning of the day is the formation of the earth 4,600 million years ago: 00.00 hours. The last stroke of midnight, 24.00 hours, marks the present moment. Thus an hour represents 191.7 million years. The first saurians (reptiles) appeared at 22.26 hours and the first pterosaurs at 22.51. At 23.13 the first birds appeared and the long-tailed pterosaurs became extinct. The short-tailed pterosaurs flourished at 23.35 and became extinct along with the dinosaurs and others at 23.39. Modern man (*Homo sapiens*) appeared 2 seconds before midnight.

Are pterosaurs reptiles at all? The modern definition of reptiles accommodates warm-blooded creatures such as pterosaurs, although reptiles are a motley crew probably without a common phylogeny.

The absence or presence of certain openings in the skull is considered a significant pointer in classifying reptiles. A distinction is made between anapsids without a temporal opening behind the eye socket (tortoises, for example), synapsids with only one, lower temporal opening (the mammal-like reptiles), euryapsids with only one, upper temporal opening (ichthyosaurs) and finally diapsids with two temporal

***Below: Scleromochlus* may be an ancestor of the pterosaurs. But its hindlimbs were much longer than its forelimbs - the reverse is true of pterosaurs.**

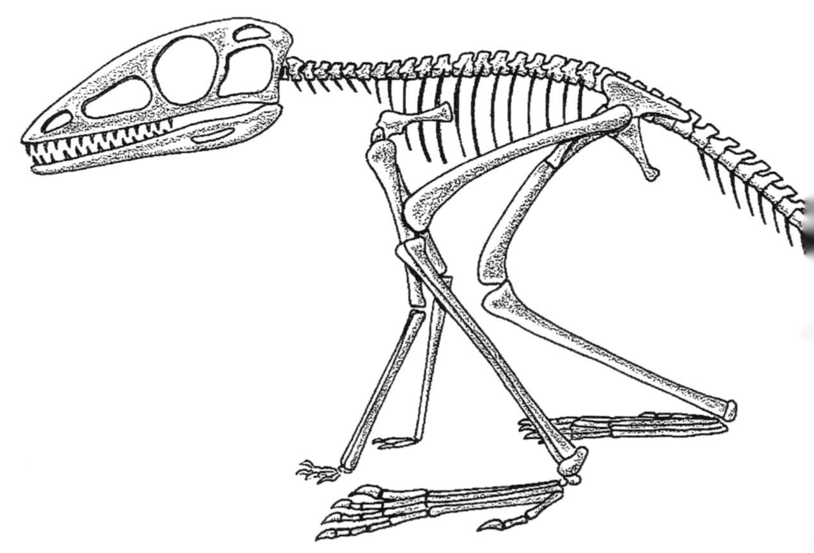

openings, an upper and a lower. According to this scheme pterosaurs are diapsids.

The earliest diapsid reptile known is from the late Carboniferous. It was a lizard-sized creature called *Petrolacosaurus*. There are two groups of diapsid reptiles, lepidosaurs and archosaurs. The lepidosaurs include lizards, snakes and the extinct rhynchosaurs and eosuchians. Crocodiles and alligators are the only remaining archosaurs, the group that also included dinosaurs. Archosaurs and pterosaurs have one significant characteristic in common: another aperture in the skull wall between the eye and nose sockets, a so-called preorbital opening. Thus pterosaurs can be classified as archosaurs.

By far the most frequent fossil pterosaur finds are made in marine strata. Most of the known species of pterosaur probably lived near the coast and fed on fish or other aquatic organisms. In rare cases soft parts, muscles, skin and connective tissue also survived as fossils - preserving imprints of flight membranes, of webs between the long toes, of a throat pouch, of respiratory tubes and of the outline of the body.

The fact that pterosaurs were flying creatures implies a high energy requirement. This can be 'financed' only by warm-bloodedness; which in turn requires a body covering of hair, feathers or fur to prevent heat loss. Pterosaurs were warm-blooded and had a body covering of hair, as fossil finds have shown.

This characteristic alone makes pterosaurs different from modern, cold-blooded reptiles like crocodiles or lizards. Another possible difference is that their young were born alive and fed for as long as they remained in the nest.

Triassic Pterosaurs

The Triassic Period at the beginning of the Mesozoic Era was highly significant for reptilian evolution. This was the time at which such diverse groups as tortoises, crocodiles and dinosaurs appeared. Fossil finds of the oldest pterosaurs so far known come from late Triassic deposits in Gloucestershire, England. Two small bones could be identified as wing metacarpals. However, they lack diagnostic characters and cannot be assigned to any known pterosaur, except to the family known as Rhamphorhynchoidea. They may even represent a new genus of pterosaur.

For a long time a fossil reptile skeleton from the middle Triassic in Besano, northern Italy, called *Tribelesodon*, was considered to be the oldest known pterosaur. Excavations in this region in 1863 and 1878 brought to light a small fossil remnant of a skeleton. Francesco Bassani identified this as a pterosaur and named it *Tribelesodon* ('three-cusped tooth'), on account of its tiny teeth with three cusps. In 1922 Franz Baron Nopcsa, a geologist and reptile expert, produced a detailed description of the putative *Tribelesodon* pterosaur, along with a drawing of the reconstructed skeleton, showing it with a long tail. The striking feature of this find, the only specimen of this creature, was a series of long bones, which both Bassani and Nopcsa took to be the elongated phalanges of a flight digit.

The Besano Triassic strata consist of black shale containing bitumen, marine deposits about 235 million years old, extending into Switzerland. Here in 1919 a palaeontologist, Bernhard Peyer, found reptile remains. They sparked off a series of excavations that continued until the mid-1970s. In September 1929 they produced an almost complete skeleton of a small reptile with extremely long cervical vertebrae. Vertebrae of this kind were already known from northern Bavaria and variously thought to be limb bones or the caudal vertebrae of a dinosaur, which Hermann von Meyer had named *Tanystropheus* ('long vertebra') in 1855. When Peyer compared the new find and the known Triassic fossils, he concluded that *Tribelesodon* was not a pterosaur, but a small *Tanystropheus*, in poor condition.

The later find solved two riddles at a stroke. First, the long *Tanystropheus* vertebrae were cervical vertebrae of a reptile with an extremely long neck (hence its other name, 'giraffe-necked saurian'). Second, the series of long bones that Bassani and Nopcsa had interpreted as long flight digit phalanges in *Tribelesodon* were in fact cervical vertebrae of *Tanystropheus*, a partially aquatic creature of the eosuchian group.

So the Triassic 'pterosaur' *Tribelesodon* stood discredited. Were the finds made in England a hundred years earlier, in 1829, in the Jurassic cliffs of Dorset, southern England, to remain the oldest pterosaurs known? *Dimorphodon* was already a perfectly developed pterosaur, which suggested that it must have had more primitive ancestors. So there must have been Triassic pterosaurs.

But there were no unquestionable fossil finds - until 1973.

Below: **This drawing shows how Franz Nopcsa reconstructed the skeleton of '*Tribelesodon*' as a long-tailed pterosaur on the basis of fossil remains from Besano. Nopcsa took the long bones to be elongated phalanges of the wing fingers. In fact they are the elongated neck vertebrae of a small *Tanystropheus*.**

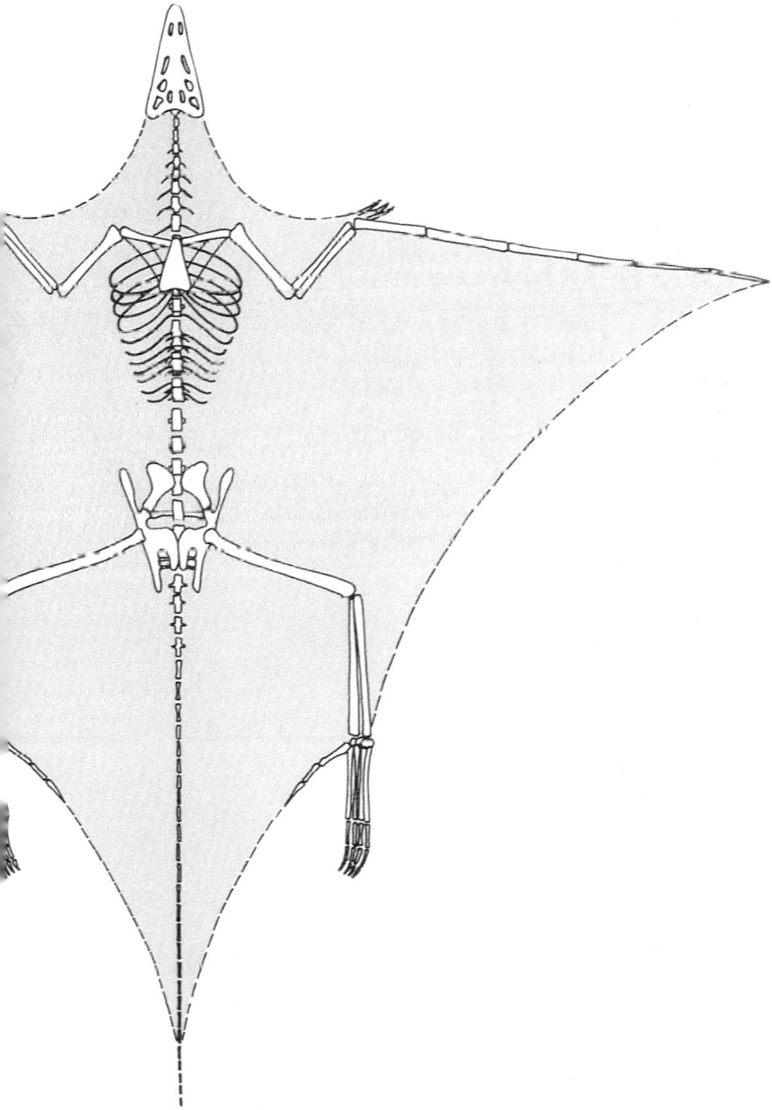

Eudimorphodon

Period: Mid-Triassic. **Family:** Eudimorphodontidae.
Where found: Italy.
Estimated wing span: 3ft 4in (1m).

In 1973 an almost complete pterosaur skeleton was unearthed from late Triassic shale, about 220 million years old, near Bergamo, Italy. This meant that the oldest pterosaur now really had been found, the first that could be conclusively proved to date from the Triassic. *Eudimorphodon* ('true two-form tooth') was a pterosaur with a wing span of about 3ft 4in (1m).

The long tail indicates why this pterosaur is assigned to the Rhamphorhynchoidea. The general structure of Eudimorphodon's skeleton is entirely characteristic of that group. The teeth are, however, unique among pterosaurs. The dentition did not consist of the usual row of teeth with a single cusp, but was divided into a few large front fangs and behind them a tight sequence of small teeth with three, five or more cusps. Altogether there were 114 teeth crammed into a jaw only 2.4in (6cm) long. Dentition of this kind indicates a fish-catcher and fossilised stomach contents have shown that *Eudimorphodon* preyed on small fishes such as *Parapholidophorus*. Juvenile individuals had a different dentition and probably caught and ate insects such as dragonflies.

The differentiated and multi-cusped teeth are not primitive reptilian characters, but a specialisation. The fact that no Jurassic pterosaur had multi-cusped teeth means that *Eudimorphodon* cannot be their direct ancestor, but represents a distinct line in the pterosaur family tree that became extinct in the Triassic.

On *Eudimorphodon*'s hand, the fourth, or wing, finger articulated with the wing metacarpal by means of a distinctive pulley-type joint on its end. This joint enabled *Eudimorphodon* to fold its wing back. It was set at a slight angle, which caused a twisting movement when the wing was folded, so positioning the flight digit against the body in such a way that the upper side of the wing faced outwards.

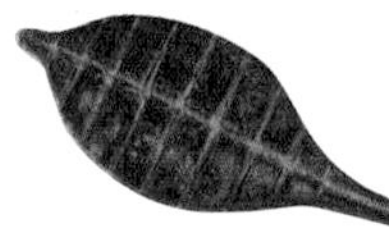

***Right: Eudimorphodon*, one of the earliest known pterosaurs, was a fully developed rhamphorhynchoid with the characteristic long tail. It had unique dentition likely to belong to a fish-eater.**

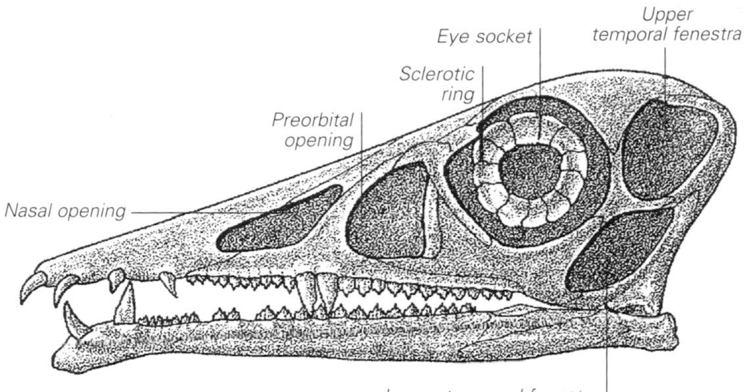

Above: **In this skull restoration the sclerotic ring around the eye and the differentiated teeth can be clearly seen.**

Peteinosaurus

Period: Mid-Triassic. **Family**: Dimorphodontidae.
Where found: Italy.
Estimated wing span: 2ft (60cm).

Following the discovery of the first *Eudimorphodon* remains five more sets of pterosaur skeletal remains were found in the Triassic limestone of the village of Cene, Italy. They were thoroughly examined in 1978. As well as *Eudimorphodon* another, smaller genus was identified, which was given the name *Peteinosaurus* ('winged reptile').

This genus turned out to be more primitive than *Eudimorphodon* in many ways. In particular, *Peteinosaurus* had only single-cusped teeth, which were flattened, with sharp cutting edges at the front and back. At the front of the lower jaw were two large teeth. The upper skull remains unknown. The dentition suggests that *Peteinosaurus* was insectivorous. In any case, this is the most primitive of the known pterosaurs. Its wings were still relatively short, only twice as long as the hind legs. In all other pterosaurs the wings were at least three times as long or longer.

Besides the type specimen of *Peteinosaurus* only one other specimen is known. Both individuals originate from the same Triassic limestone and are about the same size. In the second skeleton the skull and neck are also completely absent, but a section of the dorsal vertebral column, part of the stiff tail, typically reinforced by rod-like bony extensions, and the bones of the wings, the hind legs and the feet are preserved. The skeleton is still in articulation but was washed together by water currents before it was embedded.

Peteinosaurus has a wing span of only 24in (60cm) and can best be considered as a direct ancestor of the oldest Jurassic pterosaur, *Dimorphodon*. Both can be placed within the family Dimorphodontidae, while *Eudimorphodon* is so far the only representative of an independent family, the Eudimorphodontidae.

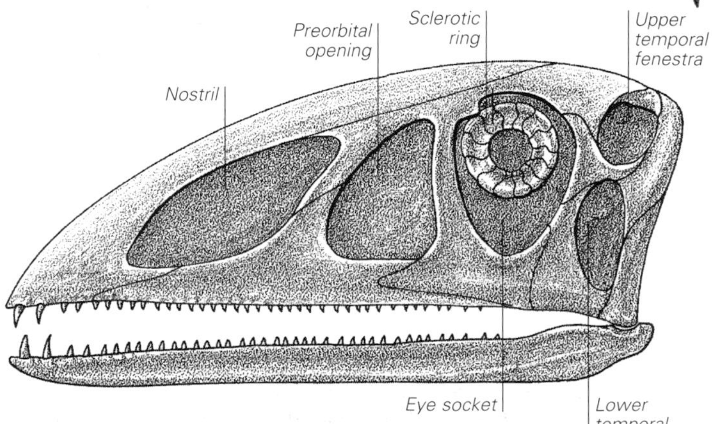

Left: This long-tailed pterosaur, which lived on the shore of the late Triassic Tethys sea, was smaller than its contemporary *Eudimorphodon*. Its dentition consists of larger anterior fangs followed by a long series of small, pointed teeth, which suggest that *Peteinosaurus* was insectivorous, perhaps catching insects on the wing.

Below: Seen here are the foot skeletons of *Peteinosaurus* as preserved (left) and as restored (right). The fifth toe is long, has no claw and could be moved in a different plane from the other four toes. Its function is not clear.

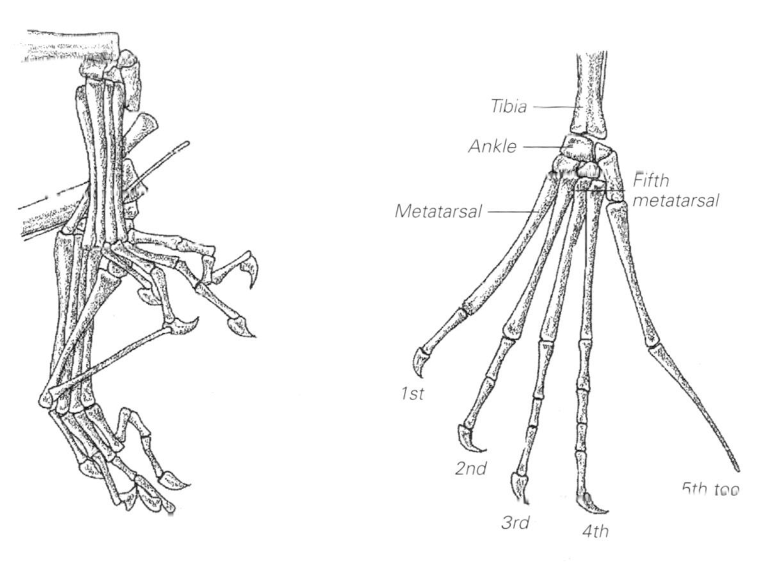

Left: This is a tentative restoration of the skull of *Peteinosaurus zambellii*. The shape of the skull is assumed to be similar to the lower Jurassic genus *Dimorphodon*.

Preondactylus

Period: Late Triassic. **Family:** Rhamphorhynchidae.
Where found: Italy.
Estimated wing span: 18in (45cm).

In 1982 a collector in Udine in northern Italy found another pterosaur skeleton in bituminous, dolomitic limestone of the late Triassic in the Preone valley in the Italian Alps. Nando Buffarini, the finder, had a stroke of bad luck that is the nightmare of every fossil hunter. The slab of rock containing the valuable fossil shattered into several pieces as it was being extracted. The bones were embedded in a marl stratum only a centimetre or two thick. When Buffarini fitted the fragments of the slab of rock together again and washed them with water, the layer of marl was washed away with the bones and lost. All that remained was the negative print of the skeleton on the surface of the rock. A cast of this negative relief was made with silicon rubber, and only then was the image of this pterosaur skeleton revealed in three dimensions and in a form that allowed it to be studied.

Analysis showed that this was a specimen of an additional pterosaur family, hitherto known only in the Jurassic, the Rhamphorhynchidae. The new genus was given the name *Preondactylus* ('Preone finger'). The dentition consists of single-cusped teeth. In 1984 one more specimen was discovered in the Preone valley. It too came from late Triassic dolomitic limestone, but from a level about 500-650ft (150-200m) deeper in the sequence of strata. The fossil consists of an accumulation of disarticulated skeletal bones. This creature, probably also a *Preondactylus*, fell prey to a predatory fish over 220 million years ago and the fish then spewed up the indigestible remains of the skeleton. This gastric pellet sank to the bottom of the sea, was covered in ooze and fossilised.

Reported pterosaur remains from late Triassic rocks in western Texas suggest that the palaeogeographical distribution of Triassic pterosaurs was considerably more extended than hitherto assumed. Although rather fragmentary, the teeth found in jaw fragments are mult-cusped and similar to those of *Eudimorphodon*.

The oldest known pterosaurs thus occur in three distinct evolutionary lines: Eudimorphodontidae, Dimorphodontidae and Rhamphorhynchidae. Such Triassic pterosaurs are apparently 'completely' developed. The evolutionary history of pterosaurs must therefore go back much further into the past than was formerly believed, perhaps to the early Triassic, possibly even to the Permian, thus in the Palaeozoic Era. No fossils have so far been found that could be interpreted as ancestors of the pterosaurs or 'proto'-pterosaurs.

***Right:* This small, long-tailed genus seems to be ancestral to the early Jurassic rhamphorhynchid *Dorygnathus* ('spear jaw'); it has similar body proportions although its dentition is different. The wings are relatively short and the legs long, proportions considered to be primitive characteristics. It is not clear whether *Preondactylus* fed on fish or if it caught insects.**

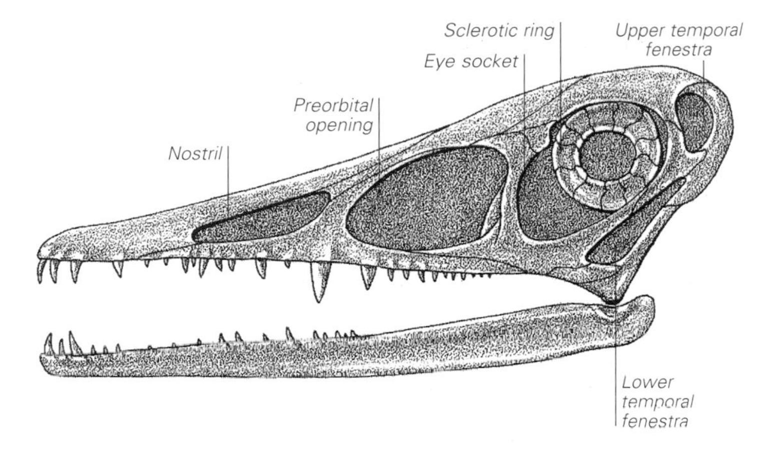

Above: **This is a tentative restoration of the skull of *Preondactylus buffarinii*. The posterior section of the skull was not preserved and is assumed to have resembled that of *Dorygnathus*.**

Jurassic Pterosaurs

The middle division of the Mesozoic Era is the Jurassic Period. It followed the Triassic Period and began about 213 million years ago. It ended 144 million years ago, and so lasted about 69 million years.

The Jurassic is generally subdivided into Lias (Lower or early Jurassic), Dogger (Middle Jurassic) and Malm (Upper or late Jurassic). A major feature of the Jurassic period was extensive flooding of continents by the sea. For this reason organisms that lived on land are particularly likely to be found in near-shore marine deposits. This is especially true of pterosaurs. The Atlantic Ocean began to open up in the Middle Jurassic but supercontinents still existed comprising present-day South America, Africa, India, Australia and the Antarctic. Asia was separated from Europe by a great seaway. The climate began to be differentiated in the course of the Jurassic but compared with today was warm and balanced.

So far Triassic pterosaurs have been proven to exist only in Europe, although it is probable that they existed in North America. In the Jurassic, however, pterosaurs were distributed worldwide and conditions were favourable for fossilisation. Pterosaur fossils have been found in Jurassic deposits in Europe, Africa, Asia, North America, Central America and South America. Various forms of pterosaur developed, adapted to different life and environmental conditions. *Pterodactylus* appeared as the first short-tailed

Right: **This drawing shows *Dimorphodon* running along on its two hind legs, with its long tail counterbalancing its head. The hypothesis that the structure of the pelvis and hindlimbs of this pterosaur made it well suited to this form of locomotion is disputed.**

pterosaur in the fossil record.

The oldest Jurassic pterosaurs were discovered in the Lower Lias limestone near Lyme Regis, Dorset, England. The first professional fossil collector, Mary Anning, worked intensively and successfully here in the first half of the 19th century. Her most famous finds were skeletons of great marine reptiles, ichthyosaurs and plesiosaurs; then in 1828 came the first pterosaur of the Lias, initially described by Oxford professor William Buckland as *Pterodactylus macronyx*. The name refers to the great claws of the small digits of the hand. At first, however, the skull of this pterosaur was not known. It was not until 1858 that Richard Owen of the British Museum in London received more pterosaur material from the Lias of Lyme Regis, including remains of skeletons with skulls, belonging to the same species.

Owen established that the skull of the genus *Pterodactylus*, formerly known only from the late Jurassic of Solnhofen, Germany, was very different. He therefore called the Lyme Regis pterosaur *Dimorphodon* ('two-form tooth'), a reference to the two kinds of teeth found in this genus.

As well as the very rare pterosaurs - so far only the species *Dimorphodon macronyx* is known - there are numerous fish and ammonites in the Lyme Regis Lias, showing that these strata are former marine deposits. They have an absolute age of about 200 to 205 million years.

Dimorphodon

Period: Early Jurassic. **Family:** Dimorphodontidae.
Where found: England.
Estimated wing span: 4ft 7in (1.4m).

Dimorphodon ('two-form tooth') is the earliest Jurassic pterosaur, discovered in early Liassic strata in southern England. It is a long-tailed form, related to the Triassic *Peteinosaurus*, which may have been its ancestor. It was about 3ft 4in (1m) long overall with a maximum wing span of 4ft 7in (1.4m). Only a few specimens of *Dimorphodon* have been found, mainly incomplete skeletal remains. They all belong to the same species, *Dimorphodon macronyx*, and come from the same rocks of the Dorset coast in England. A single specimen, consisting of only a few bones of the flight arm and the hind legs, was found in the Lower Lias on the south bank of the Severn in Gloucestershire.

Dimorphodon had a relatively large, high skull with large side apertures. These 'windows', consisting of eye sockets, upper and lower temporal openings, preorbital openings and nostrils, were separaterd by thin bars of bone only. Thus, despite its size the skull was very lightly built. It had four large front teeth on each side of the upper jaw. Behind this was a row of smaller teeth. In the lower jaw as well four or five large front teeth were followed on each side by 30 to 40 tiny but pointed teeth. This specialisation suggests that the creature was a fish-eater.

Right: **This early Jurassic pterosaur had a relatively large head and long hind legs, but short wings with a span of only about 4ft 7in (1.4m). The finger claws were quite strong and could be used for climbing on rocks and cliffs. *Dimorphodon*'s deep snout is similar to the high beak of a puffin, and the specialisation of its teeth suggest that it also was a piscivore. The long tail was largely stiffened, as is characteristic of all rhamphorhynchoid pterosaurs. It was probably used as a drag rudder. The extent of the wing membranes and the shape of the terminal tail vane can be only tentatively reconstructed here, since no soft part impressions have been preserved with any of the fossil skeletons of this pterosaur so far discovered.**

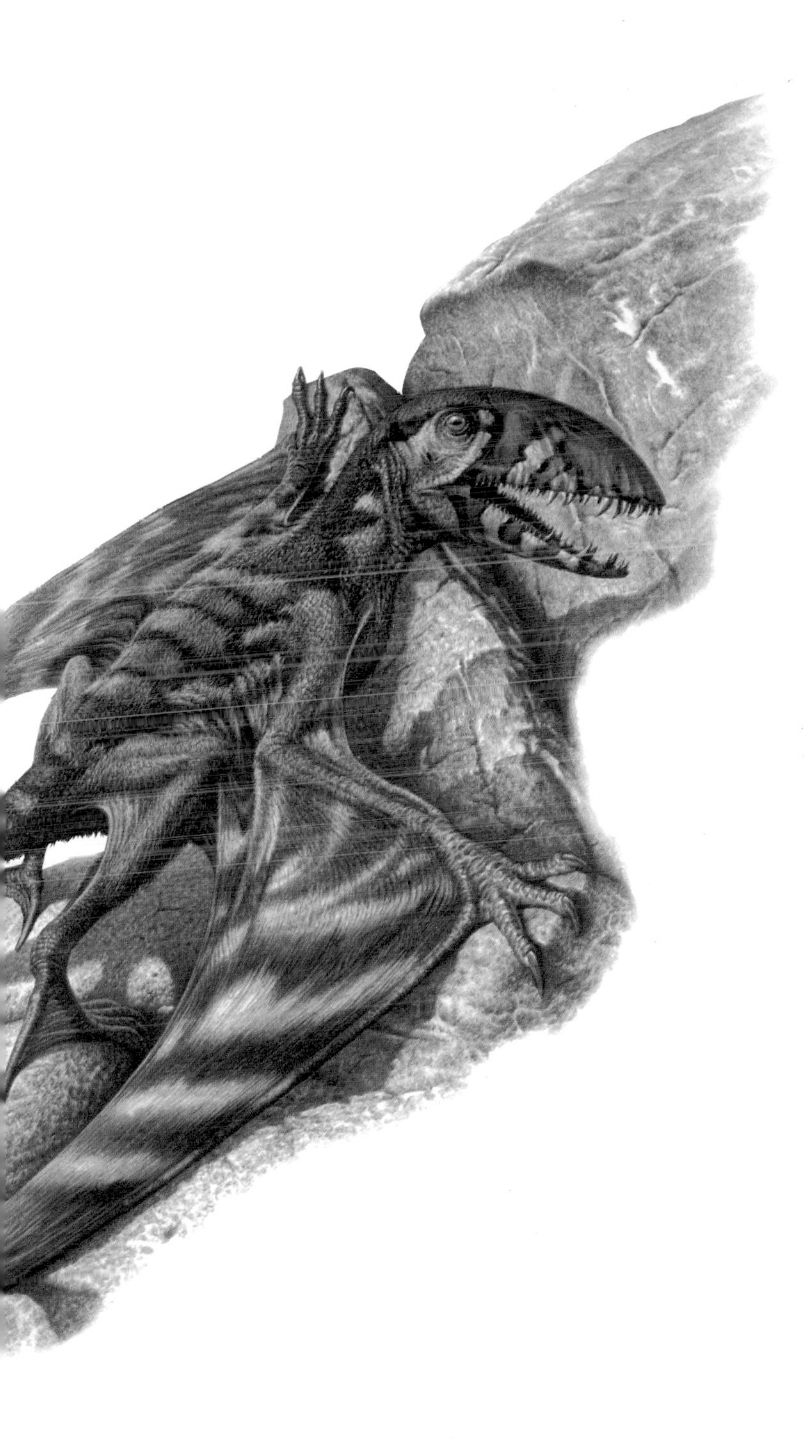

As a typical long-tailed pterosaur, *Dimorphodon* had a long vertebral tail made up of over 30 caudal vertebrae. The first five or six of these vertebrae were short and could move against each other. Subsequent caudal vertebrae were increasingly elongated and were stiffened against one another by long, thin vertebral processes. The function of this long, stiff tail, articulated at the beginning only, was to stabilise the pterosaur in flight, further emphasised by the fact that there was a small vane at the end, which was presumably used as a drag rudder.

Dimorphodon's wings were still relatively short, a primitive characteristic. It is striking that the first of the four flight digit phalanges is only a little longer than the lower arm and shorter than the second and third phalanges of the flight digit. The hind legs were extraordinarily powerfully developed and relatively long. The first four digits had claws; the fifth digit was fairly long and splayed sideways. Precise analysis of the structure of pelvis and hind leg has led to the assumption that *Dimorphodon* was well suited to bipedal, bird-like walking on the ground, the long tail balancing the large head. These problems of locomotion will be examined in greater detail in a later chapter.

Pterosaurs could probably take off from the ground by standing on their hind legs and facing into the wind with outspread wings. A simultaneous jump and stroke of the wings raised them into the air. This was more easily possible for early pterosaurs such as *Dimorphodon* and *Pterodactylus*, as they were smaller and lighter and had relatively long hind legs.

***Below:* This restoration is based upon Richard Owen's monograph. Owen thought that the function of the long fifth toe was to stretch a membrane between the tail and the hind legs, as shown in the drawing on the right.**

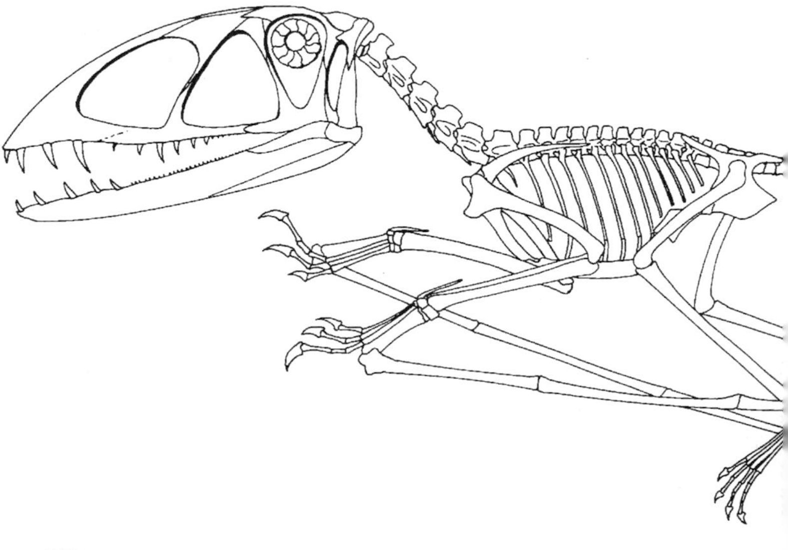

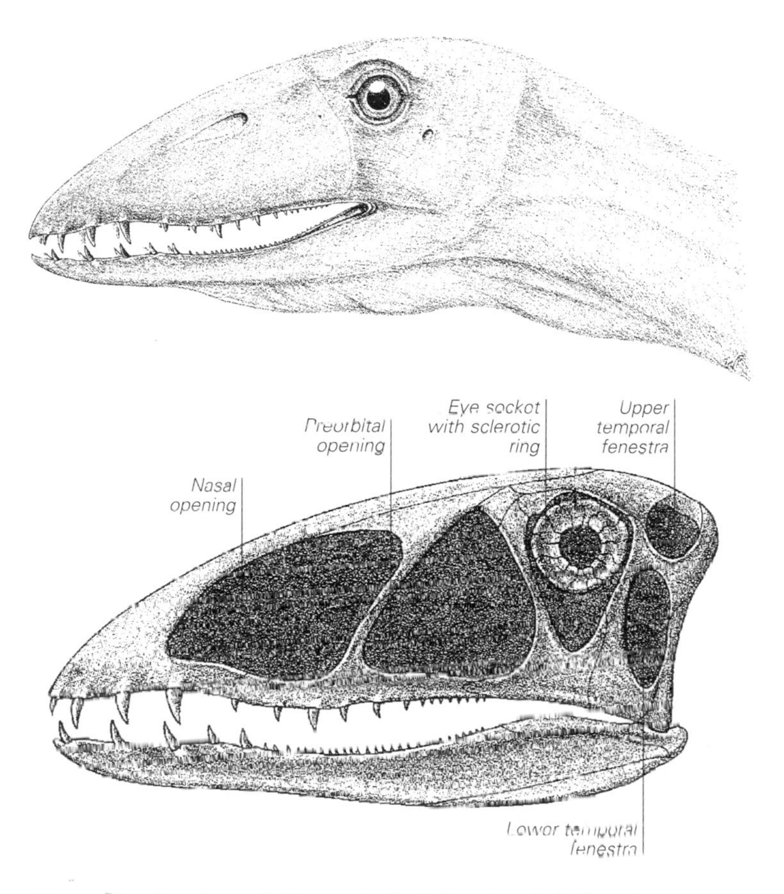

Above: **The drawings of *Dimorphodon*'s head and skull are based on the Lyme Regis finds. The skull openings separated by thin struts of bone helped to reduce the weight that this creature needed to get airborne. The bony ring in the eye socket protected the eye against deformation. The differently shaped teeth in the upper and lower jaws suggest that *Dimorphodon* was a fish-eater.**

Dorygnathus

Period: Mid-Jurassic. **Family:** Rhamphorhynchidae.
Where found: Germany.
Estimated wing span: 3ft 4in (1m).

The first Liassic pterosaur finds on the European mainland, consisting of isolated bones and jaw fragments, were made near Banz, Bavaria, southern Germany in 1830. Andreas Wagner, Professor of Palaeontology in Munich, established that the remains belonged to a new genus, which he called *Dorygnathus* ('spear jaw'), in reference to the toothless, lance-shaped point of the jaw. Elsewhere in Germany more complete *Dorygnathus* skeletons were later found, principally in Württemberg, and other finds were made in the quarries of the Holzmaden, Ohmden and Zell areas.

Those few of the slate quarries in the region that are still worked nowadays yield decorative black slate slabs for interior decoration only. Commercial mining is limited to a single stratum, the so-called Fleins, a layer 7in (18cm) thick, which gives three very firm slabs when split. This Fleins is up to 40ft (12m) below the surface of the site. All the strata above this are technically unusable, although they still contain fossils, and find their way on to the spoil heaps. Fossils are distributed throughout the profile of strata. Fossil content, especially ammonites as index fossils, means that the shale can be categorised and dated to about 190 million years ago, when an extended shallow sea flooded broad areas of central Europe.

Reptile finds from Holzmaden have become famous and are to be found in many of the world's museums today. Ichthyosaurs are particularly abundant, but plesiosaurs, marine crocodiles and even the remains of a dinosaur have been found. There are also many fish, ammonites, squids, bivalves, sea lilies and crabs. Most of the fossils are in excellent condition. The great expert on ▶

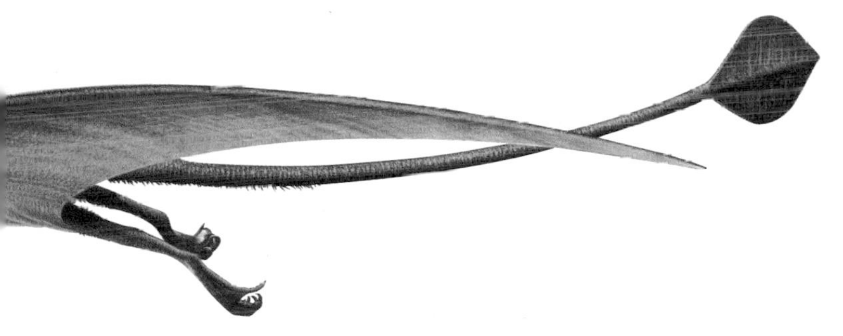

Left: **In this scene *Dorygnathus* is seen fishing on the wing a little offshore from the beach of what was in Liassic times the sea of Holzmaden, Germany. *Dorygnathus* must have been abundant in the early Jurassic, particularly in this area. It was a long-tailed pterosaur with a relatively small wing span. Its front teeth are long and point forward, thus forming a perfect gripping device for catching and holding slippery fish. It has long hind legs, and the fifth toe of the foot is also long with a bent phalanx. It may have been used to spread a small web between the toes.**

Holzmaden fossils was Dr Berhard Hauff. He began his careful preparations around 1890 and in 1937 he opened a small museum of his finds in Holzmaden, which has since been considerably extended and modernised and still attracts a large number of visitors.

The first pterosaur fossil finds from the shale of Württemberg were described in 1856, but more complete skeletons were not found until the late 19th century. Numerous outstanding pterosaurs from the slate quarries around Holzmaden and Ohmden are known today, representing two genera, *Dorygnathus* and *Campylognathoides*. The area was declared a protected area for excavation by the state in 1979 and can be considered the principal area for Liassic pterosaur finds. Other sites where only a few fragmentary pterosaur remains were found are the area around Bayreuth in Bavaria and Braunschweig in Lower Saxony.

Dorygnathus is a long-tailed pterosaur with a fairly small wing span of about 3ft 4in (1m). Its skull is elongated. The eye sockets are the largest apertures in the skull. The front teeth in the upper and lower jaw are long, powerful and forward-curving, and meshed alternately when the beak was closed. The rear parts of the jaw had only very small teeth. Dentition of this kind was a very effective organ for seizing and holding slippery prey, in other words, fish. *Dorygnathus* had a relatively small, triangular sternum. This served as an area of attachment for flight muscles. The flight digits and thus the wings were relatively short. The fifth digit of the foot was very long, however, and set at a lateral angle. Its function is not clear. Possibly it was used to spread a small web that permitted the animal to take off more easily if it had to land on the surface of the sea. The hind legs were long.

Dorygnathus is thought to have been abundant in the early Jurassic Period, particularly in the area of Holzmaden.

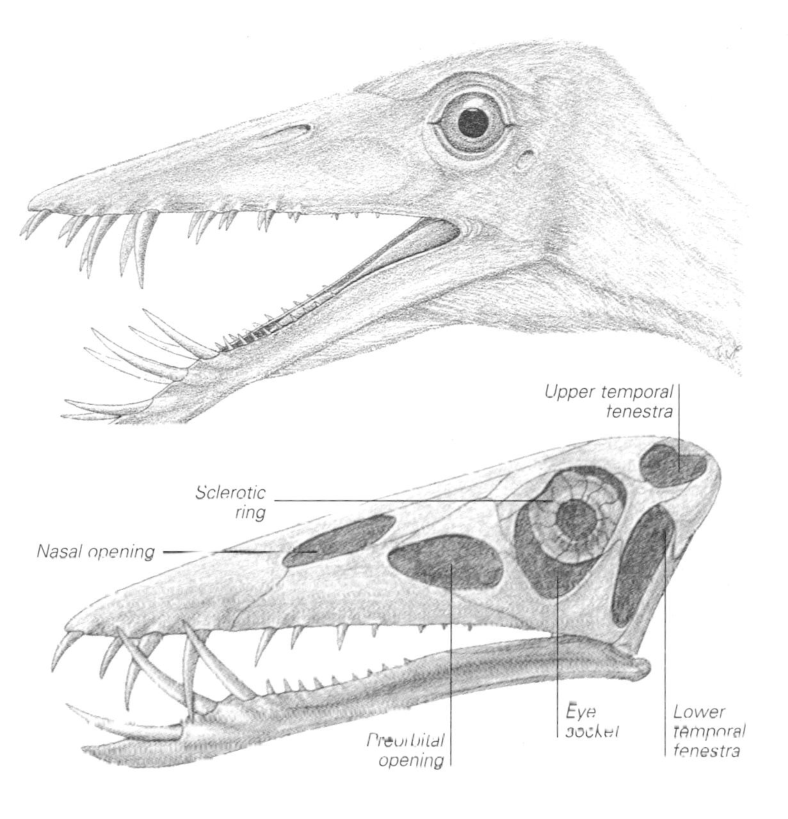

Above: **The drawings show restorations of the skull of *Dorygnathus* and a life portrait based on such fossil skulls. Note the curving front teeth.**

Left: **While *Dorygnathus* had relatively short flight digits and wings, its feet had remarkably long fifth digits, whose function is not clear. They may have served to spread a small web, which could have helped the pterosaur to paddle to get airborne after it had alighted on water.**

Campylognathoides

Period: Mid-Jurassic. **Family:** Rhamphorhynchidae.
Where found: Germany.
Estimated wing span: 5ft 8in (1.75m).

The first pterosaur specimen from the Württemberg Lias (Liassic rock) was of the genus *Campylognathoides* ('curved jaw'). However, the skeletal remains consisted of a few bones of the flight arm only. It was not until much more complete finds from the Holzmaden shale had become known that the Stuttgart palaeontologist Felix Plieninger recognised that they were a genus in their own right.

The genus has a characteristic relatively short skull, dominated by a large, circular eye socket. The end of the snout is pointed and toothed, with short, conical teeth set upright in the jaw. The sternum consists of a broad, rectangular plate of bone and has a short crest (cristopina) projecting forwards. In contrast with *Dorygnathus*, the fifth toe is very short. Two species of *Campylognathoides* are known from Holzmaden, *Campylognathoides liasicus* and *Campylognathoides zitteli*. The former had a wing span of under 3ft 4in (1m), and the latter had a span of about 5ft 8 in (1.75m).

In 1974 the Indian palaeontologist S. L. Jain described a fragment of a pterosaur skull with teeth as *Campylognathoides indicus*. The fossil came from the lower Jurassic of the Chanda district of India.

In 1986 a fossil collector found a small pterosaur pelvis that had survived in isolation in a shale quarry in the area of Braunschweig, Germany, which could also be placed in the genus *Campylognathoides*. It was particularly significant that the hip sockets in this specimen had survived in very good condition and their lateral and upward orientation indicated that pterosaurs were probably not in a position to walk on two legs like birds. Therefore the upper leg bones (femora) could not be oriented vertically, as would be needed to enable the legs to swing to and fro for walking and running on two legs.

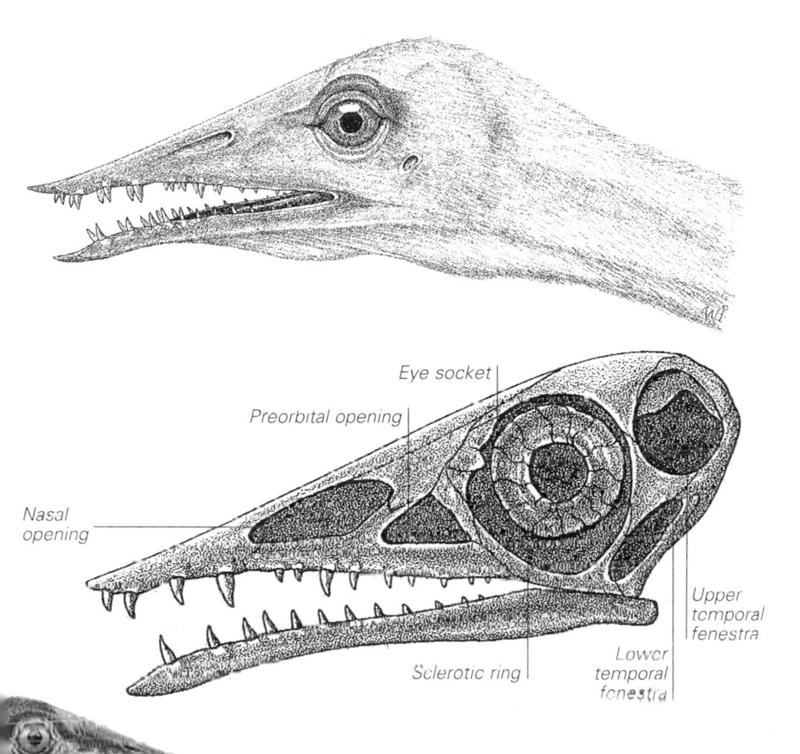

Above: ***Campylognathoides liasicus's*** **eye sockets are very large, which suggest that its eyesight was acute. Some scientists argue that such large eyes indicate a nocturnal lifestyle. The life portrait is based on the skull restoration shown.**

Left: **This pterosaur lived in the same environment as *Dorygnathus* in the Holzmaden area and elsewhere in Germany and possibly even India. It is also a long-tailed, rhamphorhynchoid pterosaur, but it has a shorter head and smaller teeth than its contemporary *Dorygnathus*. The skull is dominated by the large eye sockets. So far, two species are known, *Campylognathoides liasicus*, with a wing span of about 3ft 4in (1m), and the larger *Camphylognathoides zitteli*, with a span of around 5ft 8in (1.75m).**

Pterodactylus

Period: Late Jurassic. **Family:** Pterodactylidae.
Where found: Europe and East Africa.
Estimated wing span: 14.98in (36.25cm).

The earliest evidence of short-tailed pterosaurs, called Pterodactyloidea after the indicative genus *Pterodactylus* ('flight finger'), also comes from Solnhofen limestone in Germany. They are about as rare as the Rhamphorhynchoidea, and their principal distinctive characteristic is that they had only a short tail consisting of a few small caudal vertebrae, which was probably meaningless in terms of flight. This new, more 'modern' type of pterosaur appears in several different forms in the late Jurassic. This indicates that the Solnhofen Pterodactyloidea had already

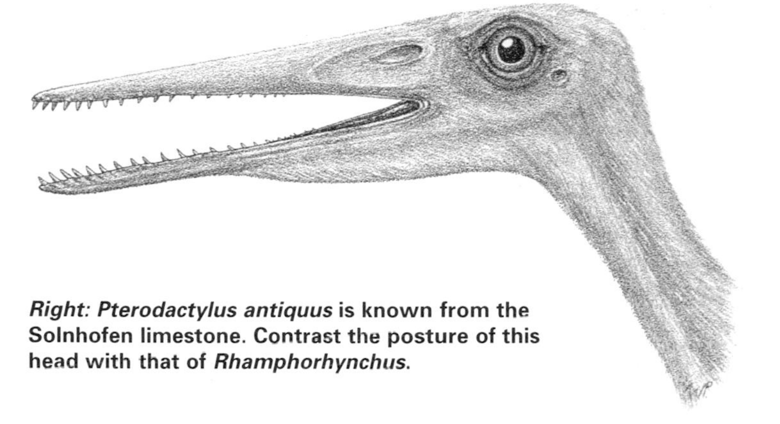

***Right: Pterodactylus antiquus* is known from the Solnhofen limestone. Contrast the posture of this head with that of *Rhamphorhynchus*.**

gone through a long phylogeny, in which different genera came into being, able to conquer differing habitats.

A gap in the fossil record means that we know nothing about the direct ancestors of short-tailed pterosaurs. But as the general structure of their skeleton corresponds basically with that of the long-tailed Rhamphorhynchoidea, we must assume that short-tailed pterosaurs were descendants of this older group of pterosaurs, from which they originated in the early or mid-Jurassic.

In order to preserve and possibly improve their ability to fly, proportions were generally altered in the Pterodactyloidea, along with the loss of the tail. The beak became more markedly elongated and the neck was clearly longer too, as a result of elongation of the individual cervical vertebrae.

The head was balanced on the neck and held like that of a pelican in flight, in complete contrast with the Rhamphorhynchoidea, which predominantly held the head extended. The two apertures in the skull before the orbital opening, nostril and preorbital opening were no longer separated by a bridge of bone, but confluent. The metacarpal bones were relatively long, often even longer than ▶

***Left: Pterodactylus* was an agile flyer, which may have fed on insects or small fish. Strikingly, its tail is much shorter than that of its contemporary *Rhamphorhynchus*. It was obviously no longer required to maintain flight stability.**

the lower arm. In contrast, the flight digit was shorter and the fifth foot digit was reduced and only rudimentarily developed.

Six species of this genus can be distinguished in the Solnhofen strata. The smallest is *Pterodactylus elegans*, diagnosed by its long, thin teeth, found only in the front part of the jaw. Its wing span is only 10in (25cm). The most common species is *Pterodactylus kochi*, of which there are fine, complete specimens in many museums and collections, some with surviving imprints of the flight membrane. A series of smaller skeletons can be identified, by the degree of ossification of the small toe phalanges, as young animals of the species. The smallest *Pterodactylus* and therefore probably the youngest had a trunk length of only 0.75in (2cm) with a wing span of 7in (18cm). This baby pterosaur could have been only a few weeks old, but was certainly already able to fly properly.

Adult *Pterodactylus kochi* reach a wing span of about 20in (50cm). Thus they were about the size of a common moorhen. Individual wing and leg bones are all that is known of the largest species, *Pterodactylus grandis*. They suggest a wing span of about 8ft 2in (2.5m), about the size of a bearded vulture and thus one of the largest of all the Jurassic pterosaurs.

Skeletal remains from late Jurassic strata in France, England and East Africa have also been assigned to the genus *Pterodactylus*. And finally, in the course of the dinosaur excavations on Tendaguru Hill in Tanzania, East Africa, *Pterodactylus* remains were found, as well as *Rhamphorhynchus* fossils, and assigned in 1931 to three different new species, *P. arningi, P. brancai* and *P. maximus*, though some palaeontologists argue that *P. brancai* corresponds better to the genus *Dsungaripterus* from the early Cretaceous of China than to the Solnhofen *Pterodactylus*.

Below: A _Pterodactylus_ skeleton is here restored in its likely flight position. The wing span of this particular specimen is about 18in (46cm).

Below right: Pterodactylus antiquus is a species known from the Solnhofen limestone of Bavaria. In contrast to _Rhamphorhynchus,_ the nostril and the preorbital opening are not completely separated by a bridge of bone, but are confluent. The length of this skull is 4.25in (10.8cm). The drawing is based on the type specimen first described in 1784.

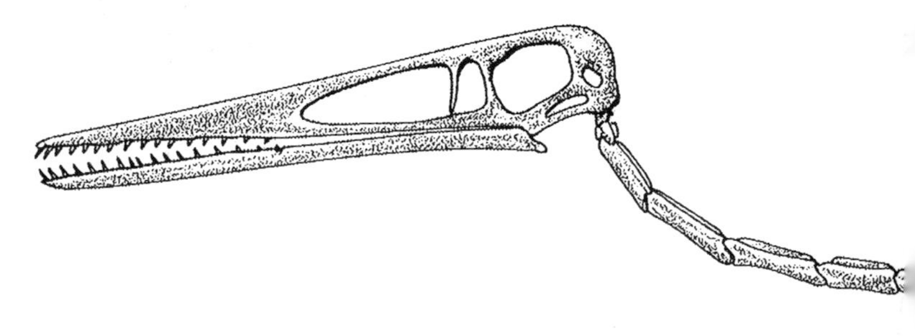

Right: **Seen here are the skulls of four different species of *Pterodactylus* from the late Jurassic limestone of Solnhofen. The length of the skulls ranges from 1.65in (4.2cm) to 4.25in (10.8cm).**

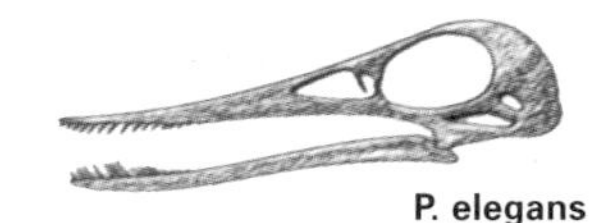

P. elegans

P. micronyx

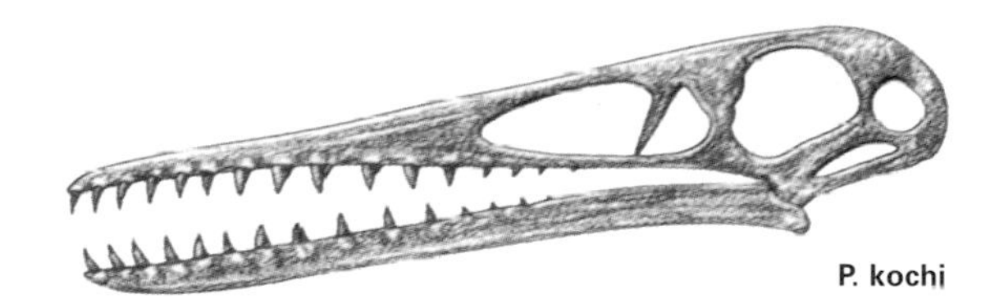

P. kochi

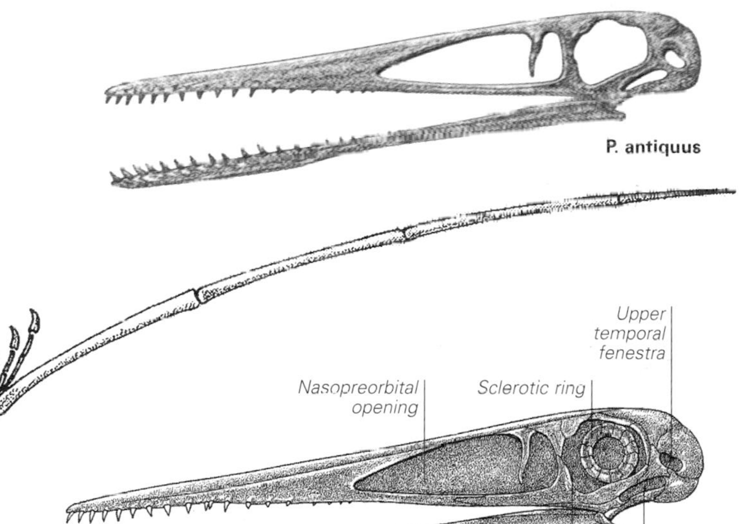

Rhamphorhynchus

Period: Mid- to late Jurassic. **Family:** Rhamphorhynchidae.
Where found: Europe and East Africa.
Estimated wing span: 16.69in (40.175cm).

The most frequently occurring genus in the Solnhofen limestone, Germany, is *Rhamphorhynchus* ('beak snout'), a long-tailed pterosaur after whom the whole sub-order is named Rhamphorhynchoidea. In the late Jurassic, 150 million years ago, they already had a long period of evolution behind them, the earliest known pterosaurs, from the late Triassic 70 million years earlier, having been Rhamphorhynchoidea as well. They preserved the long vertebrate tail into the Jurassic, a legacy of their reptilian ancestors. Thanks to good fossil preservation, we know that there was a rhomboid membrane on the end of this long tail, which was certainly used as a rudder in flight.

Solnhofen long-tailed pterosaurs may have had a long past, but there was no future for them. They had reached the peak of their evolution, but it was also almost the end. They became extinct shortly after they had populated the coasts and islands of the Solnhofen lagoon.

Rhamphorhynchus was certainly a skilful flier. The sternum, where powerful muscles originated, is a broad plate of bone and has a forward-pointing crest, or cristopina. The neck is short, with compact, short vertebrae. The skull is large and elongated and has a pointed front end. It has a large orbital opening and two smaller separate openings in the skull in front of the eyes, the nostril and the preorbital fenestra. The long, ▸

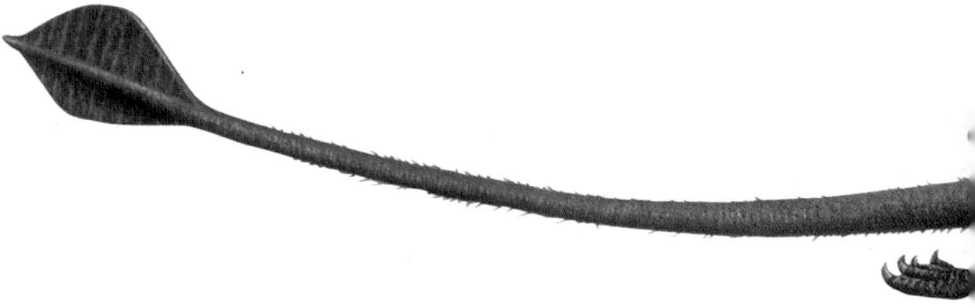

***Right:* Particularly evident in this view of *Rhamphorhynchus* are its sharp teeth and the pointed horny beaks that formed the tips of the jaws. The shape of the wing membranes and of the vertical tail rudder are known from fossil evidence.**

Above: This restoration shows the head of *Rhamphorhynchus muensteri*, the most common pterosaur found at Solnhofen. The top jaws contains 20 teeth, the lower jaws 14.

pointed, slightly curved teeth directed forwards and outwards are powerfully adapted for catching prey. When the jaw is closed they mesh alternately. There are 20 teeth in the upper jaw and 14 in the lower jaw. This dentition indicates that most species of *Rhamphorhynchus* were fish-eaters. The remains of its last prey, a small fish, were in fact found in the stomach of a Solnhofen *Rhamphorhynchus*.

So far five different species of this genus have been found in Solnhofen. The smallest, *Rhamphorhynchus longicaudus*, has a skull only 1.18in (3cm) long and a wing span of 15.75in (40cm). The largest species, *Rhamphorhynchus longiceps*, has a skull 7.5in (19cm) long and a wing span of 5ft 9in (1.75m).

The most common species, *Rhamphorhynchus muensteri*, can be divided into two groups. One has a relatively long skull and a long flight digit, the other a relatively shorter skull and shorter flight digit. This suggests sexual dimorphism: the animals with larger skulls and longer wings could be assumed to be males and the others females. There are no distinctive characters on the skeleton to make it possible to distinguish male and female individuals in any other way.

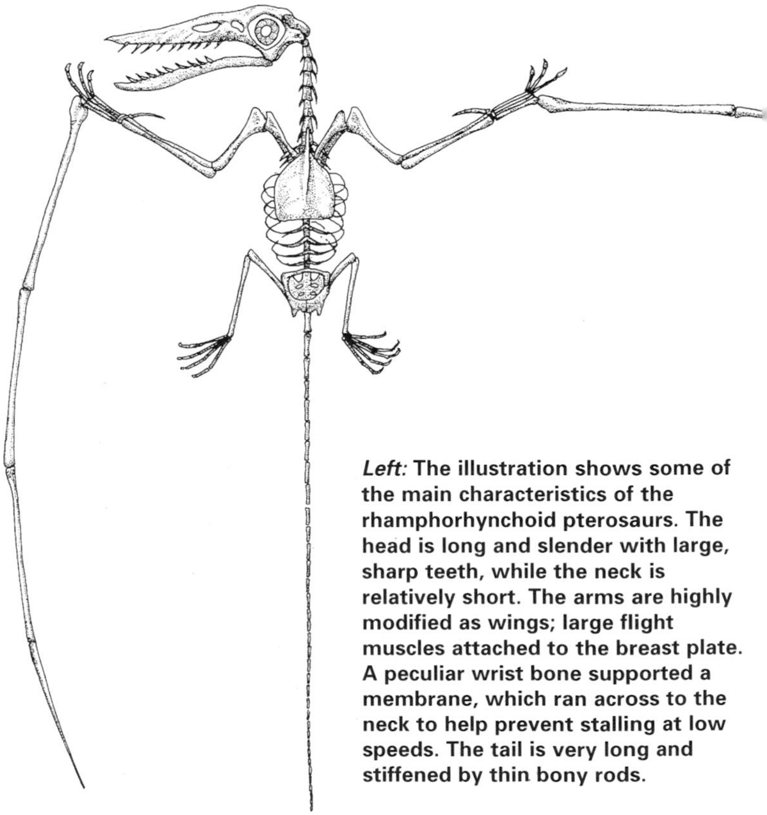

***Left:* The illustration shows some of the main characteristics of the rhamphorhynchoid pterosaurs. The head is long and slender with large, sharp teeth, while the neck is relatively short. The arms are highly modified as wings; large flight muscles attached to the breast plate. A peculiar wrist bone supported a membrane, which ran across to the neck to help prevent stalling at low speeds. The tail is very long and stiffened by thin bony rods.**

Rhamphorhynchus also occurs in late Jurassic limestone in Württemberg, southern Germany. This is the species *Rhamphorhynchus longiceps* ('long-skulled beak snout'), also known from Solnhofen in Bavaria. Remains of pterosaur skeletons from the somewhat older Oxford Clay of Huntingdonshire in England were assigned to a new species, *Rhamphorhynchus jessoni*, as were individual bones from the Tendaguru strata of Tanzania, East Africa, discovered in the course of the famous German Tendaguru dinosaur expedition of 1909 to 1913.

Individual teeth from the mid- and late Jurassic of Portugal have also been assigned to the genus *Rhamphorhynchus*.

Below: **The skulls of five different species of *Rhamphorhynchus* are shown in ascending order of size. From the top they are: *longicaudus, intermedius, muensteri, gemmingi* and *longiceps*. Their lengths in life ranged from 1.18in (3cm) to 7.5in (19cm) and the corresponding wing spans from about 1ft 4in (40cm) to 5ft 9in (1.75m).**

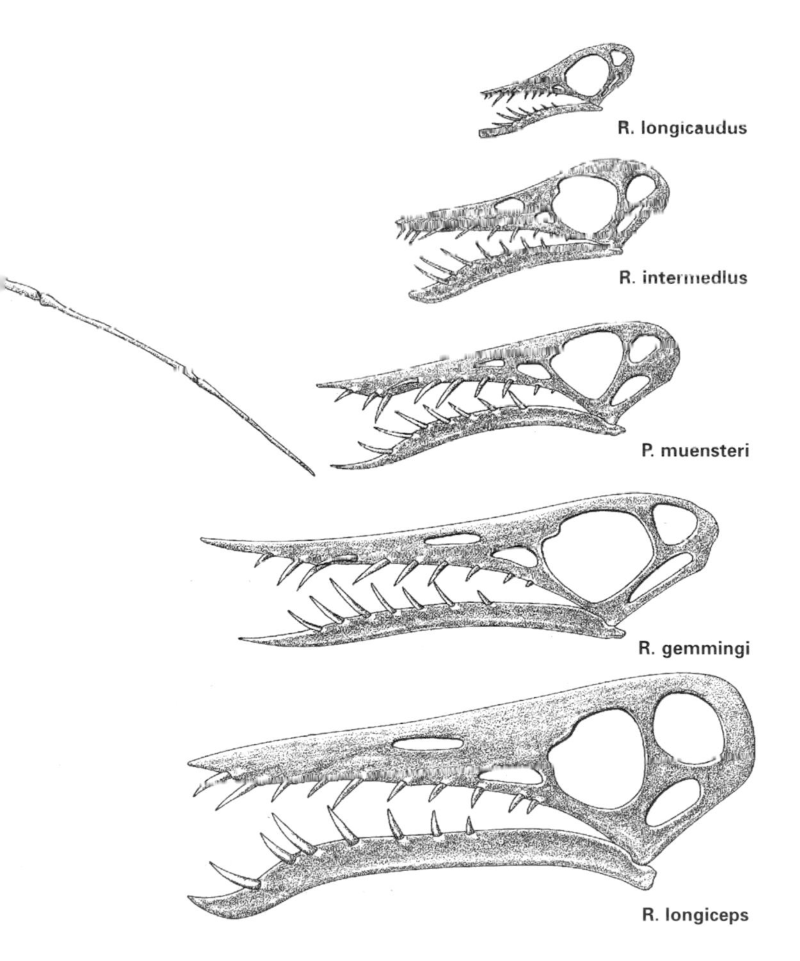

Anurognathus

Period: Late Jurassic. **Family:** Anurognathidae.
Where found: Germany.
Estimated wing span: 20in (50cm).

So far only one specimen of *Anurognathus* ('tailless jaw') has been found, and this is nothing more than a negative imprint of skeletal remains on the surface of a limestone slab at Eichstätt, Germany. It was described in 1923 as *Anurognathus ammoni*, after the Bavarian geologist Ludwig von Ammon.

This was a small and graceful pterosaur, one of the long-tailed group known as the Rhamphorhynchoidea. It occupies a special place within this group, however. It has a short, reduced tail, a kind of 'parson's nose', or pygostyle, as in birds, but has to be classified as rhamphorhnychoid because of other skeletal characteristics. Thus it has a short metacarpus, a short neck and a long fifth digit on the foot. It also has a strikingly high, short skull only 1.2in (3cm) in length, with large openings and small, peg-like teeth in broad, rounded jaws. As *Anurognathus* apparently had a wide mouth it is to be assumed that it was insectivorous. To catch its prey - dragonflies or wood wasps - in flight, it must have been an extraordinarily skilful flier. Its trunk was only 2in (5cm) long but it had extremely long wings with a span of 1ft 7in (50cm).

Right: **This is one of the strangest pterosaurs, which is known only by a single fossil specimen from the Solnhofen limestone. In its general body proportions it was rhamphorhynchoid but its tail was greatly reduced and its wings were extremely long. It must have been an agile, highly manoeuvrable flier. It had a short, deep head with a broad mouth and small, peg-like teeth and would have eaten insects such as woodwasps.**

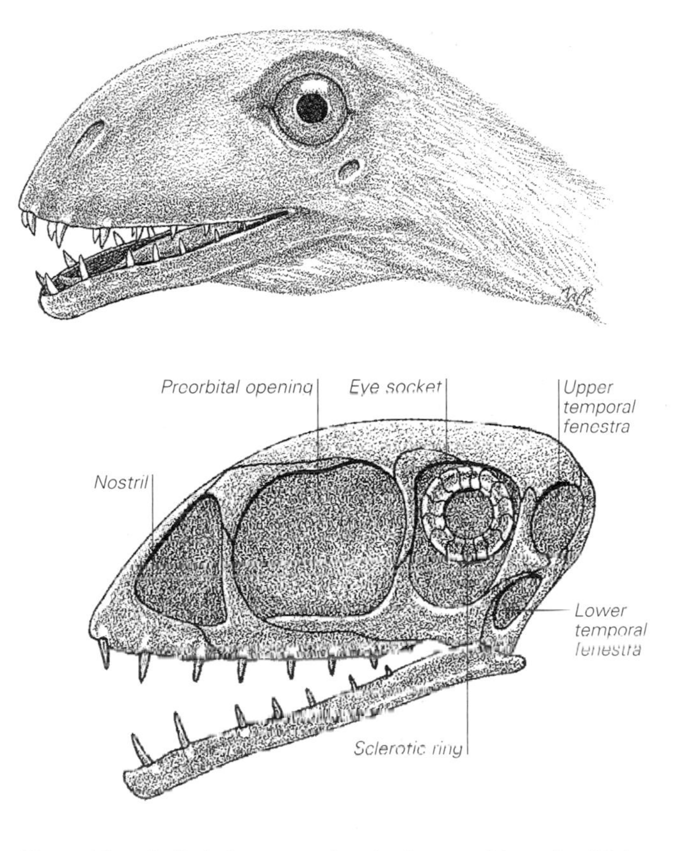

Above: **The skull of *Anurognathus* is short and broad, with large openings. It is only 1.2in (3cm) in length. Its broad, rounded jaws, which are studded with short, peg-like teeth, suggest that this pterosaur may have been an insect-eater. If that were the case, it must have been a very agile flier to hunt down its prey on the wing, just as insectivorous birds today are quick and nimble in the air. The poor state of preservation of the fossil accounts for the rather tentative restoration.**

Scaphognathus

Period: Late Jurassic.
Family: Rhamphorhynchidae.
Where found: Germany.
Estimated wing span: 3ft (90cm).

The genus *Scaphognathus* ('tub jaw') is known from two specimens only from the Solnhofen limestone. The first was one of the earliest pterosaur finds of all and was described as early as 1831 by Bonn professor August Goldfuss. As the tail region had not survived, Goldfuss thought he was dealing with a *Pterodactylus*, which he called *Pterodactylus crassirostris* ('thick-beaked flight finger'). The find was made in Eichstätt. The second specimen of *Scaphognathus* came from the Solnhofen limestone of Mühlheim near Solnhofen. Here the long tail was preserved, meaning that this genus could be classified with the long-tailed pterosaurs, the Rhamphorhynchoidea. The Mühlheim specimen is about half the size of the one from Eichstätt. The small degree of ossification in the smaller specimen indicates that this was a young animal that died before it was fully grown. But both specimens are of the same species.

Scaphognathus had a shorter, more compact skull than *Rhamphorhynchus*. Its teeth, 18 in the upper jaw and ten in the lower jaw, did not point forward, but were set upright in the jaw. The ends of the jaw do not meet at a point at the front, but are fairly blunt, like the bow of a boat, hence its name. Also the preorbital fenestrae are larger than in *Rhamphorhynchus*. The young *Scaphognathus* had a wing span of 20in (50cm) and the adult a span of 3ft (90cm). *Scaphognathus* had general body proportions and a long tail in common with *Rhamphorhynchus* but its head was somewhat shorter and the tips of its jaws less pointed.

***Right:* These drawings show a restoration of the skull of *Scaphognathus* (middle) and of its palate looking upwards into the roof of the mouth (bottom). The small holes lining the margins of the upper jaw are the sockets for the 18 teeth, which are shown in position in the life portrait (top). The skull length of this specimen is 4.5in (11.5cm).**

Above: **In its general body proportions and with its long tail, *Scaphognathus* resembles *Rhamphorhynchus*, but *Scaphognathus* had a somewhat shorter head and long teeth, which were set in an upright position. The tips of the jaws are not as pointed as in *Rhamphorhynchus*, but rather blunt. It is not clear, however, whether *Scaphognathus* fed on insects or fish.**

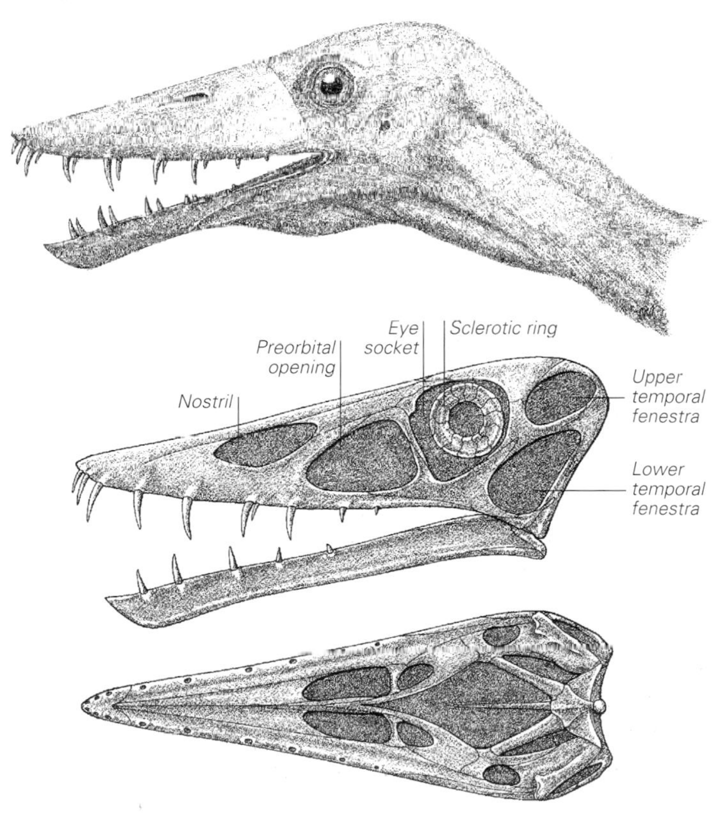

Germanodactylus

Period: Late Jurassic. **Family:** Germanodactylidae.
Where found: Germany, England.
Estimated wing span: 3ft 6in (1.08m).

The genus *Germanodactylus* ('German finger') was introduced in 1964 by the Chinese palaeontologist C. C. Young for a Solnhofen pterosaur, which C. Wiman had already described in 1925 as *Pterodactylus cristatus* ('*Pterodactylus* with crest'). So far there have been very few finds of this genus, representing two different species, *G. cristatus* from the limestone of Solnhofen and *G. rhamphastinus* from Daiting. The Daiting specimen comes from strata above the Solnhofen limestone,

Top right: **This life portrait of the smaller of the species of *Germanodactylus* currently known from late Jurassic strata shows how the head was dominated by a low cranial crest.**

Right: **These are skull restorations of *Germanodactylus cristatus* (top) and *G. rhamphastinus* (bottom), the latter coming from somewhat younger limestone in Daiting, Bavaria.**

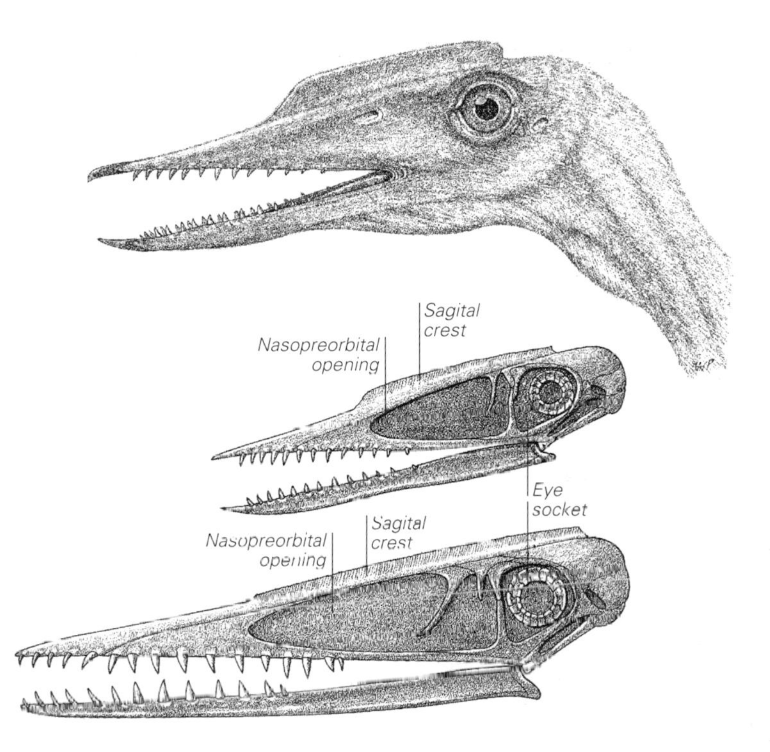

and is thus somewhat younger. It is therefore possible that in terms of phylogeny it should be seen as a descendant of the older Solnhofen species.

Germanodactylus's typical characteristic is a low bone crest on the mid-line of the skull, starting above the nostril and extending above the openings for the eye sockets. It was probably covered with a horny carina. The dentition consists of a long row of powerful and relatively short teeth. The tips of the jaws were toothless and were probably covered by pointed, horny beaks. The smaller *G. cristatus* had a skull length of 5.1in (13cm) with a wing span of 3ft 2in (98cm), the larger *G. rhamphastinus* a skull length of 8.3in (21cm) and wing span of 3ft 6in (1.08m).

David Uniwn of Reading University also assigns vertebrae, radius, ulna, a first flight digit phalanx and tibia and fibula of a pterosaur from the Kimmeridge Clay of the Dorset coast of south-east England to the genus *Germanodactylus*. This is not only the first *Germanodactylus* to be found outside Bavaria but also the oldest specimen of a pterodactyloid pterosaur, as the Kimmeridge Clay is somewhat older than the Solnhofen limestone.

***Left:* *Germanodactylus* is here hanging head down from a branch by its feet in a bat-like fashion. Whether pterosaurs could actually rest in this position has been questioned by some scientists, however. The characteristic median crest on the head is particularly evident in this view.**

Gallodactylus

Period: Late Jurassic. **Family:** Gallodactylidae.
Where found: France, Germany.
Estimated wing span: 3ft 6in (1.08m).

The name *Gallodactylus* ('Gallic finger') was introduced in 1974 by the French palaeontologist J. Fabre for a pterosaur found in late Jurassic rocks at Canjuers in the department of Var, southern France. There were many features in common with pterosaurs from contemporary lithographic limestones of Bavaria and Württemberg in Germany. Thus the first pterosaur, which had been described as Pterodactylus suevicus from Nusplingen in Württemberg by August Quenstedt, a professor from Tübingen, as early as 1855, could now be assigned to the genus *Gallodactylus*. The Nusplingen quarry has yielded only a few pterosaur fossils, of which *Gallodactylus* is one of the best-preserved examples. This species is also known from Solnhofen. There *Gallodactylus* is among the larger short-tailed pterosaurs. Like *Germanodactylus*, *Gallodactylus* did not survive into the Cretaceous.

Its particular characters were an elongated beak with a small number of narrow teeth limited to the front ends of the long, slender jaws and a short medial crest on the back of the head. The teeth pointed forwards, making a very efficient instrument for grasping slippery fish from water. *Gallodactylus* had a skull length of 5ft 11in (15cm) and a wing span of 4ft 5in (1.35m).

Top right: **This is a restoration of the skull of *Gallodactylus suevicus*. The teeth are grouped together at the front of the jaws. The skull is 5ft 11in (15cm) long.**

Right: **In general appearance *Gallodactylus* resembled *Pterodactylus*. However, it had a number of distinct characteristics, such as the short medial crest at the rear of the head and teeth that were confined to the front ends of the long, slender jaws. The forward-pointing teeth would have formed a very efficient gripping tool for grasping slippery fish from out of the water. *Gallodactylus* is known from the late Jurassic strata in France and Germany.**

Eye socket
Nasopreorbital opening
Upper temporal fenestra
Lower temporal fenestra

Gnathosaurus

Period: Late Jurassic. **Family:** Ctenochasmatidae.
Where found: Germany.
Estimated wing span: 5ft 7in (1.7m).

The last important Solnhofen pterosaur genus is *Gnathosaurus* ('jaw reptile'). This is another extremely rare pterosaur. The two specimens so far discovered are the only remains of this form, which is known from the Solnhofen limestone only. The first find, an isolated remnant of a lower jaw, was introduced as early as 1832 in Bayreuth and taken for a piece of crocodile jaw. Later the Frankfurt palaeontologist Hermann von Meyer assigned the name *Gnathosaurus subulatus* (*subulatus* is Latin for 'awl-like', after the shape of the teeth).

It was not proven that the creature was a pterosaur until a second find was made in 1951, a skull 11in (28cm) long. Nothing has so far been found of the rest of the skeleton, but it is not impossible that isolated bones from wings and hind legs of larger pterosaurs, as yet not classified with certainty, actually belong to the species *Gnathosaurus*.

Even though this was a large pterosaur with a wing span of about 5ft 7in (1.7m), we must assume that it was a filter feeder, though the teeth are more powerful than in the case of *Ctenochasma*, and less densely arranged, there being only 130. But here again the jaws have teeth extending well towards the back, with the longest at the

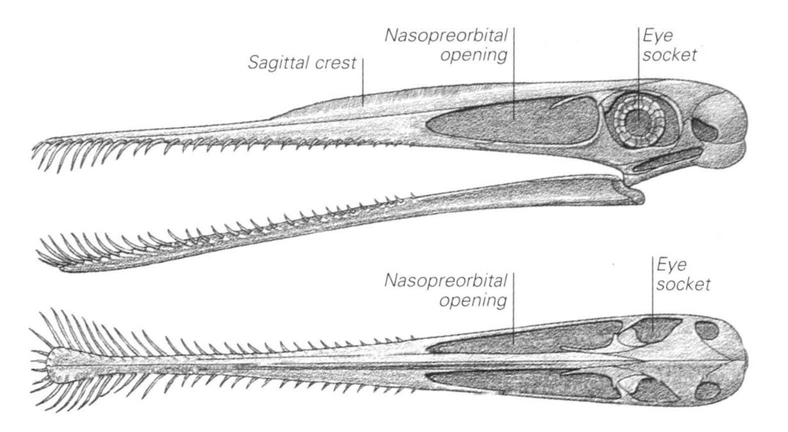

Above: **This skull restoration of *Gnathosaurus* is seen in side and top view. A low, bony crest had developed along the mid-line of the skull roof. The dense arrangement of teeth points to a diet of small marine organisms. The skull length is 11in (28cm).**

front and set around the spoon-shaped jaw end. Like *Ctenochasma porocristata*, *Gnathosaurus* also has a low bone crest on its skull.

Because of their strange filter dentition *Ctenochasma* and *Gnathosaurus* are significantly different from other pterodactyloids. For this reason they are placed together in a family of their own, which is known as the Ctenochasmatidae.

Left: **This view shows clearly the specialised dentition of *Gnathosaurus*. The long, slender jaws are lined with a series of teeth that get increasingly longer as they near the front of the snout. This suggests that *Gnathosaurus* must have been a filter feeder. When closed, the beak could be used for catching and filtering small creatures from the water.**

Ctenochasma

Period: Late Jurassic. **Family:** Ctenochasmatidae.
Where found: Germany, France.
Estimated wing span: 3ft 11in (1.2m).

This striking short-tailed pterosaur is one of the rarities of the Solnhofen limestone, although it is also known from the late Jurassic strata in France and northern Germany. The first *Ctenochasma* ('comb jaw'), consisting only of the front section of a lower jaw with numerous long, tightly packed and strong teeth, was described as early as 1851. It came from contemporary marine limestone in the Hanover area and was named *Ctenochasma roemeri*.

The first specimen from Solnhofen was described in 1862. It was only the fragment of an upper jaw. Later complete skeletons were found and named *Ctenochasma gracile*. It was not until 1981 that another species of this genus was described. It was named *Ctenochasma porocristata* because of a porous bony crest on its skull. The specimen, an isolated skull with the front section of the dentition, came from the Eichstätt quarry district.

The apt name *Ctenochasma* was chosen because of this pterosaur's large number of long, thin, inward-bending teeth, arranged in a dense row

***Below:** Ctenochasma* **was extremely well adapted as a filter feeder. It could stand in the shallows while its long jaws formed a filter basket for sifting out small aquatic planktonic organisms, such as crustaceans or the larvae of marine invertebrates.**

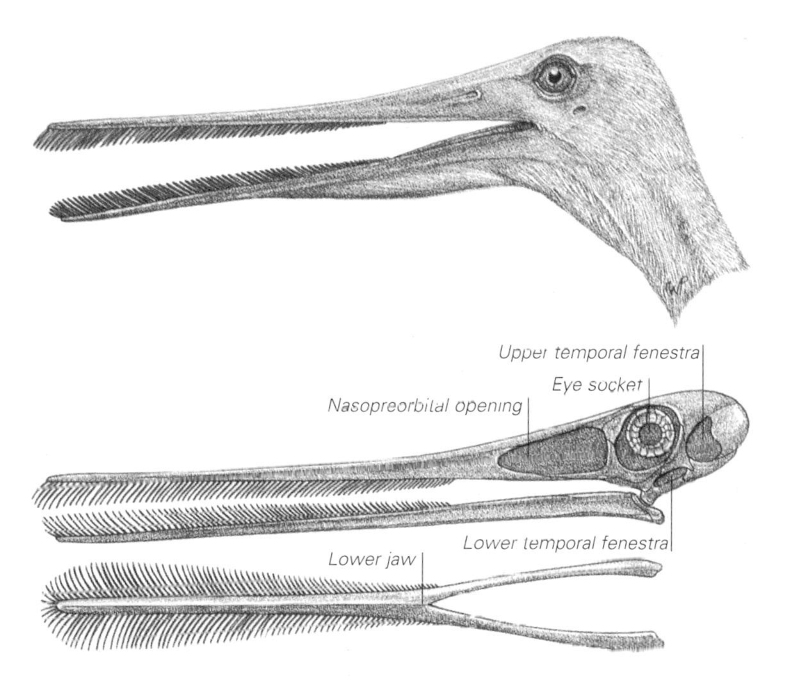

Above: **These drawings show a life portrait of *Ctenochasma gracile* (top) and a restoration of the skull and lower jaw, which is also shown from below in the bottom drawing. The jaws contain an extraordinary number of teeth - over 250 in an adult pterosaur. The skull length is 4in (10.4cm). This species had no crest on its skull. *Ctenochasma porocristata* by contrast had a long para sagittal crest running along the top of its skull, which in life was probably covered by a thin, horny crest.**

like the teeth of a comb, in the upper and lower jaw. They formed a straining apparatus, with which these creatures could filter their food out of the water. The expression 'comb dentition' is also used to describe this arrangement of teeth. *Ctenochasma* had a total of 260 individual teeth. The largest of the six specimens so far known had a skull 7.9in (20cm) long and a wing span of at least 3ft 11in (1.2m). As it can hardly be supposed that *Ctenochasma* fed in flight, these pterosaurs must have swum in the water or waded near the beach, as do most modern sea birds.

The genus *Ctenochasma* has also been proven to exist in the late Jurassic of Haute Marne, France, in the form of an isolated skull 9.5in (24cm) long, with dentition consisting of about 200 long, tightly packed teeth, indicating a typical filter feeder.

Sordes

Period: Late Jurassic. **Family:** Rhamphorhynchidae.
Where found: Central Asia.
Estimated wing span: 24.8in (63cm).

In the 1960s A. G. Sharov discovered pterosaur remains in late Jurassic strata of the Karatau mountains, including an almost complete skeleton with imprints of soft parts of the body and flight membranes. The sensational feature of this discovery was that, because of the fineness of the sediment grain in which the fossils were contained, even the thick hair that had covered the body of the creature was preserved. This was undeniable proof that pterosaurs were not naked or covered with reptilian scales but that they were hairy, an indirect proof of their warm-bloodedness. Traces of a hair covering had already been found in Holzmaden and Solnhofen pterosaurs but never the hairs themselves. Sharov called this new long-tailed pterosaur *Sordes pilosus* ('hairy evil spirit').

Sharov observed that long, dense hair covered the whole body and the curvature of individual hairs suggested ample elasticity. There was also hair on the flight membrane, digits and the skin between the foot digits, although it was sparser and shorter there. The root of the tail was covered with hair, but the rest of the tail was apparently naked. The

***Below: Sordes* is a small, long-tailed pterosaur probably closely related to Scaphognathus. The wings were short and broad. A membrane also extended between the hind legs. The body of *Sordes* was covered with dense fur, evidence of warm-bloodedness.**

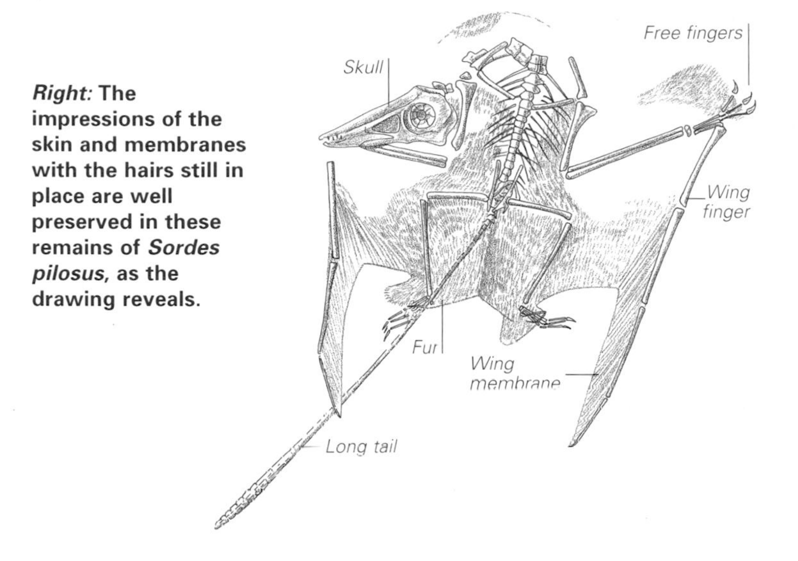

Right: **The impressions of the skin and membranes with the hairs still in place are well preserved in these remains of *Sordes pilosus*, as the drawing reveals.**

longest hairs on the body reached a length of 0.24in (6mm).

The wing membrane outlines that have survived in *Sordes* show that the hind legs were integrated into the membrane. This left the long naked tail free to move, which was vital to its function as a rudder in flight. This all resulted in a fairly broad wing area.

Sordes was a rhamphorhynchoid pterosaur with the typical features of long-tailed pterosaurs, such as a short metcarpal bone and long vertebrate tail. The end of the tail apparently flattened out slightly. There are no signs of the rhomboid terminal tail vane as in the Solnhofen *Rhamphorhynchus*. The fifth toe is very long and hoof-shaped, perhaps serving to spread the trailing edge of the flight membrane.

The skull and dentition are similar to those of *Scaphognathus* and a close relationship can thus be assumed. Both have few teeth, set upright and far apart in the jaw, and relatively short wing digits. *Sordes* can therefore also be classified as a member of the Rhamphorhynchoidae family. Three specimens of skeletons have been found. The skull was 3.15in (8cm) long and the wing span 24.8in (63cm). *Sordes* was probably piscivorous but could also have fed on insects.

Batrachognathus

Period: Late Jurassic. **Family:** Anurognathidae.
Where found: Central Asia.
Estimated wing span: 20in (50cm).

Jurassic deposits in Kazakhstan have for many years been noted for their rich fund of fossils. Late Jurassic limestone in the Karatau mountains, in the north-western foothills of the Tien shan range, have provided fossil insects in excellent condition in particular, showing great similarity with insect fauna in the Solnhofen strata in Bavaria, which are approximately the same age.

A pterosaur from Karatau was first described in 1948. These were the remains of a disarticulated and incomplete skeleton in which fragments of skull and jaw, vertebrae, ribs and bones from wings and hind legs can be recognised. In the jaws are peg-like teeth, 24 of them in the upper jaw. The shape of the jawbones suggests a high, short skull about 1.9in (48mm) long with a broad mouth like a frog's. For this reason the creature was given the name *Batrachognathus volans* ('flying frog jaw'). Very probably it was an insectivorous creature that caught its prey in flight.

Thus this form is strikingly reminiscent of the somewhat smaller *Anurognathus* from the Solnhofen strata in Bavaria. It is not known whether *Batrachognathus* from Karatau had a reduced, partly fused tail, but the preserved characteristics and skeletal proportions in *Anurognathus* and *Batrachognathus* are very similar and so seem to be related, suggesting that it would be sensible to assign both to the Anurognathidae family. It seems that only two specimens of *Batrachognathus* have been found. It was a small rhamphorhynchoid pterosaur with a wing span of about 20in (50cm).

Below: Closely related to the Solnhofen *Anurognathus, Batrachognathus* was an insect-eater. as its name ('frog jaw') suggests. It had a short head and a wide mouth with small, peg-like teeth. It is known only by incomplete skeletal remains. Here it is shown with a short reduced tail, by analogy with *Anurognathus* only.

Cretaceous Pterosaurs

The Jurassic was followed by the Cretaceous Period, which began about 144 million years ago and ended 65 million years ago. This final period of the Mesozoic Era was the longest, lasting for 79 million years.

In the late (sometimes called Upper) Cretaceous in particular there was extensive marine flooding all over the world, continents drifted apart and most of the earth's present high mountain ranges were formed. The two supercontinents, Laurasia in the north and Gondwanaland in the south, separated. At the beginning of the Cretaceous, South America and Africa were still connected, but towards the end of the period they had moved over 1,250 miles (2,000km) apart: the South Atlantic had come into being. North America and Eurasia were still connected. In the south, Australia, Antarctica and India detached themselves from Gondwana and drifted apart.

These changes also affected the climate and further development of the plant and animal kingdoms. The first flowering plants and deciduous trees appeared. Dinosaurs were still the dominant land animals and some of their evolutionary lines reached their peak. Although birds were becoming more numerous and had conquered various habitats, pterosaurs continued to dominate the air.

Cretaceous pterosaurs were found on all continents except Antarctica, again overwhelmingly in marine deposits, although only short-tailed species, the Pterodactyloidea, lived in the Cretaceous. The long-tailed pterosaurs, the Rhamphorhynchoidea, did not survive the transition from the Jurassic to the Cretaceous. The major feature of the period was enormous increase in size. The largest Jurassic pterosaurs had a maximum wing span of 8ft 2in (2.5m) but in the early (Lower) Cretaceous pterosaurs

with a 20ft (6m) wing span began to emerge and in the late Cretaceous wing spans of nearly 40ft (12m) were found as well. These pterosaurs were the largest flying creatures ever to live on earth.

Towards the end of the Cretaceous the oceans withdrew from large continental areas. Subsequently global cooling occurred and distinct climatic zones came into being on earth. Then, 65 million years ago, at the end of the Cretaceous, it was all over. In the mass extinction that took place then, dinosaurs, ichthyosaurs, plesiosaurs, mosasaurs and many fish and marine invertebrates disappeared from the earth, and the pterosaurs went as well.

The first pterosaur bones in England were found by Gideon Mantell, a country doctor, in about 1827, near Cuckfield in Sussex, at a site where a few years earlier he had found the remains of the dinosaur *Iguanodon*. The fossiliferous strata are sandy and clayey delta deposits from rivers and seas, and were formed in the south of England in early Cretaceous times. They are known as Wealden, a geological formation also found in Belgium, northern France and north-western Germany. Mantell eventually recognised the bones he had found as those of a pterosaur; they were later placed in the genus *Ornithocheirus*.

The first pterosaur remains from the late Cretaceous of England were described in 1845. They were also the first pterosaurs so far known that were larger than the largest Jurassic pterosaurs. The wing span was estimated at 8 or 9ft (2.5-2.75m). Richard Owen, the comparative anatomist who coined the term 'dinosaur', had hitherto thought it inconceivable that such huge flying animals could be warm-blooded but was forced to concede the possibility in the face of the facts.

Left: **This drawing recreates the landscape of the late Cretaceous in the area that is now Grünbach, Australia, where the remains of Ornithocheirus have been found. It shows the mouth of a river with tropical vegetation: screw trees, reeds, willows and palms. A predatory Ornithocheirus is seen soaring above the water, while turtles and crocodiles bask on sand bars by the river. A lizard is perched on a creeper, while in the foreground and background hadrosaurs can be seen foraging for food. Such fauna have been preserved in the deposits of coal that originated from the luch plant material of this locality.**

Criorhynchus

Period: Late Jurassic. **Family:** Criorhynchidae.
Where found: England.
Estimated wing span: 16ft 5in (2.5m).

Richard Owen identified a large pterosaur in the copious material from the Cambridge Greensand and called it *Criorhynchus* ('ram snout'). Only fragments of bones have been found for this species. The most marked characteristic is the front end of the jaw. It is blunt and solid, though compressed laterally. The front end of the upper jaw is slightly flattened and dented at the front. The jaws had powerful teeth, set upright, and curved slightly backwards. These typical features of the genus *Criorhynchus* were based on a fragment only of a front end of a snout. Owen did place other bones from the Cambridge Greensand in this genus, but definite classification was impossible.

Palaeontologists had always been puzzled about what *Criorhynchus*, a pterosaur with a wing span of about 16ft 5in (5m), might have looked like. The Viennese palaeontologist G. von Arthaber attempted a reconstruction of the skull in 1919. The result was a fairly short, tall head about 7in (18cm) long, which looked different from all the Cretaceous pterosaurs hitherto known. The solution came from a South American find.

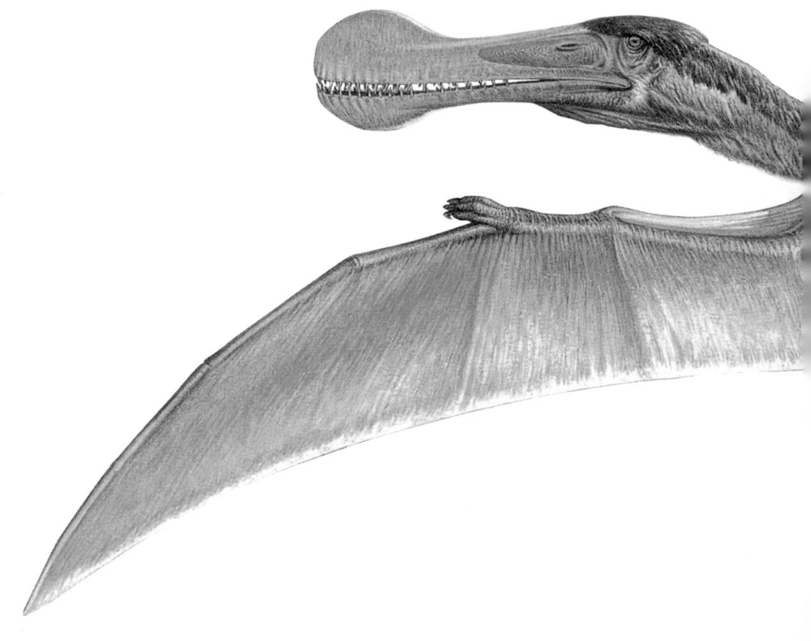

This was a complete pterosaur skull in good condition from the Santana Formation in Brazil. It was described as *Tropeognathus* ('keel jaw'). The front end of the jaw was startlingly similar to that of *Criorhynchus*. It sloped sharply at the front and extended backwards in the form of a bony crest tapering towards the top. This crest is almost semicircular at the top and limited to the front end of the upper jaw. It was presumably drawn through the water like the keel of a ship while fish were being caught in flight, and helped to stabilise the head in this phase.

It now became clear that the high snout end in *Criorhynchus* was the front part of a bone crest that may have looked similar to that of *Tropeognathus*. *Criorhynchus* must thus have had a much longer skull than Arthaber thought. The common features of these two genera meant that they were closely related and placed together in the family Criorhynchidae.

Below: **Formerly known only by fragments of the snout, *Criorhynchus* has turned out to be a close relative of *Tropeognathus* discovered more recently in early Cretaceous strata of Brazil. *Criorhynchus*, known only from England, must have looked similar, although the cranial crest at the front end of its snout was blunter and more robust. Its dentition of few, quite strong teeth suggests that this pterosaur was probably a fish-eater.**

Ornithocheirus

Period: Late Jurassic. **Family:** Ornithocheiridae.
Where found: Europe, Africa, South America, Australia.
Estimated wing span: 8ft 2in (2.5m).

Ornithocheirus ('bird hand') was described from fossil material found at English Cretaceous localities. Despite the fact that no more complete skeletons were found, but essentially only fragments of jaws, individual bones or vertebrae, a total of 36 species were distinguished. Most of them are based on specimens from the Cambridge Greensand, a marine sediment deposited by encroaching sea water at the beginning of the early Cretaceous Period. As the fossils of pterosaur bones often seem to have been worn down, frequently as a result of rolling, it is suspected that they were washed out of older strata on the seashore and redeposited. Pterosaurs of the Cambridge Greensand could thus be considerably older than their place of discovery suggests, and possibly came from the early Cretaceous.

In 1869 Harry Govier Seeley was com-missioned to arrange and catalogue the pterosaur collection for the University of Cambridge. Almost all the specimens came from the Cambridge Greensand, over 1,000 bones, all more or less broken or battered. Because of the fragmentary condition of the skeletal remains, controversy

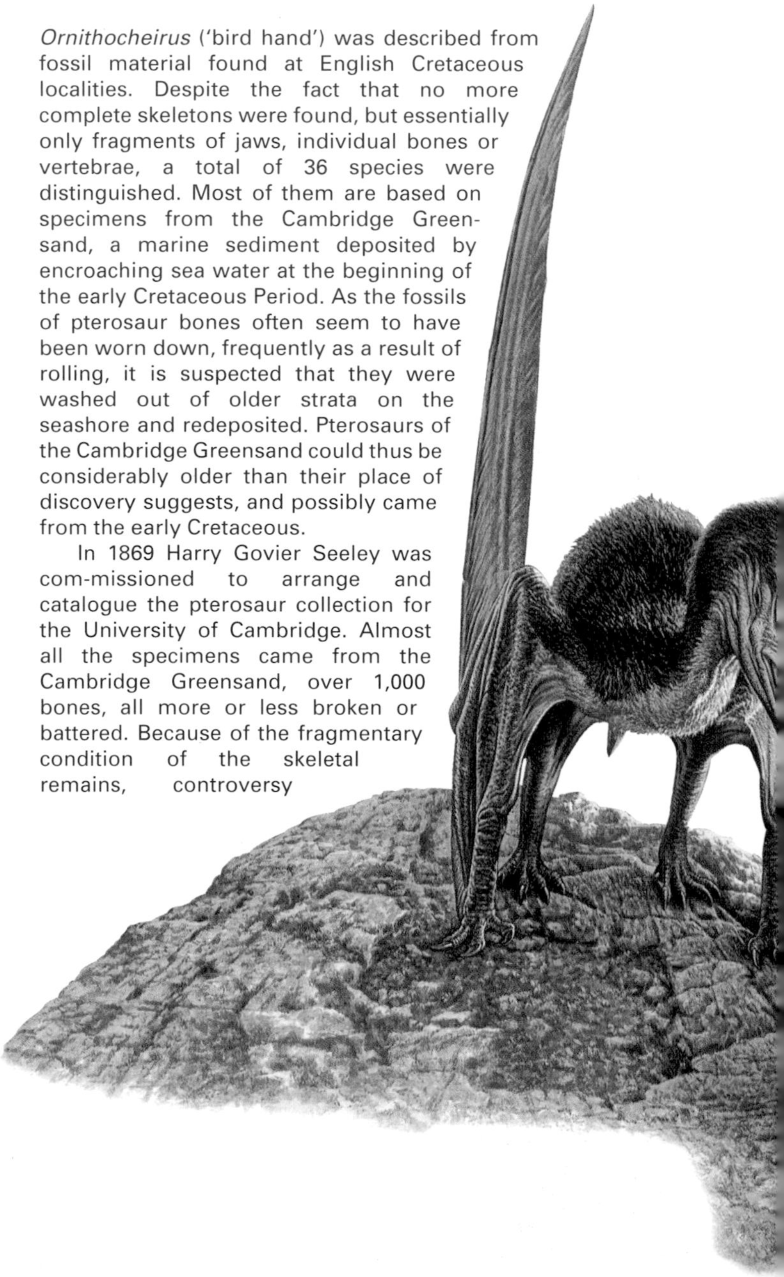

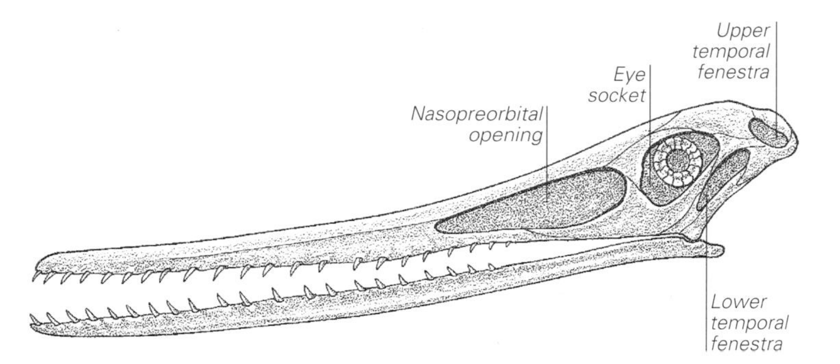

Above: **This restoration of the skull of *Ornithocheirus* is based on several fragmentary remains from the English Cretaceous. The skull is long and slender and the jaws are armed with numberous short, sharp teeth, which extend to the very front of the upper and lower jaws. It was probably a fish-eater.**

Below: Ornithocheirus **was one of the most abundant pterosaurs in Cretaceous times. Known mainly from the Cambridge Greensand, it was a medium-sized, short-tailed pterosaur, which was distributed worldwide. Its strong teeth, set in long, tapering jaws, suggest that it was piscivorous. In this scene a parent is shown feeding its young, which is picking stored fish prey out of the parental throat pouch.**

persists about what belongs to this genus and the family Ornithocheiridae named after it. In any case, they were mainly large or very large pterosaurs with long, slender skulls, some probably with a bony crest on the snout, all armed with powerful teeth coming right to the foremost point of the jaw. The vague definition of the genus meant that as time passed *Ornithocheirus* and the Ornithocheiridae became something of a 'waste bin' for many finds in England, France, Germany, Bohemia, Austria, Africa, South America and Australia.

In 1914 R. W. Hooley tried to bring an element of order into the English *Ornithocheirus* material. He distinguished between five different groups, to which he gave names of their own, particularly on the basis of jaw fragments. The latest English Cretaceous pterosaurs are known only from fragments of bones and have also been assigned to *Ornithocheirus*.

Below and right: **The drawings show fragments of different species of *Ornithocheirus* from various English Cretaceous localities. Below is a lower jaw of *O. sagittirostris* from the Wealden of Sussex. At below centre is a fragment from *O. daviesi*, which comes from the late Cretaceous in Kent. At bottom are two pictures of the upper jaw of *O. cuvieri* – seen in lateral view and from below. It comes from a chalk pit in Kent, as does *O. giganteus*, pictured top right. At right are pictured jaw fragments of *O. sedgwicki*, from the Cambridge Greensand. The four drawings show the tip of the upper jaw in lateral and dorsal views and the tip of the lower jaw in lateral and dorsal views. Despite the fact that no complete skeletons of *Ornithocheirus* are known, 36 species have been distinguished.**

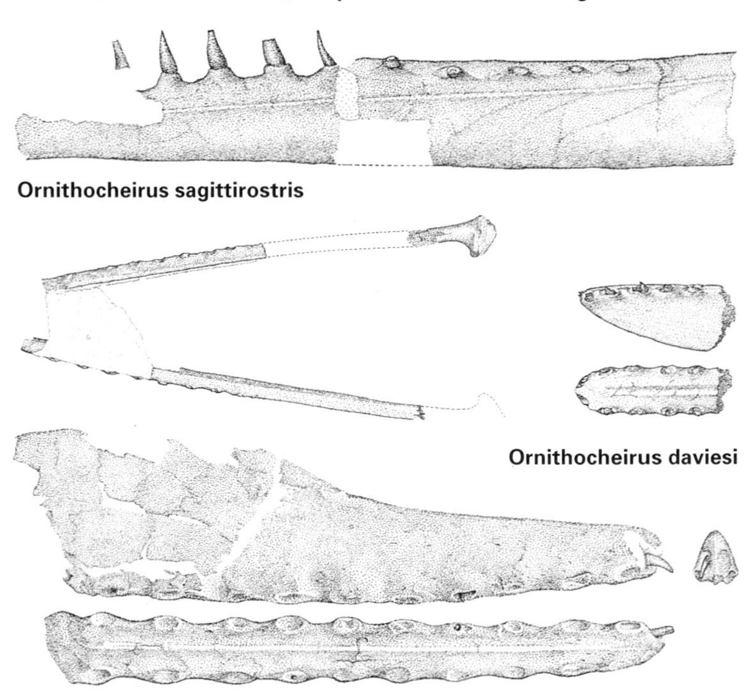

Ornithocheirus sagittirostris

Ornithocheirus daviesi

Ornithocheirus cuvieri

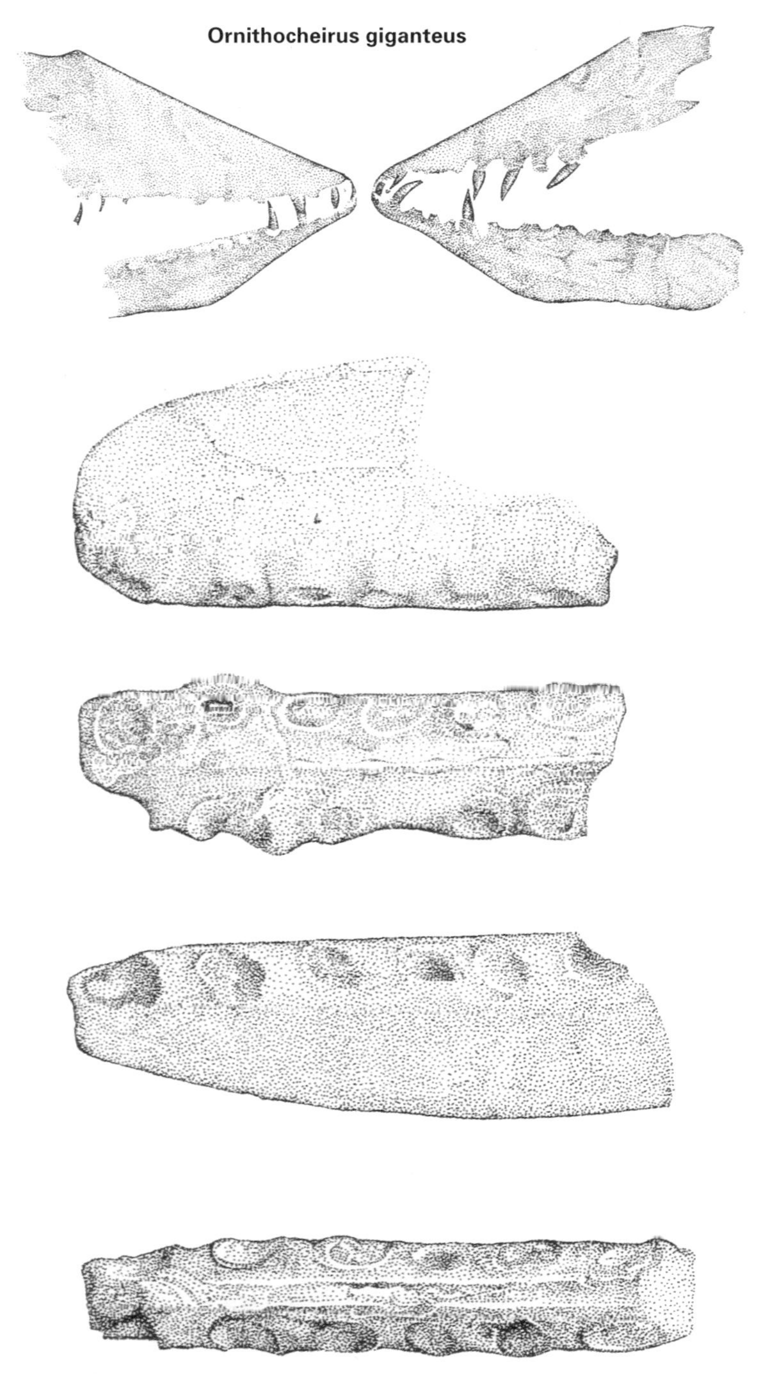
Ornithocheirus giganteus
Ornithocheirus sedgwicki

Ornithodesmus

Period: Early Cretaceous. **Family:** Ornithodesmidae.
Where found: England.
Estimated wing span: 16ft 5in (5m).

A fourth genus of Cretaceous pterosaur was discovered in England, from the Wealden of the Isle of Wight. In 1887 the English palaeontologist Harry Govier Seeley described a sacrum from the early Cretaceous at Atherfield, which he thought came from a bird and which he named *Ornithodesmus* ('bird ribbon') *cluniculus Seeley*. Later he diagnosed it as a pterosaur and also placed in this genus parts of a skull, neck and dorsal vertebrae, the breastbone and parts of the wing skeleton of an individual that also came from Atherfield in the Isle of Wight. Because of the broad teeth of this individual he called the species *Ornithodesmus latidens*.

As happens so frequently in palaeontology, there is confusion about the naming of species. The sacrum that Seeley first described came, in fact, neither from a bird nor from a pterosaur but belonged to small theropod dinosaur. Thus the generic name *Ornithodesmus* designates a dinosaur and in due course a new generic name will have to be given to the pterosaur species *Ornithodesmus latidens*. For the time being, the name *Ornithodesmus* applies to the pterosaur identified from the Isle of Wight.

Ornithodesmus was a large pterosaur with a wing span of 16ft 5in (5m). The front ends of the jaw were broad and rounded, similar to those of a duck. Sometimes called a 'duck-billed pterosaur', *Ornithodesmus* differed from a duck in having jaws that were equipped from back to front with a series of strong, lancet-shaped, laterally compressed teeth. The eye socket was small and placed fairly far back in the skull. The first six dorsal vertebrae were fused to form a notarium to which the pectoral girdle attached. The strong, alternately meshing dentition and broad snout suggest that *Ornithodesmus* was a fish-eater and that it possibly used a different catching technique from its contemporaries, the Ornithocheirids, with their pointed snouts.

The first six trunk vertebrae of *Ornithodesmus* were fused to form a notarium. The shoulder blade was supported in a shallow depression in the fused neural spines. The length of the notarium was 6.8in (17.25cm).

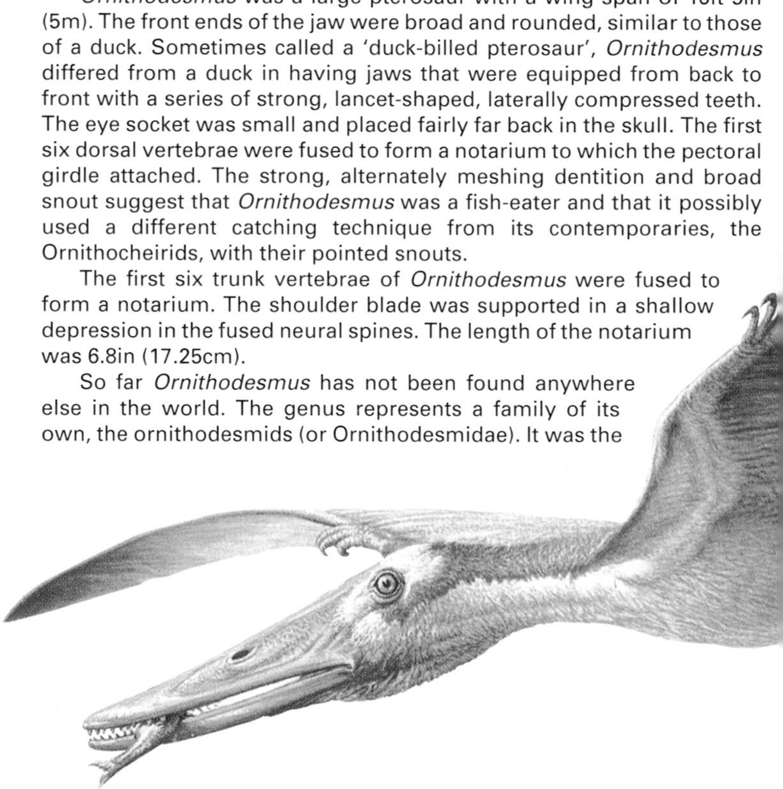

So far *Ornithodesmus* has not been found anywhere else in the world. The genus represents a family of its own, the ornithodesmids (or Ornithodesmidae). It was the fourth genus of Cretaceous pterosaur to be discovered in England, after *Ornithocheirus, Criorhynchus* and a find from the Purbeck limestone near Swanage on the Dorset coast, named *Doratorhynchus*. The latter, discovered in 1875, proved to be a large pterosaur with an extremely long neck. It was possibly an ancestor of the giant pterosaurs of Texas such as *Quetzalcoatlus*, to which it showed remarkable similarities in respect of the nature of the cervical vertebrae.

***Below:* Ornithodesmus was quite a large pterosaur with a wing span of about 16ft 5in (5m) and a skull about 22in (56cm) long. It is known from the Wealden (early Cretaceous) of England and must have been a contemporary of the *Iguanodon* dinosaurs that frequented the same landscape. To give an idea of comparative size, *Iguanodon* was about 23ft (7m) long. *Ornithodesmus* is distinguished from all other Cretaceous pterosaurs by the peculiar broad and rounded front end of its beak. This characteristic has given rise to its popular name, 'duck-billed pterosaur'. However, unlike a duck, the front of its beak was lined with short, robust, alternately meshing teeth, which suggests a fish diet.**

Phobetor

Period: Early Cretaceous. **Family:** Dsungaripteridae.
Where found: Mongolia.
Estimated wing span: 4ft 11in (1.5m).

The Junggar basin is in north-western China, between the Altai and Tien shan mountain ranges, in the province of Xinjiang. Its sequence of geological strata includes a long series of continental sediments, sandstones, slates and shales, deposited from the late Permian to the late Cretaceous. Some later Jurassic and Cretaceous horizons have produced dinosaurs. Pterosaurs have also been found in one of these formations, the Tugulu group. Their age can be given as the later part of the early Cretaceous.

In 1982 N. Bakhurina of the Moscow Palaeontological Institute described skeletal remains of a small *Dsungaripterus* (*D. parvus*; see next entry) from an early Lower Cretaceous formation of western Mongolia known as the Zagan Zabsk Formation. At first there were only bones from the wing skeleton and the hind legs. Later skulls were also discovered and there were such clear distinctions between these bones and the Chinese *Dsungaripterus* specimens that a new genus, *Phobetor* ('the frightening one'), was suggested for the Mongolian form. *Phobetor* did have *Dsungaripterus*'s toothless jaw points and a cranial crest but it also had geniune pointed teeth. Its wing span was about 4ft 11in (1.5m), only about half that of a *Dsungaripterus*.

Dsungaripterid pterosaurs apparently occurred all over the world. They lived in East Africa in the late Jurassic and in South America in the early Jurassic, as well as in China and Mongolia.

***Right: Phobetor* was a close relative of *Dsungaripterus*, although only about half its size. It had similar bony crests adorning its head. Its pointed jaws are straighter than those of *Dsungaripterus* and they contain real, conical teeth rather than tooth-like bony knobs. *Phobetor* is seen here skimming over the water and feeding in the fast-moving river shallows.**

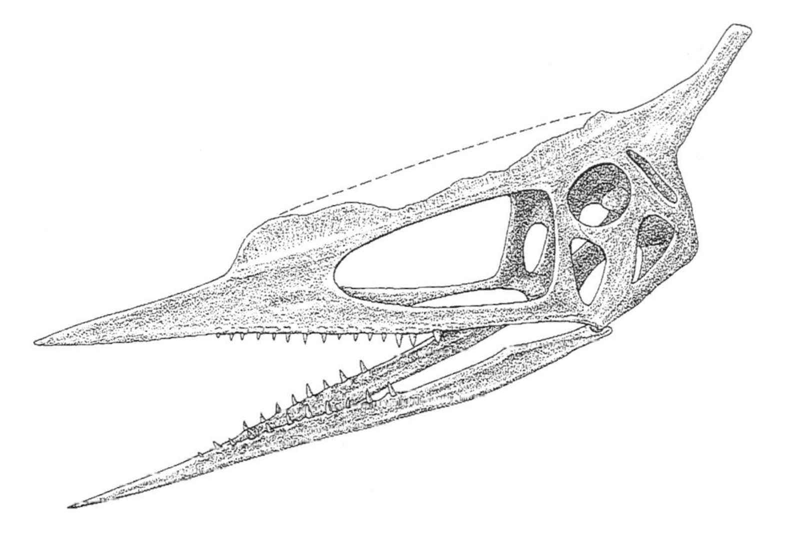

Above: **This is the skull of *Phobetor parvus* from early Cretaceous rocks of western Mongolia. This dsungaripterid pterosaur had toothless pointed tips to its jaws and crests along the top and at the rear of its skull.**

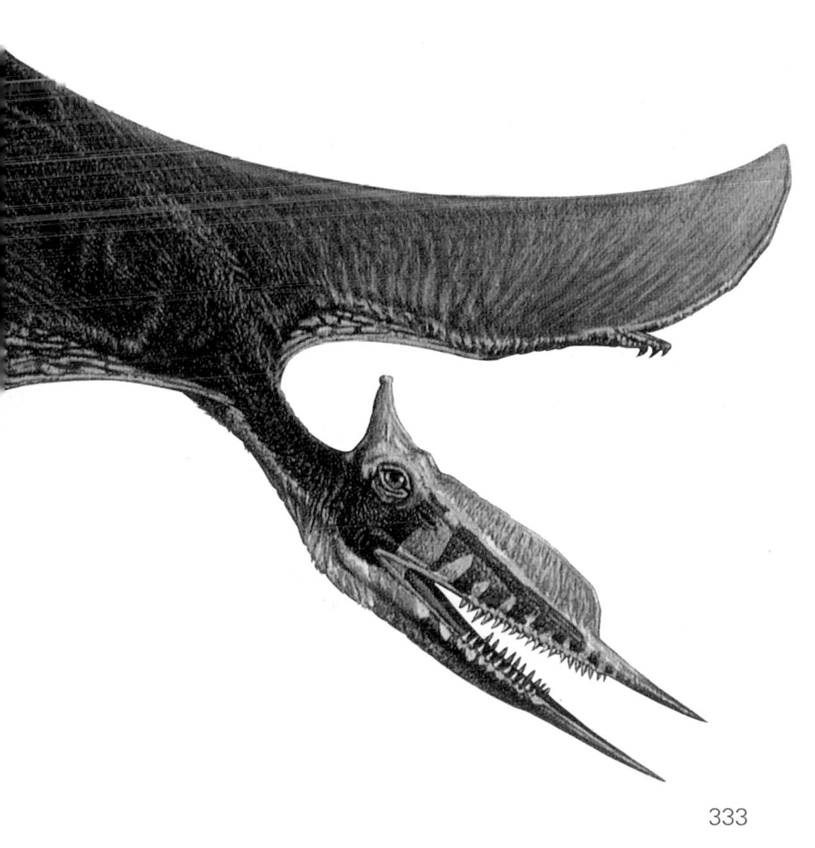

Dsungaripterus

Period: Late Jurassic to early Cretaceous. **Family:** Dsungaripteridae.
Where found: Africa, China, western Mongolia.
Estimated wing span: 9ft 10in (3m).

Professor C. C. Young, a well-known Chinese palaeontologist, discovered the first Chinese pterosaur, *Dsungaripterus* weii ('Junggar wing'). The fossil material consisted of the front sections of the skull and lower jaw and a large part of the rest of the skeleton, preserved in excellent three-dimensional condition. In 1973 a palaeontological expedition excavated more *Dsungaripterus* skeletal material on the same site near Wuerho, in the north-west of the Junggar basin, including complete skulls, a sternum, a sacrum and pelvic bones.

Dsungaripterus weii was a fairly large pterosaur with a wing span of 9ft 10in-11ft 6in (3-3.5m), with a skull up to 1ft 7in (50cm) long. The toothless tips of its jaws, slightly bent upwards, are a striking feature. They seem to have worked like a pair of tweezers. Further back, both upper and lower jaw have blunt knobs on their margins, which look like breaking tools. Perhaps *Dsungaripterus* used its jaw like the beak of a shore bird, in order to find and crack open bivalves, snails and crabs.

Other particular features of *Dsungaripterus* are cranial crests on the skull: an elongated crest on the snout along the mid-line extending over the eyes, and a short crest rising above the back of the head. The eye socket is quite high in the skull and relatively small. The largest aperture in the skull is the nasopreorbital opening. *Dsungaripterus* had a series of fused front dorsal vertebrae, a so-called notarium, and fused sacral vertebrae, a synsacrum, similarly to birds.

***Below:* *Dsungaripterus* was a moderately large pterodactyloid pterosaur with distinctive pointed and curved jaws, which may have been used like tweezers to probe for small aquatic creatures. The blunt, bony knobs further back in the jaws could have been used to crack open the shells of such organisms.**

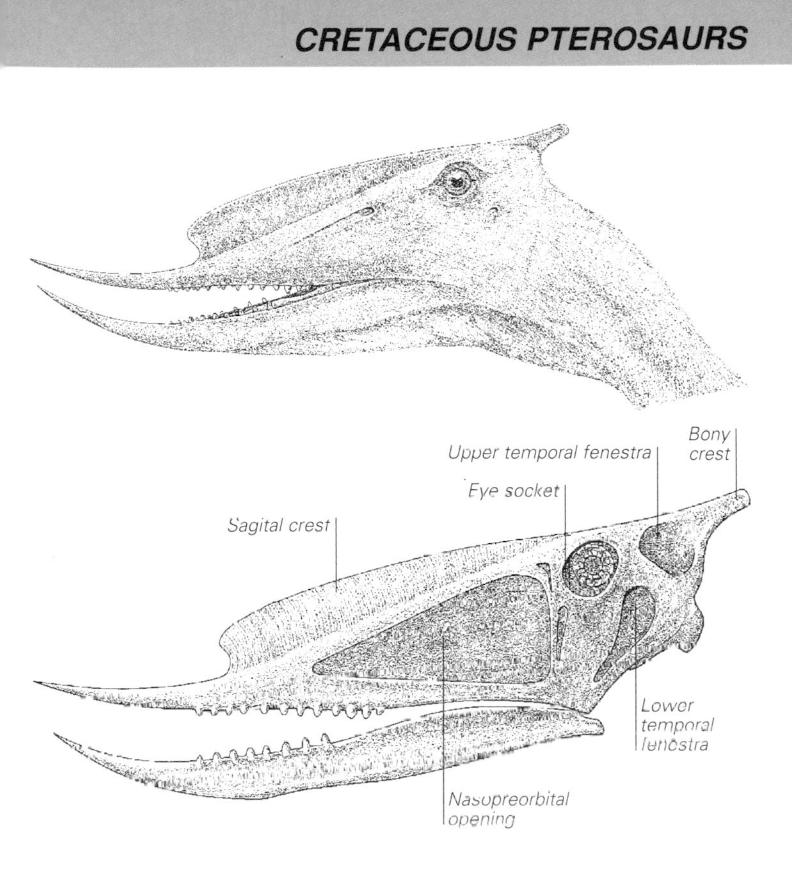

Above: **This skull restoration and life portrait of *Dsungaripterus weii* show its characteristic features: the pointed jaws, the bony crests along the mid-line and back of the skull and the unusually small eye socket.**

Tropeognathus

Period: Early Cretaceous. **Family:** Criorhynchidae.
Where found: Brazil.
Estimated wing span: 20ft (6.2m).

A complete skull with lower jaw and an isolated lower jaw documented a new pterosaur from the Santana Formation, Brazil. Its special characteristic is a tall, rounded medial crest at the front end of the snout and a similar crest on the lower side of the lower jaw, at the point where the two branches of the mandible have fused in the mid-line to form a symphysis. These crests are in the form of the keel of a ship, for which reason these pterosaurs were given the name *Tropeognathus* ('keel jaw'). Another shorter and blunter crest developed on the back of the skull. The dentition consists of a total of 26 teeth in the upper jaw and 22 in the lower.

The function of the crests on the tip of the snout was probably hydrodynamic. *Tropeognathus* also fed on fish. In flight the tip of the snout had to dip into the water and plough through the surface of the sea. The skull was so long that it had to be stabilised by the crest in this phase. This saved muscle mass on the neck and thus weight.

Tropeognathus is so far known through only two species, represented by two specimens. The skull lengths are 2ft and 2ft 2in (63 and 67cm). *Tropeognathus robustus* had a wing span of 20ft (6.2m) and is thus the largest pterosaur so far found in the Santana Formation.

The crest at the front end of *Tropeognathus*'s snout is highly reminiscent of the high front end of the snout of *Criorhynchus* from the Cambridge Greensand in England. It was therefore suggested that *Tropeognathus* should be included in the family Criorhynchidae as well.

Below: **This is one of the most unusual pterosaurs known. It was named because of the resemblance of the crests on its jaws to a ship's keel (from the Greek word *tropis*, meaning 'keel'). These crests must have served to stabilise the head when the tips of the jaws were ploughing through the water. Two species are known, *Tr. mesembrinus* and *Tr. robustus*, which can be distinguished by their different crests and feet.**

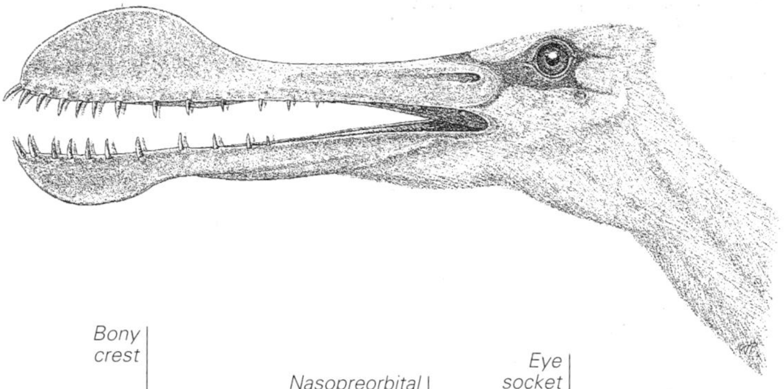

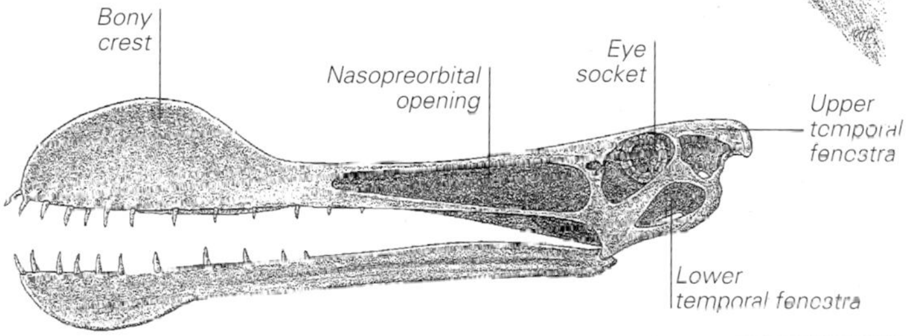

Bony crest
Nasopreorbital opening
Eye socket
Upper temporal fenestra
Lower temporal fenestra

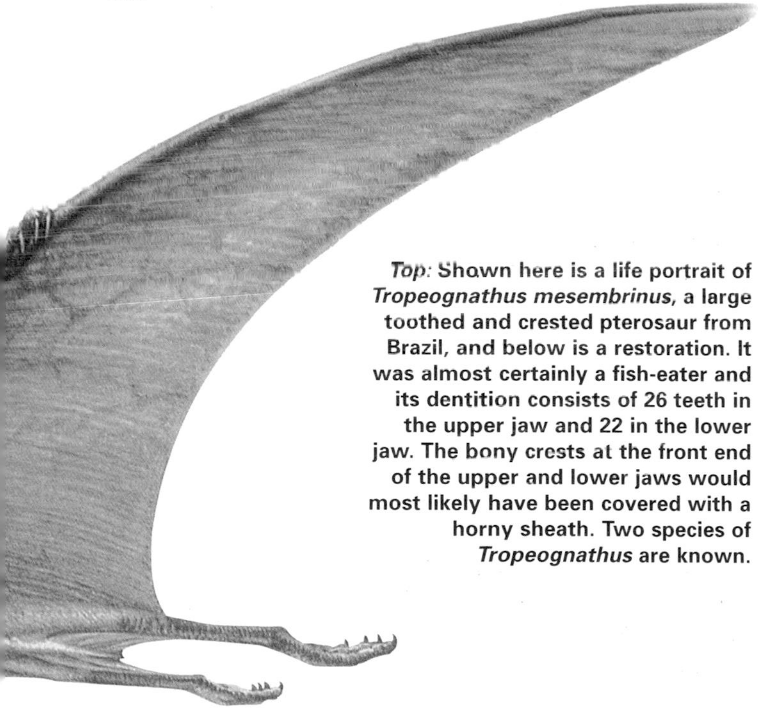

Top: Shown here is a life portrait of ***Tropeognathus mesembrinus***, a large toothed and crested pterosaur from Brazil, and below is a restoration. It was almost certainly a fish-eater and its dentition consists of 26 teeth in the upper jaw and 22 in the lower jaw. The bony crests at the front end of the upper and lower jaws would most likely have been covered with a horny sheath. Two species of ***Tropeognathus*** are known.

Anhanguera

Period: Mid-Cretaceous. **Family:** Anhangueridae.
Where found: Brazil.
Estimated wing span: 13ft (4m).

In 1951 a Brazilian named L. I. Price described the first South American pterosaur find. It was the fossilised bone of a large pterosaur with a wing span of about 11ft 6in (3.5m). It was Price again who announced the first pterosaur skeletal remains from the Santana Formation in north-eastern Brazil, from a stratum that has produced finds among the most significant and productive in the world. The Santana Formation reaches a thickness of about 656ft (200m), but it is only in the uppermost stratum that fossil concretions formed about 115 million years ago, in the early Cretaceous, in a marine environment near the coast, are to be found. ▶

***Right:* *Anhangeura* is one of the best-known early Cretaceous pterosaurs. It was quite large with very long wings and peculiar low medial crests on top of the skull and below the lower jaw. Like *Tropeognathus,* these served to stabilise the head when fishing. In this scene *Anhangeura* has just caught a fish and the front of its head on its extremely flexible neck is still ploughing through the water.**

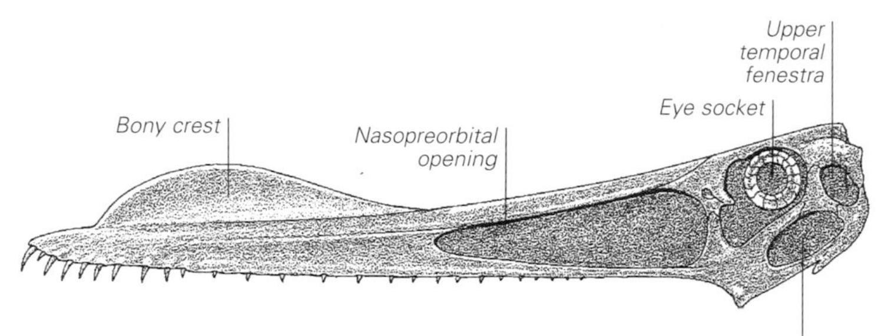

Above: **This drawing shows a restoration of the skull of *Anhangeura bittersdorffi*. The lower jaw is not preserved. The skull length is 1ft 7in (50cm). One peculiarity of *Anhanguera* is its proportions: amazingly, the skull is actually longer than the body and the wing span is enormous in relation to both.**

In 1985 D. A. Campos and A. W. A. Kellner described a new pterosaur genus from the Santana Formation, which they called *Anhanguera* ('old devil') after a name from the Tupi Indians of Brazil. The type specimen is a slender skull 1ft 7in (50cm) long with a medial crest on the snout. This crest is an outgrowth of the upper jaw bone. A similar crest may also have developed on the lower side of the lower jaw. *Anhanguera* had teeth and was probably a fish-eater. The crest on the snout was drawn through the water while the creature was fishing in full flight.

Anhanguera is now one of the best-known pterosaurs from the Santana Formation. Two more skeletal remains of this genus were found, including a fairly complete specimen, in which the skull and a large proportion of the post-cranial elements had survived, such as spinal column, ribs, pectoral girdle, pelvis and parts of the wings and hind legs. Some of the bones were found still articulated naturally in a large calcareous concretion and it was to a large extent possible to free them completely from the rocks.

The proportions of this large pterosaur with a wing span of more than 13ft (4m) are unusual: the skull is actually twice as long as the body. The great disproportion between wings and hind legs is expressed by the fact that the pectoral girdle is large and robust, but in comparison the pelvis is quite small. Neck vertebrae exhibit lateral openings: these are weight-saving devices.

Three-dimensional reconstruction of the pelvis of *Anhanguera* revealed that the hind legs could not be brought into a vertical position under the body, but were splayed slightly to the side. Thus bird-like, bipedal locomotion on the ground was scarcely possible. Orientation of the hip sockets obliquely upwards and the slight bend of the articular head of the thigh bone make quadrupedal locomotion on the ground more probable.

So far only two species of *Anhanguera* are known. A separate family, the Anhangueridae, was suggested for them. They have a characteristic crest on the snout, and complete ossification of some elements of the skeleton (skull, pectoral girdle, notarium, carpus and pelvis) did not take place until very late in the growth of the individual, perhaps not until shortly before the adult stage. The different formation of the crest in two species could also be interpreted as a sexual characteristic of male and female individuals.

Two skull specimens of *Anhanguera santanae*, preserved in New York and Munich, both regrettably are missing the bony crest that was one of the creature's striking features.

***Right:* This skeletal restoration shows *Anhangeura santanae* in a four-legged pose. This is more plausible than a bipedal posture because the hip sockets are oriented obliquely upwards and because the articular head of the thigh bone bends slightly.**

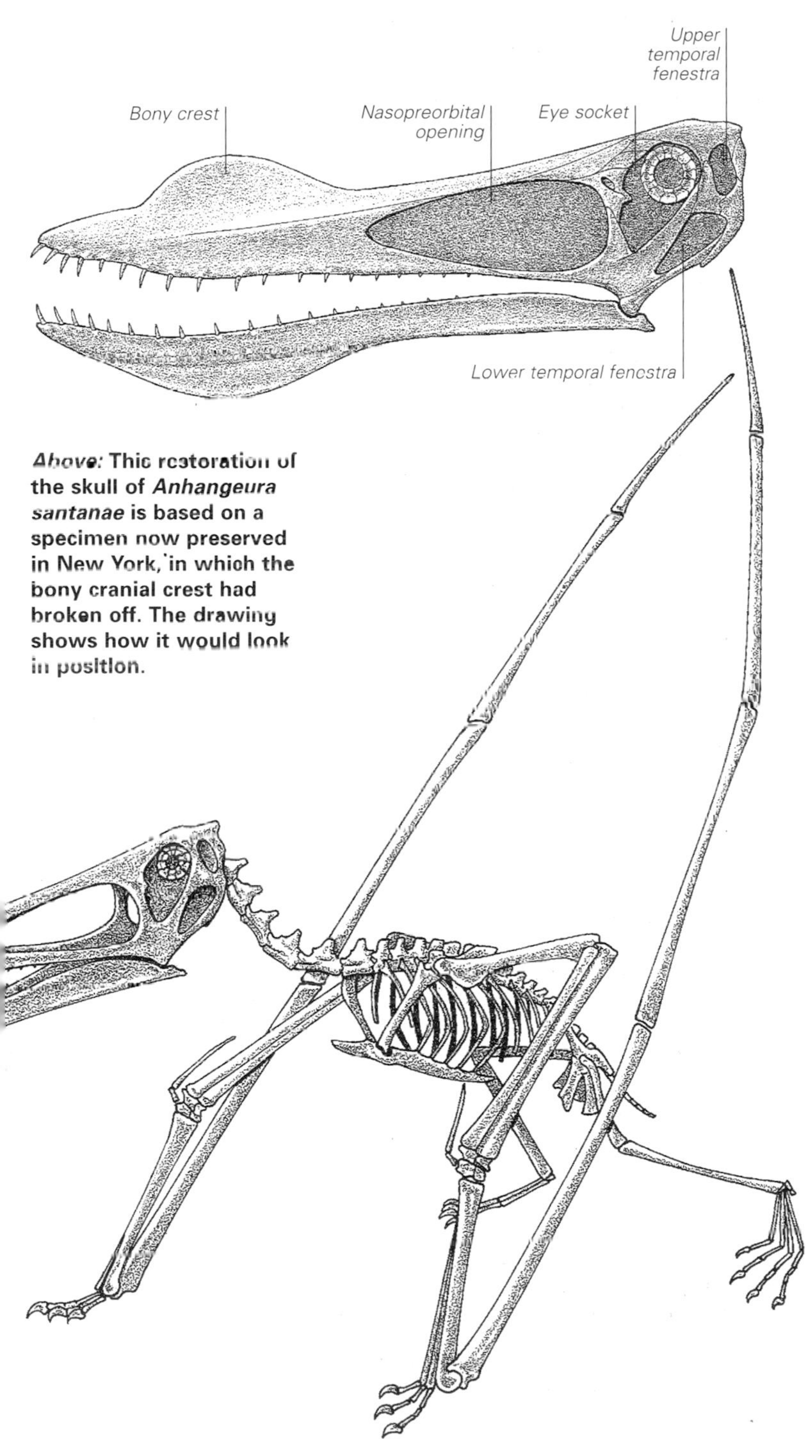

Above: This restoration of the skull of *Anhangeura santanae* is based on a specimen now preserved in New York, in which the bony cranial crest had broken off. The drawing shows how it would look in position.

Pterodaustro

Period: Early Cretaceous. **Family:** Pterodaustridae.
Where found: Argentina.
Estimated wing span: 4ft 4in (1.33m).

In 1970 Dr José Bonaparte discovered one of the most unusual pterosaurs to have been found to date. At first only a skull fragment, vertebrae and some elements of the appendicular skeleton were found, then later a complete skull and a complete skeleton including the skull came to light. They came from the early Cretaceous Lagarcito Formation in the province of San Luis in Argentina. Dr Bonaparte called this genus *Pterodaustro* ('south wing'). It is a short-tailed pterosaur with a skull 9.25in (23.5cm) long but a wing span of only 4ft 4in (1.33m). The dentition is unique.

The skull is very markedly elongated and the front parts of the jaw are bent upwards. The lower jaw has a side groove in which are set a large number of long, tightly packed, apparently elastic 'teeth', which could more properly be called bristles. About 24 such lower jaw teeth occupy a centimetre of jaw length, which means that in a jaw 7.9in (20cm) long there were almost 500 teeth in each half of the jaw - 1,000 bristles altogether. *Pterodaustro's* lower jaw was a thus a highly ▶

Below: **Dubbed the 'flamingo pterosaur', *Pterodaustro* was a remarkable filter feeder. It could not trap its food on the wing, but had to stand in the shallows and sieve small organisms out of the water with its filter basket.**

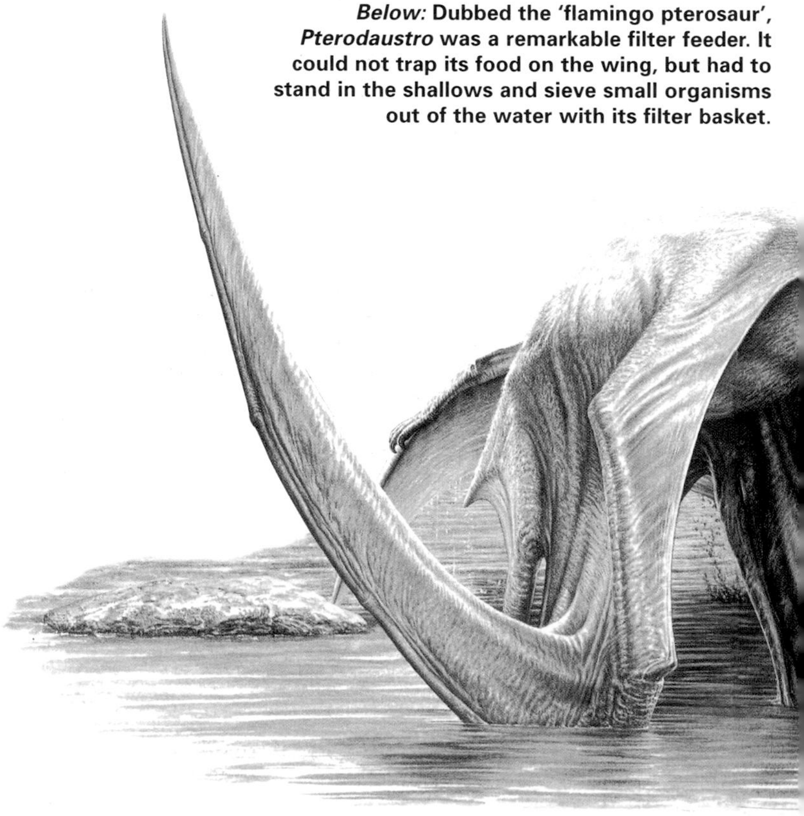

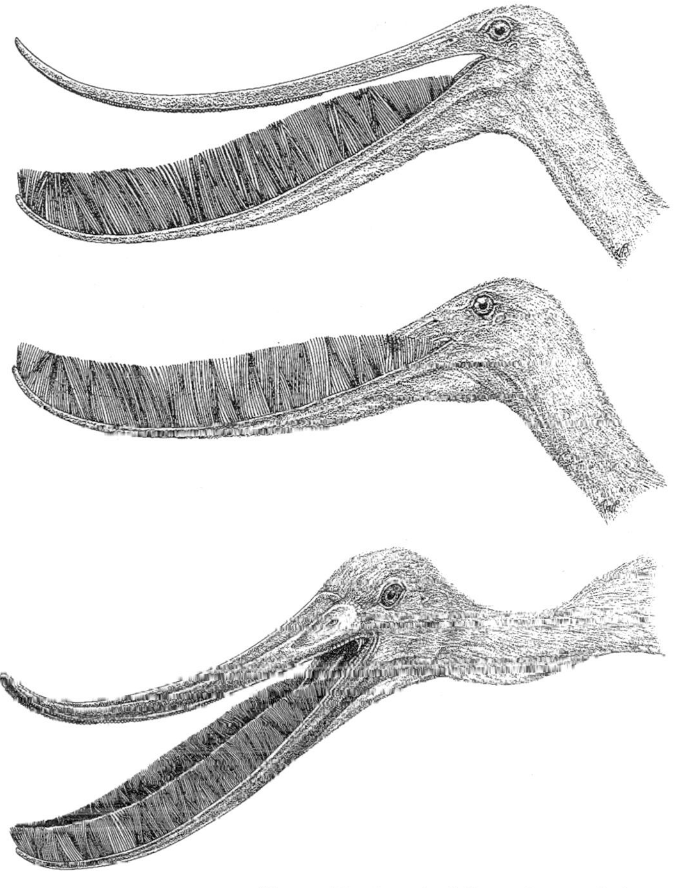

Above: The head of *Pterodaustro* is here restored as in life with its beak open and closed. Its dentition consisted of a comb-like array of long, elastic bristles (not actually teeth) in the lower jaw for sieving creatures from the water. In its upper jaw was a series of short, blunt teeth for chopping up the food into smaller pieces to be swallowed.

effective sieving apparatus for filtering small organisms out of the water. The food content of this filter basket was chopped up into smaller bits of blunt, short teeth in the upper jaw. This arrangement was far more specialised than *Ctenochasma* from Solnhofen, which had filter dentition in the upper and lower jaw but consisting of considerably fewer teeth. For this reason *Pterodaustro* was placed in a family of its own, the Pterodaustridae. *Pterodaustro* could not trap its food on the wing but had to stand in the shallows and sieve small organisms out of the water with its filter basket.

Skull fragments and a humerus of *Pterodaustro* have also been discovered in the early Cretaceous of Chile, in the province of Antofagasta. J. F. Bonaparte and T. M. Sanchez reported on a second pterosaur genus from the early Cretaceous (La Cruz Formation) of the province of San Luis in Argentina in 1975. What was found was a tibia 3.5in (9cm) long, which broadened at the end to form a bird-like roller-

***Above:* This skeletal restoration shows *Pterodaustro* in its probable flying position. This short-tailed pterosaur had a wing span of about 52in (133cm). Its skull length was 9.25in (23.5cm). The restoration is based on a drawing by Dr José Bonaparte, the scientist who first discovered *Pterodaustro* in 1970. The fossil specimens were found in early Cretaceous deposits (Lagarcito Formation) that were excavated in the province of San Luis in Argentina.**

***Above right:* This is the skull of Pterodaustro the 'flamingo pterosaur', with its mouthful of bristles.**

joint. With this were only a dorsal vertebra, a wing phalanx and a foot digit phalanx. The particular features of the tibia, which is fused with the fibula, are different from those of *Pterodaustro* and were seen as diagnostic of a new genus, *Puntanipterus* (named after natives of the province of San Luis, called *puntanos* in Spanish). Some palaeontologists argue that *Puntanipterus* belongs to the family Dsungaripteridae, which was distributed from China via East Africa to South America. *Puntanipterus* and *Pterodaustro* were contemporaries.

One of the most southerly occurrences of pterosaurs was found in early Cretaceous strata of the province of Santa Cruz in Patagonia. They are bone fragments of a small ulna, which were questionably classified as ornithocheirid. These Patagonian pterosaurs must have lived in a palaeolatitude of 51°S. Part of femur of a pterodactyloid pterosaur that cannot be any more precisely classified also came from Argentina. It was found in Lower Cretaceous deposits in Neuquén in northern Patagonia.

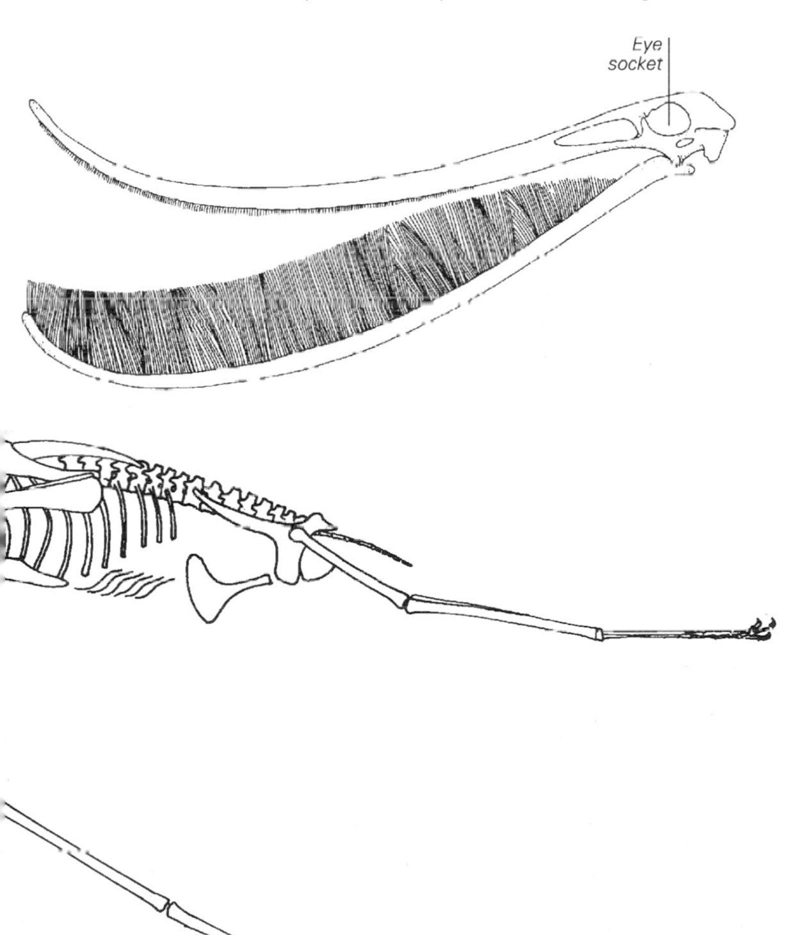

Pteranodon ingens

Period: Mid- to late Cretaceous. **Family:** Pteranodontidae.
Where found: Kansas.
Estimated wing span: 23ft (7m).

The first fossil remains of North American pterosaurs were described by Othniel Charles Marsh in 1871. In 1870 and 1871 he made many fossil discoveries at the Smoky Hill River in Kansas, among them a large quantity of pterosaur material, including skulls. It turned out that, in contrast with the English ornithocheirids, these giant pterosaurs were toothless and had a long crest at the rear end of the skull, which must have made these flying reptiles look very bizarre indeed.

For this reason Marsh thought it necessary in 1876 to distinguish the American Cretaceous pterosaurs from the English forms. He introduced the name *Pteranodon* ('toothless flier') for them and placed them in a family of their own, the Pteranodontidae, and even a sub-order of their own, the Pteranodontia. He also included another genus here, *Nyctosaurus* ('naked reptile'), which had been

Left: **Seen here in its nesting habitat is *Pteranodon ingens*, which, with a wing span of 23ft (7m), was smaller than *P. sternbergi*.**

found with *Pteranodon* skeletal remains in the Kansas chalk.

None of the skulls collected or described by Marsh was originally attached to the bones of the rest of the skeleton, with the exception of neck vertebrae. It is therefore difficult to assign skeletal bones to particular skulls. Despite this, Marsh distinguished various different species of *Pteranodon*, which differed from each other particularly in the morphology of their skulls, especially in the shape of the crest. For example, *Pteranodon ingens* had a skull 5ft 11in (1.79m) long, of which almost half consisted of the crest, rising well back over the rump. It had an estimated wing span of about 23ft (7m).

In contrast with the pterosaurs with extremely long necks such as *Quetzalcoatlus*, *Pteranodon* had a relatively short neck with powerful but short cervical vertebrae. Its long, pointed jaws are toothless, the eye socket is relatively small and placed fairly high in the skull. There is always a crest on the back of the head, but not on the snout or lower jaw. All the bones are extremely thin-walled and pneumatic, meaning that they were hollow and had small air vents, possibly to allow the penetration of air sacs, which were connected with the lung, as in modern birds. The vertebrae also have large lateral openings and are very lightly constructed.

The body weight of *Pteranodon ingens* has been calculated as a mere 36.6lb (16.6kg). With this the animal was able to achieve a maximum speed of 31mph (50km/h).

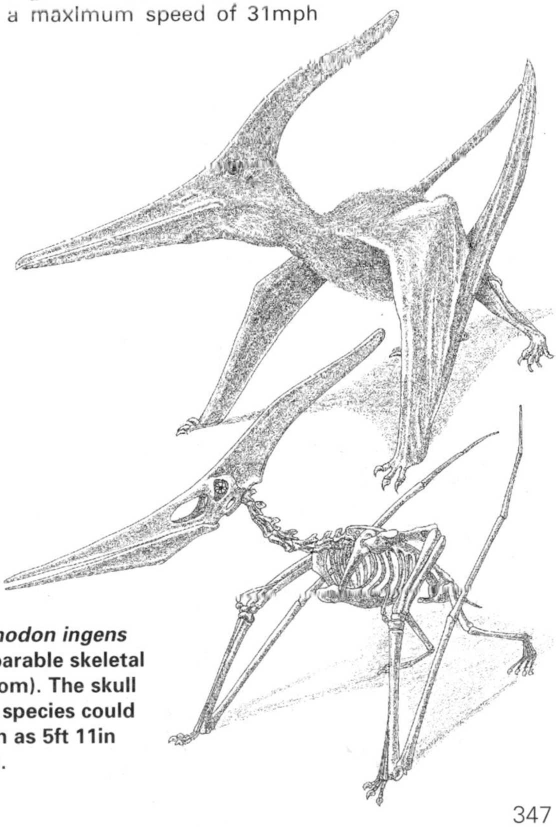

Right: **Shown here is a life portrait of *Pteranodon ingens* (top) and a comparable skeletal restoration (bottom). The skull of this particular species could measure as much as 5ft 11in (1.79m) in length.**

Nyctosaurus

Period: Late Cretaceous. **Family:** Nyctosauridae.
Where found: Kansas, Brazil.
Estimated wing span: up to 9ft 6in (2.9m).

When more pterosaur material from the Smoky Hill River in western Kansas was found in the 1870s, O. C. March recognised that it also included skeletal remains of a second form, considerably smaller than *Pteranodon*. He called this smaller form *Nyctosaurus* ('naked reptile'). In the early 1900s relatively complete skeletons were described by S. W. Williston, who also provided a first reconstruction of the skeleton.

The wing span of *Nyctosaurus* is 7ft 11in-9ft 6in (2.4-2.9m), only between a third and a half that of *Pteranodon*. Its skull is low and elongated, reaching a length of about 1ft (30cm), and ends in a long, slender beak. *Nyctosaurus* is also toothless and has only a short cranial crest at the rear of the head. As it is also different with regard to other skeletal features, this pterosaur has been grouped in a family of its own, the Nyctosauridae. Another characteristic is that the flight digit consists of only three phalanges, rather than the usual four.

Below: Nyctosaurus **was also a toothless pterosaur from late Cretaceous deposits in Kansas. However, it was smaller than** ***Pteranodon,*** **and had only a short cranial crest at the rear of its head.** ***Nyctosaurus*** **was a contemporary of the diving bird** ***Hesperornis*** **and the 'Cretaceous gull',** ***Ichthyornis,*** **both toothed birds.**

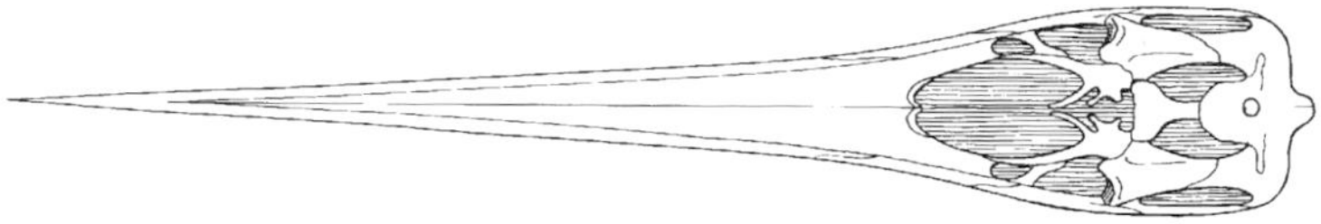

Above: **Seen here is the skull of *Nyctosaurus gracilis* from below looking up into the palate. The length of this particular skull with its long, slender beak is about 1ft (30cm).**

A humerus and fused dorsal vertebra from the marine early Cretaceous of Oregon is similar to *Nyctosaurus* but clearly a larger species, described in 1928 by C. W. Gilmore as *'Pteranodon' oregonensis*.

Pterosaur remains from late Cretaceous strata have also been found in other sites in North America, and it may be that they are pteranodontids. Relevant reports have come from Delaware, Georgia, Montana and Alberta.

Pteranodon sternbergi

Period: Mid- to late Cretaceous.
Family: Pteranodontidae.
Where found: Kansas.
Estimated wing span: 30ft (9m).

Pteranodon sternbergi ('Sternberg's toothless flier') had a crest that rose steeply and was quite broad at the top. The lower jaw alone of this species is 3.9ft (1.2m) long, thus longer by a third than that of *Pteranodon ingens*. *Pteranodon sternbergi* was thus one of the largest known pterosaurs and must have had a wing span of over 30ft (9m), compared with *P. ingens*'s wing span of 23ft (7m). This was exceeded only by the azhdarchids, such as *Quetzalcoatlus* or *Titanopteryx*.

***Below:* The scene here depicts the habitat of the late Cretaceous pterosaurs from Kansas with cliffs and nesting sites on the shore of the great mid-continental seaway that separated the western from the eastern part of North America at that time. *Pteranodon sternbergi*, the largest of the *Pteranodon* species, is characterised by the high upright crest on its skull. Its wing span could measure over 30ft (9m) in total. Almost certainly fish-eaters, these pterosaurs seem to have led a life similar to today's soaring seabirds such as albatrosses.**

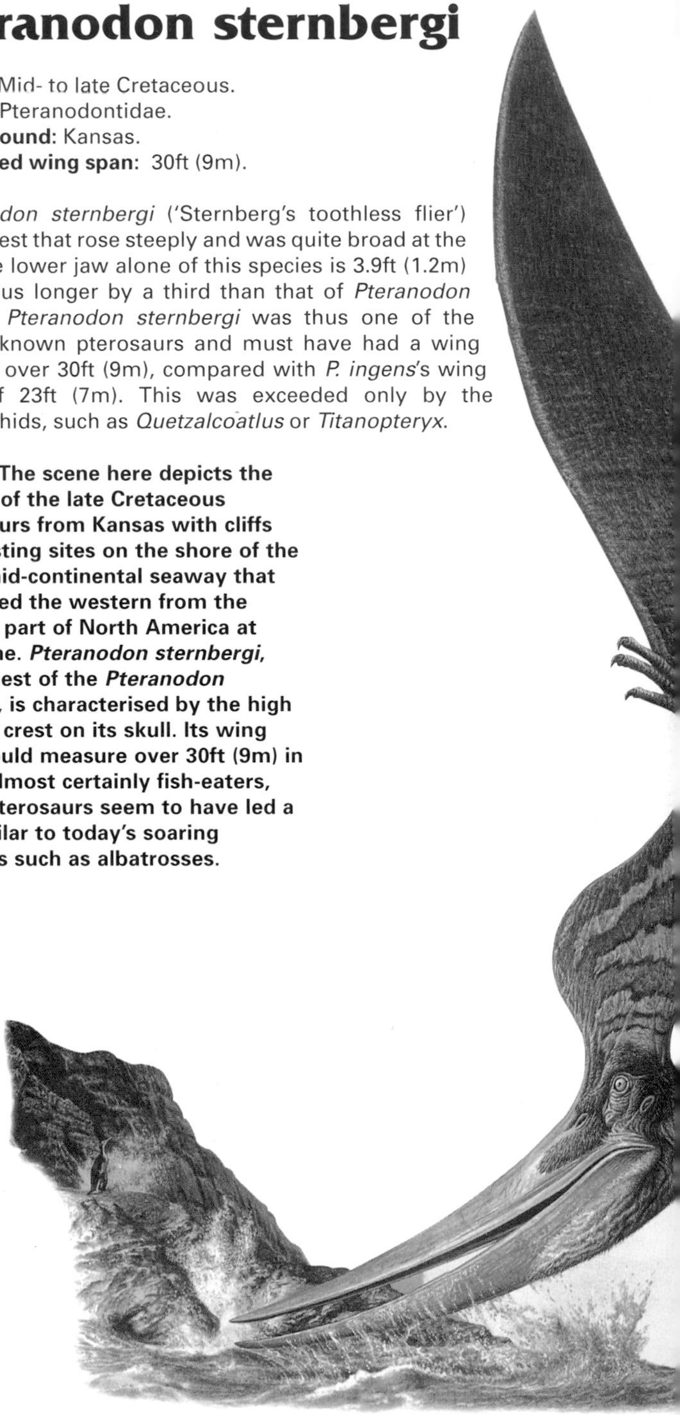

After O. C. Marsh, S. W. Williston in particular devoted himself to research into 'Kansas pterodactyls', and in 1910 G. F. Eaton, Curator of Osteology and Vertebrate Palaeontology at the Peabody Museum of Yale College in New Haven, could boast an inventory of *Pteranodon* skeletal remains featuring no fewer than 465 individuals.

Pteranodon must have been capable of sustained flying and soaring as it ranged far out over the open sea to catch fish. The western Kansas strata in which finds were made are deposits of an extended sea that ran though the North American continent in the Cretaceous as a 'mid-continental seaway'. As the sites where *Pteranodon* remains were found are at least 100 miles (160km) from what was then the coast, it can be presumed that these pterosaurs perished in or over the water, far away from their nesting or resting places on the coast. Despite their large wings their actual bodies were rather small.

Quetzalcoatlus

Period: Late Cretaceous. **Family:** Azhdarchidae.
Where found: North America.
Estimated wing span: 36-39ft (11-12m).

The Cretaceous and Tertiary strata of the Big Bend National Park on the Texas-Mexico border have long been known to contain fossils. They are particularly interesting because the transitional strata between the youngest Cretaceous and the oldest Tertiary, the Cretaceous/Tertiary boundary (K/T boundary for short), are revealed. This is one of the few places on earth where the factors that led to the extinction of dinosaurs and other land vertebrates at the end of the Cretaceous, 65 million years ago, can be studied.

In 1975 *Science* published a short report entitled 'Pterosaur from the Latest Cretaceous of West Texas. Discovery of the Largest Flying Creature'. Even palaeontologists, otherwise used to large prehistoric animals, could hardly believe that this 'Texas pterosaur', as it came to be known, had a wing span of 51ft (15.5m), as the first calculation suggested. This was twice as big as the largest pterosaurs hitherto known, pteranodontids from the Kansas chalk. The first find, in the Javelina Formation of the Big Bend National Park, yielded only a wing, a humerus and hundred of small fragments of bones. The new large pterosaur was named *Quetzalcoatlus* after the Mexican deity Quetzalcoatl, who was worshipped by the Aztecs in the form of a feathered snake. Revised calculations put the probable wing span of a large individual at 36-39ft (11-12m).

Smaller bones were also found, representing almost complete individuals. It is not yet clear whether these individuals, all found within a radius of about 30 miles (50km) from the original site, were juveniles of the large species or whether they represent a smaller species of *Quetzalcoatlus*.

Quetzalcoatlus was toothless, had sharp edges to its jaws, probably covered with horn, and a long, narrow, pointed beak with a low, slender crest. The neck vertebrae were extremely long and their articulations allowed practically no lateral movement for the neck. The long wing

***Above:* This is the last known pterosaur. With a wing span of 36-39ft (11-12m), it was also the largest flying creature of all time. Its neck was extremely long, its slender jaws were toothless and its head was topped by a long, bony crest.**

phalanges are constructed in a way that differs from other Pterodactyloidea. The first of the four wing phalanges is hollow and oval in cross-section; the other three phalanges are made of solid bone tissue, with a T-shaped cross-section. Thus nature found a perfect solution for the technical problem of the accumulation of forces during the downstroke of the wing, and combined the highest possible strength with the lowest possible weight.

Aeronautical engineers calculated that a pterosaur the size of *Quetzalcoatlus* must have weighed well over 220lb (100kg) and simply did not have enough muscular mass to raise this weight into the air and achieve continuous flapping flight. However, a glance at the massive bone crests on the humerus of *Quetzalcoatlus* is enough to show what powerful flight muscles must have been attached here. The humerus is 1ft 8in (52cm) long, and very robust in structure. One of the largest living birds, the wandering albatross, has a humerus 1ft 4in (40cm) long and a wing span of 11ft (3.4m). On this basis *Quetzalcoatlus* would have had a wing span of only 14ft 5in (4.4m). The fact that its wings stretched almost three times as far is due to the completely different structure of the pterosaur skeleton. In *Quetzalcoatlus* the humerus is the shortest bone in the wing, whereas in the albatross it is the longest. Wing length in pterosaurs is determined above all by the metacarpus and the flight digit, whereas in birds the feathers protrude far beyond the skeleton of the wing.

According to one palaeontologist's estimate, *Quetzalcoatlus* could have weighed 190lb (86kg). *Pteranodon* probably weighed between 28lb 3oz and 52lb 8oz (12.8 and 23.8kg), with a wing span of 23ft (7m). Therefore *Quetzalcoatlus*, with a wing span of 36-39ft (11-12m), may have been much lighter than the 190lb estimate, absolutely comparable in size and weight with a modern ultra-light aircraft.

Unlike most pterosaur fossils, the giant Texan pterosaurs were not found in marine strata but in sand and silt of the extensive flood plain of a river system, which, during the latest Cretaceous, was about 250 miles ▶

(400km) from the nearest sea coast. There is no geological evidence for large freshwater lakes in the area. *Quetzalcoatlus* may therefore have lived rather like the modern vulture, feeding on carrion, the corpses of dinosaurs. Its long neck would have been well adapted for this. As a good soarer with considerable stamina it was certainly able to cover large distances in search of food. Nevertheless many contradictions remain. Was the long, almost inflexible neck possibly a hindrance for an eater of carrion? And could the pterosaur tear pieces of flesh from a corpse at all with its pointed, toothless jaws? On the other hand, there is much evidence that burrowing animals lived in the area and large quantities of fossil tree trunks suggest periodic flooding. All this allows the possibility that *Quetzalcoatlus* used its slender, pointed beak to search for the molluscs and crabs that lived in the shallow pools of water.

The pterosaurs from Big Bend National Park are especially significant because they were not only the largest but also the last of these fascinating flying reptiles to live on earth. The strata in which the finds were made are dated at latest Cretaceous. They are only a few metres below the boundary layer with the Tertiary, above which neither dinosaurs nor pterosaurs are found. Thus both groups of reptiles became extinct at the same time, probably from the same causes.

***Left and above:* *Quetzalcoatlus* lived inland from the sea. Perhaps it was a carrion-feeder, although its lack of teeth makes this seem improbable. Alternatively, it may have probed for shellfish in small pools.**

Other Flying Vertebrates

In the course of their evolutionary history vertebrates often succeeded in conquering gravity and - at least for a time - raising themselves from the ground and using the air to move about in. Fish evolved species of flying fish and amphibians flying frogs, which could glide through the air for short distances, but it was above all reptiles, birds and mammals that produced effective flying forms.

Small gliding reptiles are known as early as the Palaeozoic (late Permian) *Daedalosaurus* whose fossilised skeletal remains were found on Madagascar. They showed very elongated ribs, 21 on each side of the body, used to support a gliding membrane. This lizard-like animal had a long tail and was about 16in (40cm) long. The span of the open 'wings' was about 13in (33cm). In its body structure *Daedalosaurus* is reminiscent of the modern flying dragon *Draco*, which lives in South-East Asia and is capable of flights of up to 200ft (60m).

A gliding reptile from late Triassic sediments in Kirghizia, named *Sharovipteryx* ('Sharov wing') in honour of its finder, A. G. Sharov, was a slim reptile about 10in (25cm) long, with a relatively long neck and enormously long hind legs, but very small front legs. A triangular flight membrane could be stretched between the hind legs and the front

Below: **These drawings compare gliding reptiles of the late Permian, *Daedalosaurus* and *Coelurosauravus*, and of the late Triassic, *Icarosaurus* and *Kuehneosaurus*, with the living *Draco*, the 'flying dragon', an agamid lizard from South-East Asia. The thoracic ribs of all these diapsid reptiles are greatly elongated in order to support a gliding membrane, which is stretched across them.**

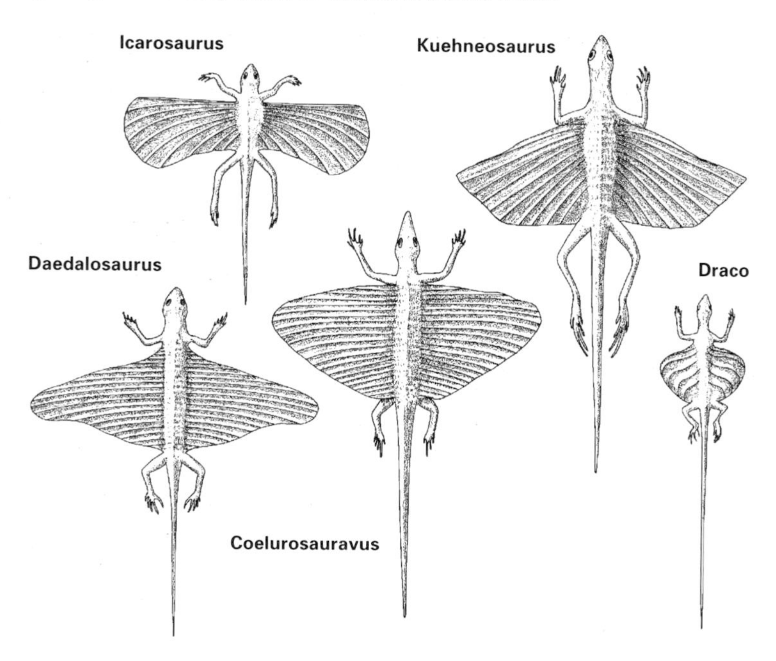

***Above:* Longisquama had a unique gliding adaptation. A double series of long, scale-like appendages were developed along its back. They could be folded and unfolded like the wings of a butterfly to form a continuous wing area.**

section of the tail, real leg wings in fact. *Sharovipteryx* could not flap these leg wings and fly actively, but it could probably glide for a certain distance.

A second reptile described by Sharov from the Kirghizia sediments is named *Longisquama* ('long scale') because of a row of enormously elongated scale-like appendages along the back. The animal is relatively small, about 4-5in (10-12.5cm) long. The appendages on the back are longer than the body and arranged in a double row one behind the other. They could apparently be folded upwards like butterfly wings or down to the sides. In the latter position they formed horizontal gliding surfaces, a kind of wing.

Longisquama was presumably arboreal and certainly did not use its wings for flapping flight, but probably for gliding. It thus documents a unique solution to the problem of gliding flight and together with the other gliders shows that even in the later Permian and Triassic there was a very wide range of aerial adaptations among the various reptile groups, long before the radiation of the actively flying vertebrates, i.e. pterosaurs, birds and bats.

***Right:* This life restoration of *Sharovipteryx* from the late Triassic of Kirghizia shows its hind legs fully extended as if in gliding position. Narrow gliding membranes are suggested behind the forelimbs.**

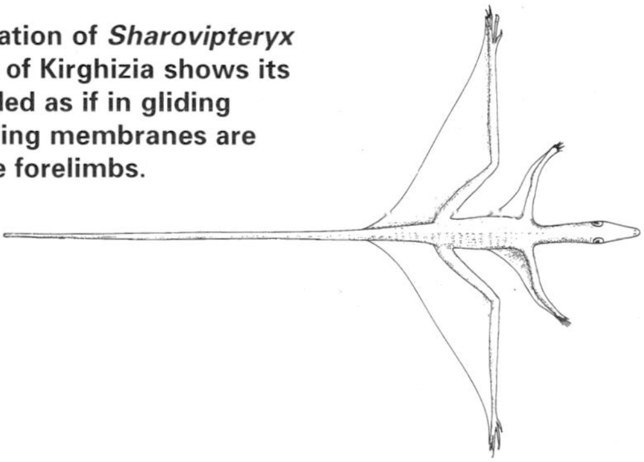

Coelurosauravus & Icarosaurus

Fossil remains have been found in Germany, England and Madagascar of another gliding reptile from the late Permian that is also related to *Daedalosaurus*. It was named *Coelurosauravus* ('hollow-tailed reptile'). The rare skeletal remains from the so-called Kupferschiefer (late Permian) marine deposits of Germany were formerly known as *Weigeltisaurus*, after Professor J. Weigelt of Halle. The remains of this creature are the oldest in the fossil record.

Similar too were two other fossil gliding lizards discovered in late Triassic rocks. One was *Kuehneosaurus*, named after Professor W. Kühne, from the Bristol Channel area in Great Britain. The other, *Icarosaurus*, comes from New Jersey, USA. *Icarosaurus* is named for Icarus, the ill-fated son of Daedalus in Greek mythology, whose attempts

to fly failed when he flew too close to the sun and his 'wings' disintegrated. It was three schoolboys who found the first specimen of *Icarosaurus siefkeri* in a piece of late Triassic shale while they were exploring an old quarry in New Jersey, across the Hudson River from Manhattan. It was studied by E. H. Colbert.

As in the case of *Daedalosaurus* and the modern *Draco* from South- ▶

***Below:* Coelurosauravus was a lizard-like, insect-eating reptile that could use its wing membranes supported by 21 elongated ribs for gliding from tree to tree or from a tree branch down to the ground. Skeletal remains of this gliding reptile, the oldest in the fossil record, were discovered in marine deposits of the late Permian, notably in Germany.**

East Asia, the wings of these two creatures were also supported by long ribs, although there were only ten to 11 pairs, which meant that the rib wings were narrower in shape. Perhaps they could also fold their wings back when climbing up tree trunks to catch insects, as can *Draco*. In any case this great area of skin, which certainly contained blood vessels, must have had a significant effect on heat regulation. The thoracic ribs of all these diapsid reptiles were greatly elongated to support a gliding membrane stretched across them. This enabled these arboreal animals to glide from one tree to another or from a branch down to the ground.

Early adaptations of vertebrates to flying in the air produced only gliding, i.e. passive exploitation of lift and drag forces, created by static aerodynamic surfaces on the body or the limbs. But in the course of vertebrate evolution the ability to fly actively emerged as well, in other words, powered flapping flight achieved by muscle power. Pterosaurs were the first vertebrates to develop active flight. The second group were the birds, which did not appear until the pterosaurs had already avchieved a high degree of diversity and worldwide distribution. The oldest fossil bird known today was *Archaeopteryx* ('ancient wing'), which lived in the late Jurassic, about 150 million years ago, and was a contemporary of pterosaurs and dinosaurs. But birds are another story and beyond the scope of this book.

***Below:* Like *Coelurosauravus*, *Icarosaurus* was able to glide by means of a membrane of skin that was supported by a series of elongated ribs. Dr E. H. Colbert described the fossil, naming the genus after Icarus, the ill-fated son of Daedalus in Greek mythology.**